Preface

The decision to compile this collection was prompted by the realization that, while a number of valuable articles were to be found in scattered periodicals, no single volume on Canadian medical history was readily available. Selected to appeal to physicians, historians, and students in either discipline, the following essays deal with a mixture of social and medical history. Doubtless those that appeal to one group of readers may appear obscure or simplistic to another. Yet it is to be hoped that the inclusion of a wide range of topics, rather than obscuring the focus of the collection, will illustrate the broad significance of the healing arts to Canadian history.

In the compilation of the volume I have received assistance from many sources. The list of contributors and the acknowledgments of locations of original publication make clear some of these obligations, but I am particularly indebted to Professor G. A. Rawlyk of Queen's University for his consistent encouragement and to Janice Dickin McGinnis and Thomas E. Brown for their bibliographic advice. As well, I have used the following repositories: the Canadian Institute for Technical and Scientific Information, the Library of the Department of National Health and Welfare, the Ottawa Public Library, the National Library, and the libraries of the University of Ottawa, the University of Western Ontario, Queen's University, and Carleton University.

S.E.D.S.

Contributors

MARGARET W. ANDREWS, a member of the Department of History of Washington State University, has published papers on the history of Canadian women and on the history of medical and other health services in Vancouver. Her current research interest is government health insurance in British Columbia and the State of Washington.

GEOFFREY BILSON is Associate Professor of History at the University of Saskatchewan and has published several articles on aspects of cholera in Canada.

MICHAEL BLISS, general editor of the Social History of Canada Series, teaches at the University of Toronto. He is the author of *A Living Profit: Studies in the Social History of Canadian Business, 1883-1911*, as well as a recent biography of Sir Joseph Flavelle.

ROBERT S. BOTHWELL, co-editor of the *Canadian Historical Review*, teaches history at the University of Toronto.

THOMAS E. BROWN received his graduate training in history at Carleton and Queen's universities and is with the Interpretive Section, Parks Canada, Prairie Region, Winnipeg.

TERRY COPP is Associate Professor of History at Wilfrid Laurier University.

JANICE P. DICKIN MCGINNIS holds a doctorate from the University of Alberta and teaches at Concordia University.

JOHN R. ENGLISH teaches history at the University of Waterloo and is the author of *The Decline of Politics: The Conservatives and the Party System, 1901-1920*.

ROBERT FORTUINE, who received his medical training at McGill University, is International Health Attaché at the United States Mission to the United Nations in Geneva.

DANIEL FRANCIS, formerly a journalist in Alberta and Ottawa, holds a master's degree in Canadian studies.

JOSEPH F. KETT, a former Fulbright scholar, is Associate Professor of History at the University of Virginia and the author of *The Formation of the American Medical Profession: The Role of Institutions, 1780-1860* and *Rites of Passage: Adolescence in America, 1790 to the Present*.

RELIEF MACKAY, a former high school teacher in Nova Scotia, holds a master's degree in history from McGill University.

ANGUS MCLAREN, Associate Professor of History at the University of Victoria, is the author of *Birth Control in Nineteenth-Century England*.

HILDA NEATBY, author of *Quebec: The Revolutionary Age, 1760-1791*, was Professor Emeritus at the University of Saskatchewan and, at the time of her death, Professor of History at Queen's University.

ARTHUR J. RAY, Associate Professor of Geography at York University, is the author of *Indians in the Fur Trade*.

CHARLES G. ROLAND, formerly senior editor of the *Journal of the American Medical Association*, is the Hannah Professor of the History of Medicine at McMaster University. His current research concerns early Canadian medical publications.

S. E. D. SHORTT, a physician and historian, is the author of *The Search for an Ideal: Six Canadian Intellectuals and their Convictions in an Age of Transition, 1890-1930* and is the Hannah Professor of the History of Medicine at Queen's University.

VERONICA STRONG-BOAG, Associate Professor of History and Women's Studies at Simon Fraser University, is engaged at present in a study of women in Canada during the 1920s.

NEIL SUTHERLAND is a member of the Faculty of Education at the University of British Columbia and the author of *Children in English-Canadian Society, 1880-1920*.

BARBARA R. TUNIS is the author of *In Caps and Gowns: The Story of the School for Graduate Nurses, McGill University, 1920-1964*.

Antiquarians and Amateurs: Reflections on the Writing of Medical History in Canada

S. E. D. SHORTT

Since the waning of the Dark Ages, European historians have charted the course of medical history. These early chronicles amounted to little more than lists of names until Renaissance scholars chose to focus primarily on the lives and works of a few eminent physicians. Enlightenment historians altered this perspective by emphasizing the evolution of medicine within the general cultural development of Europe. Though regular lectures in medical history were established at Göttingen by 1750, the subject, with its philosophical bias, was eclipsed during the early nineteenth century by interest in the developing natural sciences. It re-emerged, however, itself revitalized by the scientific method of scholarship, at the turn of the century. The year 1905, with the establishment of an institute of medical history at the University of Leipzig, marked the beginning of contemporary European medical historiography.[1]

In North America medical history as an academic discipline has had a much briefer lineage. Though lectures were given at the University of Virginia as early as 1825[2] and a number of Canadian and American physician-scholars or antiquarians produced a creditable volume of publication during the late nineteenth century,[3] the formal beginning must date from 1890. In that year Sir William Osler founded the Johns Hopkins Medical History Club. Lectures were begun in the medical school three years later and by 1903 two other American medical schools followed suit.[4] The school founded the *Bulletin of the Institute of Medical History* in 1932 and seven years later, under its present title, it became the journal of the American Association for the History of Medicine.[5] In that year a survey recorded that a total of thirty-five American and Canadian medical schools offered courses in medical history and ten "teachers of medical history" were listed in Canada. But the zenith had been reached. By 1969 only eighteen medical schools, four of which were in Canada, required instruction in medical history.[6] Though it appears, a decade later, that interest is reviving in some Canadian schools,[7] the status of the discipline is far from flourishing. Unfortunately, in Canada, unlike the United States, the declining interest in history on the part of medical schools has not been compensated for by an enthusiastic response from social historians.[8]

I

Medical historiography in Canada is American historiography writ small. The same trends and patterns, though of lesser magnitude, are evident and, in general, the same critiques apply. Much of the early literature was written by "elderly doctors,"[9] amateurs often gifted but, as one of their number confessed, "innocent of the severe disciplines of history."[10] They write, one senses, primarily to be read by other physicians, a group apparently willing to dispense with style and interpretation in preference for names and dates. The range of topics studied and the approach to these topics follows a predictable pattern. Simply stated, the standard methodology consists of little more than a chronological arrangement of biographies, linked together by brief accounts of legislation, epidemics, and institutional development.

A favoured point of departure for such historians is a description of the scurvy from which early French mariners were rescued by Indian spruce tea. The contributions of religious orders and the gradual establishment of primitive hospitals lead, via numerous epidemics of smallpox and several of syphilis, to the conquest of 1760 and the introduction of English, and particularly Scottish, medicine. The ensuing three-quarters of a century is viewed as a romantic amalgam of ingenious fur-trader-physicians, brutal military surgeons, and devastating cholera epidemics. The saga continues through fifty years of squabbles between bleeding, purging, orthodox physicians and quacks of various persuasions over issues such as licensing and medical education. The tide turns in favour of orthodoxy with the advent of scientific surgery, that is, surgery using anaesthetics and antiseptic conditions after 1870, and the simultaneous development of sophisticated hospitals and medical schools. The victory for "modern medicine," the reader is gratified to learn, is firmly established with the introduction of such discoveries as radiography by 1900 or sulphonamide antibiotics in the 1930s. A largely similar pattern of interests occupied early American historians, though more innovative and informative works have appeared with increasing frequency since 1940.[11] One cannot help but conclude that if, as has been said, European medical historians "are more than a generation ahead of their American counterparts,"[12] the state of the art in Canada has barely left the list-compiling Dark Ages.

II

Medical historiography effectively began in Canada with William Canniff's *The Medical Profession in Upper Canada, 1783–1850* (Toronto: 1894). In common with other Canadian historians of his time,[13] he emphasized the importance of the Loyalists, in this case for providing a number of physicians after 1776, and devoted considerable attention to legal and legislative developments. More striking is the fact that two-thirds of the book is composed of capsule biographies of some 260 early physicians. Though these sketches are of marginal value to anyone other than historical demographers, their significance lies in the fact that they established an enduring pattern in Canadian medical historiography. Edwin Seaborn, for example, writing *The March of Medicine in Western Ontario* (Toronto: 1944) half a century later, though beginning with an incongruous discussion of Mexican medicine, eventually adopted a biographical format. The majority of his subjects are unknown and will remain so, though the sections on Charles Duncombe, the educational theorist, and R. M. Bucke, a pioneer psychiatrist, deserve mention. Western Canada has not escaped the notice of the medical historian-biographer, as H. C. Jamieson's *Early Medicine in Alberta* (Edmonton: 1947) and Ross Mitchell's *Medicine in Manitoba* (Winnipeg: [1954]) demonstrate. That the format is, perhaps unfortunately, still considered appropriate, one need only examine W. B. Stewart's four-hundred page catalogue of practitioners and disconnected dates, *Medicine in New Brunswick* (St. John: 1974). Taken together, these studies must be considered as reference guides rather than interpretive works.

In 1928 John J. Heagerty published his *Four Centuries of Medical History in Canada* (Toronto: 1928). Though he later produced an undocumented but readable synopsis of this work, *The Romance of Medicine in Canada* (Toronto: 1940), and was echoed by W. B. Howell's brief *Medicine in Canada* (New York: 1933), the encyclopaedic two volumes remain the standard work in the field. Heagerty, the director of the federal public health services, was less concerned with style and interpretation than with employing primary sources, ranging from the Jesuit Relations to contemporary government reports in order to catalogue the major aspects of professional and institutional development. Particularly interesting are the accounts of epidemics, including smallpox

(1635–1925) and cholera (1832–71). The growth of individual medical schools and hospitals, as well as medical societies and provincial departments of public health, is clearly documented. Though a large part of one volume contains a tedious list of early physicians arranged by province, the work as a whole is a valuable source. It was complemented rather than superseded by H. E. MacDermot's *One Hundred Years of Medicine in Canada, 1867–1967* (Toronto: 1967) which focuses primarily on the development of the profession in terms of education, specialization, organization, research, and publication. Though mention is made of nineteenth-century landmarks, by dealing largely with advances in the twentieth century, this volume supplies information not available in Heagerty's earlier work.

Since 1928 several general studies limited to a single province, in addition to those mentioned earlier, have appeared. Maude Abbott's brief *History of Medicine in the Province of Quebec* (Montreal: 1931) is one of the few English sources on French Canada. It contains a readable section on the theory underlying North American Indian medicine, as well as one of the best accounts of the work of the remarkable physician and botanist Michel Sarrazin (1659–1734). William P. Bull, a non-physician, deals with the development of medicine in and near Toronto in his *From Medicine Man to Medical Man* (Toronto: 1934). The volume is presented in a readable style and primary sources are frequently cited. Particularly worthwhile is the account of the continuous conflict in the nineteenth century between orthodox physicians and unlicensed healers. As well, public health measures are considered and several pages are devoted to changes seen in general practice from 1860 to 1910. British Columbia is unusual in that the province has two recent and adequate medical histories. T. F. Rose, in *From Shaman to Modern Medicine: A Century of the Healing Arts in British Columbia* (Vancouver: 1972), has the insight to break with previous historiography and declare that far from being "romantic," much of nineteenth-century medical life was "dull" and "plodding." He realizes, too, that the medicine of the native peoples may well have equalled that of the early European physicians. The most intriguing sections of the book include an analysis of diagnoses at the Royal Jubilee Hospital (Victoria) from 1890 to 1899 and a consideration of drugs commonly used between 1860 and 1920. Well written and organized, though based largely on secondary sources, is Robert E. McKechnie's *Strong Medicine: A History of Healing on the Northwest Coast* (Vancouver: 1972). An attempt is clearly made, again in contrast to earlier works, to link medicine with the general social history of the province. Sections on Indian medicine, common illnesses among patients in the nineteenth century, and the changes brought to medical practice by twentieth-century pharmacology, are particularly worthwhile.

It is clear that Canadian medical historiography, whether following the Canniff biographical school or the encyclopaedia orientation of Heagerty, has marked limitations. In general, there is a preoccupation with eminent physicians, whether local luminaries or of the stature of Osler and Banting, or with dramatic events, particularly epidemics.[14] Even when these pitfalls are avoided, the result tends to be "internal" medical history; that is, it is concerned primarily with matters relating to the development of the profession, institutional growth, or progress in the understanding of major diseases. "External" considerations such as popular impressions of medicine, the impact of diseases on society, or the role played by paramedical disciplines are seldom considered. Almost without exception the approach of these studies is chronological and biographic rather than thematic, with no attempt to synthesize or create a larger conceptual framework. Finally, Canadian medical historians and, for that matter, Canadian historians in general, fail to consider medical history as a part—an integral part—of Canadian social history.

It is, however, unfair to make demands of past historians from the perspective of present historiographic sophistication. Most of the authors discussed were physicians for whom history was an enthusiasm pursued in addition to their medical duties. They worked with few colleagues, even fewer—one suspects—readers, and certainly no financial aid for research or publication. Despite these limitations, these writers have identified source materials, arranged events and characters into a coherent chronology, collected books, bibliographies, and documents, and generally given shape to Canadian medical history.[15] Similarly, explanations can be found for the reluctance of Canadian social historians to study seriously the medical past. Historians generally lack the technical knowledge and medical vocabulary, as well as a facility with epidemiological methods, to approach the field with confidence. Of equal significance is the uneven quality or availability of data: medical records are a relatively recent development;[16] the accuracy of early hospital and government statistics is often dubious;[17] and, finally, changing concepts of disease have resulted in confusing nomenclature and shifting classifications.[18] Considerations such as these are necessary to moderate a critique of existing historiography.

III

Perhaps of greater value than criticisms of past efforts are suggestions for historiographic developments in the future together with acknowledgement, in passing, of existing works. To establish a framework within which to consider the diverse aspects of Canadian medicine requires a detailed appreciation of the profession itself. The legal and legislative aspects of licensing have been documented and might well serve as a focus for discussing the process of professionalization and its attendant crusades against various heresies in the nineteenth century.[19] The emergence of medical associations and regulatory bodies as well as medical journals[20] is an integral part of this process and, under scrutiny, would reveal much about the social assumptions of the nascent profession. In large measure the medical profession is a reflection of the system by which it is educated, yet our knowledge of who taught what to whom, and for what reasons, is at best scanty.[21] This is particularly true in the period when the majority of Canadians sought all or part of their training abroad. As an example of the insights to be gained from a study of medical education, one has only to consider the struggle of women to enter early medical schools.[22] More significantly, such a study would clearly illustrate the links between medical history and nineteenth-century Canadian social history in general.

An equally revealing area of research is the complex nexus between organized medicine and Canadian politics and policies. An obvious inquiry is the profession's attitude towards health insurance.[23] Such a study would necessarily consider the ability of physicians to organize and function as a political lobby and would analyse the manner in which their collective views determine public policy. Indeed, a study of prominent individual physicians, such as John Rolph,[24] Sir Charles Tupper, or R. J. Manion might yield similar, though less general, conclusions. Nor should medicare be allowed to obscure other significant areas of medical and political concern. Unfortunately we know little of such topics as the public funding for medical research, the provision of medical services for groups such as military personnel,[25] inmates of prisons, or those isolated in the north,[26] or the powerful role of immigration department medical officers. The field of industrial medicine, with its implications for our appreciation of labour history, has been neglected,[27] as has the public health movement, so central to the "progressive" years. Pure food and drug legislation, physical education, public sanitation, vaccination programs, and quarantine laws remain to be closely studied.[28] An examination of these and similar topics would broaden considerably our understanding of both Canadian medicine and politics.

Though health care reaches the public in a variety of ways, central to the process is the hospital. Certainly, the infirmaries of the nineteenth century differed markedly from our contemporary institutions. Yet their metamorphosis is largely undocumented. There is evidence to suggest that in the pioneer mind they were a place of death and, if surgery was required, dismemberment, rather than healing. From newspapers, municipal or provincial committee proceedings, or the records of religious and charitable groups an accurate impression of public perceptions of the hospitals might be obtained. It is essential as well to examine what hospital records are extant to estimate the incidence of diseases in various areas, to compile statistical profiles of patients, and to determine the nature and efficacy of treatment methods. The development of hospital financing, support services, accreditation systems, and links with medical and nursing schools are further areas of investigation.[29] Finally, the emergence of specialized hospitals, such as psychiatric centres, might provide concise insight into not only the mechanics of care but also the theories of disease which underlay treatment methods.[30]

A study of hospitals supplemented by newspaper accounts, government departmental records, and the case notes of individual physicians might clarify our understanding of the role that various diseases have played in Canadian history. Epidemics, dramatic and startling in their presentation, appear to leave behind ready sources for the historian.[31] But what of more chronic maladies? Malaria was not uncommon in the Great Lakes region in the early nineteenth century, as was iodine deficiency well into the twentieth century, yet no detailed studies of these disorders exist. Similarly, the ravages of tuberculosis, especially among the native peoples, may have quietly consumed more lives than the more flamboyant cholera, smallpox, or typhoid outbreaks.[32] Such a disease, through its statistical and demographic characteristics, would provide profound insights into nineteenth-century urban class-structure. With each disease, moreover, an opportunity is gained to document and evaluate approaches to diagnosis, treatment, and research. Certainly, therapy tends to be the product of world-wide research, but there have been significant Canadian contributions, notably in the field of endocrinology.[33]

Diseases, as the surfeit of eponyms suggests, are often associated with individual physicians. In Canada, this is certainly true for Sir Frederick Banting and diabetes, but other prominent names — Sir William Osler, Norman Bethune — are known for less concise reasons.[34] Their renown, however, illustrates the unfortunate tendency to concentrate historical interest on a famous few. What of the rank and file physicians? Certain of them have left autobiographies which are often more informative than secondary works,[35] but some — such as the innovative Ontario surgeon-general practitioner, Abraham Groves — deserve further study.[36] Biography has traditionally been a strong point of Canadian historiography, a tendency which eventually will be reflected in medical history. In the interim, however, Canadian historians working in other areas might well devote, where appropriate, attention to the medical problems of their subjects.[37]

The healing arts, of course, are not the unique province of physicians, eminent or otherwise. One has only to consider the major contributions made by nursing, particularly in isolated communities or during wars and epidemics, to appreciate this point.[38] In Canada, an area of considerable significance to medical history quite unrelated to the regular profession is the practice of medicine among the native peoples. We know from accounts left by French voyageurs supplemented by archaeological evidence that Indian medicine functioned, with varying success, on three levels: the internal, using botanical medicines; the structural, which was concerned with the treatment of wounds and fractures; and the psychological, a blend of exorcism and entertainment conducted by the shaman. We do not know the efficacy of the various remedies and which of them were adopted by Europeans, nor do we fully understand the complex role of the medicine man within the community. Of greater significance to the native peoples is the terrifying impact made by European diseases. As late as the 1950s Canadian Eskimos were plagued by an epidemic of polio, yet our knowledge of this outbreak and earlier ravages by cholera, smallpox, or tuberculosis is at best impressionistic.[39] Clearly, Indian and Eskimo medicine is an area of Canadian social development requiring much closer scrutiny by historians, physicians, and anthropologists.

Much as the native peoples developed methods of dealing with disease suited to the needs of their communities and the resources at hand, so early Canadian settlers often turned to unorthodox sources for their medical needs. Itinerant peddlers of patent medicine constituted one end of a spectrum that stretched, via Thomsonian herbalist "doctors," to the quasi-orthodoxy of the homeopaths. An analysis of the appeal of these irregular healers would expose many popular nineteenth-century perceptions not just of the medical profession itself, but also of the mechanics of the human body and the nature of disease. Equally revealing would be studies of crusades and campaigns focusing on topics such as temperance, vivisection, phrenology, or eugenics.[40] These topics constitute an interface between medical and social history, the study of which would be of benefit to both disciplines.

In a review of the literature of medical history in Canada, it becomes clear that there are several significant areas in which to begin an exploration of the field. The profession itself and its societies and journals must be studied with particular emphasis on medical education and political attitudes. Methods of health care delivery, common diseases, and methods of diagnosis and treatment form the link between patients and practitioners. Finally, popular attitudes towards doctors, human physiology, and the disease process must be examined to create a solid nexus between medical and social history.

Even were Canadians to develop a sophisticated medical historiography, one might still conclude by asking the question: of what value is medical history? Traditionally, the response to this inquiry has applied only to physicians rather than historians and rests on two arguments. Time has largely annulled the first of these propositions which stated that incipient doctors could learn medicine by studying the work of their predecessors. Although this may have held some validity in the nineteenth century, few today would argue that a book of history is more clinically instructive than one of physiology. The second thesis holds that doctors, preoccupied with science, lack a "broader cultural perspective," a state of affairs remedial through the teaching of medical history. Bluntly put, this belief is nonsense; physicians susceptible to "broader culture" will find history rather than the converse, while those impervious to it will simply view history with catastrophic distaste. In reality, the value of medical history to the profession is philosophical rather than pragmatic. It reunites with a common heritage an increasingly fragmented discipline and, by describing commonly accepted but erroneous theories of the past, or those few epoch-marking flashes of medical insight, must engender a sense of profound professional humility. In an age given to technological arrogance, this surely is a major achievement. As well, to social historians medical history serves a significant purpose, for health and its preservation are perhaps the fundamental human concern. Indeed, political battles, military campaigns, or economic vicissitudes pale in importance when measured against the impact of even a single cholera epidemic. Perhaps to a steadily aging population confronted with issues of ecological survival, such an assertion will be readily intelligible. With these considerations in mind, it is time medical and social historians united to explore more fully the Canadian medical past.

Notes

1. George Rosen, "The New History of Medicine: A Review," *Journal of the History of Medicine and Allied Sciences* 6, no. 4 (1951): 5, 6–22, and "The Place of Medicine in Medical Education," *Bulletin of the History of Medicine* 22, no. 5 (1948): 594–629.
2. Henry Sigerist, "Medical History in the United States," *Bulletin of the History of Medicine* 22, no. 1 (1948): 48.

3. See, for example, Whitfield J. Bell, "Practitioners of History: Philadelphia Medical Historians Before 1925," *Bulletin of the History of Medicine* 50, no. 1 (1976): 73-92.

4. Sigerist, "Medical History in the United States," pp. 47, 49, 53.

5. Genevieve Miller, "The Missing Seal or Highlights of the First Half Century of the American Association for the History of Medicine," *Bulletin of the History of Medicine* 50, no. 1 (1976): 93-121.

6. Genevieve Miller, "The Teaching of Medical History in the United States and Canada: Report of a Field Survey," *Bulletin of the History of Medicine* 43, no. 3 (1969): 259-67. Henry Sigerist, "Medical History in the Medical Schools of Canada," *Bulletin of the History of Medicine* 8, no. 2 (1940): 303-8.

7. "Jason A. Hannah and the Hannah Chairs for the History of Medicine," *Bulletin of the History of Medicine* 52, no. 1 (1978): 125-27.

8. See Gerald N. Grob, "The Social History of Medicine and Disease in America: Problems and Possibilities," *Journal of Social History* 10, no. 4 (1977): 391-409.

9. Douglas Guthrie, "Whither Medical History?" *Medical History* 1, no. 4 (1957): 307-17, deplores this stereotype of early medical historians.

10. Dr. E. P. Scarlett, a gifted amateur, responsible for eighty-eight issues during the 1940s and early 1950s of the Calgary Associate Clinic, *Historical Bulletin*, quoted with approval by H. E. MacDermot, himself a prolific physician-historian, in *One Hundred Years of Medicine in Canada, 1867-1967* (Toronto: 1967), p. 162.

11. Grob, "The Social History of Medicine," pp. 396, 405-9.

12. Ibid., p. 391.

13. See Carl Berger, *The Sense of Power: Studies in the Ideas of Canadian Imperialism 1867-1914* (Toronto: 1970), ch. 3.

14. On the dangers of an elitist approach, see Iago Galdston, "On the Futility of Medical History," *Canadian Medical Association Journal* 93 (9 October 1965): 807-11, and Erwin H. Ackerknecht, "A Plea for a 'Behaviourist' Approach in Writing the History of Medicine," *Journal of the History of Medicine and Allied Sciences* 22, no. 3 (1967): 211-14.

15. Genevieve Miller, "In Praise of Amateurs: Medical History in America Before Garrison," *Bulletin of the History of Medicine* 47, no. 6 (1973): 586, 615; Charles Mullett, "Medical History: Some Problems and Opportunities," *Journal of the History of Medicine and Allied Sciences* 1, no. 2 (1946): 191; Bell, "Practitioners of History," pp. 73, 88.

16. For example, as late as 1956, approximately one-third of Ontario and Nova Scotia general practitioners kept no clinical records beyond obstetrical and paediatric case notes. See K. F. Clute, *The General Practitioner: A Study of Medical Education and Practice in Ontario and Nova Scotia* (Toronto: 1963), pp. 40-70.

17. Rose, *From Shaman to Modern Medicine*, p. 32, notes this limitation when describing hospital records in Victoria, B.C., during the 1890s.

18. For example, as noted by J. D. Livermore in "The Personal Agonies of Edward Blake," *Canadian Historical Review* 56, no. 1 (1975): 47, the antiquated term "neurasthenia" is difficult to interpret precisely.

19. Elizabeth McNab, *A Legal History of the Health Professions in Ontario: A Study for the Committee on the Healing Arts* (Toronto: 1970).

20. H. E. MacDermot, *History of the Canadian Medical Association, 1867-1956*, 2 vols. (Toronto: 1935 and 1958); MacDermot, *A Bibliography of Canadian Medical Publications* (Montreal: 1934); John Ferguson, *History of the Ontario Medical Association, 1880-1930* (Toronto: 1930); D. Sclater Lewis, *The Royal College of Physicians and Surgeons of Canada, 1920-1960* (Montreal: 1962).

21. Murray L. Barr, *A Century of Medicine at Western* (London: 1977).

22. Maude Abbott, "Autobiographical Sketch (1928)," *McGill Medical Journal* 28 (1959): 127-52; Elizabeth Smith Shortt, "The Women's Medical College," *Queen's Review* 3, no. 3 (1929): 80-84, no. 4: 115-20, no. 5: 153-57; Ruth M. Buck, *The Doctor Rode Side-Saddle* (Toronto: 1974); Carlotta Hacker, *The Indomitable Lady Doctors* (Toronto: 1974).

23. Robert Bothwell and John English, "Pragmatic Physicians: Canadian Medicine and Health Care Insurance 1910-1945," *University of Western Ontario Medical Journal* 47, no. 3 (1976): 14-17, and below, pp. 479-93; Bernard Blishen, *Doctors and Doctrines: The Ideology of Medical Care in Canada* (Toronto: 1969); R. F. Badgley and Samuel Wolfe, *Doctors' Strike: Medical Care and Conflict in Saskatchewan* (Toronto: 1967); D. L. Matters, "A Report on Health Insurance: 1919," *B.C. Studies* no. 21 (Spring 1974): 28-32; Malcolm Taylor, *Health Insurance and Canadian Public Policy: The Seven Decisions that Created the Canadian Health Insurance System* (Montreal: 1978).

24. Marian Patterson. "The Life and Times of the Honourable John Rolph M.D. (1793-1870)," *Medical History* 5, no. 1,

(1961): 15-33; G. D. Stanley, "Dr. John Rolph: Medicine and Rebellion in Upper Canada," Calgary Associate Clinic, *Historical Bulletin* 9 (May 1944): 1-13.

25. See, for example, Sir Andrew Macphail's suggestive and once controversial *Official History of the Canadian Forces in the Great War, 1914-1919: The Medical Services* (Ottawa: 1925). Note also W. R. Feasby, *Official History of the Canadian Medical Services, 1939-1945* (Ottawa: 1954), and G. W. L. Nicholson, *Seventy Years of Service: A History of the Royal Canadian Army Medical Corps* (Ottawa: 1977).

26. Dudley Copland, *Livingston of the Arctic* (Ottawa: 1967); Joseph P. Moody, *Arctic Doctor* (New York: 1955).

27. Michael Piva, "The Workman's Compensation Board in Ontario," *Ontario History* 67, no. 1 (1975): 39-56.

28. R. D. Defries, *The Development of Public Health in Canada* (Toronto: 1940), and *The Federal and Provincial Health Services in Canada*, 2nd ed. (Toronto: 1961); Neil Sutherland, "To Create a Strong and Healthy Race": School Children in the Public Health Movement, 1880-1914," *History of Education Quarterly* 12, no. 3 (1972): 304-33, and below, pp. 361-93; David MacLeod, "A Live Vaccine: The YMCA and Adolescence in the United States and Canada, 1870-1920," *Histoire Sociale/Social History* 11, no. 21 (1978): 5-25; Alan Metcalfe, "The Evolution of Organized Physical Recreation in Montreal, 1840-1895," ibid., pp. 144-66.

29. G. H. Agnew, *Canadian Hospitals, 1920 to 1970: A Dramatic Half Century* (Toronto: 1974); Margaret Angus, *Kingston General Hospital: A Social and Institutional History* (Montreal: 1973); W. G. Cosbie, *The Toronto General Hospital, 1819-1965: A Chronicle* (Toronto: 1975).

30. Daniel Francis, "The Development of the Lunatic Asylum in the Maritime Provinces," *Acadiensis* 6, no. 2 (1977): 23-38, and below, pp. 93-114; Cyril Greenland, "Services for the Mentally Retarded in Ontario, 1870-1930," *Ontario History* 54, no. 4, (1962): 267-74.

31. Margaret Andrews, "Epidemic and Public Health: Influenza in Vancouver, 1918-1919," *B.C. Studies*, no. 34 (Summer 1977): 21-44; Janice Dickin McGinnis, "The Impact of Epidemic Influenza: Canada, 1918-1919," Canadian Historical Association, *Historical Papers*, 1977, pp. 121-40, and below, pp. 447-77. Geoffrey Bilson, "Canadian Doctors and the Cholera," ibid., pp. 105-19, and below, pp. 115-36. Bilson, "Cholera in Upper Canada," *Ontario History* 67, no. 1 (1975): 15-30;

Bilson, "The First Epidemic of Asiatic Cholera in Lower Canada," *Medical History* 21, no. 4 (1977): 411-33.

32. George Jasper Wherrett, *The Miracle of the Empty Beds: A History of Tuberculosis in Canada* (Toronto: 1977).

33. For example, see Murray L. Barr and R. J. Rossiter, "James Bertram Collip, 1892-1965," *Biographical Memoirs of Fellows of the Royal Society* 19 (1973): 235-67.

34. Lloyd Stevenson, *Sir Frederick Banting* (Toronto: 1946); Seale Harris, *Banting's Miracle: The Story of the Discoverer of Insulin* (Philadelphia: 1946); Harvey Cushing, *The Life of Sir William Osler* (Oxford: 1925); W. R. Bett, *Osler: The Man and the Legend* (London: 1951); Ted Allen and Sydney Gordon, *The Scalpel, the Sword: The Story of Dr. Norman Bethune* (Toronto: 1952). Roderick Stewart, *Norman Bethune* (Toronto: 1974).

35. For example, William Victor Johnston, *Before the Age of Miracles: Memoirs of a Country Doctor* (Toronto: 1972); A. I. Willinsky, *A Doctor's Memoirs* (Toronto: 1960) D. W. G. Murray, *Medicine in the Making* (Toronto: 1960); Dorothy Blakey Smith, ed., *The Reminiscences of Doctor John Sebastien Helmcken* (Vancouver: 1976).

36. Abraham Groves, *All in a Day's Work: Leaves from a Doctor's Casebook* (Toronto: 1934); C. W. Harris, "Abraham Groves of Fergus: The First Elective Appendectomy?" *Canadian Journal of Surgery* 4 (July 1961): 405-10; G. D. Stanley, "Dr. Abraham Groves, 1857-1935: A Great Crusader of Canadian Medicine," Calgary Associate Clinic, *Historical Bulletin* 13, no. 1 (1948): 4-10.

37. This suggestion was made, to little effect, in "Notes and Comments," *Canadian Historical Review* 4, no. 4 (1923): 285-86.

38. J. M. Gibbon and M. S. Mathewson, *Three Centuries of Canadian Nursing* (Toronto: 1947); Margaret M. Street, *Watch Fires on the Mountains: The Life and Writings of Ethel Johns* (Toronto: 1973). Other allied professions are considered in D. W. Gullett, *A History of Dentistry in Canada* (Toronto: 1971); D. McDougall, "The History of Pharmacy in Manitoba," *Papers, Historical and Scientific Society of Manitoba*, 3rd series, no. 11, 1956.

39. Robert C. Dailey "The Midewiwin, Ontario's First Medical Society," *Ontario History* 50, no. 3 (1958): 133-38; J. Duffy, "Smallpox and the Indians in the American Colonies," *Bulletin of the History of Medicine* 25, no. 4 (1951): 324-41; Robert Fortuine, "The Health of the Eskimos, as Portrayed in the Earliest Written Accounts," ibid. 45, no. 2 (1971): 97-114, and below,

pp. 19-43. George Graham-Cummings, "Health of the Original Canadians, 1867-1967," *Medical Services Journal Canada* 23 (February 1967): 115-56; A. C. Mahr, "Materia Medica and Therapy among the North American Forest Indians," *Ohio State Archaeological and Historical Quarterly* 60, no. 4 (1951): 331-54; A. F. C. Wallace, "Dreams and Wishes of the Soul: A Type of Psychoanalytic Theory Among the Seventeenth-Century Iroquois," *American Anthropologist* 60, no. 2 (1958): 234-48; W. G. Wallis, "Medicines Used by the Micmac Indians," ibid. 24, no. 1 (1922): 24-30.

40. Thomas P. Kelley, *The Fabulous Kelley: He Was King of the Medicine Men* (Toronto: 1968); Terry Chapman, "Drug Use in Western Canada," *Alberta History* 24 (Autumn 1976): 18-27, and "The Early Eugenics Movement in Western Canada," ibid. 25 (Autumn 1977): 9-17. Accounts of temperance crusades deal only superficially with the medical aspects; for example, Graeme Decarie, "Something Old, Something New...: Aspects of Prohibitionism in Ontario in the 1890's," in D. Swainson, ed., *Oliver Mowat's Ontario* (Toronto: 1972), pp. 154-71.

The Health of the Eskimos, as Portrayed in the Earliest Written Accounts

ROBERT FORTUINE

The Eskimos of North America, although a remarkably hardy people, have borne a heavy burden of disease over the centuries since they first became known to the rest of the world. Devastating epidemics of infectious disease, notably smallpox, influenza, and measles, have changed the very course of history for many Eskimo bands across the Arctic. Whole villages have been depopulated or abandoned as a result of these terrible plagues. Even in the years since World War II, poliomyelitis, influenza, trichinosis, diphtheria, and other diseases have swept through isolated settlements, often with a high mortality and always with a great disruption of family and community life.

These infectious diseases have wreaked havoc among the Eskimos because so few individuals have had specific immunity to the causative agents, which in nearly every case were introduced from the outside at relatively long intervals.

Reprinted by permission from the *Bulletin of the History of Medicine* 45, no. 2 (1971): 97–114. Copyright 1971, The Johns Hopkins Press.

Other infectious diseases, although less dramatic, have also taken a steady toll of life and health. Tuberculosis, at times epidemic in different parts of the Arctic, for the most part has been a steady, grim companion of the Eskimos, causing death, crippling, or general poor health. Chronic otitis media, acute and chronic respiratory disease, diarrhea, meningitis, and certain parasitic infestations also cause a great deal of debility and occasionally death.

Among the non-infectious diseases, cancer, thought by Stefansson to be totally absent in "primitive" Eskimos, is now well known, and recent evidence from Alaska indicates that it may be no less common in Eskimos than in the rest of the North American population. Accidents are the commonest cause of death in all but the very old and the very young. Mental illness and alcoholism are being increasingly recognized as serious health problems. Dental decay is almost universal among the younger generation.

Some of these health problems, indeed perhaps most of them, can be associated with change in the Arctic—change which has been rapid throughout the past century but particularly in the last few decades. Nearly every aspect of the traditional Eskimo way of life has altered in some respect, and nearly every change has brought with it either a new health threat or a modification of an old one. For example, for every new snowmobile injury there is probably at least one injury less from dog bite.

It is easy to discern, in many instances, the direct and sometimes disastrous effect on health of the new technology, with its attendant behavioural changes, of newly introduced infectious agents, or of dietary changes. In a few cases it is also possible to speculate how the unfriendly arctic environment or the traditional cultural practices of the Eskimos might have contributed to the prevalence of certain disease patterns which exist today.

In order to assess the effects of change on the health of the Eskimos, of course, it is necessary to have at least a general idea of their base-line health before the change occurred. It is the purpose of this paper to try to reconstruct the status of health of the Eskimos from the earliest written records of explorers, missionaries, and traders. Since the Eskimos have no written history of their own, it is to these accounts that we must turn for information on their health at the time of their first contacts with the "outside." The record is fragmentary and discontinuous in time, since the Arctic was explored by many persons and over several centuries. Some large areas, indeed, were not even placed on the map until well into the twentieth century. The written records, moreover, have real limitations as historical documents. Many of them contain material which is inaccurate, uninformed, or prejudiced.

Often the accounts of explorers reflect the purpose of the expedition's financial backers and are thus primarily descriptions of geographical features, weather conditions, magnetic and auroral phenomena, geological formations, and natural history, often liberally spiced with narratives of man's heroic struggle (the explorer's, of course) against the elements in the white wilderness. Although many voyagers into the arctic regions never encountered Eskimos at all, even the reports of those that did frequently contain little health information, despite the fact that commonly they were written by the physician-naturalist on the expedition. The reasons are not difficult to discern. Their contact with the Eskimos was often brief, an interpreter was usually not available, the people themselves were heavily clothed, and a very few were actually hostile. The observers therefore usually had to limit their descriptions to physical features, clothing, housing, and weapons. The diseases and impairments which were mentioned were, not surprisingly, those immediately apparent even to the casual observer.

The whalers and some fur-traders, despite intimate and often prolonged contact with the Eskimos, rarely recorded their impressions of them. Although such men were usually literate and kept good business records, they cared little for descriptive accounts. In any case, they had little interest in the Eskimos as people, although they often employed them and were not above using them in less honourable ways on occasion.

Missionaries, on the other hand, were inveterate diarists and often recorded their observations of the Eskimos at length. Rarely, however, have these accounts contributed much to an understanding of health matters, except for the occasional vivid description of squalid living conditions, or of local epidemics. Most of the qualified medical missionaries arrived on the scene too late to portray conditions as they were in the earliest years of contact.

Earliest Records

The English navigator, Martin Frobisher, took an Eskimo with him on returning home from his first voyage to the Arctic in 1576. Shortly after arrival in England, however, the man became the first Eskimo victim of European civilization, for he died shortly after landing "of colde which he had taken at Sea."[1] Undaunted by the experience, Frobisher brought home from his voyage the following year an Eskimo man, woman, and child, all of whom died within two months, though not before they had been presented to Her Royal Majesty Queen Elizabeth. A Doctor Doddyngs performed an autopsy on the man and concluded that he died of pneumonia, though he also found a healed rib fracture.[2]

A few years later another Englishman, John Davis, made two voyages to the icy straits which now bear his name. He took special pains to befriend the Eskimos and described their life and customs in some detail. While at Gilbert Sound (near present Godthaab, Greenland) he observed a particularly common health problem: "These people are much given to bleed, and therefore stoppe their noses with deere hayre, or the hayre of an elan."[3]

In 1757, Hans Egede, the "Apostle of Greenland," published a book of recollections of his mission work among the people of the western coast of Greenland between 1721 and

1746. He described the Eskimos as strongly built and inclined to be fat, but afflicted with a number of problems:

> I have met with some that seemed infected with a kind of leprosy; yet (what is surprising to me), though they converse with others, and lay with them in one bed, it is not catching. They that dwell in the most northern parts are often miserably plagued with dysenteries or bloody fluxes, breast diseases, boils, and epilepsy or falling sickness, etc. There were no epidemical or contagious diseases known among them, as plague, smallpox, and such like, till the year 1734....
>
> They are very full of blood, which is observed by their frequent bleeding at the nose.[4]

He goes on to remark that few exceeded fifty to sixty years in age and that most "part in their tender infancy." The children, he found, were frequently infested with worms.

In 1767, another missionary to the Greenlanders, the Moravian David Crantz, published a two-volume history of the country in which he makes many pertinent medical observations. After remarking on nosebleeds and snowblindness, the latter the result of wind and glare, he continues:

> They are also subject to the head-ach, tooth-ach, dizziness and fainting and likewise to the palsy. There are some instances of the falling-sickness, dropsy, lunacy and madness; but these and the cancer of the mouth are not common, ...
>
> They are infested with two sorts of eruptions. One of them is a kind of rash, with little pimples, which cover the whole body except the hands, but they soon go off, and are not contagious. The other is the leprosy, attended with white putrid wounds and a scurf all over the body; this is infectious, and generally accompanies the poor creatures to the grave.... Such lepers are obliged to live apart. They are strangers to the smallpox and meazles, except a single instance in the year 1733, when a boy

brought the smallpox with him from Copenhagen and near 3000 people died of it.... ·

They have sometimes boils which spread as big as a plate....

Many drag along several years with a weakness, and defluxion in the breast, that suffocates them at last.

They know nothing of agues and fevers. But if they are troubled with stitches in the side, or rather in the breast, occasioned perhaps by settled phlegm, they first perceive a shivering, and then a little heat succeeds, which constantly continues, attended with violent convulsions in the breast. This is their common sickness, it also makes quick dispatch, and is often catching.[5]

Crantz also mentions dysentery and describes at length several epidemics, including the smallpox epidemic of 1733–34 and what is apparently an influenza epidemic in 1752. It is clear in both cases that the disease was introduced from Europe.[6]

Of particular interest is his account of "leprosy," which he, unlike Egede, considered communicable and serious, if not always fatal. In a footnote he points out that a similar disease was also prevalent in the Faroe Islands and Norway. His description of the disease in Greenland is at least compatible with leprosy, which was widespread in Scandinavia during the eighteenth century.

Because of the continuous European influence, later descriptions of health conditions in Greenland are not of much help until the late nineteenth century, when a band of isolated Eskimos was discovered and investigated around Angmagssalik, on the eastern coast of the island. There the early traders and physicians were struck by the frequency of hemoptysis, which they could not attribute with any certainty to tuberculosis.[7]

As early as the seventeenth century the Eskimos around Hudson Strait were visited and described by explorers, whalers, and traders who were heading toward the Bay and points west. The first record of health conditions among this group, however, appears to be that of Henry Ellis, who voyaged to Hudson Bay in 1746 and 1747. He found the people "of a middle Size, robust, and inclinable to be fat." He was particularly interested in the snow goggles they used to prevent "Snow-Blindness, a very grievous and painful Distemper, occasioned by the Action of the Light, strongly reflected from the Snow...."[8] This reference to inflammation of the eyes is the first of many such descriptions in the people from Hudson Strait to the mouth of the Kuskokwim River.

In 1770 Captain George Cartwright set up a fur-trading post on the Labrador coast south of Hamilton Inlet and spent sixteen years there managing a most lucrative enterprise. Under 21 July 1786, he noted in his diary: "A number of the Esquimaux are ill of most violent colds, which they are very subject to; it carries off great numbers of them."[9] From the context it would appear that such respiratory illnesses were brought in by the trading ships. Elsewhere Cartwright describes the effects of a devastating smallpox epidemic, introduced from Europe when a young Eskimo was returning to his home after a visit.[10]

In 1771 the Moravian missionaries established a permanent post in Northern Labrador, where they are still active today. Several of the early writers recorded violent epidemics among their charges, but the nature of the diseases cannot be clearly established from the available information.[11]

A final reference from the eighteenth century is that of Samuel Hearne of the Hudson's Bay Company, who travelled overland with Indian guides from Fort Prince of Wales (near Churchill, Manitoba) to the mouth of the Coppermine River in 1772. In the brief encounter he had with the Eskimos Hearne noted one old woman whose eyes "were as red as blood" and also made reference to the frequency of nosebleeds.[12]

One of the first physicians to record his impressions of the health of the Eskimos was Thomas M'Keevor, M.D., who wrote of a journey to Hudson Bay in 1812:

From personal observation I learned but little, and from enquiry still less. I may here remark, that I did not observe any appearance whatever of smallpox among them; neither had the children or parents any marks or deformity of any kind....

The only diseases which fell under my observation... were the affection of the eyelids,...epistaxis,...and hypochondriasis....

Of nosebleeds he elaborated most graphically:

I have seen the blood trickle down very copiously, without their even appearing to notice it; they allowed it quietly to trickle into the mouth, and when it took an irregular course down by the angle of the mouth, they wiped it away with the cuff of their jacket.

In the same passage he also commented on a relative infertility among the women and the apparent absence of goiter.[13]

Edward Chappell, in his narrative of a voyage to Hudson Bay during the same decade, confirms the doctor's observations on the absence of deformity and the frequency of epistaxis. He mentions accidentally inducing "a torrent of blood" in a young girl to whom his men had given snuff. "The fact is," he writes apologetically, "as we afterward discovered, that bleeding at the nose is a most common incident among the *Esquimaux*, and it is certain to follow the least exertion."[14] Sore eyes were mentioned as being especially common among the young men but infrequent in women or old men. Chappell also remarked on what was another recurrent theme—the fact that the standard of personal hygiene was different among the Eskimos. "Many of the women," he relates, "had very pleasing features; but they were so disfigured with dirt, and their persons smelt so strongly of the seal oil, that it required a stout heart to salute even the prettiest of them."[15]

At the other end of the continent, in 1817, a Russian ship under the command of Otto von Kotzebue passed north of the Bering Straits and into what is now Kotzebue Sound. Dr. Eschscholtz, the surgeon on the voyage, found the Eskimos of St. Lawrence Island and the mainland "of a middle size, robust make and healthy appearance." Their manner of making friends, however, the good doctor found somewhat less than hygienic: "Each of them embraced me, rubbed his nose hard against mine, and ended his caresses by spitting in his hands and wiping them several times over my face."[16]

Captain Beechey, of the H.M.S. *Blossom*, visited the same general area in 1826 and found "ophthalmia" to be very prevalent, despite the fact that snow goggles were widely employed. In general, he found the people much less attractive than others did, describing them as "extremely diminutive, dirty and forbidding. Some were blind, others decrepit; and, dressed in greasy worn-out clothes, they looked perfectly wretched."[17] Beechey saw a number of cripples on his voyage, including one so handicapped he went about on all fours.

The Royal Navy's Half Century

The first voyage of Captain John Ross in 1818 marked the beginning of a whole new era in arctic exploration. Although valuable work was done by the Hudson's Bay Company and later by the Americans, ships' officers, and men of the British Royal Navy dominated the arctic scene for nearly fifty years, first in the quest of the elusive Northwest Passage and later principally in search of the ill-fated expedition under Sir John Franklin.

Ross's expedition took him to Baffin Bay. What few Eskimos he saw on this trip, mostly on the coast of Greenland, impressed him with their white, regular teeth and their generally corpulent physiques.[18]

Lt. John Franklin's first expedition took him through Hudson Strait in 1819 on his way to the great arctic land mass to the west. Near Resolution Island the ship's party met a large band of Eskimos, most of whom Franklin also noted to be stout. He, too, recited the now familiar formula in his diary: "Most of the party had sore eyes, all of them appeared of a plethoric habit of body; several were observed bleeding at the nose during their stay near the ship."[19]

In the same year, W. Edward Parry, in the ships *Hecla* and *Griper*, pushed far to the west through Lancaster Sound and what is now Parry Channel. In September 1820 he encountered a party of seventeen Eskimos on the western coast of Baffin Island but saw no sign of disease among them, "except that the eyes of the old couple were rather blear, and a very young infant looked pale and sickly." The group in general appeared well fed, had beautiful teeth, and were cleaner than he had been led to expect. It is of incidental interest that these Eskimos refused rum offered to them, even when it was diluted with water.[20]

Parry's second voyage, which lasted from 1821 to 1823 and during which he explored the northern and western coasts of Hudson Bay and the surrounding regions, is an exceptionally good source of health information.

He made his first contact with the Eskimos on the north shore of Hudson Strait, where he found their personal hygiene less than optimal. He gained quite the opposite impression, however, at Lyon Inlet on the south side of the Melville Peninsula, where he was greatly taken by the cleanliness of the Eskimos who frequented his ship. He had ample chance to observe this group closely, since his ships became frozen into the ice for the winter not far from their camp. Parry noted several cases of chronic disease in the settlement, including an elderly infirm man who walked with a stick and an eight-year-old child who was "quite an idiot, deaf and dumb from his birth, and squinting most horribly with both eyes."[21]

During this first winter in the ice, Parry had occasion to observe a serious outbreak of respiratory disease. "Almost the whole of these people," he wrote, "were … affected with violent colds and coughs, occasioned by a considerable thawing that had lately taken place in their huts, so as to wet their clothes and bedding." He noted that as the huts became colder again (and hence less wet), the epidemic seemed to subside. John Edwards, the ship's surgeon, treated many cases of catarrhal disease, including a single case of pleurisy.[22]

The following winter, while the ships were frozen in further north near the settlement of Igloolik, another severe disease outbreak occurred among the Eskimos. Although Parry describes in detail the circumstances of many of the victims, he gives tantalizingly little information on their symptoms and signs. Even Dr. Edwards gives very little to go on in his account: "[It] appeared to be acute inflammation of some of the abdominal viscera, very rapid in its career." The illness attacked young and old alike. Some of the patients seemed to linger with a wasting disease characterized by diarrhea, whereas others suffered a rapidly fatal outcome within one or two days. By February 1823 the situation had become so bad that Parry set up a small hospital tent, with six beds, adjacent to the ship, so that better care could be provided to those who were critically ill. (Perhaps an ulterior motive for the establishment of this first arctic hospital was that the ship's own sick bay was now swarming with lice from its recent Eskimo occupants.) Edwards and the others did their best to help those who were sick and frequently made trips to the village to visit the new cases. Lack of food in the settlement, occasioned by the illness of the hunters, only worsened the situation. At least one patient who was treated for an extended time at the ship developed scurvy, presumably as a result of his long exposure to navy rations. Despite close contact with the sick and dying, none of the ship's officers or crew appears to have become ill. Among the Eskimos, however, the disease took a heavy toll. Eighteen of the 155 persons at the camp died that winter.[23]

Dr. Edwards commented at length on the health of the Eskimos, but his descriptions, though graphic, leave something to be desired for the twentieth-century diagnostician.

For example, he considered the epidemic to have resulted from exposure to the "putrid exhalations from the decomposing relics of offals,"[24] not an unusual view in his day. He also had a theory on the origin of nosebleeds. In his view, the frequent eating of animal food induced "a highly plethoric state of the vascular system" leading to a condition of "vicarious hemorrhage...having no small share in maintaining a balance in the circulating system." Generally, however, he thought the Eskimos enjoyed excellent health, at least during the summer months, and that "abdominal and thoracic inflammations" were the only common diseases plaguing them. He observed no exanthematous disorders. Like so many others, he noted snow blindness and the white, regular, but often worn teeth. He described several chronic diseases, including rheumatism, epilepsy in a deaf mute boy who died in the epidemic, and a cleft palate in a young woman.

G. F. Lyon, who commanded the ship *Hecla* in Parry's squadron, found pot bellies common in both sexes and noted that the women were inclined to be fat. "The teeth," he observed, "are strong, and deeply fixed in the gums. They are formed like rounded ivory pegs, and are as flat on the upper end as if filed down. Old people have them worn quite even with the gums, and it is but rarely that any are decayed."[25] In another place he noted a woman "who squinted abominably," a defect he had seen in Eskimos elsewhere.[26]

Sir John Ross, on his expedition to Boothia Peninsula between 1829 and 1833, found several persons with crippling conditions, including a highly respected woman with a club foot, a man with a broken or diseased thigh, and a third who had lost a leg in an encounter with a bear. The ship's carpenter made an artificial leg for the latter, for which he was exceedingly grateful.[27]

It might be noted here in passing that Dr. George M'Diarmid, the surgeon on this expedition, attended members of his own crew with "pneumonia, colds, simple fevers, and some cases of gastric disease" during the voyage. The armourer, moreover, died of "confirmed consumption" in July 1829. It is easy to imagine how such diseases could have spread to the Eskimos during their regular visits to the ship.[28]

Franklin's second expedition in 1826 brought him into contact with Eskimos near the mouth of the Mackenzie River. There he remarked on the general robustness of the people, noting particularly the great proportion of elderly individuals, all of whom seemed well fed, even obese, and in excellent health. The whole party, except the young, he found afflicted with sore eyes, two old men being nearly blind.[29] Dr. Richardson, a physician who was second in command on the expedition, was particularly impressed with the cleanliness of the group he encountered.[30]

Thomas Simpson of the Hudson's Bay Company also noted that the Eskimos of this region were "stout, well-looking people," with only a few cases of eye inflammation among them. Further west near Point Barrow, however, he encountered a huge Eskimo cemetery which he speculated might have resulted from an extensive epidemic.[31]

The most detailed observations on health from the western Arctic are those of Alexander Armstrong, M.D., who was surgeon on the M'Clure expedition around the middle of the century. Speaking of the Eskimos living near Cape Bathurst, he wrote:

> I was unable to ascertain with any degree of accuracy, what were the prevailing diseases among them; cutaneous diseases and chest affections appear the principal....
>
> I saw several old people afflicted with chronic bronchitis, and asthma, and one or two had wens on the head and neck.... They all appear to suffer more or less from ophthalmia—in the old people it is very common, with eversion of the eyelids. Several appear to have lost their vision from opacity of the cornea, the result of frequent attacks, produced by the combined influence of snow and sunshine. I saw none labouring under any form of congenital disease or deformity, and from what we could learn, there is seldom any mortality except

amongst the old people and very young children, resulting in the latter, I should say, from the effects of exposure.

Elsewhere Armstrong comments on the low fertility of the
women and the white, worn teeth.[32]

Alaska: Explorers and Scientists

There was no serious interest in the exploration of western
and northern Alaska until relatively late. In the early part of
the nineteenth century, as we have seen, Kotzebue and
Beechey stopped briefly near what is now Kotzebue Sound,
while others visited the north coast on their way to or from
the region around the Mackenzie River delta. In 1833 the
Russians established a trading post called St. Michael near the
mouth of the Yukon. The coast southward from here to Cape
Newenham, however, where large numbers of Eskimos lived,
was left relatively untouched, in part because the shallowness
of the offshore waters made landings difficult.

One of the few Russians who left an account of southwestern Alaska was Lt. L. A. Zagoskin of the Imperial Navy,
who explored on foot the lower Yukon and Kuskokwim
basins between 1842 and 1844. He made his journey only a
few years after a devastating smallpox epidemic had swept
through the region from the south. A number of abandoned
village sites he described bore mute testimony to the deadly
effects of this disease on a population which had had no previous exposure to it. Around St. Michael itself, Zagoskin particularly noted lice, carbuncles, sore eyes, and consumption.
Already, he noted, the Eskimos were showing the bad effects
of their contacts with the Russian traders. Syphilis, he was
glad to report, had not yet reached this area, although it was
wreaking havoc with the Aleuts to the south. On the whole,
he found the people in good health. "Really and truly," he
wrote, "the natives never seem to catch any cold."[33]

Nearly forty years later, however, Dr. Irving Rosse of the
U.S. Revenue Steamer *Corwin* had an opportunity to observe
the same Eskimo group and found, significantly, pulmonary

diseases and syphilis to be very prevalent, as were rheumatism, alimentary disorders, and hysteria.[34] Captain Hooper's account of the same voyage adds that the hair and clothing of these Eskimos were "alive with vermin."[35]

John Simpson, surgeon on the H.M.S. *Plover*, spent the two winters of 1851–52 and 1852–53 at Point Barrow, where he had ample opportunity to observe closely the health of the local people. In a village of 309, there were at the outset 166 males and 143 females in fifty-four households. During the first winter an epidemic of respiratory diseases, presumably influenza, carried off no less than forty persons. In the second year of his stay he counted twenty-seven deaths, mostly from famine, and only four births. This group, clearly, was losing ground in its battle for existence. Simpson noted that the people, understandably, were "inclined to sparseness" in their physiques. The maimed and the crippled were again prominent. In one group of fourteen summer tents, he found "one crippled old man, a blind and helpless old woman, two grown-up women with sprained ankles and one other old invalid, besides children of various ages, carried by their families."[36]

After transfer of Alaska to the United States in 1867, the U.S. Army sent out a number of exploratory expeditions to the Territory. Captain Charles Raymond, in charge of one of the first of these, wrote of his experiences among the Eskimos of the lower Yukon in 1869. Although he found most of them "vigorous and healthy," he was struck by the prevalence of "consumption, colds, asthma, rheumatism, and croup," the last of which caused a high mortality among the children. Their homes were swarming with vermin. Although liquor was freely available to these people through the traders at St. Michael, Raymond found no intoxication and stated, "I do not believe them to be intemperate."[37]

Ivan Petroff, who surveyed southwest Alaska for the 1880 Census tabulation, found the people riddled with disease, particularly consumption, but also "paralysis," "inflammation of the bowels," "fits," and general debility. Indeed, he could not help expressing admiration for these people who were "wonderful in their patience when suffering all the ills that flesh is heir to in their lonely, desolate homes."[38]

The *Corwin*'s voyage of 1884 provides some insight into conditions among the Eskimos of the Kobuk and Nowatak rivers, who had probably had less previous contact with the whites than the groups already described. J. C. Cantwell wrote that pulmonary complaints and rheumatism were the principal types of illness and that epidemic diseases were of rare occurrence. He found the ubiquitous sore eyes but, like Petroff, related it to poor ventilation in the homes rather than to snow glare.[39]

John Murdock visited Barrow at a time (1881–83) when the village was well known to explorers, whalers, traders, and missionaries. His account is still useful, however, because of his intimate and prolonged association with the Eskimos and the fact that he also summarized the views of his predecessors:

> Diseases of the respiratory and digestive organs are the most frequent and serious ailments from which they suffer. The former are most prevalent toward the end of summer and early in winter.... Nearly everyone suffers from coughs and colds in the latter part of August [arrival of ships?], and many deaths occur at this season and the beginning of winter from a disease which appears to be pneumonia. A few cases, one fatal, of hemorrhage of the lungs were observed.... The people suffer from diarrhea, indigestion, and especially from constipation.
>
> Gonorrhea appears common in both sexes, but syphilis seems to be unknown in spite of the promiscuous intercourse of the women with the whalemen. One case of uterine hemorrhage was observed. Cutaneous diseases are rare. A severe ulcer on the leg, of long standing, was cured by our surgeon, to whose observations I am chiefly indebted for what I have to say about the diseases of these people; and one man had lost the cartilage of his nose and was marked all over the body with hideous scars from what appeared to be some form of scrofulous

disease. A single case of tumor on the deltoid muscle was observed. Rheumatism is rather frequent. All are subject to snow blindness in the spring, and sores on the face from neglected frost bites are common. Many are blind in one eye from what appears to be cataract or leucoma, but only one case of complete blindness was noticed....

Injuries are rare. One man had lost both feet at the ankle and moved about with great ease and rapidity on his knees. All are subject to bleeding at the nose....

Natural deformities and abnormalities of structure are uncommon, except strabismus, which is common and often, at least, congenital.[40]

Discussion

Murdock's account is a fitting place to close this brief survey of the early documents bearing on Eskimo health. Not only does it confirm many of the observations made by earlier writers, but it also demonstrates well many of the adverse effects on health of the increasing contact with outside influences. Indeed, nearly all the Alaskan sources quoted, as well as some of the later ones from Greenland, Labrador, and the Canadian Arctic, reflect the harmful effects of imported diseases or changing environmental conditions.

The early written accounts are remarkably consistent in their descriptions of health conditions, despite the fact that they span over 300 years in time and many thousands of miles in distance. This consistency would perhaps warrant some tentative general conclusions about the health status of the Eskimos at the beginning of their intimate contact with western culture. What follows can of course give only a partial and distorted picture of health conditions as they were. The early observers could only comment on what they saw, or what they heard, or what they were interested in describing, or perhaps what they thought was important during their often brief contact. Most of them were not qualified to diagnose disease.

Throughout the Arctic the early records are consistent in describing the Eskimos as generally healthy, well fed, and even fat. In some cases obesity may have been assumed on insufficient evidence, bulky arctic clothing and the rounded facial configuration of the Eskimos giving a false impression of stoutness. In any case, it is probable that before the days of overhunting, commercial whaling, and the fur trade, the Eskimos generally had an adequate food supply except when, occasionally, they missed the caribou migration, or when adverse weather and ice conditions prevented them from hunting sea mammals.

Almost all the early writers were also in agreement that the teeth of the Eskimos were white, straight, often worn down, but virtually free of decay. Even today this state of affairs may be observed in many of the older people, particularly those who subsist largely on native foods.

The specific health condition most frequently mentioned, perhaps because it was so obvious even to the non-medical observer, was nosebleeds. From the first encounters in the sixteenth century, epistaxis has a prominent place in many of the writings. The frequency, severity, spontaneous onset, and the Eskimos' peculiar susceptibility to the condition are all clearly described. Nearly everyone also had a theory about its cause, but none of these explanations ring true today. There is no mention in the writings that the explorers themselves or other Caucasians suffered an undue incidence of the condition, a fact which would tend to negate such ready explanations as the cold, dry air. There is furthermore little evidence that this condition is unusually common today in Eskimos or whites, at least in western Alaska. The nosebleeds, therefore, remain a minor enigma.

Almost everyone who described the appearance of the Eskimos commented on the problem of sore eyes. Red, inflamed, and weeping eyes, of course, were obvious to the most casual observer, whether medically trained or not. In addition, many of the explorers, traders, and missionaries suffered from the condition themselves and were therefore particularly conscious of it in others. Although a number of theories on its causation were suggested, it seems likely that most of the Eskimos were afflicted with snow blindness, caused by their heavy exposure to a combination of sun, wind, and reflected glare. The condition seemed to be most common in the spring, when days were long and bright and the ice and snow still prevalent. It also predominated in the adult men, who of course were most heavily exposed during their hunting activities. A second possible explanation mentioned by several writers was that sore eyes resulted from constant exposure to the smoky interiors of their homes, particularly in the wood-burning areas of southwestern Alaska. A third possibility, at least in the later years, may have been phlyctenular keratoconjunctivitis, the condition which probably accounts for most cases of blindness in Eskimos today. Since this condition is thought by most to be related to tuberculosis, it is not likely to have been prevalent before the middle of the nineteenth century.

A number of people were described as being crippled or maimed in some way. Some were undoubtedly the victims of accidents, others seemed to have arthritic conditions, and some were deformed at birth. In addition to those with musculoskeletal defects, several persons observed children and adults with obvious mental retardation, convulsive disorders, or severe mental disturbances. The remarkable thing, in view of the widespread myth to the contrary, is the fact that the Eskimos seemed to take special pains to render faithful care to these unfortunates, who must have been a heavy burden to their families.

One might speculate on the causes of some of these crippling conditions. The Eskimos have always depended on large animals such as caribou, walruses, bearded seals, polar bears, and even whales for food, and the hazards of stalking and killing such quarry may be easily imagined. The cruel arctic weather has also always taken its toll. Mental retardation, mental disease, and epilepsy no doubt had a variety of causes, as in our own day, many of them totally obscure.

Trauma at birth or later head injury may have accounted for some cases, and infection of the central nervous system may have been implicated in others. The rather frequent mention of congenital disorders such as strabismus and cleft palate, however, suggests that some cases of cerebral dysfunction may have been genetically determined. The Eskimos, of course, lived for the most part in small isolated bands and relatively close intermarriage must have been common. Some Eskimo groups today are known to have an unusually high prevalence of genetically determined diseases, the best studied example being the Yupik Eskimos of southwestern Alaska, in whom arthrogryposis (Kuskokwim disease), methemoglobinemia, the salt-losing adrenogenital syndrome, and pseudocholinesterase deficiency have all been found to be relatively common.

The evidence on infectious diseases is difficult to interpret. There is little doubt that lice and certain helminths were indigenous to the people of the Arctic long before the arrival of Europeans. It is also difficult to imagine that the Eskimos would not have had their own complement of viral and bacterial diseases to plague them, just as every other segment of humanity has. Several of the earliest writers mention boils and other skin infections, diarrhea, and respiratory disease when describing the usual state of health of the people they encountered.

It is abundantly clear, however, that other infectious diseases were introduced from the outside. No exanthematous diseases were known in the Arctic until the Greenland smallpox disaster of 1733. Both this and the later Labrador and Alaskan epidemics point up the people's total lack of previous experience with this disease. The "Great Sickness" of 1900 in southwestern Alaska depopulated many villages and is still spoken of with awe by the few remaining survivors. Whether this plague was influenza or a combination of diseases is still uncertain. Whatever its nature, however, it attacked only the Indians and Eskimos to any degree. Measles was another disease which, when it struck, carried off victims of all ages. Although there are no specific early references to them, other epidemic diseases such as mumps, chickenpox, and rubella are still attacking isolated arctic villages with a high morbidity in our own generation.

The exquisite susceptibility of the Eskimos to diseases previously unknown to them is apparent from several of the writings already quoted and is again strikingly illustrated by the story told by a Hudson's Bay Company trader in 1834. Near Fort Chimo he met a group of six Eskimo families who had never previously seen a European. "We had been ill of a cold on their arrival," he wrote, "and six of them died in the course of twenty-four hours. The poor people left us in a great hurry, they left their dead also exposed upon the rocks; I offered to lend a hand to bury them but they would not wait an hour."[41]

Whether tuberculosis was introduced to the Arctic from the outside or was endemic there must remain unresolved, at least on the basis of the early writings. Almost everyone who was on hand long enough to observe a chronic wasting respiratory disease was also there long enough to have been a source of infection himself. Undoubtedly a number of arctic visitors, such as ship's crewmen, were themselves afflicted with tuberculosis and by their activities could easily have introduced the disease through a long winter contact with a settlement. From the written records it appears that tuberculosis was already firmly established in various parts of the Arctic by the second half of the nineteenth century.

Finally, several writers mentioned the apparent infertility of the Eskimo women they encountered. This inference seemed to be based on the observation that families were small and that children were not much in evidence. A few mothers were seen breast feeding children as old as four years, a practice which undoubtedly did lower the birth rate somewhat. A high perinatal and infant mortality probably also kept the average family small.

Quite the opposite situation prevails today. Although mortality is still higher than it should be, many more Eskimo children than formerly live to grow up, because of their access to modern medical care. Breast feeding, particularly beyond one year, is becoming less common. As for fertility itself, the Eskimos, in fact, have one of the highest birth rates of any population known. In a careful study of twenty-seven villages in western Alaska, the crude birth rate was found to be 53/1000.[42] Recent estimates from Canada are in line with this figure.

In conclusion, it seems clear from the available evidence that the health of the Eskimos prior to their prolonged contact with western culture was good, if not exceptional. The Eskimos showed that they had reached a remarkably effective adjustment to an unkind world and seemed to be thriving, despite some of the usual kinds of ills that all mankind is heir to. This balance was badly upset by the coming of men from other lands—men with new ways, new ideas, a new technology, and, most of all, new diseases. The effects of this encounter for the Eskimo people have been profound.

Notes

The research for this paper was for the most part carried out at the Library of the Arctic Institute of North America, in Montreal, and at the Stefansson Collection, Dartmouth College Libraries, Hanover, N.H. My thanks are due to the staffs of both these libraries for their courtesy and willing assistance.

1. V. Stefansson and E. McCaskill, eds., *The Three Voyages of Martin Frobisher* (London: Argonaut Press, 1938), 1: 50.
2. Ibid., 2: 23.
3. A. H. Markham, *The Voyages and Works of John Davis the Navigator* (London: Hakluyt Society, 1880), p. 19.
4. H. Egede, *A Description of Greenland* (London: Allman, 1818), pp. 119-21.
5. D. Crantz, *The History of Greenland,...* (London: Society for the Furtherance of the Gospel Among the Heathen, 1767), 1: 234-35.
6. Ibid., pp. 333-39.
7. A. Høygaard, "Tuberculosis in Eskimos," *Lancet* 235 (1938): 758-59.

8. H. Ellis, *A Voyage to Hudson's Bay by the Dobbs Galley and California in the Years 1746 and 1747* (New York: Johnson Reprint Corp., 1967), pp. 132, 137.

9. C. W. Townsend, *Captain Cartwright and his Labrador Journal* (Boston: Estes, 1911).

10. D. Jenness, *Eskimo Administration 3: Labrador* (Montreal: Arctic Institute of North America, 1965), p. 10.

11. Ibid., pp. 43–44.

12. S. Hearne, *A Journey from Prince of Wales's Fort in Hudson's Bay to the Northern Ocean, 1769-1772* (Toronto: Macmillan Co. of Canada, 1958), pp. 102, 209.

13. T. M'Keevor, *A Voyage to Hudson's Bay during the Summer of 1812* (London: Phillips, 1819), pp. 37–38.

14. E. Chappell, *Narrative of a Voyage to Hudson's Bay in His Majesty's Ship Rosamond* (London: Mawman, 1817), pp. 73–74.

15. Ibid., p. 66.

16. O. v. Kotzebue, *A Voyage of Discovery into the South Sea and Beering's Straits for the Purpose of Exploring a North-East Passage Undertaken in the Years 1815-1818* (London: Longman et al., 1821), 1: 191–92.

17. F. W. Beechey, *Narrative of a Voyage to the Pacific and Beering's Strait, etc.* (London: Colburn & Bentley, 1831), 1: 365.

18. J. Ross, *A Voyage of Discovery....* (London: Murray, 1819), 1: 172.

19. J. Franklin, *Narrative of a Journey to the Shores of the Polar Sea in the Years 1819, 1820, 1821 and 1822* (London: Dent, 1924), p. 22.

20. W. E. Parry, *Journal of a Voyage for the Discovery of a Northwest Passage from the Atlantic to the Pacific, Performed in the Years 1819-1820, in His Majesty's Ships Hecla and Griper* (London: Murray, 1821), pp. 280, 287.

21. W. E. Parry, *Journal of a Second Voyage for the Discovery of a Northwest Passage from the Atlantic to the Pacific; Performed in the Years 1821-23, in His Majesty's Ships Fury and Hecla* (London: Murray, 1824), pp. 90, 159–66.

22. Ibid., pp. 180–84.

23. Ibid., pp. 389–416, 492.

24. Ibid., pp. 544–47.

25. G. F. Lyon, *The Private Journal of G. F. Lyon of H.M.S. Hecla* (London: John Murray, 1825), pp. 308, 311.

26. G. F. Lyon, *A Brief Narrative of an Unsuccessful Attempt to Reach Repulse Bay Through Sir Thomas Rowe's "Welcome" in H.M.S. Griper in the year 1824* (London: Murray, 1825), p. 59.

27. J. Ross, *Narrative of a Second Voyage in Search of a North-West Passage and of a Residence in the Arctic Regions During the Years 1829, 1830, 1831, 1832, 1833* (London: Webster, 1835), p. 243.

28. Ibid., Surgeon's Report, pp. cxx, cxxvii.

29. J. Franklin, *Narrative of a Second Expedition to the Shores of the Polar Sea, in the Years 1825, 1826, and 1827* (London: Murray, 1828), p. 117.

30. Ibid., p. 196.

31. Th. Simpson, *Narrative of the Discoveries on the North Coast of America, Effected by the Officers of the Hudson's Bay Company During the Years 1836-1839* (London: Bentley, 1843), pp. 110, 121, 157.

32. A. Armstrong, *A Personal Narrative of the Discovery of the North-West Passage* (London: Hurst & Blackett, 1857), pp. 197, 193-95.

33. L. A. Zagoskin, *Lieutenant Zagoskin's Travels in Russian America, 1842-1844*, ed. H. N. Michael (Toronto: University of Toronto Press, 1967).

34. *Cruise of the Revenue-Steamer Corwin in Alaska and the North West Arctic Ocean in 1881.* Medical and Anthropological Notes by Irving C. Rosse, M.D. (Washington: Government Printing Office, 1883), pp. 21-23.

35. C. L. Hooper, *Report of the Cruise of the U.S. Revenue Steamer Thomas Corwin in the Arctic Ocean, 1881* (Washington: Government Printing Office, 1884), p. 103.

36. J. Simpson, "Observations on the Western Eskimo and the Country They Inhabit; from Notes Taken during Two Years at Point Barrow," in *Arctic Geography and Ethnology* (London: Murray, 1875), pp. 237-49.

37. C. P. Raymond, "Reconnaissance of the Yukon River," in *Compilations of Narratives of Explorations in Alaska* (Washington: Government Printing Office, 1900), p. 33.

38. I. Petroff, *Report on the Population, Industries, and Resources of Alaska* (Washington: Government Printing Office, 1882), pp. 43-44.

39. M. A. Healy, *Report of the Cruise of the Revenue Marine Steamer Corwin in the Arctic Ocean in the Year 1884* (Washington: Government Printing Office, 1889), p. 83.

40. J. Murdock, *Ethnological Results of the Point Barrow Expedition 1881-1883.* Smithsonian Institution, Bureau of American Ethnology (Washington: Government Printing Office), pp. 39-40.

41. N. Finlayson, Letter of 3 October 1834. Quoted in K. G. Davies, ed., *Northern Quebec & Labrador Journals and Correspondence 1819-35* (London: Hudson's Bay Rec. Soc., 1963), p. 240.
42. J. E. Maynard and L. M. Hammes, *Arctic Health Research Center Infant Morbidity and Mortality Study, Bethel Area, Alaska, October 1960-December 1962*, Anchorage, Alaska, Administrative Report, AHRC, May 1964.

Diffusion of Diseases in the Western Interior of Canada, 1830-1850

ARTHUR J. RAY

Much has been written about the effects of certain European diseases, most notably smallpox, on Indian populations; yet few scholars have attempted to assess the impact that a series of epidemics had on Indian life in various areas of North America. According to the anthropologist John C. Ewers, the paucity of such studies has probably led scholars to underestimate the havoc that diseases wreaked. He contends that scholars should consider the cumulative effects which these visitations of death had on population trends, band sizes and structures, tribal movements, balances of power, and the customs of Indians.[1] For most areas of North America, however, before these questions can be dealt with effectively the historical record must be examined to construct an inventory of diseases. Also, the geography of epidemics must be worked out in as much detail as possible to determine the frequency with which diseases occurred regionally, the origins and patterns of dispersals of the various epidemics, and the diffu-

Reprinted by permission of the American Geographical Society from the *Geographical Review* 66, no. 2 (April 1976): 139-57.

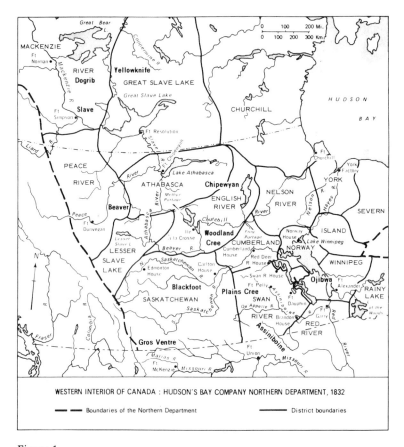

WESTERN INTERIOR OF CANADA : HUDSON'S BAY COMPANY NORTHERN DEPARTMENT, 1832

- - - Boundaries of the Northern Department ⸻ District boundaries

Figure 1

sion processes that produced these spatial patterns. This paper focuses on a portion of the western interior of Canada between 1830 and 1850 and attempts to achieve these latter objectives. It should also illustrate the type of work that can be done and should be a useful building block for further studies in the historical population geography of western Canada.

The area chosen for examination comprises the former Northern Department of the Hudson's Bay Company. This department covered a vast territory and was divided into eighteen districts for administrative convenience (Fig. 1). The physical and cultural geography of the department was highly varied. The central and southern portions of the Red River, Swan River, and Saskatchewan districts were grassland areas, home of nomadic bison-hunting Indian groups such as the Blackfoot, Plains Assiniboine, Cree, and Ojibwa. Arching from the east bank of the Red River northwestward across the northern sections of the Swan River and Saskatchewan districts was a transitional vegetational zone known as the parklands. Here prairie meadows were interspersed with sections of woodlands. The vast boreal forests of the subarctic stretched east of Lake Winnipeg and north of the Swan River and Saskatchewan River districts. These lands were inhabited by Woodland Indians such as the Ojibwa, Cree, Assiniboine, and Chipewyan. In the northern section of the Churchill District and the northeastern portion of the Great Slave District, the forest yielded to open tundra. This region came to be known as the barren lands. An analysis of the diffusion of diseases in the Northern Department thus affords an opportunity to consider how a variety of physical and cultural ecological factors may have influenced patterns of dispersal.

Of significance to diffusion processes, in certain sections of the Northern Department large numbers of Indians followed seasonal patterns of migration (Fig. 2). For example, in the Saskatchewan, Swan River, and Red River districts, Plains Indians such as the Assiniboine, Cree, and Ojibwa passed the winters in the sheltered river valleys and forested portions of the parklands. They spent the summers in the open grasslands, hunting the massive bison herds and travelling south to trade with horticultural Indians and American Fur Company traders in the Missouri River valley. Their Woodland Cree, Ojibwa, and Assiniboine relatives inhabited the woodlands during the warmer months of the year but often joined the Plains groups in the parklands during the middle and late winter in order to hunt bison.[2] Large-scale seasonal shifts of population also took place in the northeastern portion of the department in the vicinity of the boreal forest-tundra zone, where bands of Chipewyan Indians followed the migratory barren-ground caribou. These caribou passed the summer

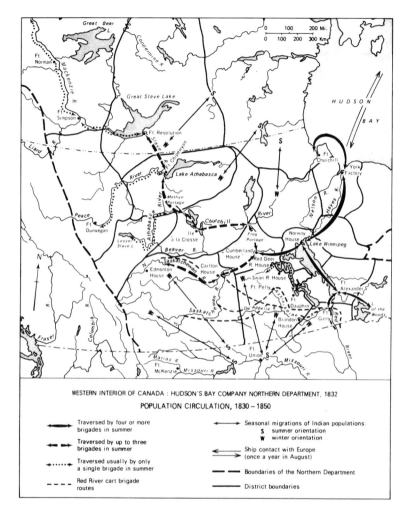

Figure 2

grazing in the open tundra and retreated to the shelter of the northern edges of the forest in winter.

The spatial concentration of Indian populations also varied seasonally. In all areas summer was the time when Indian groups came together to form larger villages. In the wood-lands, fishing encampments of two or three hundred were common, whereas in the grasslands, bison camps of one to four thousand were frequently reported. In the grassland and woodland areas, the Indians dispersed into smaller bands during the winter. These bands varied greatly in size depending on local resources. In the woodlands they often consisted of twenty to thirty individuals; in the parklands some camps of up to a thousand people were reported, but most were probably much smaller.[3]

A large portion of the non-Indian population of the department was also highly mobile, being involved in the inland transport business of the London-based Hudson's Bay Company. The company's extensive network of posts were linked together by boat, canoe, and cart brigades (Fig. 2). The boat and cart brigades were largely manned by Métis of mixed Indian and European ancestry. Severe winter weather and transportation technology precluded any extensive movement of goods during the winter, so almost all of the traffic between posts occurred during the summer, with the peak volume between the middle of June and the middle of August. Boat brigades were usually dispatched from the various district headquarters to Norway House and/or to York Factory. The latter was the chief port of entry for the Northern Department and a terminal point for brigades of the Rainy Lake, Winnipeg, Island, Swan River, and Cumberland districts. The flow of traffic was heaviest between York Factory and Norway House because of the key functions they served in the trading network. These two posts also had frequent contacts with the Red River Colony in the vicinity of Fort Garry.

Because of the relatively short open-water season, boat transport operated on a tight schedule and every effort was made to avoid delays. The late dispatch of a brigade often meant that a district ran the risk of not receiving critical winter supplies. This was particularly the case with the more northerly Mackenzie River and Great Slave Lake districts, where brigades often did not complete their return voyage until late autumn or early winter.

In addition to the summer movement of cargo between posts, there was limited contact during the winter, when letters were exchanged among traders via the so-called winter express. However, relatively few men were involved as couriers, so the possibility of transmission of disease at that time was limited.

In southern Manitoba and the adjacent portions of Saskatchewan, the Red River cart brigades carried a considerable volume of trade between the various posts during the summer season. These cart trains, consisting of horse-drawn two-wheeled carts, followed well-established routes (Fig. 2) and played an increasingly important role in the company's transport business as time passed.

In short, during the period between 1830 and 1850 there was a considerable amount of interaction of population between the various sections of the Northern Department. This interaction was facilitated by the migratory habits of certain Indian groups, by their trade at Hudson's Bay Company posts, and by the movement of men and material between the various posts by boat, canoe, and Red River cart. Furthermore, there was a marked seasonality to these patterns of interaction. Interregional, Indian–European, and Indian–Indian contacts were all more intensive during the summer, and the possibilities of transmitting diseases were therefore greatest at that time.

Influenza

During the period under consideration, a series of major and minor outbreaks of contagious diseases occurred.[4] Epidemics of influenza, most frequently reported, were recorded in 1835, 1837, 1843, 1845, 1847, and 1850. Influenza is a viral infection, with an incubation period of one to four days. Symptoms vary, but individuals generally experience a fever during the first twenty-four hours and suffer from inflammation of the respiratory and/or alimentary canal. General body aches and weakness are common. Significantly, since the dis-

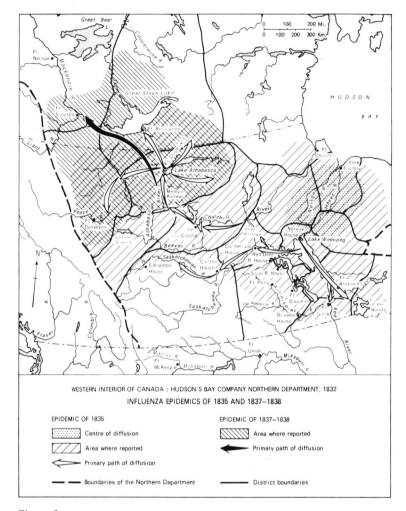

WESTERN INTERIOR OF CANADA : HUDSON'S BAY COMPANY NORTHERN DEPARTMENT, 1832
INFLUENZA EPIDEMICS OF 1835 AND 1837–1838

EPIDEMIC OF 1835

- Centre of diffusion
- Area where reported
- Primary path of diffusion

EPIDEMIC OF 1837–1838

- Area where reported
- Primary path of diffusion

- Boundaries of the Northern Department
- District boundaries

Figure 3

ease usually affects primarily the respiratory passages, the first appearance of the illness may lead an untrained observer to diagnose it as a bad cold.

The influenza epidemic of 1835 was first reported almost simultaneously at Norway House and York Factory (Fig. 3). The journal entry for Norway House for 22 June reads, "Several of the people laid up with a most severe cold." The following day, Don Ross, chief trader at the post, added, "The whole establishment...[was] much afflicted with sickness, somewhat resembling a cold but of a much more serious nature."[5] On the 26th the disease was said to be spreading in every direction. On 29 June Ross wrote, "We are all severely affected with the prevailing sickness, Influenza, no one escapes it: there are now upwards of 120 individuals young and old, including Indians, labouring under it at and about the Establishment."[6] Ross was the first to diagnose the disease as influenza.

At York Factory the first man to be reported sick was one of the crewmen of the Red River boat brigade. On 21 June this brigade departed for Norway House, but the sick man remained at York Factory. Five days later, chief trader James Hargrave said that six men were suffering from severe colds and sore throats. The number of men sick continued to increase, and on 5 July Hargrave wrote, "Severe colds, sore throats, pains in the breast, headaches, etc. still prevail very generally both in the establishment among the crews of the inland brigade and also among the Natives."[7] Hargrave never indicated that the disease was influenza, but his men were suffering from the same symptoms as those of the people at Norway House. On the basis of the information contained in the York Factory and Norway House journals, it therefore appears that the source area of the epidemic was in the York Factory, Island Lake, Nelson River, and Norway districts.

Illness spread quickly to other brigades that arrived at Norway House or York Factory from the interior. For instance, on 1 and 2 July the Red River and Rainy Lake brigades arrived at York Factory healthy, but three days later many of the crewmen were sick. The tight time constraints under which the company operated made it necessary to dispatch the boats anyway, and the sick crews were sent into the interior on 5 July.[8] Because of their weakened condition they took twenty-seven days to reach Norway House.[9] On arriving at this post they reported that most of the other inland brigades were laid up along the route to York Factory. Among these were the crews from the Swan River and English River districts, who had been forced to stop at Oxford House.

Meanwhile, on 12 July the Athabasca brigade of four boats arrived at Norway House in good health. Eight days later they were ready to head inland again, but many of the boat-men and Edward Smith, who was in charge of the brigade, were too sick to proceed.[10] They finally departed on 23 July, with many of the crewmen still suffering from the effects of influenza.[11] Although the Athabasca brigade was thus a car-rier of the disease, as were the other brigades, the epidemic apparently preceded the brigade as far to the northwest as Ile à la Crosse. According to Roderick Mackenzie, "the few Indi-ans that we found at the Establishment [Ile à la Crosse] on arrival were laid up with Influenza; which broke out among them early in August."[12]

Farther to the north, the Indians did contract the disease from the Athabasca brigade, which arrived at Fort Chip-ewyan on 3 October. Smith wrote, "Shortly after our arrival at this station Influenza broke out among the people that pass the summer inland and the families. The Indians being all about us at this season did not escape the effects of the disease."[13] By 12 October the sickness was reported to be raging throughout the country. The rapid spread of the epi-demic to the Chipewyan Indians in the hinterland of Fort Chipewyan was apparently a consequence of the fact that when the brigade arrived at the post, 162 Indians were wait-ing to trade. They bartered their furs for the goods they wanted and then dispersed to their winter hunting grounds, inadvertently carrying the disease with them. On 22 January 1836, Smith learned the illness had reached the "Caribou" Indians in the forest-tundra zone.[14]

The diffusion of influenza to the north and west of Fort Chipewyan seems to have been the result of dispatching company men and supplies in those directions. For instance, on 3 October, men departed from Fort Chipewyan for Forts Vermillion and Dunvegan, in the Peace River District. Three days later crews departed for Fort Resolution and the Mackenzie River District. On 19 December, Smith received a letter from the Peace River brigade informing him that the influenza epidemic had broken out in that region.[15]

Although the Mackenzie River brigade no doubt carried the disease with them when they left Fort Chipewyan on 6 October, influenza apparently did not break out in the Mackenzie River Valley during the winter. No references to the contagion are found in the journals of posts located in that district. The late arrival of the disease-carrying brigades may account for the failure of the epidemic to spread; by the time the crews arrived, the Indians had already scattered to their winter hunting grounds.

Farther to the southwest, the epidemic seems to have been spread to the Saskatchewan District by brigades from that area which arrived at Norway House between 25 June and 2 August 1835. Like the other inland crews, they contracted the disease at the post and left before they were fully recovered. All of the Saskatchewan boats embarked for the trip home by 3 August. Unfortunately, the records for the Edmonton District for this period are incomplete, and no journals have survived for this year for Edmonton House. Thus it is difficult to obtain a clear picture of the diffusion of disease in this quarter. Nonetheless, judging from the information contained in a letter addressed to Governor George Simpson by John Rowand at Edmonton House on 31 December 1835, it is clear that the epidemic broke out during the summer but apparently affected only the Woodland Assiniboine and Cree.[16] The Plains Indians may have avoided exposure because most of them were farther south in the open grasslands.

In 1837 influenza broke out again in the Northern Department (Fig. 3). Although information concerning this epidemic is less complete than was the case with the preceding one, its diffusion can be outlined. The 1837 epidemic seems to have erupted in the Athabasca and Peace River districts. On 30 December 1837, Alexander McLeod informed Governor Simpson from Fort Chipewyan that "a bad cough or Influenza afflicted the Natives all over this District, since the middle of summer."[17] A journal entry for Fort Dunvegan for 29 May 1837 states that most of the Indians living in the district were ill. As late as 28 February 1838, the post journal indicates that many Indians were still suffering from the "prevailing illness."[18]

The records from York Factory, Norway House, and Fort Edmonton contain no references to influenza during the summer and autumn of 1837, suggesting that the epidemic did not spread southward. Rather, it seems to have diffused northward, into the Mackenzie District. For instance, the journal for Fort Resolution for the summer of 1837 indicates that on several occasions company men suffered from bad coughs. Also, one of the Indian crewmen of the Mackenzie River brigade became ill on 3 July and was left at Fort Resolution to recuperate. Considering that the brigade had just come from the Athabasca District, where influenza was widespread, it seems highly likely that the Indian was suffering from the same illness. Unfortunately, no diagnosis was offered in this case, or for the "bad cough" suffered by the other men at the post. In any event, although influenza may have been present at Fort Resolution, it did not spread to the adjacent parts of the district as no contagion was reported among the Indians.

The epidemic did reach the Mackenzie River District, however. The timing of its appearance there suggests that the Mackenzie brigade which passed Fort Resolution on 3 July was the carrier. A letter dispatched to Governor Simpson from Fort Simpson on 27 November 1837 states that, "a kind of Epidemic disease or Influenza got among the Indians towards the latter end of summer, and still continues.[19] Assuming that "latter end of summer" was August, the disease broke out after the Mackenzie brigades arrived home.

Although the epidemic spread to Indians in the vicinity of Fort Simpson, it does not appear to have reached much farther down the Mackenzie River Valley or east of the

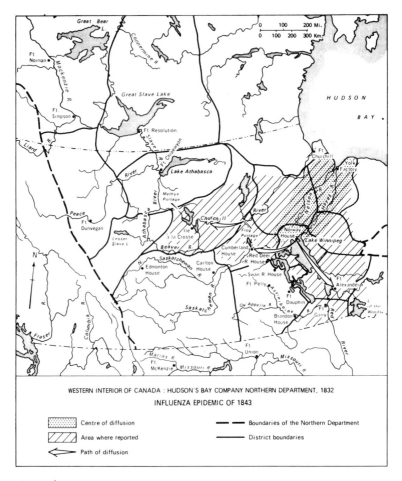

WESTERN INTERIOR OF CANADA : HUDSON'S BAY COMPANY NORTHERN DEPARTMENT, 1832

INFLUENZA EPIDEMIC OF 1843

Centre of diffusion	▬ ▬ Boundaries of the Northern Department
Area where reported	▬▬▬ District boundaries
Path of diffusion	

Figure 4

Coppermine River area. Not one of the dispatches from Fort Norman includes any references to influenza or to any other diseases. Thus, as Figure 3 shows, the influenza epidemic of 1837 was apparently more localized than was that of 1835.

Six years later, in 1843, yet another epidemic of influenza occurred (Fig. 4). Initial reports of the disease came almost simultaneously from York Factory and Norway House. Letters from these two posts indicate that it broke out in July and persisted through August. During the late summer and autumn, Indians in the vicinity of Fort Alexander were said to be sick with influenza.[20] To the northwest, the epidemic spread as far as Ile à la Crosse, in the English River District. It apparently reached that area in September, for between the 21st and the 26th the Ile à la Crosse journal indicates that many Indians were sick and refused to leave the post.[21] The records from Forts Chipewyan, Dunvegan, and Edmonton contain no references to widespread sickness during the summer, autumn, or winter, so the epidemic does not seem to have extended beyond the English River District.

During the summer of 1845, influenza hit sections of the Northern Department for the fourth time in ten years (Fig. 5). According to the York Factory journals, the disease was first contracted by the boat crews of the Red River colony in the spring. These crews carried it northward to Norway House and York Factory. Influenza was widespread in the vicinity of Norway House by mid-July, and an Indian died from the illness at that post on the 21st of that month. From then until 29 August the disease is mentioned frequently in the journal. That no reference is made to it thereafter suggests the epidemic had subsided.

Influenza apparently did not reach York Factory until mid-July, for it was first mentioned in the post journal on the 17th of the month: "In the afternoon four Oxford House boats received cargoes [they had arrived on the 15th] . . . and took their departure. . . . The Crews of these boats are generally affected with Influenza, a disease prevalent this summer among the Natives and servants in the low country."[22] On 19 July, just four days after this Oxford House brigade arrived, a servant at York Factory was reported sick with influenza. Two days later, four more were sick; the disease began to spread. The rapidity with which this epidemic diffused to the area around the post led Hargrave to write: "The disease,— Influenza—broke out . . . and although on two previous occa-

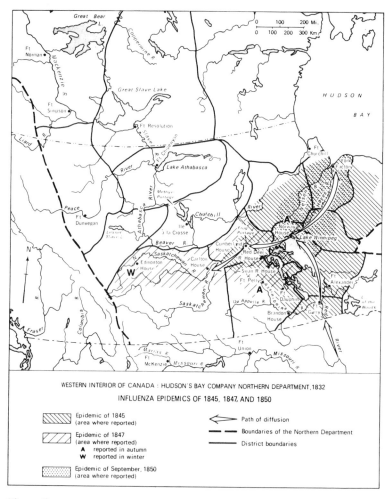

WESTERN INTERIOR OF CANADA : HUDSON'S BAY COMPANY NORTHERN DEPARTMENT, 1832

INFLUENZA EPIDEMICS OF 1845, 1847, AND 1850

Epidemic of 1845
(area where reported)

Epidemic of 1847
(area where reported)
A reported in autumn
W reported in winter

Epidemic of September, 1850
(area where reported)

Path of diffusion

Boundaries of the Northern Department

District boundaries

Figure 5

sions of a similar nature I had witnessed more mortality, at no time within these last twenty years did the contagion spread so widely or produce such effects upon the physical strength of the convalescents."[23] Not until the first week of September did the outbreak begin to subside in the area around York Factory.[24]

Although the debilitating effects of the epidemic brought the freighting business between York Factory and Norway House to a virtual standstill in late July and August, Hargrave indicated that the sickness did not interfere with the inland brigades.[25] The fact that most of the brigades had left for the interior before the disease reached epidemic proportions may explain why it does not appear to have spread to the English River area or to other districts to the northwest. Why the epidemic did not spread to the Saskatchewan District is not clear, however. One Saskatchewan brigade left Norway House on 28 July, and many of the crewmen were sick. Thus the disease was carried into the district, even though it did not cause an epidemic.

In 1846 influenza was reported again in the English River, Athabasca, and Great Slave districts, but the symptoms that fur traders diagnosed as influenza may have been complications resulting from measles, which was prevalent that year. The following year, however, influenza did make its appearance once more, this time primarily in the Saskatchewan Valley and the lands to the south (Fig. 5). According to Ross, a "severe" epidemic broke out in the Norway District in the autumn.[26] From there it spread to the west and southwest. William Todd reported that influenza was also widespread around Fort Pelly in the Swan River District in autumn, affecting Plains and Woodland Indians alike.[27] A letter from John Harriott at Edmonton House indicates the epidemic reached that area in early winter and that its effects were felt most strongly in the parkland area. No other posts reported the disease, so it appears to have been confined to the area shown in Figure 5.

In the autumn of 1850, the sixth outbreak of influenza in twenty years took place. As on three preceding occasions, it appeared almost simultaneously at York Factory and Norway House in the month of September.[28] Like the epidemic of 1847 it was relatively localized and seems to have been confined mostly to the York, Norway, and contiguous districts (Fig. 5). The epidemic probably did not spread more widely because it broke out in autumn, after most of the transport business had been completed.

The mortality rates from the various influenza epidemics varied considerably. In 1835, eight Indians at York Factory died and two children of employees at Norway House succumbed.[29] The York journal reveals that the post's medical doctor made daily visits to the lodges of nearby Indians to administer medicine. It adds that his efforts and the food supplies sent out from the post to aid the weakened Indians helped to reduce the death toll. Although the loss of life thus appears to have been moderate in these two districts and to have been confined mostly to the young and the old, particularly women, it seems to have been much greater in the Saskatchewan area. There the "prevalent sickness carried off so many," mostly Woodland Cree and Assiniboine, that Rowand, who was in charge of the district, expected it seriously to reduce the fur returns from the region.[30] The toll was also high in the English River District, where at least forty or fifty Indians perished.[31] The loss of life in the Athabasca and Peace River districts, said to be great, led the journalist of Fort Chipewyan to remark that "the present distressing situation of the Indians is without parallel during my thirty-six years residence among them."[32] Even though the record of fatalities is incomplete, most of the victims again appear to have been women and children.

The influenza epidemic of 1837 seems to have been much milder and reportedly produced no fatalities around Fort Simpson or in the Athabasca District. Loss of life was widespread only in the vicinity of Fort Dunvegan, in the upper Peace River Valley.[33] The toll there may have been boosted by malnutrition, for food was in short supply that year. Similarly, the influenza epidemics of 1843, 1845, 1847, and 1850 were relatively mild and caused few deaths. However, the death rates for the influenza epidemics of 1843 and 1845 may have been underestimated, because other illnesses, such as scarlet fever in 1843 and whooping cough and perhaps dysentery in 1845, were prevalent in the Manitoba lowlands. Most of the deaths reported in those two years were attributed to these other illnesses.

Scarlet Fever

Scarlet fever is caused by streptococci. Significantly, an attack of scarlet fever does not confer immunity to the victim; on the other hand, the typical scarlet fever symptoms of early high fever, redness of the throat and tonsils, and a blotchy red rash, are rarely observed twice in the same individual. Rather, repeated attacks usually produce other responses, such as strep throat. Thus the first outbreaks of the disease in the early nineteenth-century Canadian West could have been identified easily, but subsequent visitations of the fever would be more difficult to diagnose and thus may not have been recorded. Also, although scarlet fever is communicable, it rarely occurs in epidemic form.[34]

The epidemic of 1843 was probably the first occurrence of scarlet fever in the Canadian West for at least a generation, because most of the people afflicted by it had readily identifiable symptoms. The disease seems to have appeared first among the Red River colonists in mid-summer and to have persisted there until December.[35] By late summer it had spread among the Indians along the lower Winnipeg River in the vicinity of Fort Alexander. In October it broke out among the Indians along the Berens River on the eastern shore of Lake Winnipeg when they came to pick up their winter supplies.[36] Whether the disease reached the Norway or Island Lake districts is not clear. Ross's letters from Norway House to Governor Simpson indicate that influenza was common in his district as well as to the south and to the northeast. He also mentioned the scarlet fever epidemic in the Red River and Berens River areas. Presumably, if the fever had been present in his district he would have said so. Given the lack of references to scarlet fever and given the fact the disease is less contagious than influenza or measles, it probably was localized in the Red River and Winnipeg districts of southeastern

Manitoba. Even so, loss of life was reportedly heavy among Indians and Europeans alike in the affected area. Mortality rates were not spread evenly over the populations, however, and the victims were usually children.[37]

Measles

The epidemic of measles that began in 1846 lasted almost a year in the Northern Department (Fig. 6). Like the influenza epidemic of 1835, its effects were widely felt. Measles is a viral disease, one of the most communicable known.[38] The disease causes an inflammation of the mucous membrane of the nose and air passages within ten days of contact. Three or four days after these symptoms are manifest, a rash appears on the face, abdomen, and extremities. It generally attacks children under the age of fifteen, but when the disease is introduced into a population not previously exposed, an extremely high proportion of people of all ages, often more than 90 percent, will contract it.[39]

The measles epidemic of 1846 first appeared in the Red River area in the early summer. Again the boat brigades seem to have been the primary carriers. On 7 June four boats arrived at Norway House from Red River, and Ross reported that the crews were sick with measles.[40] He quickly loaded their canoes and sent them on to York Factory, hoping to avoid the contagion. The same day the Methey Portage brigade arrived from Ile à la Crosse and remained for two days. On the 9th, boats from Rainy Lake arrived. All of these crews were healthy. On the 13th all of the district Indians arrived to trade, and in the afternoon a boat came in from the Berens River. On 17 June Ross reported that several of his men were sick with measles. This happened ten days after their first exposure to the disease and thus corresponds closely to the normal incubation period for the illness.[41] The same day the English River brigade arrived at Norway House and informed Ross that eighteen of the men of the Methey Portage brigade, which they had passed on the way, were sick with measles.

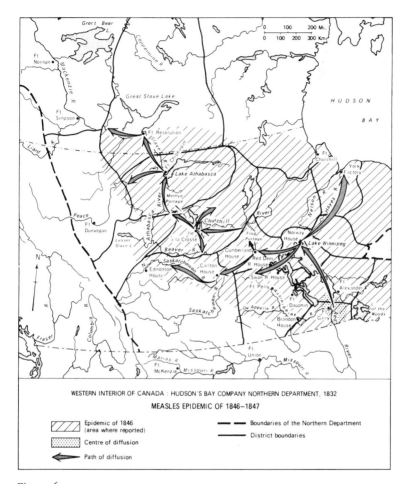

Figure 6

Measles were now widespread from Norway House to York Factory and southward to the Red River colony. Meanwhile, other brigades continued to arrive at Norway House: the Saskatchewan on 26 June, the Swan River on 8 July, the Athabasca on 15 July, and two more from the Red River on 25 July and 4 August. All were exposed to the disease for varying lengths of time and then departed for home, usually with some of the men suffering from the illness.

Initially the disease appears to have spread most rapidly northeastward from the centre of diffusion. This is not surprising, however. Until midsummer most crews were heading for Norway House and/or for York Factory. Westward and northwestward expansion of the epidemic accelerated as the crews left for home. As the arrival-departure information for Norway House indicates, this began in mid-July. On 29 July half of the men stationed at Cumberland House were said to be sick from measles.[42] Considering the incubation period for the disease, the post would have been exposed as early as 19 July, perhaps by the Athabasca brigade that had left Norway House on 16 July. By 9 August measles was widespread around Carlton House, suggesting that the population there had been exposed at least as early as the first of the month.

Because of the greater travel distances, the disease spread to the north of the Saskatchewan River more slowly. Roderick Mackenzie indicated that the outfit from York Factory did not arrive at Ile à la Crosse until 10 September. This was later than normal, owing to the debilitating effects which the measles had on the crews. When the brigade arrived, he reported, "We found nearly the whole of our Chipewyans in camp here apparently in good health." But "early in October the Measles and Influenza broke out violently among our unfortunate Indians."[43] Mackenzie's observations thus leave little doubt that the Ile à la Crosse brigade carried the disease into the English River District.

Farther to the north, the Athabasca brigade arrived at Fort Chipewyan on 17 September. Measles among the crews was again cited as the reason for their late arrival.[44] On 29 September, boats were dispatched to Forts Vermilion and Dunvegan in the Peace River Valley to the west and to Forts Resolution and Simpson to the north. On 3 December some of the men at Fort Chipewyan were sick with the measles and influenza. A week earlier a Chipewyan had complained that sickness was widespread among them in their winter camps. The disease was not specified, but in all probability the Indians were suffering from measles.

Measles apparently did not spread westward to the Peace River area that winter, for a letter from Fort Chipewyan dated 24 December stated that everyone there was enjoying good health. Similarly, the epidemic does not seem to have diffused northward to the Indians in the upper Mackenzie District. A probable explanation is that the disease had so delayed the crews that they did not arrive at Fort Simpson until after the Indians had completed their autumn trading and had scattered to their winter camps. Somewhat surprisingly, it does not appear to have affected the men at Fort Simpson either that winter, or the following summer.

The measles epidemic of 1846–47 was not only widespread but also took a heavy toll of life among all ages. On 10 August, Hargrave reported that thirty-one Indians had died around York Factory, including "only those in the immediate vicinity and buried by the company's Servants."[45] Nicol Finlayson dispatched a letter to Governor Simpson from Fort Alexander on 3 August in which he remarked that "sickness had made such ravage among the natives this summer, and the last which has more the appearance of a pestilence than an epidemic."[46] Similar reports came from the Red River, Norway House, and Oxford House. The loss of life and the debility of the survivors was such that the company was unable to find enough able-bodied men to take the boats to the Red River, Norway, Oxford, and York districts.[47] The disease had equally devastating results in other areas, and with the exception of the smallpox epidemic of 1838, the measles epidemic seems to have produced the highest mortality rate.

Judging from the information provided by Hargrave at York Factory, it may be that many of the deaths resulted not directly from measles but from subsequent complications. Commenting on the heavy loss of life, he observed that "inflammation of the heart and of the chest generally followed the disease that originally attacked them, and the greatest mortality resulted from that cause."[48] Measles can produce serious consequences that affect the respiratory system, the ears, and the brain.[49] Hargrave's observations indicates that the Indians were prone to the first of these sequelae. As has been noted, the records of Ile à la Crosse, Fort Chipewyan, and Fort Resolution all reveal that influenza broke out along with measles in 1846. The coughing and respiratory troubles reported as influenza may well have been complications associated with the measles.

Smallpox

Smallpox was undoubtedly one of the most dreaded of all European diseases to which the Indians were exposed. It broke out in the Northern Department in 1837 (Fig. 7). Initial symptoms of smallpox are fever, chills, headaches, and prostration, which continue for three or four days. The temperature then begins to fall, and a rash appears and evolves into a number of pustules. Crusts form and the scabs finally fall off about the end of the third week. Smallpox varies from a mild disease with a fatality rate of less than 1 percent to a severe condition with a fatality rate of 30 percent or more. The severity of a given epidemic is directly proportional to the residual immunity of the population and therefore decreases over time after exposure.[50] The epidemic of 1837 was the first major outbreak in the Northern Department since 1780. Consequently, it is not surprising that many of the Indian groups who contracted the disease suffered terrible losses. The fur traders estimated that the Indians, chiefly Assiniboine, Blood, Sarsee, Piegan, Blackfoot, and Gros Ventre, lost up to three-quarters of their populations.[51]

Figure 7 traces the diffusion of the epidemic. Significantly, the pattern is similar in most respects to two other smallpox epidemics that struck the Northern Department in 1780 and 1869.[52] Furthermore, it contrasts sharply with the patterns outlined for the influenza, scarlet fever, and measles epidemics. The smallpox epidemic first broke out in June 1837 at Fort Union. The source of the contagion was an American Fur Company supply boat that had been dispatched from St. Louis. When it arrived at Fort Union, one man on board was suffering from smallpox. Although the American Fur Com-

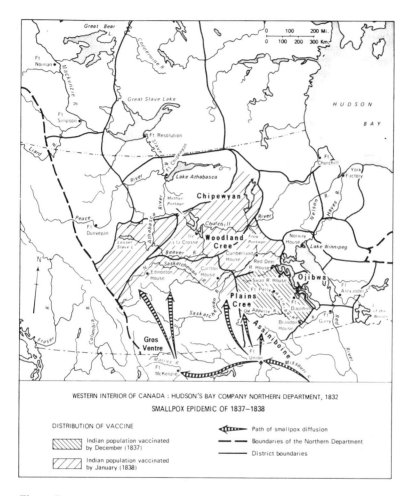

WESTERN INTERIOR OF CANADA : HUDSON'S BAY COMPANY NORTHERN DEPARTMENT, 1832

SMALLPOX EPIDEMIC OF 1837–1838

Figure 7

pany traders attempted to prevent the spread of the disease in the vicinity of the post, their efforts failed. A party of more than 1,000 Indians ignored warnings to stay away from the fort, and they contracted smallpox soon after their arrival. Only 150 survived.[53]

The epidemic was transmitted farther up the Missouri River valley by another supply boat of the American Fur Company. Shortly after the steamboat had arrived at Fort

Union a longboat was sent on to Fort McKenzie, on the Marias River a short distance upstream from its confluence with the Missouri River. The crew of the longboat became ill shortly after leaving Fort Union, and an attempt was made to quarantine them in the vicinity of the Judith River. However, a party of more than five thousand Blackfoot and Piegan, who were waiting at Fort McKenzie to trade, insisted that the supply boat proceed. Trade began as soon as the boat arrived, and shortly thereafter the Blackfoot and Piegan fell victim to the epidemic.[54]

Smallpox was quickly carried northward into the Northern Department by the equestrian Assiniboine, Cree, Blood, Blackfoot, Gros Ventre, and Piegan Indians, who fled in the misguided belief that they could run away from contagion. By autumn the disease was reported in the Qu'Appele River valley, and by November it had reached the Indians living in the parklands along the North Saskatchewan River between Carlton House and Edmonton House. Further diffusion of the epidemic to the east and north was arrested by an extensive vaccination program of the Hudson's Bay Company, so the Woodland Indians escaped the ravages of the disease.[55]

The Trading Network and the Diffusion of Disease

Outbreaks of contagious diseases that affected populations in two or more districts occurred nine times between 1830 and 1850. In addition, several other, more localized, epidemics occurred.[56] In most instances the Hudson's Bay Company boat brigades served as the primary carriers of the diseases. With the exception of the smallpox epidemic of 1837, the process was essentially one of hierarchical diffusion, similar to what one would expect in a well-developed central place system.[57]

The key position of certain posts, such as Norway House and York Factory, in the transport system no doubt accounts in part for the greater frequency of disease experienced there. Indeed, the Norway District appears to have been the most unhealthy, with ten different epidemics. Norway District was also the most central location, in frequent contact with the west, northwest, northeast, and south. The ecological situation of Norway House and York Factory may also have been important, for both were situated in marshy lowland areas.

The timing of the outbreak of a disease was clearly critical in determining how widely it diffused. Generally, epidemics that began in midwinter remained relatively localized because the Indians had little contact with the posts, because they were widely dispersed, and because traffic between districts was minimal. On the other hand, if an epidemic erupted in midsummer it generally spread rapidly, especially if it was highly contagious. At this time of the year, Indians gathered together in larger encampments, visited the trading houses frequently, and there was a high volume of boat and canoe traffic between districts.

Diseases were less frequent in the peripheral areas, such as the Mackenzie River and Great Slave Lake districts, which were so distant from the usual point of origin in Manitoba that the brigades did not arrive until early winter, or later in epidemic years, owing to the debilitating effects of disease on the crews. By that time the local Indians often had already dispersed to their winter camps. Thus the timing of transmission also helped to reduce the prevalence of disease in the northernmost areas. Elsewhere, large trading parties of Indians would await the arrival of the supply boats. During the trading that followed, the Indians often contracted disease and spread it to the hinterlands of the posts as they fanned out to their winter hunting grounds.

The smallpox epidemic of 1837–38 was an exception to the general pattern. Rather than breaking out in the York Factory–Norway House–Red River area, it erupted in the Missouri River valley. Initial transmission was via American Fur Company supply boats, but subsequent dispersal was caused by the northward flight of Indians who sought to escape from the dreaded disease. The disease failed to diffuse through the network of woodland posts of the Hudson's Bay Company because of the vaccination program which the company carried out as a countermeasure.

The impact of these repeated epidemics on the population growth rates of the various districts has not been dealt with in detail here, for information regarding losses of life is still sketchy. The epidemics of influenza in 1835, of smallpox in 1837, and of measles in 1846–47 caused heavy losses in areas affected; most other epidemics were said to have taken light to moderate tolls. Verification or refinement of these general statements, however, must await meticulous analysis of the population estimates and tallies taken at various times.

Notes

I wish to thank the Hudson's Bay Company for permitting me to consult and quote from its microfilm collection in the Public Archives of Canada, in Ottawa; the Canada Council, for defraying my travel and research expenses; and C. F. Godfrey, M.D., and the late Andrew H. Clark, for their comments and suggestions on earlier drafts of this paper. I would also like to thank the York University cartographic office, particularly Robert P. Ryan, for drafting the maps.

1. John C. Ewers, "The Influence of the Fur Trade on Indians of the Northern Plains," in *People and Pelts: Selected Papers of the Second North American Fur Trade Conference*, ed. Malvina Bolus (Winnipeg: Peguis Publishers, 1972), pp. 1–26, reference on p. 20.

2. Arthur J. Ray, *Indians in the Fur Trade: Their Role as Trappers, Hunters, and Middlemen in the Lands Southwest of Hudson Bay, 1660–1860* (Toronto: University of Toronto Press, 1974), pp. 166–81.

3. Charles A. Bishop, *The Northern Ojibwa and the Fur Trade: An Historical and Ecological Study* (Toronto: Holt, Rinehart and Winston of Canada, 1974), pp. 277–89.

4. The Hudson's Bay Company records are an excellent source of information regarding diseases and the general health of the Indians. The traders in charge of the various districts of the Northern Department generally wrote two to four letters a year to Governor George Simpson, in which they reported on

the general state of the fur trade in their respective areas. Since epidemics almost always disrupted trade, they were usually reported. Frequently these reports include accounts of when and where a disease broke out. Supplementing the correspondence are the journals of the posts. The daily entries in many of these journals make it possible to pinpoint the date on which an epidemic erupted and the length of time it lasted.

The principal difficulty with the data relates to the fact that many of the posts lacked trained medical personnel to diagnose illnesses. Compounding the problem is the fact that some diseases, such as smallpox and measles, have similar symptoms in their early stages and that others produce classic symptoms in an individual only once, making subsequent attacks of the illness hard to diagnose. Finally, in some years, such as in 1843, several diseases reached epidemic proportions at almost the same time. For these reasons, the traders' diagnoses of illnesses must be viewed with caution, particularly when the epidemics were localized. Generalized outbreaks afford an opportunity to do more cross-checking of sources, so that correct diagnoses are more likely.

5. Norway House Journal, 1835, Public Archives of Canada, Hudson's Bay Company Collection (micro-film) (henceforth referred to as HBC), B 154/a/26, p. 6.
6. Ibid., p. 8.
7. York Factory Journal, 1834–35, HBC 239/a/148, p. 60.
8. Ibid.
9. Norway House Journal, 1835, HBC B 154/a/26, p. 12.
10. Ibid.
11. Ibid., p. 13.
12. Governor George Simpson, Letters Inward to Simpson (henceforth referred to as Simpson Inward), Roderick Mackenzie, Ile à la Crosse, 10 January 1836, HBC D 5/4, p. 152.
13. Simpson Inward, Edward Smith, Fort Chipewyan, 31 December 1835, HBC D 5/4, p. 148.
14. Fort Chipewyan Journal, 1835–36. HBC B 39/a/31, p. 79.
15. Ibid., p. 72.
16. Simpson Inward, John Rowand, Edmonton House, 31 December 1835, HBC D 5/4, p. 143.
17. Simpson Inward, Alexander McLeod, Fort Chipewyan, 30 December 1837, HBC D 5/4, p. 364.
18. Fort Dunvegan Journal, 1838, HBC B 56/a/6, p. 4.
19. Simpson Inward, McPherson, Fort Simpson, 27 November 1837, HBC D 5/4, p. 346.

20. Simpson Inward, Nicol Finalyson, Fort Alexander, 1 December 1843, HBC D 5/9, p. 313.
21. Ile à la Crosse Journal, 1843, HBC B 89/a/22, p. 29.
22. York Factory Journal, 1845, HBC B 239/a/161, p. 47.
23. Simpson Inward, James Hargrave, York Factory, 10 August 1845, HBC D 5/14, p. 253.
24. Simpson Inward, James Hargrave, York Factory, 8 September 1845, HBC D 5/15, p. 39.
25. Simpson Inward, James Hargrave, York Factory, 10 August 1845, HBC D 5/14, p. 253.
26. Simpson Inward, Don Ross, Norway House, 10 December 1847, HBC D 5/19, p. 629.
27. Simpson Inward, William Todd, Fort Pelly, 23 April 1848, HBC D 5/22, p. 169.
28. Simpson Inward, Don Ross, Norway House, 27 November 1850, HBC D 5/25, p. 253; and Simpson Inward, James Hargrave, York Factory, 1 December 1850, HBC D 5/25, p. 298.
29. York Factory Journal, 1834-35, HBC 239/a/148, pp. 60-62; and Norway House Journal, 1835, HBC B 154/2/26, pp. 9-16.
30. Simpson Inward, John Rowand, Edmonton House, 31 December 1835, HBC D 5/4, p. 143.
31. Simpson Inward, Roderick Mackenzie, Ile à la Crosse, 10 January 1836, HBC D 5/4, p. 152.
32. Fort Chipewyan Journal, 1835-36, HBC B 39/a/31, p. 71.
33. Simpson Inward, McPherson, Fort Simpson, 27 November 1837, HBC D 5/4, p. 346; and Fort Dunvegan Journal, 1838, HBC B 56/a/6, p. 4.
34. Jacques M. May, M.D., *The Ecology of Human Disease*, A.G.S. Studies in Medical Geography no. 1 (New York: MD Publications, Inc., 1958), p. 252.
35. Simpson Inward, Nicol Finlayson, Fort Alexander, 1 December 1843, HBC D 5/9, p. 313.
36. Ibid.
37. Ibid.
38. May, *Ecology of Human Disease*, p. 264.
39. Ibid., pp. 264-65.
40. Norway House Journal, 1846, HBC B 154/a/46, p. 3.
41. Ibid., p. 4.
42. Simpson Inward, Colin Campbell, Cumberland House, 29 July 1846, HBC D 5/18, p. 85.
43. Simpson Inward, Roderick Mackenzie, Ile à la Crosse, 12 January 1847, HBC D 5/19, p. 65.
44. Fort Chipewyan Journal, 1846, HBC B 39/a/42, p. 21.

45. Simpson Inward, James Hargrave, York Factory, 10 August 1846, HBC D 5/18, p. 180.
46. Simpson Inward, Nicol Finlayson, Fort Alexander, 3 August 1846, HBC D 5/18, p. 105.
47. Simpson Inward, James Hargrave, York Factory, 10 August 1846, HBC D 5/18, p. 180.
48. Ibid.
49. May, *Ecology of Human Disease*, p. 264.
50. Jacques M. May, M.D., ed., *Studies in Disease Ecology*, A.G.S. Studies in Medical Geography no. 2 (New York: Hafner Publishing Co., Inc., 1961), pp. 1–4.
51. Ray, *Indians in the Fur Trade*, p. 188.
52. Ibid., pp. 107, 191.
53. Edwin T. Denig, *Five Indian Tribes of the Upper Missouri*, ed. John C. Ewers (Norman: University of Oklahoma Press, 1961), p. 71.
54. Arthur J. Ray, "Smallpox: The Epidemic of 1837–38," *The Beaver*, Autumn 1975, pp. 8–13.
55. Ray, *Indians in the Fur Trade*, pp. 188–89.
56. Most of these illnesses were confined to a single district and produced few fatalities. Many cannot be identified because descriptions of symptoms are insufficient. For instance, "sore eyes" were common in the western English District during the autumn and winter of 1844 and in the northern Saskatchewan District in January 1840. In December 1840, many Indians in the Norway District suffered from "putrid fever." Identifiable but localized epidemics included three outbreaks of whooping cough, one in the Nelson River District in 1834, one in the Norway District in 1843, and one in the Ile à la Crosse area in 1845; mumps, in the York District in 1841 and in the Ile à la Crosse region in 1844; and dysentery, in the Norway District in 1845 and 1846.
57. Gerald F. Pyle, "The Diffusion of Cholera in the United States in the Nineteenth Century," *Geographical Analysis* 1 (1969): 59–75.

Poor Relief and Medicine in Nova Scotia, 1749-1783

RELIEF MACKAY

No society is free from those helpless individuals who through illness, old age, mental defects, shiftlessness, or bad luck are dependent on the charity of their fellow citizens. Pre-Loyalist Nova Scotia seems to have had more than her share of these unfortunates, and she dealt with them in typical eighteenth-century fashion. The economic condition of the province and the character of a part of the population combined with certain actions of the government to increase the number of undesirables. For example, the council, observing that "it seems to be one of the ends and advantages of New Colonys to serve as a refuge to unfortunate debtors that by labour and industry they may have an opportunity to retrieve their fortunes and be again useful," was disposed to offer certain privileges to such persons, although "it was observed on the other side that a regulation of this sort makes a colony the refuge of Cheats, Rogues and fraudulent Bankrupts."[1] The

Reprinted by permission, and slightly abridged, from
Collections of the Nova Scotia Historical Society 24 (1938):
33–56.

result of their deliberations was a resolution that settlers were not to be liable for debts contracted previous to their emigration except for goods imported into the colony.[2] This resolution was made law by the first assembly in 1758,[3] and continued in force until 28 August 1762.[4] It was revived in the session of October 1763 "in favour only of those persons...who have come into this Province and have been under the protection and sanction of the aforesaid laws before the said twenty eighth day of August one thousand seven hundred and sixty two," and was continued until 1769.[5] Such a regulation was bound to attract the unscrupulous as well as the honest, and one of the first concerns of the assembly was an attempt to check this undesirable immigration. An act "to prevent the importing disabled, infirm and other useless persons into the Province"[6] was intended to mitigate the evil; but it was repealed by His Majesty[7] because the terms of description were too loose and the penalty to be inflicted on masters of vessels at the discretion of overseers of the poor, too great.[8] A similar act without these defects was submitted for royal approval in 1768,[9] and was again disallowed.[10] The result was an "Inundation of persons who are not only useless but very burdensome to the Community, being not only those of the most dissolute manners, and void of all Sentiments of honest Industry, but also Infirm, decrepit, and insane, as well as extremely indigent persons, who are unable to contribute anything toward their own maintenance."[11]

Halifax, the capital and chief port of a province whose contact with the outside world depended entirely on water communication, was the chief sufferer from these "inundations." Many a ship left behind some of her most undesirable passengers, and indigent immigrants, intended for the out-settlements, were loath to leave the source of government philanthropy. Even some of those who did settle in the outlying districts seem to have gravitated to Halifax as their fortunes declined, for in 1767 the overseers of the poor complained that many of their charges belonged to different parts of the province, and that it was unfair to tax the Haligonians for their support.[12] Then, too, the presence of the army and navy led to certain social problems. When the troops came to Halifax after the evacuation of Boston in 1776, they brought with them more than 2,000 camp followers,[13] and even before that time the authorities complained that "great inconveniences have arisen, from the numbers of Idle, helpless and indigent Women left in this Town by Regiments on their departure from this Province, together with a very heavy expence to the Inhabitants for their support and maintenance"; it was requested that "the Women which have been brought here by the Troops may be obliged to embark with them."[14] Obviously such an overwhelming number of dependent persons was out of all proportion to the permanent population, and it is little wonder that "the Industrious Inhabitants, especially of the Town of Halifax, esteem themselves subject to a grievous tax thereby, and are disabled from affording the Relief they are willing to do to their honest poor."[15]

While most of those persons on relief were cared for in their own homes, the city boasted a time-honoured institution for the reception of homeless and unruly paupers. As early as 1752 it was suggested that a "Bridewell or workhouse" be established where able-bodied dependents could be made to work for their keep instead of being a burden on the community.[16] After a series of delays the building seems to have been finally erected in 1759 with £500 from the duty money,[17] and in that year an act was passed for regulating it. The inmates were to be "all disorderly and idle persons, and such who shall be found begging, or practising any unlawful games, or pretending to fortune-telling, common drunkards, persons of lewd behaviour, vagabonds, runaways, stubborn servants and children, and persons who notoriously misspend their time to the neglect and prejudice of their own or their family's support." Such persons were to be set to work at useful tasks, and punished for idleness or disobedience by being whipped, fettered and shackled, or deprived of their food until they were reduced to better behaviour. It was hoped that the institution would be self-supporting, and that there would be a sufficient surplus from the workers' earnings to provide for those idiots, lunatics, and invalids who were cared for by a special keeper.[18] Apparently this scheme was unsuccessful, for in 1763 an additional act required that three rooms in the workhouse should be set aside for a poorhouse, to be supervised by the overseers of the poor and supported by the Halifax poor taxes.[19] Indeed, the dream of a self-supporting workhouse was rapidly fading, and in 1764 it was taking £500 annually from the duty money besides £100 assessed on the inhabitants.[20] Such an expense was too much for the impoverished treasury, and in 1765 the keeper was informed that the workhouse must be closed.[21] It seems probable that this order was carried out, for there is no mention of the workhouse in an estimate of the annual expenses of the provincial government, dated 16 June 1766.[22] However, it was reopened later, for in 1797 the authorities were advertising for a keeper for the House of Correction.[23]

Another public institution of even earlier foundation was the orphanage, which was opened on 8 July 1752.[24] There was great need of such an establishment especially after the arrival of the German and French Protestants, many of whom died on the voyage because of the crowded and unsanitary conditions. One ship reached Halifax with eight newly made orphans on board, and within twelve days their number was increased to fourteen.[25] Moreover, the Orphan House sheltered poor children, whether orphans or not. Belcher says that between 1752 and 1761 the majority of those cared for *were* orphans,[26] but his figures belie his words, for 161 of the 275 children admitted were *not* orphans.[27] These were children left destitute through the death of one parent and the illness of another, or more often the desertion of both, "of which more instances have happened here than in common, from the great Concourse of dissolute abandoned Women, followers of the Camp, Army, and Navy."[28] Laws "to provide for the support of Bastard Children, and the punishment of the Mother and reputed Father"[29] were, of course, powerless to stop the evil, and the government found itself responsible for the support of these unwanted waifs.

Before the establishment of the Orphan House the children were cared for in private homes at the public expense, the foster parents (as we should call them today) being allowed 3s. or 4s. a week, exclusive of clothing and provisions. This arrangement proved most unsatisfactory, as the children were often neglected and "generally trained up in almost every Vice, without the common Principles or seeds of Industry." The guardians of the Orphan House went to the other extreme in their effort to "avoid Idleness and irreligion." Every minute must be accounted for. A schoolmaster of the Society for the Propagation of the Gospel was employed to teach them to read, "instructing them in their duty to God and their Neighbour from Nine to Twelve O'clock in the Morning—and from 2 to five in the Afternoon."[30] During the rest of the day the girls were employed in housework, carding wool, spinning, and knitting stockings, while "such boys as were capable of doing anything have been preserved from Habits of Idleness (in the Intervals of School Hours) in attempting to pick Oakum during Winter, and in Summer in Weeding, gathering Stones and other little Offices in the Hospital and Orphan House Gardens."[31]

It is not hard to visualize this pathetic procession with its "Decent and Orderly appearance." Of the 275 children who lived in the Orphan House at one time or another between 1752 and 1760, 173 were sickly, crippled, deaf, dumb, blind, or feeble-minded. Their diet consisted of beef, pork, bread, molasses, and spruce beer—the latter being substituted for rum because it was "so conducive to health."[32] Later there were some additions to this fare, for when Governor Legge carried out his investigation in 1774, he found that the menu was as follows: Breakfast, broth, hasty pudding, or milk; dinner, fish three or four times a week, meat two or three times, bread and cheese once; supper, bread and beer.[33]

Judging by the wholesale purchase of checked linen and "oznabriggs," the decent and orderly appearance of these

foundlings must have been further enhanced by a strict uniformity of dress—unless, of course, there was some scope for
individual taste in such articles as the "2 Dozen ratt nawed
Hatts" received from His Majesty's stores.[34] Naturally, no
very elaborate or individual costumes could be contrived on
an annual clothing allowance of £1 per child.[35] Nevertheless
it is unfair to criticize the directors too severely, since they
were hampered on every side by financial restrictions. The
Orphan House was supported by the annual grant from
Parliament and was therefore a matter of concern to the
parsimonious Lords of Trade.

The third public institution which undertook to care for
the more unfortunate members of society was the hospital,
which was built in 1750.[36] In these days when state medicine
is regarded as a modern and revolutionary plan, it is interesting to note that similar measures were undertaken in the dim
and distant eighteenth century. Perhaps the term "state
medicine" is misleading; there was no system of social insurance, and the responsibility of government did not extend to
self-supporting citizens. Rather, the care of the sick and
infirm was looked on as a part of the poor relief, and the
hospital had very little in common with our modern institutions of the same name. It was a sort of refuge for the necessitous inhabitants said to be "used by soldiers of Hopsons
Regiment and a few miscreants of the town, for no sober
industrious people will go there for a 'cure' to live among
Soldiers and in the greatest riot and confusion—as the people
who go into this Hospital are of the violent sort."[37] However,
the Parliamentary grant, besides supporting the hospital, also
made due allowance for the sensibilities of "sober industrious
people" by paying the salaries of a few surgeons for so long as
the indigence of the settlers prevented them from supplying
their own medical attendance in their homes.

The first expedition in 1749 carried with it seventeen surgeons and twelve surgeon's mates and assistants,[38] a number
which was intended to supply the five settlements originally
planned. When the Lords of Trade found that only one
settlement was established, they ordered Cornwallis to dis-

charge from the government service all those who were not needed for Halifax.[39] These surgeons were engaged for one year only,[40] apparently in the hope that by that time the settlers would be self-supporting. In 1752 their Lordships were complaining of the expense (estimated at £1,145 in 1751),[41] "as there must be now many Families both used and very well able to bear such expenses."[42] As usual, their Lordships were too early in their demands for economy, but the number of public practitioners was being gradually reduced. In 1759, besides the hospital surgeon and his assistant, one surgeon and one midwife were included in the estimate, and £20 for medicine money.[43] In 1762, after a further remonstrance from Whitehall, the allowance for the surgeon and medicine money was omitted, and two midwives shared the salary which had formerly gone to one.[44] In 1764 Governor Wilmot wrote that he would punctually observe their Lordships' orders to reduce the charges for midwives, as he had intended anyway to omit them from the estimate.[45] He proceeded to do so. Thereafter, even this very necessary service was the concern of the inhabitants, and midwives began to advertise their qualifications in the local papers.[46]

The town of Lunenburg shared this official philanthropy, and managed to remain on the establishment even longer than Halifax. Although Lunenburg was still receiving the services of two midwives, one surgeon, and one assistant surgeon as late as 1767,[47] there is no evidence that the New Englanders and other late arrivals were supplied with similar medical attendance. They were apparently intended to look after themselves, but in 1777 the council received a petition from a doctor who wanted to be reimbursed for his expense in inoculating sixty-two poor persons in the townships of Windsor, Newport, Horton, and Falmouth during the smallpox epidemic of 1775-76.[48] Generally speaking, however, the authorities were chiefly concerned with the health of the Haligonians.

Unfortunately, most of our information about the hospital is furnished by a surgeon named John Grant, whose penchant for writing memorials seems to have almost equalled that of

Alexander McNutt. His main theme was the "injustice in the present medical service in Nova Scotia by which he and other surgeons are prevented from making a living."[49] In other words, Mr. Grant had a grievance, and since he was "agin the government" it is very difficult to know whether or not his facts are reliable. The governor assured the Lords of Trade that he (Grant) was "a most audacious and impudent fellow" who made a practice of breeding discontent among the people and encouraging contempt for the government;[50] and their Lordships, "Having been assured of Grant's true character by the Proceedings of the Council…realize that his accusations were without foundation."[51] If this conclusion was justified, there would be no excuse for quoting Grant's remarks. But might not the governor and council have been prejudiced?

Mr. Grant's contention was that a great deal of expense could be saved by contracting with one surgeon (i.e., Mr. Grant!) instead of employing so many in the government service. They were said to be so busy looking after the government officials who kept them in their positions that they had no time to care for the poor.[52] Moreover, in addition to their salaries they were paid 6d. per day for every patient in the hospital,[53] an arrangement which did not tend to reduce the number of patients.

A further scheme for economy was to exclude certain persons from the privileges of the hospital. This list gives an illuminating picture of the inmates of that institution. Incurables were not to be admitted, and venereal cases should be made to work for their cure in the workhouse. In order to prevent "miscreant inhabitants" from being "entertained" for long periods at the public expense they were to be examined by two surgeons before entering, and every two months thereafter. Any patients "detected in liquor" or who absented themselves from the hospital for more than two hours at a time were to be turned out. Grant maintained that if these undesirable persons were eliminated, the number of patients would be reduced from thirty to ten.[54]

At least one of Grant's statements is of doubtful reliability. He says that the hospital was occupied by "profligate soldiers," whereas Governor Lawrence, anxious that the institution should be kept on the civil rather than the military establishment, writes that "the necessitous Inhabitants (not the Troops) have constantly occupied the Hospital."[55] The passage already quoted can hardly be used to substantiate Grant's evidence, as it bears all the earmarks of having been written by Grant himself. Nevertheless the Lords of Trade disregarded Lawrence's advice, and after 1761 the hospital was included among the military expenses.[56]

Like the workhouse and the orphanage this hospital came to an untimely end; in 1767 the council advised that it be granted for the use of an almshouse[57]—a curious recommendation, when the poorhouse was still in existence. Perhaps the "objects of charity" were to be transferred from the old workhouse to the hospital building. During the next few years the infirm poor of Halifax must have made use of the almshouse, but in 1780 the Court of Quarter Sessions for Halifax, having considered the "usual practice of Some of the neighbouring Colony's respecting the appointing Frequently young Gentlemen that became Qualified in their Medical Capacity's (and more Especially Natives) to take Care of the Diseased Poor, as an Encouragement to such Qualifications," appointed to this position Malachy Salter who had come from London with recommendations from eminent medical professors.[58]

So much for the organization of "state medicine." But what of the conditions behind the organization? What diseases were most common, how were they treated, and with what success? These questions are of great interest to the social historian. Doubtless the medical interpretation of history has been over-emphasized by some of its exponents, particularly certain modern biographers, but at the same time health, or lack of it, is apt to have far-reaching effects which are not always confined to the social sphere. For example, it was reported in the fall of 1775 that the Americans had planned an invasion of Nova Scotia but had postponed it partly on account of the epidemic of smallpox at Halifax.[59] Would it be too absurd to suggest that a microscopic germ might claim some credit for keeping Nova Scotia within the British Empire?

The climate was considered remarkably healthy and "not subject to Epidemical Diseases," a fact which Captain John Knox attributed to "the myriads of venomous reptiles and insects that absorb the noxious vapours, and purify those misty exhalations,[60] which might otherwise naturally be supposed to be offensive and unwholesome"![61] Yet in spite of the salubrity of the air and the outdoor life of most of the people, they did fall victim to certain diseases, of which the most common was the smallpox. Ex-Governor Mascarene wrote in 1752 that he did not want his son to go to England until "he had got over that evil which most people are liable to go through once in their life."[62] Most of the inhabitants, however, did not regard the "evil" with such resignation; there are several instances of jurymen asking to be excused from their duties because they had not had the smallpox,[63] and elaborate measures were taken to prevent its spread. Although one gentleman writing in the local paper asserted that "this Distemper was not Contracted by Contagion which probably indicates a disposing influence to this Malady either in the generality of Constitutions or the Air,"[64] it seems to have been generally understood that it was contagious. In 1760 the assembly passed an act "to Prevent the Spreading of Contagious Distempers" which was particularly concerned with preventing infection from ships entering the harbour. Any vessel carrying "any Plague, Small-Pox, Malignant Fever, or other Contagious Distemper" was to anchor at least two miles below the town, and must obey the governor's orders "for the performing Quarentine, for the Airing and Cleansing the Passengers, Vessel, and Goods on board, and for removing the infected and sick persons out of the said Vessel."[65] Later in the same year it was ordered that all vessels be stopped at George's Island (in Halifax Harbour) and the passengers examined before being allowed to land.[66]

These measures seem to have been reasonably successful, for there was no real epidemic until 1775. In August of that year the inhabitants of Windsor requested a proclamation to prevent the spread of the smallpox "during the continuance of the Harvest,"[67] and were informed that since there was no law on which to base such a proclamation, they must make their own regulations.[68] This request may have led to an act passed a few months later which gave explicit directions for the segregation and care of victims, and for defraying the expense in the case of indigent persons;

> Provided that any person or persons desirous of being Inoculated (for the small-pox) themselves or of having their families Inoculated, may Proceed therein, provided that the house or place wherein they dwell or reside during all the time of being Injected with the small-pox shall be at least one hundred and sixty rods distance from any other house or dwelling, and that they take care to prevent and restrain all persons infected from going from thence further than eighty rods from such House, and also that their desire of Inoculating be made known in the Townships where they dwell, and a flag hung out at their said house, to the end that all persons may take note thereof and avoid, if they see cause, going near such houses or places.[69]

Strangely enough, nothing in this act was to apply to the town of Halifax. Possibly the houses were too close together to make such segregation practicable.

The act seems to have had some effect. At Liverpool the justices and overseers of the poor were kept busy "consulting for the safety of the town." They hung out flags, measured the required distances, and set up a "hospital" for inoculated patients.[70] At Horton the Grand Jury presented two men "for Introducing the small-pox into this Town Contrary to a law of this Province," and both acknowledged that they had inoculated their families, but pleaded that they did not understand the law.[71] The precautions required during the period of inoculation were very necessary, for in the days before vaccination[72] the matter injected was taken from a human smallpox sore, and although the patient thus treated usually contracted the disease in a mild form, anyone taking it from him would suffer the usual violent effects. The inoculated person, by protecting himself, might easily start a serious epidemic,[73] and it was this danger which the legislators wished to avoid.

It seems somewhat remarkable that the practice of inoculation was so commonly accepted in Nova Scotia at this time. Only fifty years earlier Lady Mary Montagu had tried to introduce it into England, with conspicuous failure. She had been impressed by its widespread use in France where "thousands undergo this operation and the French ambassador says pleasantly that they take the small-pox here by way of diversion...there is no example of anyone that has died of it, and you may well believe I am satisfied of the safety of the experiment, since I intend to try it upon my dear little son."[74] But the English public did not see her point of view, and Cotton Mather, who took up the cause in Massachusetts, met with the same opposition. Yet while the English and New England clergy held forth on the wickedness of thwarting the will of Providence, the sermon in favour of inoculation by the Rev. Dr. Breynton, rector of St. Paul's, "has been the means of conquering the Prejudices, and preserving the lives of many People,"[75] and the SPG missionary De La Roche wrote from Lunenburg:

> As soon as it was spread enough to be certain that inoculation could not be charged with the further propagation of it, I gave the example and inoculated my eldest child.... But this method was not relished by the generality. It had not made its way to their native town and villages in Germany and other Parts before they emigrated; and so, prejudice and fanaticism played their parts with such success, that not above a hundred sub-

jects have been inoculated; all of which did very well, not one being ill enough to keep the bed.[76]

The robust constitutions and outdoor life of the Germans must have stood them in good stead, for not everyone escaped so easily. Dr. Breynton wrote that the disease was peculiarly fatal to Americans, and that all his persuasive powers had been necessary to overcome their aversion.[77] The Indians, too, were most susceptible, and "have so great dread of it, as to be entirely disheartened upon the first symptoms and cannot be prevailed on to use any means for their recovery."[78] Such fears were not without foundation; in spite of Lady Mary Montagu's assurances, inoculation frequently proved fatal. The following figures given as late as 1801 are somewhat startling: of ninety-one persons who died of smallpox in Halifax during that year, seventy had taken the disease "in the natural way" and twenty-one by inoculation.[79] The pages of Simeon Perkins contain frequent mention of deaths from inoculation, and on 25 March 1776 he wrote: "The people meet concerning the small-pox, and generally sign an agreement not to be inoculated."[80] The other towns seem to have been more willing to take the risk: in Kings County the "Inhabitants Generally resolved on Enoculation";[81] and an enthusiastic Halifax surgeon expressed the view that "The happy Effects of inoculating for the Small-Pox is too well known to need any Arguments to persuade a reasonable Person to prefer Inoculation, to taking this Disorder in the natural way." This doctor, however, had a reason for his optimism. He charged ten shillings for inoculation, medicines, and attendance, and six dollars for private patients who wished to make use of his commodious house furnished with candles, beds, and a nurse.[82] The popularity of this practice is shown by the following notice:

It will undoubtedly be agreeable to the public, at this critical Juncture, to hear from unquestionable Authority, that Messrs. Phillips and Faries's first Class of Patients, consisting of between one and two Hundred, inoculated for the Small-Pox, are now by the Blessing of God, all save over the Disease; without having had one bad, or unpromising symptom. The Patients were of all Ages from Fifty Years down to less than One.[83]

The method used may be of some interest. One philan-thropic surgeon published in the Halifax paper "A few hints on method of Inoculation which may be of use to Poor fami-lies unable to pay a Practitioner," in which minute directions are given concerning diet and medicine. The patient must abstain from meats, spices, butter, wine, and all highly sea-soned food, and must avoid "severe Exercise, violent Passions, or Warm Rooms." Powdered jalap, "Calamel," and "Tart Emittick" are recommended, as well as barley water sweet-ened with brown sugar, "and one ounce of powdered Cream Tart in half a Gallon of the Decoction." With reference to the actual operation, the best method was "by small Punctures of a Lancet dipped in the various matter."[84] This was probably the same process as that described with such spirit by our friend Lady Mary Montagu:

> The old woman comes with a nutshell full of matter of the best sort of small-pox, and asks what vein you pleased to have opened. She immediately rips open that which you offer to her with a large needle (which gives you no more pain than a common scratch) and puts into the vein as much venom as can lie upon the end of a needle, and after binds up the little wound with a hol-low bit of shell; and in this manner opens four or five veins.[85]

It must not be supposed that smallpox was the only dreaded disease. There are occasional references to yellow fever among the troops at Halifax[86] and on at least one occasion a fever was said to have been caused by the great quantity of rum sold to the soldiers by unlicensed retailers.[87] Indeed, the presence of the troops was responsible for many undesirable conditions in Halifax, particularly the prevalence of venereal disease. Grant had mentioned the large number of such patients in the hospital, and had claimed to be able to effect a cure for forty shillings.[88] Probably a more popular remedy was the use of "Keyser's Pills well known for their efficacy, in curing the Venereal disease with secrecy and dispatch."[89]

A complete catalogue of Nova Scotian ailments would be tiresome and unnecessary; it is fortunate that a concise summary is ready to hand, for surely nothing was omitted from the list of disorders which would be immediately cured by that all-powerful patent medicine "Sal Salutis or Salt of Health." The list included jaundice, leprosy, scurvy, king's evil, hectic fevers, consumptive weaknesses, fresh colds, rheumatism, female weaknesses, constipation, ulcerated legs, and yellow fever.[90] Yet in spite of this imposing inventory, the people were not unhealthy. Outdoor exercise, active lives, and nourishing food made up for the lack of modern sanitary knowledge. In pioneer life it is generally the mind that is neglected, not the body, and these Nova Scotians were no exception. We have examined some of the measures, official and otherwise, which were intended to hold together the bodies and souls of poor, infirm, neglected, and diseased individuals, and while these measures may seem primitive to us today, they were at least as enlightened as current practice elsewhere in the eighteenth century.

Notes

1. Public Archives of Nova Scotia (hereafter PANS), vol. 209, Minutes of Council, 2 February 1749–50.
2. Ibid., and 14 January 1750–51.
3. PANS, Manuscript Acts of Assembly, 32 Geo. II, c. 30.
4. Ibid., 33 Geo. I, c. 20.
5. Ibid., 3 and 4 Geo. III, c. 13; 6 and 7 Geo. III, c. 8.
6. Ibid., 33 Geo. II, c. 7.
7. Public Archives of Canada, Nova Scotia (hereafter PAC, NS), A, 66, Lords of Trade to Belcher, 8 May 1761.

8. Ibid., A, 65, Lords of Trade to His Majesty, 15 April 1761.
9. Ibid., A, 83, Francklin to Hillsborough, 15 August 1768.
10. PANS, vol. 212, Minutes of Council, 2 April 1770.
11. PAC, NS, A, 77, Green to Lords of Trade, 24 August 1766.
12. PANS, vol. 212, Minutes of Council, 3 January 1767.
13. Ibid., 3 June 1776.
14. Ibid., vol. 136, Campbell to Lieut.-Col. Bruce, April 1771.
15. PAC, NS, A, 77, Green to Lords of Trade, 24 August 1766.
16. PANS, vol. 209, Minutes of Council, 22 December 1752.
17. Ibid., Manuscript Acts of Assembly, 32 Geo. II, c. 9.
18. Ibid., 33 Geo. II, c. 1.
19. Ibid., 3 and 4 Geo. III, c. 9.
20. PAC, NS, A, 74, Wilmot to Lords of Trade, 24 June 1764.
21. PANS, vol. 211, Minutes of Council, 2 July 1765.
22. PANS, Journals of Assembly, 16 June 1766.
23. *Royal Gazette and the Nova-Scotia Advertiser*, 2 May 1797.
24. PAC, NS, A, 55, State of the Orphan House at Halifax, 1754.
25. Ibid., A, 49, Hopson to Lords of Trade, 16 October 1752.
26. Ibid., A, 66, Belcher to Lords of Trade, 3 November 1761.
27. Ibid., Account of Orphan House, 8 June 1752–31 May 1761.
28. Ibid., Belcher to Lords of Trade, 3 November 1761.
29. PANS, Manuscript Acts of Assembly, 32 Geo. II, c. 19.
30. PAC, NS, A, 55, State of the Orphan House at Halifax, 1754.
31. Ibid., A, 66, Belcher to Lords of Trade, 3 November 1761.
32. Ibid., A, 55, State of the Orphan House at Halifax, 1754.
33. Ibid., Dartmouth Mss. 1.2. 975, Burrow to Legge, Report on Orphan House, 10 May 1774.
34. Ibid., NS, A, 55, p. 254, Account of His Majesty's Stores received for the use of the Orphan House.
35. Ibid., A, 62, Estimate for Orphan House for 1759 (enclosed Lawrence to Lords of Trade, 26 September 1758).
36. PANS, vol. 35, Cornwallis to Lords of Trade, 19 March 1749–50.
37. Ibid., vol. 284, doc. 13, Petition to the Lords of Trade, 1758?
38. T. B. Akins, ed., *Selections from the Public Documents of the Province of Nova Scotia* (Halifax, 1869), 1: 506–57.
39. PAC, NS, A, 36, Lords of Trade to Cornwallis, 16 February 1750.
40. Ibid.
41. Ibid., A, 40, Estimate for Nova Scotia, 1751. Whitehall, 19 February 1751.
42. Ibid., A, 46, Lords of Trade to Cornwallis, 6 March 1752.

43. Ibid., A, 62, Estimate of Civil Establishment for Nova Scotia, 1759.
44. Ibid., A, 66, Estimate of Civil Establishment for Nova Scotia, 1762.
45. Ibid., A, 74, Wilmot to Lords of Trade, 24 June 1764.
46. *Nova-Scotia Gazette and the Weekly Chronicle*, 1 November 1774.
47. PAC, NS, A, 78, Estimate of Civil Establishment for 1767.
48. PANS, vol. 301, doc. 19, Memorial of Michael Head, Surgeon, Windsor, 5 June 1777.
49. PAC, NS, A, 57, Memorial of John Grant, Halifax, 13 January 1755.
50. Ibid., A, 58, Lawrence to Lords of Trade, 28 June 1755.
51. Ibid., Lords of Trade to Lawrence, 9 October 1755.
52. Ibid., A, 57, Memorial of John Grant, Halifax, 13 January 1755.
53. Ibid., A, 62, Estimate for Hospital for 1759.
54. Ibid., A, 57, Memorials of John Grant, 21 October 1754 and 13 January 1755.
55. Ibid., A, 63, Lawrence to Lords of Trade, 20 September 1759.
56. Ibid., A, 64, Estimate for Civil Establishment for 1761.
57. PANS, vol. 212, Minutes of Council, 13 November 1767.
58. Ibid., vol. 298, doc. 87, Record of General Quarter Sessions of the Peace held at Halifax, December 1780. This gentleman is apparently a son of Malachy Salter, Esq., the Merchant. The *Nova-Scotia Gazette* of 10 December 1782 announced the death of Doctor Malachy Salter, aged 25 years.
59. PAC, NS, A, 94, Legge to Dartmouth, 20 December 1775.
60. He is referring to the fogs.
61. Captain J. Knox, *An Historical Journal of the Campaigns in North America*, ed. A. G. Doughty (Champlain Society, 1914), 1: 320.
62. PAC, Brown Mss., Mascarene to King Gould, 17 October 1752.
63. PANS, Chipman Mss., 1778, doc. 15.
64. *Nova-Scotia Gazette and the Weekly Chronicle*, 4 July 1775.
65. PANS, Manuscript Acts of Assembly, 1 Geo. III, c. 6.
66. Ibid., vol. 211, Minutes of Council, 11 December 1760.
67. Ibid., vol. 212, Minutes of Council, 29 August 1775.
68. Ibid., vol. 136, Bulkeley to Deschamps, 29 August 1775.
69. Ibid., Manuscript Acts of Assembly, 15 and 16 Geo. III, c. 2.
70. Ibid., Diary of Simeon Perkins, 13 and 16 February 1776.
71. Ibid., Chipman Mss., 1776, doc. 1.

72. The pioneer work in this field was done by Jenner, who published his "Inquiry into the Causes and Effects of Variolae Vaccina" in 1798.

73. H. W. Haggard, *Devils, Drugs and Doctors* (New York, 1929), p. 225.

74. Lord Wharncliffe, ed., *Letters of Lady Mary Wortley Montagu* (London, 1837), 1: 309.

75. PAC, SPG Records, Anonymous letter, no date, but probably about 1776.

76. Ibid., De la Roche to the Society, Lunenburg, 26 August 1776.

77. Ibid., Dr. Breynton to the Society, Halifax, 12 January 1776.

78. Knox, *Historical Journal of Campaigns in North America*, 1: 146, note.

79. G. W. Hill, "History of St. Paul's Church," Nova Scotia Historical Society, *Collections* 2: 95.

80. PANS, Diary of Simeon Perkins, 25 March 1776.

81. Ibid., vol. 301, doc. 19, Memorial of Michael Head, Surgeon to Governor and Council, Windsor, 5 June 1777.

82. *Nova-Scotia Gazette and the Weekly Chronicle*, 1 August 1775.

83. Ibid., 8 August, 1775.

84. Ibid., 4 July 1775 and 29 August 1775.

85. Wharncliffe, *Letters of Lady Mary Wortley Montagu*, 1: 308.

86. PANS, Diary of Simeon Perkins, 26 August 1777.

87. Akins, "History of Halifax City," Nova Scotia Historical Society, *Collections* 8: 49.

88. PAC, NS, A, 57, Memorial of John Grant, 13 January 1755.

89. *Nova-Scotia Gazette and the Weekly Chronicle*, 16 February 1779.

90. Ibid., 12 October 1779.

The Development of the Lunatic Asylum in the Maritime Provinces

DANIEL FRANCIS

Late in the year 1835 some two dozen reputed lunatics who had been imprisoned in the county gaol in Saint John were removed first to the city's almshouse and then, early the next year, to the basement of a small, wooden building on Leinster Street. This building, constructed originally as a cholera hospital but as of February 1836 housing fourteen lunatics in its depths and as many sick paupers upstairs, was Canada's first mental institution. It would be another twelve years before New Brunswick had a permanent treatment centre and another twenty-three years before its sister province of Nova Scotia had one.[1] Yet this little hospital, inadequate as it was, represented an important change in the treatment of the insane in the Maritimes. At last it was being recognized that the most important thing about the mentally ill was that they were mentally ill, not poor or violent or criminal, and that they required a specific kind of supervision in a specific kind of institution. It had not always been so.

Reprinted by permission from *Acadiensis* 6, no. 2 (1977): 23-38

The first law regarding the insane in the two colonies was a 1759 statute establishing a workhouse in Halifax. No special accommodation was provided for insane paupers in the building who were lumped indiscriminately with "all disorderly and idle persons, and such who shall be found begging, or practising any unlawful games, or pretending to fortune telling, common drunkards, persons of lewd behaviour, vagabonds, runaways, stubborn servants and children, and persons who notoriously misspend their time to the neglect and prejudice of their own and their family's support." Special consideration was given only to the retarded and lunatics who were physically incapable of labouring. Others were to be put to work alongside their fellow inmates and with them to be whipped "moderately" upon entering the workhouse and strenuously if they proved "stubborn or idle."[2] In 1774 a second statute entitled "An Act for Punishing Rogues, Vagabonds, and other Idle and Disorderly Persons," provided that persons "furiously mad and dangerous to be permitted to go abroad" should be "safely locked up in some secure place."[3] In New Brunswick an 1824 statute directed dangerous lunatics to be "kept safely locked up in some secure place" and if necessary chained, a practice which was already being followed.[4] Lunatics who fell afoul of the law were thus placed in conditions which could only aggravate their illness and then expected to behave normally or suffer for it.

Yet the insane certainly were not actively persecuted. If they caused no problems and could look after themselves, they were left to wander at will. Those who were either wealthy themselves or had wealthy relations were usually packed off to a private madhouse in the United States or Britain. Far from seeking out inmates for the prisons and poorhouses, the authorities hoped a mentally ill person's family would assume the responsibility of caring for him at home. But since many of the insane were quite understandably paupers, those who could not support themselves or rely on their families were placed in almshouses or workhouses. From their beginnings the two colonies adopted the British poor law system which was based on the administrative principle that each town or parish had to support its own poor by a compulsory assessment of the inhabitants.[5] While able-bodied unemployed were either gaoled for being "idle and disorderly persons" or set to work by an overseer of the poor, some kind of accommodation was found for the infirm poor, often in private homes or in buildings rented for the purpose. A major drawback to this system of relief was that many communities did not have the resources to care for their poor and as a result the practice of auctioning off paupers developed.[6] Overseers of the poor were authorized to pay local residents to take paupers into their homes and support them for a year. The price was arrived at by a process of down-bidding at a public auction. The person willing to take the pauper for the least amount of money won his or her services. Originally the practice was regulated but gradually controls were relaxed and the system became one of brutal abuse. Paupers became a kind of slave labour in the backwoods of the provinces and people began to use the auctions as a means of making an income and as a source of subsidized labour. Clearly, many of the victims of the auction block, at least before asylums were built, would have been paupers suffering from mild forms of mental illness.

In Nova Scotia the mentally ill first were provided for in the Halifax Poor's Asylum in 1812. It was originally intended that they be confined apart from the healthy paupers but as the institution became overcrowded this distinction was not enforced. In 1832 a legislative committee touring the poorhouse reported that "every room from the cellar to the garret is filled to excess" and told of one room with eighteen beds which nightly held forty-seven persons.[7] The committee urged the erection of a hospital but did not consider a separate lunatic asylum necessary. It was not really until Hugh Bell became mayor of Halifax in 1844 that an energetic movement for the establishment of an asylum began. Bell had arrived in the colony from Ireland in 1782 at the age of two years and had been in turn a journalist, a Methodist preacher, a successful brewer, and a politician. He was sixty-four when, apparently influenced by a term as commissioner of the Poor's Asylum, he undertook to persuade the government to build an asylum.[8] His first move was to pledge his own salary as mayor to a special asylum fund. Next, he organized public meetings to gather similar private pledges, hoping to force the government's hand. Bell's campaign was supported by a number of wealthy Haligonians and endorsed by at least two Halifax newspapers, the *Novascotian* and the *Times*, but the scheme did not seem to capture the imagination of the populace. As the *Times* reluctantly reported, Bell's activities "do not appear to be well seconded."[9] In 1845, prompted by an abortive suggestion from New Brunswick that it, Nova Scotia, and Prince Edward Island build a joint asylum, a commission was established with Bell as the chairman to investigate the possibility of establishing an asylum in Nova Scotia. The Bell Commission enthusiastically endorsed the project the next year but no action was taken and in 1848 another legislative committee argued that "it would be improper at this time to recommend any appropriation of the public monies which would require so great an expenditure."[10] Early in 1850 Dorothea Dix, the American psychiatric reformer, delivered an impassioned plea to the legislature on behalf of the mentally ill but she failed to prompt any action and not until 1852 did "an Act for Founding a Lunatic Asylum" pass the assembly and not until January 1859 were the first patients admitted.[11]

A number of factors may have contributed to this delay. During the 1840s, when Hugh Bell was trying to get government backing for an asylum, the assembly was preoccupied with the noisy struggle for political power between James Johnston's faction and the "Liberals" led by Joseph Howe. Another explanation, the one advanced at the time, was that other demands were being made on the provincial treasury.[12] For the first half of the century the hospital annexed to the Halifax Poor's Asylum was the only public hospital in the city. During the typhus epidemic in 1847 this facility was woefully overcrowded and the local medical community began to petition the government for a new hospital. In 1849 a legislative committee conducted an investigation into the matter which resulted in funds being allotted. Since at the same time the assembly was financing the construction of a new prison, the legislators apparently felt justified in putting off the asylum recommended by the 1846 commission. Furthermore, in the early 1850s railway fever absorbed the attention and the revenues of the province. "Provincial finances were completely compromised by railway legislation and there was a powerful aversion to new taxation for any other purpose."[13]

Agitation for the reform of treatment of the mentally ill began earlier in New Brunswick than in its neighbouring colony, perhaps because in the former the social dislocation associated with higher rates of immigration made the plight of the insane more evident and more urgent. The movement was led by a medical man, Dr. George Peters. Peters had been born in Saint John in 1811 but had been exposed to more advanced ideas about insanity during his years as a medical student in Edinburgh.[14] In the 1830s he was the visiting medical officer at the Saint John almshouse and county gaol and it was the degraded condition in which he found the insane incarcerated in these institutions which prompted him to petition the assembly for the provision of an asylum. In the gaol Peters was horrified to find that warders were making no attempt to separate the mentally ill from other criminals and he discovered many lunatics under heavy restraint, "some of them perfectly naked and in a state of filth."[15] At the almshouse Peters found similarly inadequate conditions. This institution had been built in 1819 to house sixty persons.[16] In 1836 it held 140 paupers, forty of whom required medical treatment and were kept in a makeshift two-room infirmary, big enough to handle eight people comfortably.[17] Sick patients overflowed these two rooms into the section of the almshouse reserved for the mentally ill. It was this situation which provoked Peters into seeking permission from the government to move the insane from the almshouse to the basement of the cholera hospital. Unfortunately, the situation did not improve. Lunatics were able to mingle freely with the sick paupers who were being treated in the upper stories of the hospital and the building was too crowded to allow Peters to practise any kind of treatment. The temporary asylum was really just an extension of the almshouse; as Peters himself described it, it was "essentially a pauper institution."[18]

At the same time as the temporary asylum was opening in 1836, the justices of the peace in Saint John County, alarmed at the growing number of mentally disturbed inmates in the gaols, petitioned the assembly to establish a more permanent asylum.[19] A legislative committee was appointed with instructions to gather information from the United States and Europe about the treatment of the insane and to plan a permanent facility. Although this committee reported in December of that year, it was a decade before the assembly was convinced of the inadequacy of the temporary building and appropriated funds that allowed construction of the new asylum to begin.[20] It is not difficult to account for this reluctance to commit provincial funds to the asylum project. While it is true that between 1838 and 1841 the newly acquired control over the revenues from the crown lands swelled the provincial coffers, the decentralized manner in which these funds were dispensed meant that provincial projects did not always receive financial support. As MacNutt has pointed out, the individual assemblyman had control over how and where government money was spent in his constituency.[21] Control of the purse strings was crucial to him because by deploying the money skilfully he could ensure electoral support. He might be reluctant, therefore, to surrender any portion of his patronage money to projects of a more general purpose. Yet the parochialism of legislators should not be exaggerated. The late 1830s and early 1840s were years of heavy immigration and economic crisis in the colony and the assembly was faced with a variety of immediate needs. In response, it undertook in the years between

1834 and 1847 four major welfare measures aside from the asylum.[22] In 1834 a cholera hospital was opened in Saint John; in 1836 funds were authorized for the construction of a county gaol in the city and a house of correction; in 1838 a new almshouse-workhouse-infirmary complex was approved; and in 1847 the Emigrant Orphan Asylum opened its doors in Saint John. Proponents of a mental asylum had to vie with all these different interests for a share of the public funds and were actually at a disadvantage since gaols and poorhouses could if necessary double as mental institutions.

The Maritime mental institutions which eventually were established in the 1840s and 1850s were designed to accommodate a specific treatment technique known as moral treatment. A few simple drugs, both tranquillizers and purgatives, were administered to control behaviour; assorted bathing techniques were advised for manic or depressed patients; and blood-letting had not entirely been discredited. But moral treatment, or the humane method, was the principal therapeutic technique. It was to the nineteenth century what psychoanalysis became to our own. Moral treatment had its origins in the last decade of the eighteenth century in Europe where it developed out of the practical experiences of Philippe Pinel in France and William Tuke in England. Pinel (1745–1826) attained legendary stature in the history of psychiatry by being the first to strike the chains from the insane and free them from confinement in dungeons, first at the Hopital de Bicêtre in Paris in 1793 and two years later at the Saltpetrière, a hospital for women. His major work, *A Treatise on Insanity*, was published in an English translation in 1806 and his theories were known in the Maritimes as he was referred to approvingly in the New Brunswick report of 1836. Tuke (1732–1822), an English tea merchant and Quaker, pioneered moral treatment in the York Retreat for the Insane which he founded in 1792. His grandson, Samuel Tuke, wrote *Description of the Retreat* in 1813, which was published in the United States the following year and became a standard text for reformers throughout the English-speaking world. Really not treatment in a medical sense at all, the moral method employed compassion and lenience within a strictly controlled environment in an attempt to coax the mind back to sanity. The intention was first of all to relieve the patient's fears and then to distract the mind from its morbid preoccupations. In this manner the patient was encouraged to exercise self-control and to reassert the primacy of will over passion. At mid-century this technique was extended by John Conolly, a British asylum doctor, to include the complete abolition of all mechanical and physical restraints.

The principles of moral treatment were carried into the Maritimes by reform-minded laymen such as Hugh Bell and, more importantly, by doctors who had been educated in Europe or the United States. At the beginning of the century most Maritime medical men were trained as apprentices but by the 1830s a number were being educated at universities in Great Britain and this was certainly true of the doctors who became medical superintendents at the new asylums and the main exponents of moral treatment in the two colonies.[23] George Peters, the original superintendent of the New Brunswick institution, and his successor John Waddell, superintendent for twenty-seven years, both received their degrees from Scottish universities affiliated with mental hospitals where modern treatment techniques were employed. James DeWolf, the first superintendent of Mount Hope, likewise was a graduate of Edinburgh University. Later in the century aspiring doctors began to attend American medical schools; for example, James Steeves, Waddell's successor, studied in Pennsylvania and New York.[24] Even when these early alienists were not formally trained in the United States, their annual reports indicate that they kept a close watch on developments there and frequently toured the more famous American institutions where moral treatment was practised. While the broad principles of moral treatment were endorsed by all the asylum superintendents, there were differences in the way these principles were applied. This was especially true of the elimination of physical restraints. In New Brunswick Waddell early on rejected the "indiscriminate and frequent use" of mechanical restraints but argued that sometimes they had to be applied for the good of the patient and this moderate position was adopted by his successors.[25] In Nova Scotia, on the other hand, there were quite radical differences of opinion at different points in time. Dr. DeWolf invoked Conolly and endorsed "the total disuse of mechanical restraint" whereas his successor, Dr. A. P. Reid, defended physical restraints as a form of discipline.[26] Despite these differences of emphasis, however, medical personnel at the Maritime asylums shared a perception of themselves as practitioners of moral treatment.

Moral treatment enjoyed such unequivocal allegiance because it was believed to be effective. The decades of the 1840s and 1850s were a period of unbridled optimism regarding the curability of mental illness. "It is the decided opinion of most persons who have investigated the subject," the New Brunswick commissioners reported in 1836, "that insanity is on the increase. But at the same time it is consolatory to observe, that the disease is not now considered of so formidable a nature as it used to be, because it is found easily to yield to judicious treatment timely applied."[27] In the United States optimism reached a high point in the period 1830–1850 and it is not surprising that the same is true of the Maritime colonies since they looked across the border for proof that their asylums would be successful.[28] The Bell Commission, for example, reported recovery rates of 82½ percent and 86½ percent respectively at the Worcester Asylum in Massachusetts and Boston's McLean Asylum and concluded confidently that "Wherever an Asylum is established, there the numbers of Insane in proportion to the population begin to diminish."[29] An important qualification invariably made was that a lunatic was curable primarily in the very early stages of his illness, usually in the first three months. If madness could be detected at the outset and the afflicted person removed from his home to an asylum before temporary symptoms became permanent illness, then cure was virtually assured. If not, if family or friends hesitated before bringing the mentally ill to the asylum, then doctors promised nothing. In fact, they hinted at the worst. When John Waddell stated categorically that "No insane man recovers at home" he was speaking for all his colleagues.[30] Insanity demanded moral treatment and moral treatment demanded the asylum.

A clear idea of the aim of moral treatment is best obtained by examining how it was intended to be implemented in the new Maritime asylums. Practitioners began with the building itself. The ideal location was on a height of land commanding a scenic view, right at the edge of civilization. Such a site offered the insane the scenery which was expected to soothe their frenzies and divert their attention. Advocates of moral treatment had great faith in the remedial influence nature exerted over the deranged mind: "... the sounds caused by rushing water is the music of nature, and is always in harmony with, and soothing in its effects on, the nervous organism."[31] Diversion was also a rationale for building the asylum on the edge of a city, remote enough so that the insane were insulated from the excitement of urban life but close enough so that they had "constant proofs that they are in a world of hope, and among beings who are engaged in the every day business of life."[32] These asylums were not built on secluded sites far from the centres of population. On the contrary, as examples of the charitable character of the populace, they were trophies to be displayed.

The physical appearance of the institution was an important aspect of moral treatment. As in all things, the emphasis was on symmetry and good taste, what came to be called "moral architecture."

> As it is found that the external appearance, as well as the internal economy of the Hospital for the Insane, exert an important moral influence... it is a principle now generally recognized and acted on, that good taste and a regard for comfort, should characterize all the arrange-

ments both external and internal, as calculated to induce self-respect and a disposition to self-control.[33]

As important as the countenance of the asylum was the arrangement of its buildings. Within the Maritime asylums certain classes of patients were to be isolated from each other. For example, patients were segregated by sex and special accommodation was provided for "frantics" whose violent behaviour might disturb the other inmates. Another criterion for separating patients was social class. In part the rationale for this practice was economic. Asylum administrators hoped to attract wealthy patients whose fees would contribute to the upkeep of the institutions. It was thought necessary to offer this class of patient comfortable surroundings and assurances that it would not be subjected to the unsettling manners and morals of lower class lunatics.[34] This reasoning also betrays a therapeutic rationale. Patients had to be insulated from all that was offensive to them and which might cause them to retreat into their derangement. Segregation by class was one of the practices asylum personnel anticipated would make Maritime institutions superior to their American counterparts in which conditions were distressingly democratic.[35] As it turned out, however, overcrowding and lack of funds kept asylums in Nova Scotia and New Brunswick from achieving a rigorous separation of social classes. It was a recurring complaint throughout the century that the indiscriminate mixing of classes was diverting wealthier patients to foreign institutions, thereby losing local asylums desperately needed funds.[36]

As for the organization of time within the asylum, moral treatment combined three elements—work, play, and worship. The most important of this trinity was work, physical labour within the asylum itself or in the gardens surrounding the institutions. Useful employment was intended to have a variety of effects, not the least of which was to defray the expenses of maintaining the institution. More important, labour had therapeutic value, if for no other reason than it exhausted the patients, improving their sleeping habits and their physical health. Like the scenery, physical work, by forcing the patient to concentrate on something other than himself, diverted his attention from his sickness, theoretically weakening the irrational forces in their struggle with the will. Since many of the insane seemed to suffer from excess energy which made their behaviour frenzied and unpredictable, regular labour was intended to divert and give vent to some of this energy in a more useful and healthy way. But perhaps the most important influence labour was expected to have on the insane was its moral influence. If a patient was to rejoin society as a productive member, then he or she had to be taught independence, industry, and self-respect. Useful employment was as much a way of instilling moral values as it was of healing broken minds.[37] But work could not occupy all the time nor all the patients in an asylum. It was anticipated that upper class inmates, who apparently did not require the moral lessons of useful employment, would be exempt from physical labour. For them, and for the lower classes in their spare time, instructive recreation had to be provided. As well, regular religious observances were scheduled, though for reasons more behavioural than spiritual. Religion was useful as another distraction and the services, because of their communal nature, were considered excellent opportunities for practising decorum and restraint.[38]

The final element of moral treatment, and one which circumscribed all the others, was isolation. While it was considered healthy that the mentally ill be aware of, and to some degree witness to, the daily life of society beyond the asylum walls, it was also considered crucial that the individual patient be removed from the immediate social surroundings which had been witness to his fall from reason.

The first and most important step is to remove the patient from his own home and from all the objects which he has been accustomed to see. His false notions and harassing impressions are associated in his mind with the objects exposed to his senses during the approach of his disease. His relations have become to him stale and uninteresting, and afterwards cause of angry irritation.... The most favourable situation is a retirement, where the patient will be surrounded by objects which have a composing influence.[39]

The mind, once shattered, needed a quiet place, a kind of laboratory, in which it could be carefully reconstructed. Throughout the century medical men repeatedly warned the public that the insane could not be treated at home, that they had to be surrendered up to the asylum if they were not to become forever incurable.

When all these elements were combined, the result was a self-enclosed, tightly organized institution, the aim of which was the reformation of its inmates' behaviour into socially conventional patterns. Perhaps the most revealing statement about moral treatment can be found in the Nova Scotia report of 1846—"without system there cannot be success."[40] The asylum was a system. Everything from its location to the table manners of its inmates was interrelated to transform behaviour. In charge of this process was the medical superintendent, "the very light and life of the Institution," who was expected not to practise medicine but to attract the confidence, the obedience, and the emulation of his charges.[41] The system ignored causes because the understanding of them was rudimentary.[42] Instead, doctors concentrated on symptoms— the hallucination, the frenzy, the melancholy—and tried to eliminate them by reinforcing the patient's self-control. This was the moral system and it flowered in a brand new institution, the asylum.

At the same time as the new Maritime asylums were opening their doors, a noticeable change occurred in the attitude of the law to the incarceration of the insane. Prior to this time statutes had illustrated a reluctance on the part of the lawmakers to take responsibility for the care of the mentally ill.

However, as the asylum began to be emphasized as the only proper place for treatment, legislators became much more aggressive in their attitude toward the insane. In New Brunswick the original bylaws governing the new asylum restricted inmates to "lunatics proper" and refused admission to all but exceptional cases of idiocy and delerium tremens.[43] This changed in 1852 when "An Act to Amend the Law Relating to Lunatics and Insane Persons" provided that "any person furiously mad or so far disordered in his reason as to be dangerous when at large" was to be taken forcibly to the asylum and incarcerated there on the orders of two justices of the peace.[44] No doctor need be consulted and the superintendent of the asylum could not refuse a patient. Seven years later the law was changed to ensure that no one was admitted to the provincial asylum without first being certified by a doctor but the asylum's superintendent still had no right to refuse admittance to anyone so certified, be they senile, retarded, or epileptic.[45] The legal emphasis was on making it as easy as possible to get the mentally ill into the asylum. In Nova Scotia the situation was similar. Prompted by four murders committed within a year, all by men who were subsequently found to be insane, the legislature passed a law which allowed two justices of the peace to hold in custody any person who "seemed" to be insane and "seemed" to have "a purpose of committing some crime."[46] If found to be mentally disturbed by a doctor, the individual was held either in gaol or in the poorhouse, or in the asylum when it opened four years later. The Nova Scotia asylum superintendents had more discretionary power than their New Brunswick counterparts. From the beginning the Nova Scotia asylum at Mount Hope was governed by a law which allowed recent and acute cases of insanity to be given preference over more chronic cases.[47] This meant that when the institution became crowded, which it very soon did, mental defectives and cases of long-term illness were refused admittance. While at no time were persons ever legally committed to the Nova Scotia asylum without certification by a physician, there was a perceptible shift in the legal attitude. An 1858 statute, "An Act For the Management of the Hospital for the Insane," provided for the incarceration of any person who could be proven to be "by reason of insanity, unsafe to be at large or suffering any unnecessary duress or hardship."[48] By 1872 the law made no reference to public or personal safety. It merely stated that "any lunatic being at large may be apprehended."[49]

Unhappily, the medico-legal campaign to institutionalize the mentally ill had an effect quite opposite to that intended by reformers and medical men. To be effective, moral treatment required a small number of patients, all of whom were in the acute stage of their illness, and a large staff to work with them. What happened, however, was that the asylums were immediately and continuously overcrowded, especially with what were considered chronic incurable cases, and had neither the staff nor the facilities to be anything more than places of confinement. The heady optimism of mid-century evaporated into exasperation, and sometimes plain brutality, as asylums proved unable to fulfil their role as successful treatment centres.

The New Brunswick asylum opened in December 1848 and in his report for the following year the medical superintendent, John Waddell, was already asking that the institution be enlarged.[50] When completed, it was intended to handle 180 patients in a complex of three buildings, but these were not finally built until 1864, at which time the daily average of patients at the asylum was 194.[51] Demands for expansion continued but it was not really until 1885, when a farm annex capable of handling 150 of the more long-term cases was built, that a satisfactory patient population was achieved.[52] New Brunswick now had facilities for 320 acute cases and almost half that many chronics, and complaints about overcrowding were seldom heard. In Nova Scotia the Mount Hope Asylum was also constantly overcrowded from its opening in 1859 until the commencement in 1886 of the county asylum system. The county institutions were meant to accommodate "harmless insane, idiotic persons, and epileptic persons who are insane but who have not manifested symptoms of violent insanity."[53] By 1897 there were fifteen of them throughout Nova Scotia.[54] Crowded conditions at the asylums made the successful treatment of patients almost impossible and cure rates never approximated the heady forecasts of 80 and 90 percent. By 1882 Dr. A. P. Reid was admitting that at Mount Hope only about 10 percent of the patients had much hope of regaining their mental health.[55] In 1891 the superintendent of the New Brunswick institution admitted that "Out of four hundred and forty-two patients, only sixteen were expected to be restored to mental health."[56] That is barely more than 3 percent. The asylum had become a place of confinement for hundreds of mentally ill people who were given next to no hope of recovery.

Not only were the asylums hopelessly overcrowded, they were also poorly staffed. At first, the superintendent was the only medically qualified staff member. Later in the century he was given an assistant. It was the intention of both asylums that these doctors make daily visits to all the patients but evidence given at a number of enquiries suggests that these duties were frequently neglected. Daily care of asylum inmates devolved upon a small number of attendants who had no training and often, because of overwork or simple meanness, no sympathy. Since turnover in these jobs was rapid and steady, the insane seldom even had the benefit of experienced care. Given these conditions, it is not surprising to find that there were a number of publicized incidents of attendants abusing patients. In New Brunswick, just a year after the asylum opened, two attendants were dismissed for what was delicately called "gross misconduct."[57] A short while after Mount Hope opened in Nova Scotia the institution's steward, Amos Black, was dismissed by a committee of investigation, apparently for having sexual relations with a number of the patients. In any event Black and DeWolf, the superintendent, were frequently at odds, the committee terming the situation at the asylum a "civil war" between the two men with the patients neglected as a result.[58] Five years after the Black incident, the bruised, lice-ridden corpse of Richard Hurley became the centre of a controversy about the standard of care at the asylum. During the twenty-four-year-old Hurley's six-month stay at Mount Hope no members of his family were permitted to visit him until the day the father was summoned to take the consumptive body of his son home to die. A committee investigating the incident concluded that parts of the asylum were indeed overcrowded and filthy, although it declared that there was "no evidence to fix any blame on either Dr. DeWolf or any of the attendants."[59]

While unqualified attendants were undoubtedly the cause of some abuse, the biggest problem in the asylums was lack of space. In 1877 Dr. James Steeves, superintendent of the New Brunswick hospital from 1876 to 1896, travelled to Fredericton to try and convince the legislature to finance an addition to the building. There were 284 patients in an institution built to accommodate only 200, Steeves told the Saint John *Daily Telegraph*, and 100 of these did not have the separate rooms they required for proper treatment. "The evils involved in this simple fact are such as could not well be described in our columns," wrote the interviewer, "for the details would be offensive and even shocking."[60] In Nova Scotia the "offensive" details of overcrowding were described publicly, as a result of an investigation into conditions at the asylum in May 1877.[61] It was established that because of crowding, patients were being neglected, wards were filthy and no treatment was being carried out. Kate Cameron, an attendant at Mount Hope for four years, told the committee that she had once seen a female patient stripped, bound, and left unattended in a room with no bed and no heat, simply because she had torn her clothes. It was December and the woman froze to death but no inquest was held into the incident.[62] Michael Meagher, another attendant, told the following story:

A patient named Graham was in the dark room (solitary confinement) while I was at the Hospital. It was in the

Winter time. The glass was broken, and the rain came in and wet the floor. Graham was lying on the floor on a mattress. The room was in a very dirty condition. There was straw on the floor, and human excrements. I saw the snow not melted on the floor. We put the food in over the door sometimes. The doctor would occasionally enquire how he was....He never went to see him. A man put in the dark room was entirely neglected. Graham was subject to fits; he might have died without assistance during the night: he was left entirely to his own resources after locking him up. Graham was a powerful, muscular man. It was the practice of the attendants to give as little food as possible to patients in that state to reduce their strength; just enough food to sustain them. The doctors never enquired into the quantity of food given them. Graham was in the dark room from one to three weeks. The room was bitterly cold; it was hardly fit for a dog; it was not fit for a human being.[63]

These abuses at Mount Hope may have been aggravated by Superintendent DeWolf, an arrogant man with whom most of his employees found it difficult to work. But the fact that both the New Brunswick and Prince Edward Island asylums were also, in different degrees, found to be inadequate institutions, suggests that Mount Hope was not the exception but the rule.[64]

The evidence indicates that the Maritime asylum failed to live up to its founders' expectations. Instead of a place of treatment it had become a place of confinement. Good intentions were one thing, but lack of adequate space and facilities meant inevitably that the emphasis at the asylums was on custody, not treatment. Organization became paramount as the logistics of caring for hundreds of mentally ill inmates became complicated and costly. Behaviour was subordinated to a rigidly controlled pattern of daily institutional life. The county asylums built in Nova Scotia after 1885 epitomized this trend. The regulations for one of these institutions warned that "any inmate guilty of drunkenness, disobedience, obscenity, disorderly conduct, profane or indecorous language, theft, waste or who shall absent himself or herself from the premises without the permission of the Superintendent or who shall injure or deface any part of the house or furniture therein, or who shall commit waste or destruction of any kind in regard to property connected with the Asylum shall be subject to merited punishment."[65] "Merited punishment" included solitary confinement on a diet of bread and water for up to twenty-four hours. All activity at these institutions—getting up in the morning, eating meals, taking exercise, going to bed at night—was done en masse and regulated by the sounding of bells. Given the intolerable conditions of the asylum, the humane aspect of moral treatment had been sacrificed to the requirements of the system. The Maritime asylum had become more a jail than a hospital.

Notes

The author would like to express his gratitude to Professor S. F. Wise, Department of History, Carleton University, for his invaluable assistance with the thesis from which this article is excerpted.

1. Prince Edward Island is not considered in this article because not until very late in the period under discussion was a hospital for the mentally ill constructed on the Island. An asylum was opened near Charlottetown in 1847 but it doubled as a house of industry and in construction resembled a workhouse more than a hospital. This building, chronically overcrowded and underfinanced and poorly lit and ventilated, remained the only facility for the mentally ill until 1879 when the first proper hospital built for the purpose was opened. See R. N. Stalwick, "A History of Asylum Administration in Canada Before Confederation" (Ph.D. thesis, University of London, 1967), pp. 89 passim; Henry Hurd, ed., *The Institutional Care of the Insane in the United States and Canada* (Baltimore, 1917), 4: 203 passim. When the term Maritime is used in the article, therefore, it is meant to refer to New Brunswick and Nova Scotia only.

2. *Statutes of Nova Scotia*, 32 Geo II, c. 1.

3. Ibid., 10 Geo III, c. 5.

4. *Consolidated Statutes of New Brunswick*, 5 Geo IV, c. 9.

5. For the following discussion of poor relief I am indebted to Brereton Greenhous, "Paupers and Poorhouses: The Development of Poor Relief in Early New Brunswick," *Social History* 1 (April 1968): 103–26, and James Whalen, "New Brunswick Poor Law Policy in the Nineteenth Century" (M.A. thesis, University of New Brunswick, 1968), part of which was published in *Acadiensis* 2, no. 1 (1972).

6. See Greenhous, "Paupers and Poorhouses," and Grace Aiton, "The Selling of Paupers by Public Auction in Sussex Parish," *Collections of the New Brunswick Historical Society* 16 (1961): 93–110.

7. Nova Scotia, Legislative Assembly, *Journals*, 1832, App. 49 (hereafter references to Assembly journals in the Maritimes will be to *JLA*).

8. Henry Hurd, *Institutional Care of the Insane*, p. 549.

9. *Novascotian*, 25 November 1844, and *Times*, 5 November, 22 December 1844.

10. Nova Scotia, *JLA*, 1846, App. 32; *JLA*, 1848, App. 54.

11. Ibid., 1850, App. 72.

12. *Novascotian*, 23 March 1846.

13. W. S. MacNutt, *The Atlantic Provinces* (Toronto, 1965), p. 261.

14. Hurd, *Institutional Care of the Insane*, p. 584.

15. George Peters to Executive Council, 28 November 1836, New Brunswick, Records of the Executive Council, Health and Sickness, vol. 2, Provincial Archives of New Brunswick (hereafter PANB).

16. Whalen, "New Brunswick Poor Law Policy," p. 55.

17. *New Brunswick Courier* (Saint John), 24 December 1836.

18. George Peters to Executive Council, 3 May 1845, New Brunswick, Executive Council Papers, vol. 118, p. 1442, PANB.

19. Hurd, *Institutional Care of the Insane*, p. 37.

20. Report of the Commissioners, December 1836, New Brunswick, *JLA*, 1836–37, App. 3.

21. W. S. MacNutt, *New Brunswick* (Toronto, 1963), pp. 258–59.

22. Whalen, "New Brunswick Poor Law Policy."

23. See K. A. MacKenzie, "Nineteenth Century Physicians in Nova Scotia," *Collections of the Nova Scotia Historical Society* 31 (1957): 119–20, and J. W. Lawrence, "The Medical Men of St. John in its First Half Century," *Collections of the New Brunswick Historical Society* 1 (1897): 273–305

24. Hurd, *Institutional Care of the Insane*, pp. 561, 584, 591, 595.

25. Report from the Medical Superintendent of the Provincial Lunatic Asylum, New Brunswick, *JLA*, 1851, App.
26. Report of the Medical Superintendent of the Nova Scotia Hospital for the Insane, Nova Scotia, *JLA*, 1872, App. 20; 1881, App. 3A.
27. New Brunswick, *JLA*, 1836-37, App. 3.
28. See Norman Dain, *Concepts of Insanity in the United States, 1789-1865* (New Brunswick, N.J., 1964), p. 114.
29. Nova Scotia, *JLA*, 1846, App. 32.
30. Report of the Medical Superintendent, New Brunswick, *JLA*, 1849, App.
31. Ibid., 1875, App. 6.
32. Report of the Commissioners, New Brunswick, *JLA*, 1836-37, App. 3.
33. Nova Scotia, *JLA*, 1846, App. 32.
34. Report of the Commissioners, New Brunswick, *JLA*, 1836-37, App. 3.
35. Report of the Medical Superintendent, New Brunswick, *JLA*, 1849, App.
36. See, for example, New Brunswick, *JLA*, 1850, 1851, App., and Nova Scotia, *JLA*, 1860, App.; 1874, App. 6.
37. See Report of the Commissioners, New Brunswick, *JLA*, 1836-37, App. 3, and Nova Scotia *JLA*, 1846, App. 32.
38. Report of the Commissioners, New Brunswick, *JLA*, 1836-37, App. 3.
39. Ibid.
40. Nova Scotia, *JLA*, 1846, App. 32.
41. Ibid.
42. For a detailed discussion of contemporary theories of insanity and its causes see my thesis, "That Prison on the Hill; The Historical Origins of the Lunatic Asylum in the Maritime Provinces" (M.A. thesis, Carleton University, 1975).
43. Correspondence, Reports and Returns, New Brunswick, Records of the Executive Council, vol. 118, Lunatic Asylum, 1843-57, pp. 1540-46, PANB.
44. Report of the Medical Superintendent, New Brunswick, *JLA*, 1854, App.
45. *Consolidated Statutes of New Brunswick, 1903*, vol. 1, c. 101.
46. *Nova Scotian*, 1 January 1855; *Statutes of Nova Scotia*, 1855, c. 34, ser. 1-6.
47. Nova Scotia, *JLA*, 1859, App. 10.
48. *Statutes of Nova Scotia*, 1858, c. 38.
49. Ibid., 1872, c. 3.

50. Report from the Medical Superintendent, New Brunswick, *JLA*, 1850, App.
51. Ibid., 1865, App. 14.
52. Ibid., 1886, App.
53. *Statutes of Nova Scotia*, 1886, c. 44.
54. Report of the Medical Superintendent, Nova Scotia, *JLA*, 1899, App. 3A.
55. Ibid., 1883, App. 3A.
56. Report from the Medical Superintendent, New Brunswick, *JLA*, 1891, App.
57. *Morning News* (Saint John), 7 December 1849.
58. Nova Scotia, *JLA*, 1861, App. 6; *Novascotian*, 28 May 1860.
59. Report of Committee on Humane Institutions, Nova Scotia, *JLA*, 1867, App. 38.
60. *Daily Telegraph*, 28 August 1877.
61. Report of Commission to investigate the condition and general management of the Provincial Hospital for the Insane, Nova Scotia, *JLA*, 1878, App. 10.
62. Nova Scotia, *Supplementary Evidence as to the Management of the Hospital for the Insane* (Halifax, 1872).
63. Ibid.
64. In 1874 a Grand Jury visited the Prince Edward Island asylum and reported that they "find it difficult to ask your Lordships to believe that an institution, so conducted, would be allowed to exist in a civilized community. In a cell below the ground, about six feet by seven feet, they found a young woman, entirely naked, beneath some broken, dirty straw. The stench was unbearable. There were pools of urine on the floor, evidently the accumulation of many days, as there were gallons of it." The superintendent of the institution was apparently "an ordinary labourer" and the jury concluded that "the whole Asylum is one state of filth." (Grand Jury Presentment on the state of the Asylum, PEI, *JLA*, 1875, App. G)
65. *Bylaws*, Cumberland County Hospital for the Insane, 1895, Public Archives of Nova Scotia.

Canadian Doctors and the Cholera

GEOFFREY BILSON

Cholera ravaged Europe and North America at intervals during the middle years of the nineteenth century. There were major epidemics in Canada in 1832 and 1834 and again in 1849 and 1854 and minor outbreaks in the early 1850s. The disease was a terrible one, which struck very hard at the poor where they were crowded together in filthy cities. The cholera raised questions about the nature of disease, about public health and sanitation and about the need for international cooperation for health needs. Doctors had no convincing explanations about cholera and no effective cures for it and the efforts of government to deal with the disease took place against a background of fear that could erupt into riot or rebellion in the right circumstances.[1] Cholera demanded attention and it stimulated action in many European countries.

It is now known that cholera is caused by the cholera vibrio which enters the human body through the mouth and multiplies rapidly in the intestines. In patients severely affected the

Reprinted by permission of the Canadian Historical Association from *Historical Papers*, 1977, pp. 105-19.

disease causes a massive purging of fluid which dehydrates the body and upsets its chemical balance. As it progresses, the patient suffers severe cramps in his intestines and limbs, the body becomes cadaverous and turns blue. The patient's blood grows thick, his bodily processes slow and fail and without treatment over half the victims severely affected will die. Nowadays, the patient is treated with antibiotics and intravenous infusions of fluid. Rigorous hygiene, clean water supplies and efficient sewage disposal are the best defences against the disease which still claims most of its victims amongst those denied these benefits.

The way in which cholera spreads and is carried raises difficulties for public health officials in the twentieth century. Cholera can be carried by people who give no indication that they have the disease and these apparently healthy carriers play a large role in spreading the disease. During an epidemic, many victims have the disease in a mild form indistinguishable from a minor upset and they can effectively spread the disease by contaminating water supplies. The large number of subclinical cases help to maintain cholera even when the epidemic appears to have subsided.[2] The disease is still not fully understood at the present time.

In the nineteenth century, cholera baffled the doctors.[3] It fitted no known pattern of contagion, people in contact with victims were often left unscathed, the disease could break out apparently simultaneously in widely separated parts of a town. For these reasons, many doctors argued that cholera was epidemic—that it occurred where particular conditions of soil, climate, atmosphere, and exhalations from filth or stagnant water produced an epidemic atmosphere. People who for one reason or another had predisposed themselves to the disease, by intemperance, by fear, by immoderate diet, by fatigue, by getting too hot or cold fell ill. In 1851, the British delegation at the first international sanitary conference denied that cholera was contagious and insisted that it was epidemic.

At the same time, there were those doctors who looked for a specific cause of the disease and for a mechanism by which it spread which would answer the questions that non-contagionists raised. In England, William Budd and John Snow postulated in the late 1840s and early 1850s that water supplies infected by some matter from the discharges of cholera victims spread the disease. In Italy in 1854, Filippo Pacini of Florence described the cholera vibrio which he had seen through his microscope and suggested the way in which the vibrio multiplied and later suggested that fluid loss was the cause of death. By 1854, the nature of the disease and its mode of transmission were understood but few members of the profession accepted the explanations of Pacini and Snow. They continued to argue for a greater or lesser degree of contagiousness, and to put the major emphasis on the atmosphere as the agency for spreading the disease. In 1859, the British delegation at an international conference argued that cholera was not contagious and should be removed from the list of diseases requiring regulation.

Not until the idea that a specific germ could cause a particular disease began to dominate the profession would the work of Snow and Pacini come to seem overwhelmingly convincing. The germ theory was merely one among a number of explanations in the 1860s and without the technical skill that microscopic study demands, the germ theory was not absolutely convincing. It had to take its place amongst theories which suggested that disease was a process of fermentation or a product of miasma or produced by spontaneous generation.[4] When Robert Koch isolated and cultured the cholera vibrio in 1885 he swung most of the profession behind the germ theory but many remained unconvinced that the vibrio could cause the disease without specific atmospheric conditions which made the vibrio poisonous. To prove this point, Max von Pettenkoffer drank a tumblerful of water laced with the cholera vibrios. Much was invested in the opposition to germ theory. Efforts to clean up the cities were justified by warnings of the danger of miasma and effluvia, warnings which might lose their effect if germs were the explanation. A disease spread by germs and human contact might be stopped by quarantine, but trading nations did not welcome quarantine.

The idea of contagion produced fear and panic, leaving the victims without aid and threatening social order. With these disadvantages, the germ theory needed very convincing evidence to win over the profession and for the years in which cholera visited Canada, the debate was unresolved.

Doctors, for the most part, were practical men concerned with making a living. When cholera attacked their patients they could not simply say that it was a strange disease about which they could do nothing, although that was the truth, but were forced to do something about it. There opened the "grotesque chapter" of cholera therapy, which has been described as "a form of benevolent homicide." The therapy included bleeding and huge doses of calomel (a preparation of mercury) and opium. Physical treatments were often brutal and included cauterization of the spine and blisters by cantharides or boiling water applied to the stomach. Anything seemed worth trying, including electric shocks and intravenous injections of various liquids. The injections were normally confined to the most desperately ill and were usually fatal. The only advance in therapy in the century was that the most brutal treatments were gradually abandoned.[5] One consequence of the grotesque therapy, which was part of the usual range of therapies applied to disease, was that people began to abandon the regular medical men and turn to those who offered less daunting regimens. They turned to Thomsonians, who practised a form of medicine based on formulae of plants devised by Samuel Thompson or they turned to homeopathic doctors who used minute doses of drugs heavily diluted. These may not have cured, but they did little harm. In the cholera years in the United States, Thomsonians made great gains at the expense of the regular medical men.[6]

The Canadian Medical Profession

During the cholera years in Canada, the medical profession was forming itself with difficulty against opposition and in the face of internal divisions. The chief means by which regular doctors sought to make theirs an exclusive profession were education, examination, and licensing. Some of the major efforts toward achieving professional standing were made between the early 1830s and the later 1860s, but they were made at a time when the doctors were losing public esteem. At the beginning of the period the regular doctors were trained by apprenticeship and by study at a medical school, usually outside Canada, where part of the training included work on a hospital ward.[7] In both Lower and Upper Canada, doctors trained in medical schools demanded that schools be established in Canada. Their motives were mixed. The normal pattern by which a school was established was that a group of doctors (or occasionally a single doctor) would begin to teach classes in medicine and attempt to introduce their students into a hospital with which they had an affiliation. In this way, for example, Dr. William Caldwell and his colleagues established the Montreal Medical Institution in 1823, Dr. Charles-Jacques Frémont and his colleagues established the Ecole de Médecine de Québec in 1845, and Dr. John Rolph set up his own school in Toronto in the early 1830s which became the Toronto School of Medicine on his return from exile in 1843. The schools were set up because their founders wanted to teach medicine on lines that they approved. In Montreal, French doctors resented English domination of medical education and established their own schools. For some, it was a source of income, and John Rolph seems to have used his political influence to protect his school from competition by the University of Toronto in 1852. A degree of public support came from those who wanted Canadian doctors to be trained in Canada. In Upper Canada there was much fear, expressed by John Strachan and by members of the profession that without a medical school in the province, too many young men were going to United States schools, where they were inadequately trained and exposed to democratical principles.[8] Unlike the United States, where medical schools became commercial operations and lowered standards of entry in their pursuit of students,[9] those in Canada sought affiliation with universities and maintained high standards of entry. Entry requirements usually included Latin, and a university degree in medicine was thought sufficient qualification to practice. One purpose of the education was to produce gentlemen who would raise the tone of the profession and make it clearly superior.

In the mid-century, students at a Canadian medical school attended lectures on Materia Medica and therapeutics, Anatomy and Physiology, Principles and Practice of Medicine, Principles and Practice of Surgery, Midwifery and the Diseases of Women and Children, and Medical Jurisprudence. In some schools they attended lectures on chemistry. They spent more or less time at a hospital, according to the connection that their school had with an institution. In anatomy, the students dissected, usually under the guidance of a demonstrator rather than the professor; in some schools, such as Laval after 1862, they might be offered the chance to use the microscope in anatomy but there was little laboratory work.[10] By the early 1870s, McGill was said to be the best medical school north of Philadelphia. William Osler went there from Toronto, and found a strong emphasis on work in the wards, but little difference in education from what had been set up forty years before. Not until Osler returned from Europe to take a chair at McGill in the mid-1870s would the European medical science based on laboratory work and the microscope be introduced at McGill with the help of a batch of microscopes which Osler had shipped to Montreal.[11] It was at the same time that McGill first began to offer lectures on public health to its students. Medical schools in Canada did not produce graduates likely to contribute to medical advance.

The medical school and the university were institutions which could define the profession, but while many members had not been educated in that way, licensing offered a method of defining the profession. The struggle over universities and over licensing and regulating the medical profession gives some clues to public attitudes to doctors in Canada.

From the late eighteenth century there were efforts to license medical practitioners by boards of examiners. In Lower Canada these efforts to define who should be in the profession produced tension between French and English doctors in 1831 and again in 1846. Proposals to form a College of Physicians and Surgeons of Lower Canada provoked bitterness until the moderate French and English doctors agreed to form the college, for fear that if they did not get together eclectics and irregular physicians would gain legal standing.[12] In Upper Canada, the profession had less success in making itself exclusive. Efforts to set rigorous standards of admission to the practice of medicine failed in the early nineteenth century because they were impractical. When the medical men proposed that they be allowed to form a corporation to regulate themselves, as the lawyers had done, the proposal was rejected in the early 1830s. A College of Physicians and Surgeons was set up in 1839 but the legislation was disallowed by the imperial government for infringing the liberties of the Royal College of Surgeons of London. In 1869, the Ontario Medical Act defined medical practitioners and included homeopaths and eclectics against whom regular doctors had been waging a long campaign.[13]

The public was not as convinced as were the regular doctors of the need for limited entry to the profession. In the 1850s a medical journal complained that Upper Canada was flooded with "a horde of root doctors, steamers and quacks" who divided "with the regularly qualified physicians the scanty subsistence the neighbourhood is capable of affording" by "ingratiating themselves into the good opinions of the farmers and country shopkeepers, and descend[ing] to familiarities with the lower classes, to which educated gentlemen cannot stoop and soon the latter finds his ignorant and low competitor is preferred to himself, or at least divides pretty equally, public confidence."[14]

The quotation suggests something of the complex of attitudes which were present among the regular doctors—a fear of declining scientific standards, uncertain social standing, and too effective competition for the health care dollar. It also points to the reality of medical practice in mid-century Upper Canada—that many people chose irregular practitioners because they preferred them and because there was no social or scientific reason for choosing regulars. In all parts of Canada people gave work to unlicensed and irregular practitioners until the late 1860s and beyond. It must have been especially galling for doctors to be told by the Crown lawyers in Britain that corporate or collegiate organization would "have a tendency to establish a monopoly which might be found highly injurious to the inhabitants of the Province" and by the lawyers in Upper Canada that medicine should be a trade open to all, with the law the remedy against error.[15] On the other hand, when the medical faculty of the University of Toronto was abolished by the legislature in 1852, it was done on the grounds that the public should not finance education for men entering such lucrative professions as medicine. Thus, doctors found themselves in low public esteem with their claims to professionalism not widely respected even while their profession was regarded as lucrative.

The regular doctors were not well placed to command public confidence on any question and regular doctors made efforts in the mid-century to build their sense of professionalism and to justify professional standing. One method was to organize medical societies which would serve to bring medical men together and encourage discussion of medical questions. In 1826, Dr. Joseph Morrin had set up the Quebec Medical Society for these purposes and to press for legislation against abuses.[16] Medico-Chirurgical Societies were established in most of the major centres of Upper and Lower Canada and out of the societies came a move to organize a single association to represent the profession. In 1844, Dr. Joseph Painchaud proposed such an association, which would also undertake to supply governments with "statistical and hygienic" information, but efforts to establish the association failed because of the resistance of doctors who could see no clear advantage to themselves and feared the burden of offering advice to the public "without remuneration."[17] Not until 1867 would Confederation offer the occasion to organize the Canadian Medical Association.

The medical profession did not present a united front to the world during the mid-nineteenth century. Even as it struggled to define itself it was shaken by disputes between French doctors and English doctors, between country practitioners and those in the city, between those trained in Britain and those trained in Canada, and even between those trained in different parts of Britain. In 1836 doctors complained that the Province of Upper Canada made invidious distinctions between licentiates of the Colleges of Surgeons of Dublin, Edinburgh, Glasgow, and those of the Royal College of Surgeons of London.[18] Divided, distrusted, and with little public respect or support, the medical profession further undermined public confidence in itself by its failure either to explain or to deal with cholera when it came to Canada.

Canadian Doctors and the Cholera

When cholera threatened Canada in 1832, laymen and doctors alike had access to information about the disease which was widely published in the press. The British government sent the governor general copies of the reports of the investigations of various commissions which had visited Russia. He, in turn, made them available to the Quebec Medical Board. The British government also sent copies of the recommendations of the Central Board of Health for the consideration of Canadian doctors. It was on the basis of this British information that the Quebec Medical Board made the recommendations on which the quarantine act of 1832 was based.[19] Interested doctors, such as Dr. Joseph Painchaud, collected and distributed among their colleagues what writings they could find on the disease.[20] Some military men had served in India and had seen the disease there and military surgeons were familiar with the recommendations of their colleagues in India. The first impulse of most doctors interested enough to study the question was to form their opinion on the basis of European authors. They would continue to do so, modifying what they read by what they observed in their own practices.

They were, therefore, plunged immediately into the question of whether or not the disease was contagious; a question made more pressing by the huge number of emigrants entering the St. Lawrence each season. Opinion was divided, but the bulk of the Canadian doctors decided that cholera was not contagious but that it required an epidemic influence to develop. A group of American doctors visiting Canada reported that in the opinion of many Canadian doctors "the disease has not been imported, but has originated in Canada under circumstances favorable to its development [*sic*] and increase."[21] Thus confidence in an atmospheric explanation soon produced difficulties as the disease had appeared with the emigrants. Some doctors claimed to have seen cholera before the first emigrant arrived and others pointed out that the emigrants had been coming for weeks before cholera appeared. What was the connection between emigrants and cholera?

One possible explanation could be found in the idea of predisposing causes—that something one did or did not do predisposed one to a disease which was epidemic. Diet, intemperance, immoderate habits, and dirt might be predisposing causes. The conditions under which the emigrants were transported, crushed together in filthy ships, weakened by poor food, and suddenly exposed to a new climate would render them particularly liable to the disease. In Canada, the cholera had ravaged the French-Canadian population, it was said, and their habits had remained unchanged since the conquest. They lived on vegetables, soup and bread, paid little attention to comfort or cleanliness, and were usually intemperate. The English, on the other hand, had "good substantial nutriment."[22] If the disease originated in Canada, what was the justification of quarantine? The Quebec Board of Health did consider closing the station at Grosse Isle when cholera appeared in the city, but decided to keep it as a place where people could clean themselves before finishing their journey.[23] In future years, quarantine would be kept although logic did not support it, because it served as a means of preventing obviously sick people from landing in Quebec.

In the face of the emigrant tide, many doctors continued to emphasize that cholera was not contagious. Dr. A. F. Holmes stated flatly that the pattern by which the disease spread, the fact that it first attacked the French Canadians and the fact that it appeared in Quebec before cases were reported at Grosse Isle were "sufficient ground to repudiate the idea of its having spread from one point, or its having been introduced by emigrants." He then agreed that the fact that it spread along commercial routes did raise questions but felt "forced to leave the subject without attempting to solve the problem." Holmes had believed that once the disease appeared in a community it could not be passed from person to person, but "from personal observation" he was forced to the conclusion that in some circumstances cholera could become infectious and pass from person to person. The disease, said Holmes, was "generally devoid of infectious power, but subject, under circumstances favorable to it, to acquire that power."[24]

The observed facts struggled against the theory of non-contagion. There could be no clearcut agreement. Dr. Joseph Workman presented a thesis for his M.D. at McGill in May 1835. In it, he argued that all cases of the disease were found among people who had had contact with victims and that "its close adherence to emigrants proved still more incontestably the agency by which it is transmitted from country to country." The thesis, said Workman, was not challenged by the faculty.[25]

In the fifteen years after the epidemic of the 1830s, Canadian medical training had changed and a number of medical journals were being published in the country. These offered their readers a combination of reports gleaned from foreign journals, thus serving as channels to bring the latest European ideas to Canada, and as forums for Canadian doctors. As most of the local doctors were practitioners not especially interested in the theory of disease, local contributions were limited in number.[26] The discussions in the journals do suggest that experience in the 1840s and 1850s had led most doctors to accept the idea that cholera was contagious to some extent. George Douglas, medical superintendent of Grosse Isle, was prepared to argue that "to assert that cholera is contagious in the same degree as typhus fever or small pox is against all observation and experience." He pointed out that not one doctor, clergyman, or nurse who attended cholera victims was in anything like the danger that similar attendants of typhus victims faced.[27] That might be true, but did it mean that cholera was not contagious? "When we reflect that contagious diseases frequently exhibit themselves in a form apparently epidemic and that epidemics assume many of the features of contagious diseases, it becomes a matter of exceeding difficulty to draw the line of demarcation between them," wrote Dr. Archibald Hall.[28] The atmospheric argument remained strong, but in the aftermath of the 1849 epidemic there were doctors who were prepared to argue for contagion. Dr. William Marsden argued that cholera could be transmitted from person to person by direct or indirect contact either by a virus (like smallpox) or by a miasmata from the sick person (like the plague). For Marsden it was the beginning of a lifelong campaign to convince his colleagues that cholera was contagious.[29]

If the profession was beginning to incline toward the idea that cholera was contagious, it was no more convinced of the argument than were doctors elsewhere. In Canada, the reasons for rejecting contagionism were strong. As Dr. Anthony von Iffland, a man with extensive experience, pointed out, the doctrine of contagion was a doctrine which struck terror into people and produced panic and, interestingly, gave the medical profession an undeserved reputation as "a preserver endued with courage to confront, and skill to disarm, the unseen destroyer."[30] On the other hand, a resolution of the

Medico-Chirurgical Society of Montreal, that cholera was "essentially non contagious" was condemned by many doctors and laymen.[31]

In 1866, something of an official opinion on the question was given by a panel of doctors called together by the Bureau of Agriculture. These "unbiased and well informed minds" agreed that cholera was "portable" and that it was best to assume "that it is carried by persons, effects and merchandize and even by the winds of the air and currents and streams" and that it could "make a jump over distances of several hundred miles." The practical consequences were that quarantine should be maintained to "delay" and "limit the spread" of a disease it could not prevent. The pamphlet was reissued without amendment by the bureau in 1873, in the face of the expected return of cholera.[32] In that same year, the *Canada Medical and Surgical Journal* stated flatly "of the contagious character of cholera there can be no doubt" and quoted the example of Halifax, which had successfully contained an outbreak of cholera to the ship on which it occurred by a rigorous quarantine in 1871. The editor, having made that bold claim, retreated to the argument that quarantine "if it does not prevent the introduction of disease, at least induces a feeling of public security, which is in itself beneficial."[33] The debate over contagion revealed that the profession was confused and had no clear opinion that was incontrovertible. In that, doctor and layman were alike and why, then, should the layman listen to the doctor or look to him for advice?

There was no clearer answer to the question of the nature of the disease or its action on the body. Doctors and laymen alike could see and describe the manifestations of the disease but doctors needed to know how it was acting internally. The disease struck at the "gastric and intestinal functions."[34] Autopsies were performed to discover the exact nature of the disease but there was no agreement. The disease might be one of the intestines, but it could also be one where the intestinal upset and discharges were only the consequences of the body's efforts to purge itself of a poison affecting the lungs, the nervous system, or the blood. In the 1830s, the tendency was to see cholera as a disease of the blood, "the sudden abstraction of saline particles from the blood" which had to be restored if health was to return.[35] This was the basis for saline treatments of the disease. It was also possible that it was a disease which by fermentation produced a poison that over-loaded the digestive system or that it was a disease which depressed the nervous system and stopped all the body func-tions. When Dr. Hall published accounts of microscopic examinations from European journals he thought they held "the probability of results of great magnitude," suggesting as they did the possibility that a specific agent was involved in the disease.[36] No Canadian doctor seems to have followed this approach to the disease.

The centre of the relationship between doctor and patient was the doctor's ability to cure his patient or to make him feel that what the doctor offered was worth having. If a man could reassure the patient, he would have his gratitude and he did not have to be a regular physician to do that. The treatments which Canadian doctors hurled against a disease they did not understand were as barbarous as any used else-where in the world and cannot have reassured the patient. In the 1830s, the favoured treatments were bleeding, calomel in doses large enough to make the gums bleed, opium, and counter irritant therapy by cautery and blistering. Some of the hardier patients survived. Private Patrick Mullany of the 32nd Regiment was one. He was taken ill on duty at Quebec City in 1832. He hid from the doctors until he was seen to be sick and was taken to hospital on 17 July at 9:00 a.m. He was bled thirty ounces, given fifteen grains of calomel and two of opium, given a turpentine enema and rubbed with turpen-tine to ease his cramps, fed ginger tea, and allowed to rest. At 2:00 p.m. he was given another three grains of calomel and put on a course of ⅛ grain of opium every half hour with calomel every third hour. That evening he was dosed with castor oil. 18 and 19 July passed with calomel, opium, castor oil, an enema, but also a glass of port wine every two or three hours. On 20 July he was given an acidulated drink, warm wine, lemonade, beef tea, and had a blister applied to his stomach. On 21 July he was dosed with rhubarb, had twelve leeches applied to his stomach, followed by a second blister and was fed beef tea and arrowroot. By 22 July he was able to eat oatmeal porridge for breakfast, but the mercury had begun to affect his mouth. He was given bicarbonate of soda every three hours and beef and arrowroot teas. On 23 July the medicines were ended and he improved slowly until 30 July and was able to return to duty on 11 August.[37] Perhaps he was right to hide on 17 July; but he was receiving the best treatment of the day.

In both Lower and Upper Canada, efforts were made in 1832 to transfuse solutions into the veins. Dr. George Griffin described one such experiment. Private James Williams of the 26th Regiment when almost dead was given a transfusion of seventeen pints of soft rain water "carefully filtered" and mixed with 180 grains of muriate of soda, 206 grains of carbonate of soda, 204 grains of phosphate of soda. After ten minutes, Williams lost the blue colour and opened his eyes, saying that he felt better. "About twenty five minutes after the commencement of the transfusion, when about eight pints of the fluid had been introduced, he suddenly vomited...and died in a few minutes." It was the usual outcome of these experiments.[38] Perhaps it is not surprising that people looked to other medical help than that of the regular doctors.

The only major shift in therapy in late epidemics was that bloodletting was less used. It was going out of style in general practice. Dr. F. C. Mewburn remarked in the 1880s that "in medicine, the furious bloodletting are gone, and well would it have been had we retained the lancet, using it moderately, instead of doing as we did about 1845, by taking up stimulants, and, like bleeding, carrying it to excess."[39] There were those who regretted its passing in cholera therapy. Dr. Wm. Marsden made a strong plea for its use, based on his experience in 1832. "My practice was then *bleeding whenever blood could* be obtained, even in collapse and I am not sure that any better practice could be adopted now in very many cases." Marsden combined bleeding with massive doses of calomel "of upwards of 200 grains within a few hours." His own practice and the experience of doctors in India and France convinced him that bleeding restored the circulation.[40] The enthusiasm for transfusion treatment also declined in these epidemics, presumably because of the lack of success. Dr. James Bovell of Toronto did experiment with transfusions of milk in 1849, but his experiments were not repeated.

Marsden obviously felt that bleeding needed a strong defence against his colleagues' growing scepticism, but he need have no fears for the calomel. Dr. Archibald Hall, writing as lecturer in Materia Medica at McGill, argued that the evidence of autopsies convinced him that the cause of death was "an impression of the nervous system" which impeded the vital body functions. Hall rejected stimulant therapies and concentrated on checking the vomiting and purging and restoring "the various secretions by excitation of the glandular viscera." Calomel in large doses, combined with morphia, should be given at first, followed by smaller doses every half hour or hour.[41] Dr. George Gibbs reported that he had followed the suggestions of the English Dr. Ayre of Hull (whose suggestions had been reported in the Canadian medical press) and given large doses of calomel. "I have never regarded the quantity of calomel taken as of any moment in such a dreadful disease, trusting to combat its ill effects by proper treatment after subduing the cholera."[42] One can imagine the effects of that attitude on patients with previous experiences with the effects of calomel, and doctors did meet resistance from patients who had the strength to resist. By the 1850s, there were reports in the medical press of treatments being used in England which were designed to maintain the patient's strength while nature made the cure—but those treatments smacked of homeopathy and the regular physicians seemed to prefer an assault on the disease and on the patient. Doctors always claimed that early treatment was the key to a cure, but many patients knew better and treated themselves or their friends.

Few Canadian doctors showed any interest in microscopy but some of them were interested in the statistical approach to epidemiology which yielded important results in mid-nineteenth-century Europe. The collection of statistics showed that certain parts of a city were less healthy than others and lent strength to the arguments of sanitary reformers. As early as 1834, William Kelly, a surgeon of the Royal Navy, had read a paper on medical statistics to the Literary and Historical Society of Quebec. In it he had shown that the mortality in the towns of Lower Canada was twice that in the country and suggested that increasing ratio of mortality at a time of commercial growth was the result of failures to keep the cities clean and well supplied with water. He argued that it was particularly important to supply the poor with water "as the scarcity of water is perhaps the only one of the sources of disease peculiar to them, that can be met by municipal regulations." Self-interest supported action because "when disease begins among the poor, it sooner or later spreads to the rich." Kelly's studies were hampered by inadequate statistics and "slovenly" record-keeping at the hospitals.[43]

It was a complaint frequently repeated in the future. The statistics collected by local government were inaccurate and uninformative. The need for accurate statistics seemed especially pressing when the country was subject to the large influx of emigrants it experienced each year. "There are very few cities in the United States of any note, and as few also in Great Britain and the European Continent, whose civic authorities have not bestowed some attention to this matter, the weekly or monthly results being published in the form of bills of mortality," said one commentator in 1845. The figures which did exist suggested to him that mortality was decreasing in Montreal, which he attributed to sanitary improvement.[44] Dr. Joseph Painchaud's experience, referred to earlier, in which doctors failed to act on his suggestion that they create an association which would supply statistical information to government because of the burden it would impose on them, suggests the general attitudes of the profession toward the question in the mid-1840s. The situation did not improve until the late 1860s, when the new Canadian Medical Association set up, as one of its first committees, a committee on statistics. The lack of record-keeping by all levels of government hampered all attempts to underpin medical suggestions with solid evidence.

Whenever an epidemic struck Canada, local boards of health were set up to enforce quarantine and to suggest and enforce local sanitary laws. They met considerable opposition and inertia, were short-lived, and had little impact on the conditions of the towns of Canada. The relations between boards of health and the medical profession were often strained. Boards were usually largely composed of laymen and therefore quickly aroused the professional pique of the doctors. In Lower Canada in 1832 relations deteriorated very quickly between the boards and the doctors who felt that they were being too harshly criticized. Similar professional complaints were raised in 1849 when the Central Board of Health was accused of being a lay body "armed...with almost despotic powers, controlling the Profession and the Local Boards throughout the province." A certain bitterness crept into the complaint that "Every one, now-a-days, dabbles in Physic... and it is but one step further to attribute to every one an intricate and intuitive acquaintance with the causes of disease and the means for their prevention and removal...fitting them at once to be able members of a Board of Health, and capable of immediate legislation for the profession and the public, on some of the most subtle and intricate questions which can possibly engage the attention of men." "The profession will not voluntarily submit itself to the control of a Board in which a lay constitution is so monstrously predominant."[45] That was just the point—many laymen could not see how the medical profession was any better qualified to comment on cholera than were laymen, but they did recognize that medical men claimed a professional expertise that had little basis in knowledge. Part of the failure to act to clean up Canadian cities lay in the fact that there was no clearly obvious scientific reason why the cities which were filthy in the years before and after the epidemics needed to be clean to prevent epidemics.

Conclusion

Cholera was a hideous disease which created fear, panic, and a demand for action. By its nature, it raised a number of troublesome questions to which there were no clear answers before the germ theory was generally accepted and the mode of transmission suggested by Budd and Snow was acknowledged. Canadian doctors were aware of the debate over the question of contagion and contributed to it from their own experience in some of the most fatal epidemics in the West. Their contributions helped to undermine their standing in the public's eye because it led laymen to think that the profession was merely confused. When they added to that confusion a barbaric therapy against a disease which they clearly did not understand, they sacrificed further public respect.

This disillusionment of the public with the profession was reflected in the wide support for the irregular practitioners who had always flourished in the frontier conditions of Canadian life. The irregulars now gained greater followings as they offered systems of medicine which were no more harmful, and often less brutal, than that of the regulars. The regular medical men thus found themselves striving through the cholera years to organize themselves in the face of public indifference and hostility. Attempts to improve medical education led to the setting up of a number of medical schools, but they offered relatively little training in areas which would prove useful in the fight for public health measures. This weakness was reinforced by the fact that governments did not collect the statistics on which epidemiology could rest. Doctors were thus denied by the nature of their own training and by failures of society the access to the techniques which were proving fruitful in Europe. Medical men claimed a position in society which their scientific knowledge did not sustain, but they undermined that claim by internal feuds which often divided them and reduced their prestige. They sometimes appeared to the public as a self-interested group of squabbling poseurs. Their relations with boards of health, where they were set up, often reflected this fact. Not until cholera had ceased to be a threat to Canada did developments take place in medical science and in medical education in Canada which could permit the profession to make valid the claims it had advanced to scientific expertise and the right to a professional standing in the community. When those changes occurred progress was made in public health.

Notes

1. Discussions of the social impact of cholera can be found, for example, in Asa Briggs, "Cholera and Society in the Nineteenth Century," *Past and Present* 19 (1961): 76–96; Louis Chevalier, *Laboring and Dangerous Classes in Paris during the First Half of the Nineteenth Century* (New York, 1973); Roderick E. McGrew, *Russia and the Cholera 1823–1832* (Madison, Wis., 1965); and Charles E. Rosenberg, *The Cholera Years* (Chicago, 1962).

2. J.J. Dizon, "Cholera Carriers," and E.J. Gangarosa and Wiley H. Mosley, "Epidemiology and Surveillance of Cholera," in Dhiman Barua and William Burrows, eds., *Cholera* (Philadelphia, London, and Toronto, 1974).

3. The fullest discussion of the debate over the disease can be found in Norman Howard-Jones, "The Scientific Background of the International Sanitary Conferences 1851–1938," *W.H.O. Chronicle* 28: 159–71, 229–47, 369–84, 414–61.

4. J. K. Crellin, "The Dawn of the Germ Theory: Particles, Infection and Biology," in F. N. L. Poynter, ed., *Medicine and Society in the 1860s* (London, 1968).

5. Norman Howard-Jones, "Cholera Therapy in the Nineteenth Century," *Journal of the History of Medicine and Allied Sciences* 27 (1972): 373–95.

6. Rosenberg, *Cholera Years*, pp. 70-72.
7. Maude E. Abbott, *History of Medicine in the Province of Quebec* (Montreal, 1931), p. 49.
8. William Canniff, *The Medical Profession in Upper Canada 1783-1850* (Toronto, 1894), pp. 53, 176
9. William G. Rothstein, *American Physicians in the 19th Century* (Baltimore, 1972), p. 85.
10. Canniff, *Medical Profession in Upper Canada*, p. 185; George W. Spragge, "The Trinity Medical College," *Ontario History* 58 (1966): p. 69; C-M. Boissonnault, "Charles-Jacques Frémont," *DCB*, vol. 9 (Toronto, 1976).
11. Harvey Cushing, *The Life of Sir William Osler*, 1 (Oxford, 1925): 70-71, 144.
12. Abbott, *History of Medicine*, p. 72; Sylvio Leblond, "La médecine dans la Province de Québec avant 1847," *Les Cahiers des Dix* 35 (1970): 81; H. E. MacDermot, *History of the Canadian Medical Association 1867-1921* (Toronto, 1935), p. 3.
13. Canniff, *Medical Profession in Upper Canada*, pp. 20-21, 31, 36, 62, 64, 67, 153; MacDermot, *History of the CMA*, p. 8.
14. *Canada Medical Journal*, July 1852, quoted in Spragge, "Trinity Medical College," p. 64.
15. Canniff, *Medical Profession in Upper Canada*, p. 153; MacDermot, *History of the CMA*, p. 11.
16. John J. Heagerty, *Four Centuries of Medical History in Canada*, 1 (Toronto, 1928): 282-83.
17. MacDermot, *History of the CMA*, pp. 17, 19.
18. Canniff, *Medical Profession in Upper Canada*, pp. 87-88; G. M. Craig, "Two Contrasting Upper Canadian Figures: John Rolph and John Strachan," *Transactions of the RSC*, series 4, 12 (1974): 247. Abbott, *History of Medicine*, p. 72.
19. G. Bilson, "The First Epidemic of Asiatic Cholera in Lower Canada," *Medical History* 21, no. 4 (October 1977): 411-33.
20. Public Archives of Canada (PAC), Records of the Governor General, RG7 G18, vol. 16-17, Dr. George Roberts to Lord Aylmer, 31 May 1833.
21. J. E. DeKay, J. R. Rhinelander, *Report of the Commissioners employed to investigate the origins and nature of the Epidemic cholera of Canada* (New York, July 1832).
22. Samuel Jackson, Charles Meigs, Richard Harlan, *Report of the Commission appointed by the Sanitary Board of the City Councils to visit Canada for the investigation of the Epidemic Cholera ...* (Philadelphia, 1832), pp. 6-7.
23. Bilson, "Lower Canada."

24. Martyn Paine, "History of the Cholera at Montreal," *Boston Medical and Surgical Journal* 8 (1833): 54–55. This was a questionnaire answered by Dr. Holmes.

25. Dr. Joseph Workman, "Cholera in 1832 and 1834," *Canada Medical Journal* 2 (1865–66): 485–89.

26. E. H. Bensley, "Archibald Hall," *DCB*, 9: 358.

27. George Douglas, "Asiatic Cholera," *British American Journal of Medical and Physical Sciences* 3 (1847–48): 262.

28. *British American Journal of Medical and Physical Sciences* 4 (1848–49): 220.

29. *British American Journal of Medical and Physical Sciences* 5 (1849): 198; *Canada Medical Journal*, vols. 4 and 5 (1868–69).

30. A. von Iffland, "The Quebec Board of Health, the Cholera at Beauport and its Treatment," *British American Journal of Medical and Physical Sciences* 5 (1849): 199–200.

31. *British American Journal of Medical and Physical Sciences* 5 (1849): 108.

32. *Memorandum on Cholera* (Ottawa, Bureau of Agriculture and Statistics, 1866, 1873).

33. *Canada Medical and Surgical Journal* (1873), p. 426.

34. Jackson, *Report*, pp. 21–22.

35. George Griffin, "Observations," *British American Journal of Medical and Physical Sciences* 4 (1848–49): 293.

36. *British American Journal of Medical and Physical Sciences* 4 (1848–49): 178, 209.

37. Griffin, "Observations," p. 269.

38. Ibid., p. 295; and see Bilson, "Lower Canada."

39. Canniff, *Medical Profession in Upper Canada*, p. 517.

40. William Marsden, "On Bloodletting in Cholera," *British American Journal of Medical and Physical Sciences* 5 (1849), pp. 141–45.

41. A. Hall, "On the Calomel Treatment in Algide or Asiatic Cholera," *British American Journal of Medical and Physical Sciences* 5 (1849): 86.

42. George D. Gibbs, M.D., "On the Successful Treatment of Cholera in Canada," *Lancet* (1854), p. 5.

43. William Kelly, M.D., "On the Medical Statistics of Lower Canada," read 19 April 1834, *Transactions of the Literary and Historical Society of Quebec*, 3, 1st series (reprinted 1927): 193–221.

44. See, for example, *British American Journal*, 15 January 1845; ibid., 15 July 1845.

45. *British American Journal*, 2 July 1849, p. 75.

Medical Licensing in Lower Canada: The Dispute over Canada's First Medical Degree

BARBARA R. TUNIS

Canada's first medical degree was awarded by McGill University, Montreal, on 24 May 1833.[1] The conferring of this degree precipitated a legal controversy over the right of a medical graduate of a Canadian university to practise medicine without further examination by licensing authorities. Such a right was finally achieved in 1835, when the Medical Board of Examiners for the District of Montreal was forced to accede to an order of the court.

A conflict of this nature is not unique in the history of medical licensing. In Great Britain similar disputes had occurred two centuries earlier between the universities and the Royal College of Physicians of London.[2] In France bitter rivalry had arisen over the same issues.[3] But in the present instance the controversy was closely related to political events in Lower Canada in the early nineteenth century.[4]

Reprinted by permission of the author and the University of Toronto Press from *Canadian Historical Review* 55, no. 4 (1974): 489–504.

A court case surrounding McGill's degree resulted when the Montreal Medical Board refused to grant its licensing certificate to the candidate, William Logie, unless he submitted to further examination before the board. This Dr. Logie declined to do. The dispute that followed was the culmination of a series of problems and ambiguities concerning the function and powers of the medical licensing body which had plagued the board since its election in 1831. But the basic issues were more complex, and involved the structure and control of the medical board itself. Logie, caught in a legal entanglement between the university and the medical board, was a victim of circumstance around whom the conflict reached its climax.

The underlying problems were intensified by the varying relationships of those involved to the political authorities and the political disputes of the period. The growth of French-Canadian nationalism and the increasing activity of members of the medical profession in the Legislative Assembly further complicated the issue. In effect, the struggle for control of the medical boards, elected *v* appointed, reflected, in microcosm, the larger political scene. To understand the case it is necessary to examine the backgrounds of the protagonists, the Montreal Medical Board of Examiners and the McGill Medical Faculty.[5]

The Montreal Medical Board was one of two licensing bodies in Lower Canada. Elected under the Medical Act of 1831,[6] it had replaced a previous board appointed by the governor. An appointed board, of varying composition, had been in existence since 1788, when an act of the British Parliament,[7] designed primarily to prevent unlicensed persons from practising medicine in the Province of Quebec, had empowered the governor, Lord Dorchester, to appoint a number of medical men to examine prospective practitioners of medicine.

Accordingly, district medical boards were formed in Quebec and Montreal, members being selected by the governor from among the medical men of each district. Every person wishing to practise medicine in the province was required by law to appear before one of these boards. If satisfied with the "character, fitness and capacity" of the candidate, the members issued him a certificate which, along with payment of a fee and the governor's approval, entitled the holder to a licence to practise. Candidates with degrees in medicine, which at the time could not be obtained in British North America, were usually granted the certificate of the board without further examination. Those whose credentials did not satisfy the board, or those who had received their medical education by apprenticeship, were required to submit to the board's examination. Only those who received the certificate of the board could be licensed to practise. Not all members of the medical profession were satisfied with this arrangement. Some resented the appointment of the boards by the governor rather than by the practitioners; others complained that the majority of those appointed were British.[8]

By 1822 the active members of the Montreal Board of Examiners had dwindled to three. One of these was Dr. William Robertson, a founder of the Montreal General Hospital. The other two were Dr. Daniel Arnoldi and Dr. Henry Loedel, who had served on the board for more than ten and thirty years respectively.

Dr. Robertson was also one of the medical officers seeking to establish a medical school in conjunction with the hospital. As a part of this plan he suggested the reconstitution of the Montreal Board of Examiners to include the other medical officers of the hospital. The governor, Lord Dalhousie, agreed, dismissed the previous board, and created a new one in 1823.[9] This board was to consist in future of "persons holding diplomas or testimonials from Medical Institutions in Great Britain, of those who are at present the Medical Officers of the Montreal General Hospital."[10]

The board was now composed of five men, all medical officers of the Montreal General Hospital and founders of the Montreal Medical Institution, a medical school connected with the same hospital.[11] Robertson and his colleagues, John

Stephenson, Andrew Holmes, William Caldwell, and Henry P. Loedel, Jr., all had received their medical education in Scotland. Four of the five were of British origin and only two were born in Canada. This created an uneasy situation in the profession. But more serious was the fact that those who already conducted the only public medical school in Montreal were now the sole possessors of the power to license practitioners. Adverse criticism appeared in *The Free Press*, regretting the appointment of the medical officers of the Montreal General Hospital

> as the sole examiners of all those who wish to be admitted to practise the medical profession in Canada. This accomplished, no young man, however superior his natural and acquired abilities might be, who had not walked the Montreal General Hospital, and attended the lectures of the learned officers of this enlightened medical school, would pass this Board; in fact, none who had not been reared by these *soi-disant* lecturers would be admitted to the practice of the profession here.[12]

Dissatisfaction with the Medical Act of 1788, which had made all this possible, increased. Unsuccessful attempts to repeal the act had been made in the Legislative Assembly in 1820 and 1822. These were followed by renewed efforts vigorously pressed, Arnoldi and Loedel, Sr., joining the ranks of those petitioning the legislature for repeal of the act. Urged on by representatives of the medical profession in the Legislative Assembly, the government had the act repealed and passed a new one in March 1831.

The new act[13] placed the appointment of the Boards of Examiners in the hands of the physicians themselves. On 11 July 1831 forty-one of the medical practitioners of the District of Montreal met to choose a new board.[14] At this meeting, the members of the board of 1823, Drs. Robertson, Holmes, Stephenson, and Caldwell,[15] were conspicuously absent from those elected and it was this new board which faced William L. Logie, M.D., in 1833 when he requested a licence to practise.

Logie had received his degree that same year from the McGill Medical Faculty, the other protagonist in the conflict. The McGill Medical Faculty was the direct successor to the Montreal Medical Institution, and was composed of precisely those officers of the Montreal General Hospital who had constituted the previous Board of Examiners. They became a faculty when the Montreal Medical Institution, unable to secure degree-granting privileges, negotiated an amalgamation with McGill College, founded (but in name only) by Royal Charter in 1821. By this agreement of 1829, the Montreal Medical Institution became the Medical Faculty of McGill College.[16] Dr. Robertson received the rank of professor, Drs. Holmes, Stephenson, and Caldwell that of lecturer. All four were to receive the rank of professor once the charter of the college had undergone remodelling to allow the medical school to grant degrees.

Negotiations to obtain the necessary alterations in the charter were immediately undertaken, but official approval met with repeated delays. In October 1831 the McGill Medical Faculty, then entering its third session, reiterated its request for authority to confer degrees, and, in a petition to the governor, Lord Aylmer, deplored the fact that a medical degree could not be obtained in Canada. Students seeking a degree were forced to go "...abroad...an expense too great to many, or to the United States, where they are in danger of imbibing principles inimical to our Government and our Institutions."[17] Four students from McGill College, for example, had applied that year for entrance to the University of Vermont at Burlington.[18] Others had gone to Europe where, Dr. Stephenson said, students from McGill College were well received, obtaining a degree "after successful examination... immediately after their arrival and without attending any other classes there."[19]

In reply to the petition, the solicitor general of Lower Canada, C. R. Ogden, requested the submission of the "Statutes, Rules and Ordinances of the Medical Faculty" for royal approval. He later raised one objection to the statutes as outlined. If English were to be the only language of instruction in the science of medicine, wrote Mr. Ogden, French-speaking students would continue to be forced to go abroad to seek a degree. "I incline to think," he concluded, "that this evil would be aggravated if the restriction [of language] were suffered to exist."[20]

Nevertheless, the statutes received royal sanction the following May, professorships were granted to all four members of the Medical Faculty, and McGill College obtained the right to confer degrees in medicine in July 1832.[21]

How the McGill degree would be regarded by the new medical board was not known. The members of the McGill Medical Faculty, no longer medical examiners for the district, were doubtless eager that their graduates be licensed without undergoing further examination. But, aware of the authority of the board as a licensing body, they had concluded their petition of the previous year:

> ...every person wishing to practise the different branches of the Medical Profession in the Province, is bound by Law to appear before the Medical Board of Examiners...before he can obtain a Licence, whether he have a Degree or Diploma, or not and...your memorialists therefore beg leave respectfully to point out that the object [of the petition] does not in any way interfere with the Prerogatives of the Medical Board.[22]

Certain circumstances, however, may have caused the McGill professors to foresee difficulties with the board. Firstly, ambiguity in the wording of the Medical Act, especially in relation to candidates with degrees, was creating problems of administration for the medical boards. Secondly, the new composition of the Montreal board focused attention on divergent political views within the medical profession. These had been apparent at the time of the election of the board in July 1831. *La Minerve* described as "très animée"[23] the meeting where, as we have seen, Drs. Robertson, Holmes, Stephenson, and Caldwell were rejected. Each in turn was proposed and seconded, only to be defeated by a "decided majority."[24]

Prominent among the members of the new medical board were several representatives of the Legislative Assembly, two of whom, Alexandre Demers and Jacques Labrie, had served on the committee to review the Medical Act. Labrie, a distinguished historian and graduate in medicine from the University of Edinburgh, was not to see the results of his efforts as he died before the end of the year. He was succeeded on the board by Dr. J. B. Lebourdais. Other members of the new board included Pierre Beaubien and G. J. Vallée, both graduates of Edinburgh, J. B. Meilleur, author and educationist, F. C. Duvert, R. S. Bourdages, and T. Kimber.

Also elected to the board were three brothers, Drs. Wolfred, Robert, and John Nelson, of whom the first two had been members of the Legislative Assembly from 1827–30. Wolfred Nelson, like William Robertson, had served in the War of 1812, subsequently establishing a medical practice in St. Denis on the Richelieu River. Of Loyalist extraction, he had early associated himself with the reform movement in Lower Canada. Robert Nelson, a prominent surgeon and teacher of surgery in Montreal, was a friend and supporter of Louis-Joseph Papineau, Speaker of the Legislative Assembly and leader of the Reform party. Both brothers were to play leading roles in the political uprisings of 1837 and 1838. The third brother, John, died prematurely in 1833. President of the new board was Daniel Arnoldi, whose service on an earlier board had been terminated by the commission of Lord Dalhousie.

The Montreal *Gazette* deplored the defeat of the board made up of the McGill professors and expressed regret that, in electing the new board, "where professional merit only ought to have been the test and qualification required of candidates for the honourable situation of Examiner, party politics should have been introduced, and the whole proceedings conducted in a manner resembling that of a political association, striving to put their partisans into authority."[25]

The act[26] governing the new board, composed of twelve members, was to remain in force until 1 May 1837, during which time the board was to meet every three months. A new board was to be elected every three years and vacancies in membership were to be filled by ballot. Official recognition of the Montreal board was not obtained for several weeks, and then only after Arnoldi and Robert Nelson made representation to the governor.[27] Almost immediately, problems arose in the administration of the act.

From the outset, certain clauses of the act provided for more than one interpretation, and, in fact, in the two years preceding William Logie's application, interpretation of these portions of the act presented some difficulty. Article V was clear enough, stipulating the need for a "regular and continued apprenticeship of at least five years" with a licensed physician or a recognized medical school. But Article VI exempted from the board's examination all those already licensed as physicians and surgeons, or those holding degrees from a university or college provided that the degree had been obtained from the said university or college "in conformity to the rules thereof, and after five years' study at least, and not otherwise." A matter for interpretation here was whether or not the applicant spent all five years in the same institution. As will be seen, Logie could be faulted on the technicality that the school (the Montreal Medical Institution) became, after his first year, the Medical Faculty of McGill College, and hence a different institution.

A second provision of Article VI required that the diploma or licence conferring the degree be produced and verified "to the satisfaction of the Board." This latter clause gave almost unlimited power for the board to reject a diploma, since it did not say what criteria for this "satisfaction" should be.

An opportunity was given to assess the actions of the Montreal board and its interpretation of the Medical Act at meetings held in 1831 and 1832. At the first meeting of the board in October 1831, James Robertson, son of Dr. William Robertson, was granted a certificate on the simple presentation of his medical degree from Edinburgh. Two other candidates successfully passed the board's examination. Another failed and one was not examined "in consequence of an interruption in his studies."[28] This last candidate, G. M. Abbott, had dropped out for one season, thereby running afoul of the clause which required every candidate to have served a regular and uninterrupted apprenticeship of at least five years. But the board must have exercised a certain flexibility in the administration of the act, because at its next meeting Abbott was examined and admitted.[29] At this same meeting, held in January 1832, the interpretation of the act again caused confusion. Two candidates, Cyrille Coté and Seraphim Viger, in requesting a licence to practise, presented the board with degrees acquired in the United States. They had commenced their studies at McGill College (or its predecessor, the Montreal Medical Institution), but had later registered at the University of Vermont, where they received diplomas after three months of lectures. The board refused to admit them without examination and on this ruling sought the advice of the executive of the government as to the interpretation of Article VI of the Medical Act, concerning candidates holding university degrees. The solicitor general of the province upheld the decision of the board "in refusing certificates to candidates who have not complied with provisions of the Act referred to."[30]

Meanwhile, Coté and Viger, together with another graduate of Vermont, J. B. Allard, took their case to the medical board in Quebec City.[31] M. Coté, *Le Canadien* reported, was the first candidate called. The question was raised as to whether the Quebec board should examine candidates rejected by the Montreal board, but after discussion and in order to avoid any conflict between the two boards, Coté agreed to withdraw his diploma and appear before the board as "un simple élève." Viger likewise agreed to submit to examination. But Allard, appearing before the board in exactly the same situation as the other two candidates—that is, possessing a diploma of the University of Vermont obtained after two courses of medical lectures there—requested licence to practise without examination by the board "according to Article VI of the Medical Act."

The Quebec board, in this case, decided exactly the opposite to the Montreal board in the case of the other two candidates. Allard was admitted without examination, on the presentation of his diploma and on swearing by oath that he had received it after five years' study. The Quebec board interpreted Article VI to mean only that five consecutive years of study were required, whereas the Montreal board held that the five years must be passed in the same school or university from which the diploma was obtained. As has been seen, the decision of the Montreal board was upheld by the solicitor general of the province. But it seems that the executive of the government had forwarded its opinion unsolicited, to the Quebec board. The latter, *Le Canadien* concluded, refused to act according to this opinion, feeling that the board should retain the independent character it had been granted by the passing of the act.[32]

A move towards more uniformity in the operation of the two boards was made in the ensuing months. A general meeting of the medical profession was called by the Quebec board for mid-November,[33] in order to consider proposed changes in the Medical Act. In January 1833 Robert Nelson of the Montreal board sought the cooperation of the Quebec board in laying specific amendments to the act before the Legislature,[34] and in July a joint meeting of the two boards was held to discuss the matter further.[35]

Meanwhile, a candidate who had failed his examination as a physician before the Montreal board in 1832, and who had been recommended for licence as a surgeon only, filed an appeal to the governor. The governor requested the Montreal board to reconsider the case of Joseph Breadon, a retired medical officer in the Royal Navy. When the Montreal board met in January 1834 and upheld its previous decision, the governor referred the case to the Quebec board. In contrast to its earlier decision concerning the students from Vermont, the Quebec board was hesitant as a body to give an opinion which might approve or disapprove of the actions of the Montreal board. The president of the Quebec board, Joseph Painchaud, pointed out that the courts were designed to handle complaints against the board, but that he personally felt that the members of his board would agree with the decision of the Montreal board in the case of Mr. Breadon.[36]

Apart from the conflict over the meaning of the Medical Act as interpreted by the medical boards, one other event of 1832 may be relevant to the ensuing events surrounding Logie's application. It is possible that election riots of that year, in which individual members of the medical profession were involved, may have contributed to antagonistic feelings. As has been noted, a number of medical practitioners were among the leaders of the Reform party in the Legislative Assembly. A vacant seat necessitated a by-election in the West Ward of Montreal in the spring of 1832. The successful candidate was a doctor and journalist, Daniel Tracey, whose imprisonment on a charge of libel earlier in the year had angered members and supporters of the Reform party. Tracey's election by a narrow margin on 21 May was followed by a riot in Place d'Armes in the vicinity of the poll, where troops fired into the crowd, killing three persons. William Robertson of the McGill Medical Faculty, one of two magistrates on duty at the poll, read the Riot Act and was later accused of ordering the troops to fire.[37]

The events of 21 May were heatedly reviewed in the newspapers the following autumn and in the Legislative Assembly, where the official enquiry was debated. Sworn testimony of witnesses included that of Robertson, William Caldwell,

Arnoldi, and Magistrate Benjamin Holmes, brother of Dr. Andrew Holmes. The acquittal of the troops early in 1833 and the failure to punish anyone led to increased resentment and bitterness in the assembly. But Tracey, the central figure, had died of cholera only two months after his eventful election.[38]

Windows of McGill College, located in Place d'Armes, were "shivered to atoms" during the riot when the lecture rooms were given to the troops as "shelter...from the inclement weather." The *Courant*, recalling the event, observed: "We believe that the feelings of some individuals in this city, relative to this medical school, are not to be considered as altogether unconnected with this outrage."[39]

It was in the midst of this dispute in July 1832 that McGill College received degree-granting privileges, and May of the following year when Logie received his degree. The public ceremony, at which he was the only candidate, attracted considerable attention in the *Gazette* and the *Courant*, whereas *La Minerve* stated simply that McGill College had conferred its first degree.[40]

Logie's application for licence to practise was made before the Montreal Medical Board the following July. Eight members of the board[41] were present at the meeting, chaired by Dr. W. Nelson, vice-president, in the absence of Dr. Arnoldi. An official report of the meeting, at which the degree was rejected, appeared in *La Minerve*: "M. Logie présenta un Diplôme de M.D. de l'Université du Collège McGill. Ce Diplôme fut rejeté unaniment, n'étant point conformé à la loi, ni appuyé par des documents à la satisfaction du Bureau. En ayant été informé, on lui offrit d'examiner, ce qu'il refuse."[42] The *Gazette* made this observation: "...of course the University and the Medical Board are now in complete collision. From the present composition of the Board, we are not surprised at their late decision, for the University of McGill College has been regarded with a jaundiced eye for some time past by a political party in the country...merely because it is a University likely to introduce into the country, the rudiments of a British education."[43]

Logie had received his degree under authority of the Charter of McGill, "in conformity with the Statutes, rules and ordinances of the said College." He also had been given two certificates attesting to the successful completion of his studies. One signed by Dr. Stephenson stated that "during five successive years" he had attended the required lectures of the university as well as the medical and surgical practices of the Montreal General Hospital; the second affirmed that during this entire period he had studied under Dr. Robertson "as an indentured apprentice."[44]

There is no indication that these documents were ever produced before the board; on the contrary, evidence would seem to show that Logie sought exemption from the board's examination under Article VI of the Medical Act, on the simple presentation of his diploma. Although Article VI had earlier been a source of disagreement between the Montreal and Quebec boards, by 1833 differences of opinion between these boards had been resolved. In addition, agreement had been reached on a new matter for interpretation, this time concerning the Statutes of McGill College.

At a joint meeting of the medical boards of Quebec and Montreal held early in July, a resolution moved by Dr. Painchaud and seconded by M. Couillard, both of the Quebec board, endorsed the Montreal board's position. By a vote of 15-1 the two boards moved that the diplomas of McGill College not be admitted by the medical boards until the legislature had given its opinion on the rights accorded by the Charter of McGill College.[45]

Just as Article VI had proved to be a source of ambiguity for applicants with degrees, so the Statutes of the McGill Medical Faculty were also found to be unclear as to the years of study necessary to obtain a degree. For instance, Chapter II, Statute 4 stated that students must have attended at least three years of lectures and two years of hospital practice, but those who wished to practise in Lower Canada could not receive their degree until after five years' study "unless they consent to undergo the examination required by the [Medical Act]."

On the other hand, Chapter II, Statute 6 stated that any person who had attended two years of lectures at another recognized medical school could enrol at McGill College, attend one full course of lectures, "thus completing the period of study required by these statutes," and obtain a degree after passing the examination.[46] This clause would suggest that it was possible to obtain the Degree in Medicine and Surgery from McGill College after three years of study. Indeed, the 1832 newspapers had published an official announcement of the proposed conferring of degrees by McGill College to the effect that "the time of study required to obtain a degree is three years."[47]

Logie, meanwhile, decided to contest the decision of the board, paid notice of his intent appearing in newspapers in Montreal, Quebec, and Kingston early in July.[48] Then Logie, "deeming himself aggrieved" by the action of the Montreal Medical Board, filed an affidavit in the Court of King's Bench.[49] The court was presided over by the chief justice of the district, in this case the Honourable James Reid, who, as governor of McGill College, had officiated at the ceremony at which Logie had received his degree.

The affidavit, dated 12 October 1833, stated that Mr. Logie held a diploma from McGill College constituting him Doctor in Medicine and Surgery "fit and qualified to practise medicine and surgery in all its branches."[50] It had been granted to him by the principal and professors of McGill College, a "chartered body corporate," after he had studied the science of medicine during five successive years and had passed a course of study in conformity to the rules of the college. The affidavit further stated that the board, having examined the diploma and administered an oath, "did refuse and doth yet refuse" to grant its certificate. An extract from the minutes of the 1 July meeting of the board was appended. At the same time, Logie's lawyers filed a motion that members of the board appear before the court the following February to show cause why a writ of Mandamus should not be issued to them ordering them to grant their certificate. Their client, they claimed, had verified his diploma before the board and had "proved that he was a fit and proper person to obtain a licence."[51]

The February date was later postponed until 9 April when Dr. Arnoldi laid the reply of the board before the court. His representation consisted of the resolutions of the board passed at a meeting held two days previously, at which the case had been reviewed. First, the board disputed Mr. Logie's right to appeal under Article XII of the Medical Act, denying that he had suffered in any way from anything done "by the authority of the Rules and Regulations of the Board." Second, the board denied the court's ruling that Mr. Logie had proved that he was a "fit and proper person to obtain a licence," quoting the 1 July minutes of the board to this effect. The diploma, declared the board, was a "mere certificate of the Knowledge and Ability of the Candidate ... to practise Physic and Surgery, in the opinion of those who granted the same." Furthermore, it did not indicate the period of study required at McGill College, which by law could not be less than five years. Logie had been asked for other documents which would verify this fact "to the satisfaction of the Board," but had refused to produce the documents requested. When the board offered to adjourn to the following day in order to give him time to produce them, Logie again refused; an examination offered by the board was also refused.

The board's statement then referred to the Charter of McGill College, and concluded that "if the Rules and Regulations of the University stipulate a less time than that statuted in the Law ... the Board feels itself bound to refuse every degree that may emanate from such University inasmuch as the degree is nothing more than a special Certificate and cannot imply under any circumstances a period of Study either longer or shorter than the period stipulated in its Charter."[52] In support of this opinion, the board cited the case of another candidate who had applied for a licence on the same day as Logie. G. W. Campbell, holding a degree from the University of Glasgow obtained after four years of study, had been refused the certificate of the board until he had successfully passed the board's examination.

Logie's lawyers decided to pursue their case on the interpretation of the questionable portion of Article VI. An affidavit was filed by T. W. Jones, M.D., who had been granted the certificate of the Montreal Medical Board in January 1834. He had commenced his medical studies at McGill College, completed them at the University of Edinburgh, but received his certificate on the presentation of his degree, and on making oath that he had studied five years. He had not been required to swear that he had spent the five years at the same university. Mr. Jones also referred to the case of the late James Robertson, M.D. (Edin.), who had received the certificate of the Montreal board in 1831 on the simple presentation of his diploma.[53]

On the basis of these submissions, the court came to a decision. A writ of Mandamus dated 12 May 1834 and witnessed by Chief Justice Reid was issued against the board, ordering it to grant its certificate to Mr. Logie or to "shew cause to the contrary thereof."[54]

The board's reply was filed on 12 June by Dr. Arnoldi. Written in French, precisely stated, seven reasons for refusing the certificate were listed. They were in effect a summary of the reasons presented to the court in April, but the changed, almost inflexible, wording seems to indicate the deadlock which had become apparent.[55] Logie's refusal to comply with the request of the board either to present the necessary documents or to take the examination had left the board with only one alternative—the recognition of Logie's degree under Article VI. This the board was not prepared to do.

Logie's lawyers filed a notice of motion that the return be quashed and a peremptory writ of Mandamus be issued, "the whole with costs." Three reasons were given in support of this action:

1st) Because the said return does not answer the said writ nor deny the facts in the said writ set forth and alledged [*sic*].
2nd) Because the said return is argumentative and contains conclusions of law or legal deductions.
3rd) Because the said return is wholly insufficient.[56]

At the hearing scheduled for 7 October, the Court of King's Bench ruled that "a peremptory mandamus be issued... commanding [the board] to grant the certificate."[57]

For the board, the case of "The Crown *v* Logie" was a matter of "degrees *v* licences," a test of the authority of the Medical Board of Examiners as a licensing body constituted by the Medical Act of 1831. For McGill College, the status of its degree was at stake, the outcome of the case a matter of interest to the faculty of the college and to all of its prospective students who might be planning to practise medicine in Lower Canada.

The full text of the judgment, published in the *Gazette* in November, began with the assertion that McGill College was recognized by the same statute under which the Board of Examiners was constituted, and that the existence of the university and the right to confer degrees were not in any manner denied or contested.

The study of medicine during five successive years was considered by the court to be the indispensable factor in the obtaining of a licence. Under Article IV, each candidate was required to swear to this fact under oath. Article VI, it was decided by the court, extended the right of exemption from examination by the board to all who had obtained a degree or diploma from a university "...in conformity to the rules thereof, and after five years study of the science of medicine, whether wholly or in part performed in such University.... Had the legislature otherwise intended, that intention would have been clearly and absolutely expressed, for there is no economy or sparing of words in statutes...."[58] The second provision of Article VI, that the diploma must be produced and verified "to the satisfaction" of the board, was not mentioned.

The court dismissed the other reasons put forward by the board as "argumentative" and "insufficient." The fact that Logie's diploma did not state that he had studied medicine during five successive years was considered by the court to be non-essential, as Article IV already required every candidate to make this declaration under oath. Logie's degree, the judgment concluded, should have been considered by the board as "sufficient and complete."

Although three more students of McGill College had received degrees in medicine in May 1834, the possibility that McGill's degree would be recognized by the Montreal Medical Board again became problematical, as relationships within the profession deteriorated.

The legal proceedings against the Montreal Medical Board coincided with a period of increased political tension in Lower Canada and increased political involvement by individual members of the medical profession. Robert Nelson, for instance, a member of the Legislative Assembly from 1827–30, was elected to Montreal's first City Council which replaced rule by magistrates in June 1833.[59] Among those removed from office was William Robertson. In October 1834 Nelson was chosen with Louis-Joseph Papineau to represent the West Ward of Montreal in the coming elections to the assembly and in November both candidates were elected.[60] This was the same district in which the riots surrounding Tracey's election two years previously had taken place, with the result that the 1834 elections revived all the animosities of the earlier event in which Robertson had played a prominent part. Again, following the election, a heated dispute in the newspapers between Robertson and Papineau almost resulted in a duel.[61]

The election of a new medical board in the summer of 1834 was the occasion of open disagreement between Robertson and Nelson and among other members of the profession. Under the provision of the Medical Act of 1831, seventy-one practitioners of the District of Montreal met on 7 July to elect a new board. The meeting, presided over by Arnoldi, was described by the *Gazette* as "far from orderly and peaceable."[62] Differences of opinion resulted in the withdrawal of a "minority" of the members, led by Robertson and Stephenson, and the election of the new board by the remaining "majority" with little opposition. As in 1831, no member of the McGill faculty was elected to the board.

Argument arose first over the proposition of Stephenson that a second secretary should be appointed and again when the question was raised concerning the right to vote for non-practising physicians. In the ensuing confusion, Robert Nelson rose and "le plus grand silence règne dans la salle."[63] He said it was an insult to the profession to ask if a physician had a practice, and urged the meeting to proceed with the business at hand. Wolfred Nelson then nominated Arnoldi, Sr., as president. Robertson opposed the motion and once again confusion reigned. Calls for the vote were made in great disorder.

A major split occurred over the method of voting. Robert Nelson requested division as followed in the Legislative Assembly where those for the motion stand to the right, those against to the left. Robertson opposed, he and Stephenson requesting that each member present a list of twelve names, voting to be "à vive voix." In the argument that ensued, Arnoldi called for the vote by division and the motion was passed 46 to 25. "Messrs. Stephenson, Robertson, McCulloch et autres sortent de la salle, en déclarant qu'ils n'ont point voté, considérant les votes comme illégaux." The remaining members of the board were nominated and voted for in the same way, but before the voting was completed, Stephenson returned to the hall to register a written protest with Arnoldi. This, too, was ignored: "Ce papier, supposé être une espèce de Protèt, fut mis de côté sans être ouvert, par le Président et par l'assemblée, qui la regardèrent comme irregulier, et comme devant point arrêter les procédés."[64]

Although the decision of the court in the case of "The Crown *v* Logie" was made known in October 1834, the board was not expected to meet again until the following January. Recognition of McGill's medical degree, in compliance with the order of the court, was to meet outright resistance by the medical board, as Dr. Robert Nelson, its newly elected president, and the board appeared to ignore the decree.

On 6 January 1835, the following item appeared in the *Gazette*:

> The Medical Board of this District ought by Law to have met yesterday, but we are somewhat surprised in learning that the medical sages who comprise it, and who have never omitted meeting on any previous occasion, were generally absent, only one of the Board having appeared. The cause of this extraordinary circumstance is said to be their unwillingness to obey the recent judgement of the Court of King's Bench, ordering the Board, by a peremptory mandamus, to grant a licence to Dr. William L. Logie, a graduate of McGill College. We do not know what course will be pursued in this strange position of affairs, but should imagine that these sons of Escalapius [*sic*] have rendered themselves liable to be proceeded against for a contempt of court.[65]

In April, at which time the next meeting of the board should have occurred, *La Minerve* reported: "Le Bureau de Médecine qui devait s'assembler aujourd'hui s'ajourna au 4 mai, faute de quorum, plusieurs des membres qui avaient le fleuve à traverser, pour se rendre en cette ville, n'ayant pu le faire, vû le mauvais état des glaces."[66]

The *Gazette* did not refer to the problems of transportation involved in the postponement of the April meeting, but pointed out that some candidates for licences in the Montreal district were "under the necessity of going to Quebec to be examined in consequence of the late extraordinary conduct of the Montreal Board."[67]

The board, however, could not avoid the issue indefinitely. On 4 and 5 May 1835 two meetings of the Montreal Medical Board took place, attended by nine of its twelve members, and presided over by Wolfred Nelson. Both the president, Robert Nelson, and the vice-president, R.J. Kimber, were absent. Robert Nelson, who had left Canada in December on political business,[68] was absent in Great Britain as the board acquiesced to the order of the court. The *Gazette* reported:

> The Montreal Medical Board, which omitted to hold its last quarterly meeting, assembled on Monday last.... An examination of candidates for licences was held [and five admitted].... The Board then adjourned to the next day, 5th May, when...Messrs. Patrick McNaughton and John McMillan, with diplomas, were each admitted to practise medicine, the last having submitted to an examination.
>
> Dr. McNaughton, who was admitted on the simple presentation of his diploma, was a graduate [of 1834] of McGill College, and thus it will be seen that the Medical Board have [*sic*] conformed to the judgement of the Court of King's Bench in the case of Dr. Logie.[69]

La Minerve carried a short account of the meeting without mention of the legal suit.[70]

Meanwhile, the political situation in Lower Canada was becoming explosive; both McGill College and the Montreal Medical Board were affected by the resultant turmoil. McGill College, which conferred three degrees in 1835 and four in 1836, was forced by political clashes of that year to close for several sessions.

The Montreal Medical Board of 1834 ceased to exist when the Medical Act expired in May 1837. Furthermore, the outbreak of armed rebellion in November of that year precluded any possibility of the act continuing. The Medical Act of 1788 was revived, with the result that when McGill College reopened in 1839, William Robertson was once again president of the Montreal Medical Board.[71] He remained in this position, and as senior member of the McGill Medical Faculty, until his death in 1844. Similarly, Stephenson and Holmes were also appointed to the 1839 board. Of the 1834 Board of Examiners, however, only two members were included in the new board, Daniel Arnoldi[72] and O. T. Bruneau. The Nelson brothers, directly involved in the events of 1837–38, were exiled from Canada, Robert spending the rest of his life in the United States, Wolfred returning to Montreal when political amnesty was declared.[73]

Although the dispute over Canada's first medical degree was settled, it is perhaps ironic that the man who precipitated the controversy never claimed his licence to practise in Lower Canada. Buried in the text of the judgment of the Court of King's Bench was the seventh reason given by the board for its refusal to grant him its certificate. The court referred to "an immaterial fact, the absence of Mr. Logie from this Province since the issuing of the mandamus."[74] William Logie, for reasons unknown, had left Lower Canada before the end of 1833. He applied for and received a licence to practise medicine in New Orleans, Louisiana, in January 1834, and spent his entire professional career in the United States. He died in 1879, and is buried in Geneva, New York.[75]

Since the first publication of this article in 1974, the following sources relevant to the dispute over medical licensing in Lower Canada have been found: J.-Edmond Roy, *Histoire du notariat au Canada* (Lévis, 1900), pp. 498–516; Ignotus [Thomas Chapais], "La profession médicale au Canada," *Bulletin des recherches historiques* 12 (1906): 143–50. As well, a transcript of the documents "Ex parte William Logie," no. 1880, was located in the *Journal of the Legislative Assembly of the Province of Canada*, vol. 3, 24 November 1843, pp. 54–63.

Notes

The preliminary research was aided by a grant from the Humanities and Social Sciences Division of the Canada Council to support studies of the history of the Faculty of Medicine of McGill University. The author acknowledges with gratitude the advice and encouragement of Dr. E. H. Bensley and Dr. Donald G. Bates, Professor of History of Medicine, McGill University.

1. H. E. MacDermot, *One Hundred Years of Medicine in Canada* (Toronto, 1967). For the career of Canada's first medical graduate, which was previously unknown, see B. R. Tunis and E. H. Bensley, "William Leslie Logie: McGill University's First Graduate and Canada's First Medical Graduate," *Canadian Medical Association Journal* 105 (December 1971): 1259-63.

2. Sir George Clark, *A History of the Royal College of Physicians of London* (Oxford, 1964-66)

3. Francis R. Packard, *Guy Patin and the Medical Profession in Paris in the XVIIth Century* (New York, 1925).

4. For the political background of this period the author has drawn on Helen Taft Manning, *The Revolt of French Canada 1800-1835: A Chapter in the History of the British Commonwealth* (Toronto, 1962).

5. Standard references on the history of McGill University and medical history in Canada do not deal with this dispute. Cyrus Macmillan, *McGill and Its Story, 1821-1921* (Toronto, 1921), p. 94 refers to a legal dispute between the university and "rival authorities" but does not elaborate; Maude E. Abbott, *History of Medicine in the Province of Quebec* (Toronto, 1931) describes in detail the origin of the McGill Medical Faculty, but does not mention the dispute or the medical boards of 1831; Sylvio Leblond, "La Médecine dans la Province de Québec avant 1847," *Les Cahiers des Dix* 35 (1970): 79-85, discusses the problems of the medical boards of 1831, but not the legal case which ensued.

6. 1 William IV, c. 27, "An act to repeal a certain Act or Ordinance therein mentioned, and to provide effectual Regulations concerning the Practice of Physic, Surgery and Midwifery."

7. 28 Geo. III, c. 8, "An Act or Ordinance to prevent persons practising Physic and Surgery within the Province of Quebec, or Midwifery in the Towns of Quebec and Montreal without licence."

8. Charles-Marie Boissonnault, *Histoire de la faculté de médecine de Laval* (Québec, 1953), pp. 62-67.

9. Minute Book of the Montreal Medical Institution, McGill University Archives, Montreal.

10. A. W. Cochran to Dr. Arnoldi, 11 February 1823, Public Archives of Canada (hereafter PAC), Civil Secretary's Letter Book, RG 7, G 15C, vol. 31, 267.

11. H. E. MacDermot, *A History of the Montreal General Hospital* (Montreal, 1950); Abbott, *History of Medicine*, pp. 56–60.

12. *The Free Press*, 27 March 1823.

13. 1 William IV, c. 27.

14. Election of Members of the Medical Board, 11 July 1831, PAC, Civil and Provincial Secretaries' Office, RG 4, B 28, vol. 53.

15. The fifth member, Henry Loedel, Jr., had died of typhus in 1825.

16. Abbott, *History of Medicine*, p. 60; E. H. Bensley, "The Beginning of Teaching at McGill University," *McGill Journal of Education* 6 (1971): 23–24.

17. Memorial of the Medical Faculty of McGill College to Lord Aylmer, 29 October 1831, PAC, Secretary of State Papers, RG 4, A 1, vol. S-270, 135.

18. Lester J. Wallman, "Benjamin Lincoln, M.D., Vermont Medical Educator," *Vermont History* 29 (1961): 196–209. The four students, Cyrille Coté, J. B. Allard, Sylvestre Cartier, and Seraphim Viger, are named in a letter to E. H. Bensley, McGill University, from Lester J. Wallman, 30 October 1963.

19. J. Stephenson to Col. Craig, civil secretary, 2 November 1831, PAC, Secretary of State Papers, RG 4, A 1, vol. S-271, 12.

20. C. R. Ogden to Lord Aylmer, 11 November 1831, PAC, Civil and Provincial Secretaries' Offices, "S" series, RG 4, A 1, vol. 271, 64.

21. L'Université Laval, founded in 1852, was the first French-language institution in Canada to confer degrees in medicine. L'Ecole de Médecine et Chirurgie, founded in Montreal in 1843, spent many years in search of degree-granting privileges. It affiliated for this purpose, in turn, with McGill College, Victoria University (Cobourg), and l'Université Laval (Montréal), which became l'Université de Montréal in 1919.

22. Memorial of the Medical Faculty of McGill College to Lord Aylmer, 29 October 1831, PAC.

23. *La Minerve*, 4 juillet 1831.

24. Election of members of the medical board, 11 July 1831, PAC.

25. Montreal *Gazette*, 12 July 1831.

26. William IV, c. 27.

27. Sylvio Leblond, "La Médecine dans la Province de Québec avant 1847," pp. 80-81.
28. Montreal *Gazette*, 8 October 1831.
29. *La Minerve*, 6 janvier 1832.
30. Col. Craig, civil secretary, to Dr. Lebourdais, 21 January 1832, *Rex* vs *Logie*, Archives de la Cour Supérieure de Montréal (hereafter ACSM), Court of King's Bench, no. 1880, 1834.
31. Like the Montreal board, the Quebec Medical Board had been elected in July 1831. Its members are listed in John J. Heagerty, *Four Centuries of Medical History in Canada* (Toronto, 1928) 1:324; see also, Leblond, "La Médecine dans la Province de Québec," p. 80.
32. *Le Canadien*, 4 avril 1832. Whether these candidates had indeed studied five years is questioned by Leblond, "La Médecine dans la Province de Québec," pp. 81-84.
33. *Le Canadien*, 19 octobre 1832.
34. Leblond, "Le Médecine dans la Province de Québec," p. 84.
35. *Le Canadien*, 12 juillet 1833.
36. Case of Joseph Breadon, Soliciting a Licence to practise Physic in Canada, PAC, Civil and Provincial Secretaries' Offices, RG 4, B 28, vol. 53.
37. Manning, *The Revolt of French Canada*, pp. 149-50.
38. Emmet Mullally, *Dr. Daniel Tracey, A Pioneer Worker for Responsible Government in Canada* (Montreal, 1935).
39. *Canadian Courant and Montreal Advertiser*, 10 October 1832.
40. *La Minerve*, 27 mai 1833; Montreal *Gazette*, 25 May 1833; *Canadian Courant*, 25 May 1833.
41. These were R. Nelson, T. Kimber, G.J. Vallée, J.B. Lebourdais, O.T. Bruneau, L.M.R. Barbier, T. Bouthillier, and A.W. Robinson. The latter four members had replaced A. Demers, R.S. Bourdages, and J. Nelson, deceased, and F.C. Duvert, resigned.
42. *La Minerve*, 4 juillet 1833. This was an almost verbatim extract from the minutes of the board.
43. Montreal *Gazette*, 4 July 1833.
44. A draft copy of Logie's degree, dated 24 May 1833, and the two certificates are preserved in the Osler Library, McGill University.
45. *Le Canadien*, 12 juillet 1833.
46. Statutes of the Medical Faculty, 1832, McGill University Archives.
47. *Canadian Courant*, 5 September 1832.
48. *The Vindicator and Canadian Advertiser*, 5 July 1833.

49. Article XII, 1 William IV, c. 27, stated: "...that any person who shall deem himself aggrieved by anything done under the authority of the said rules and regulations shall have the right of appealing therefrom to the Court of King's Bench for the District."

50. Affidavit of said W. L. Logie, fyled 12 October 1833, *Rex* vs *Logie*, ACSM. The extract from the board minutes had been reproduced in *La Minerve*, 4 juillet 1833. As far as can be ascertained, the Minute Book of the Montreal Medical Board of Examiners for 1831–39 is no longer in existence.

51. Ex parte W. L. Logie, motion fyled 12 October 1833, *Rex* vs *Logie*, ACSM.

52. Ex parte W. L. Logie, fyled 9 April 1834, *Rex* vs *Logie*, ACSM.

53. Affidavit of Thomas W. Jones, fyled 11 April 1834, ibid.

54. Writ of Mandamus issued 12 May 1834, ibid.

55. Reply of Board fyled by Dr. Arnoldi, 12 June 1834, ibid. The board had just hired Messrs. Cherrier and Laberge, advocates, as Counsel for Defence. An earlier request made by Dr. Arnoldi for legal assistance from the crown had been refused. The case of Mr. Logie was prosecuted by Messrs. Buchanan and Andrews.

56. Notice of Motion, fyled 17 June 1834, ibid.

57. Unlabelled slip of paper dated 12 October 1834, ibid.

58. Montreal *Gazette*, 15 November 1834.

59. Léon Trépanier, "Le Premier Gouvernement de Concordia," *Les Cahiers des Dix* 28 (1963): 214.

60. *La Minerve*, 17 novembre 1834.

61. The exchange of words which precipitated the quarrel appeared in *La Minerve* and the *Montreal Herald* in December 1834. See Aegidius Fauteux, *Le Duel au Canada* (Montréal, 1934).

62. Montreal *Gazette*, 8 July 1834.

63. *La Minerve*, 10 juillet 1834.

64. Ibid.

65. Montreal *Gazette*, 6 January 1835.

66. *La Minerve*, 6 avril 1835.

67. Montreal *Gazette*, 11 April 1835.

68. *La Minerve*, 1 juin 1835; Trépanier, "Le Premier Gouvernement de Concordia."

69. Montreal *Gazette*, 12 May 1835.

70. *La Minerve*, 7 mai 1835.

71. J. Nelson, *The Quebec Almanack and British American Royal Kalendar* (Quebec, 1840); Leblond, "La Médecine dans la Province de Québec," p. 88.

72. Daniel Arnoldi became the first president of the College of Physicians and Surgeons of Lower Canada, formed in 1847.

73. J. Lacoursière, ed., *Les Troubles de 1837-1838* (Montréal, 1959). Wolfred Nelson was re-elected president of the Montreal Medical Board in 1846 and played a leading role in the incorporation of the medical profession in Lower Canada. He and Dr. Arnoldi received honorary degrees from McGill College in 1848.

74. Montreal *Gazette*, 15 November 1834.

75. B. R. Tunis and E. H. Bensley, "William Leslie Logie: McGill University's First Graduate and Canada's First Medical Graduate."

The Medical Profession in the North-West Territories

HILDA NEATBY

In recent years the romantic aspects of the medical profession have been so thoroughly exploited by journalists, novelists, and Hollywood, that the mere historian can hardly fail to be dull. In order to be really dull, this article will ignore the thrilling and curious aspects of the doctor's life in territorial days, and devote itself to a theme which, with no appeal for Hollywood, has yet profound and permanent significance for one who too often is reduced to a merely symbolic role in medical drama, the patient. The development of public organization and control of the medical profession in the Territories is an interesting local phase of an old and widespread practice in the western world. Formerly guilds and similar organizations exercised rather rigid controls over all trades and callings. After a brief trial of the *laisser faire* method, public control was resumed, this time by national governments, which today are expected to protect the anxious customer to the last thread. In the learned professions, where the scientist

Reprinted by permission from *Saskatchewan History* 2, no. 2 (1949): 1-15.

is also an artist, and therefore prone to excessive individualism, public control can be most usefully exercised through the members themselves. The early relations between government and the doctors in the Territories, the increasing need for some organization and control of the profession, and the resulting organization and activities of the College of Physicians and Surgeons of the North-West Territories, may be without romantic glamour, but are certainly not without interest, human and professional.

Early doctors came out to the Territories in various capacities, and followed a wide variety of callings. The earliest came as medical officers of the North-West Mounted Police. Dr. A. L. Jukes, who arrived in 1880, was the son of an East India Company surgeon and became a prominent early citizen of Regina. He was one of a group of hard-working men who not only did much for the health and comfort of the police, but apparently attended the general public, Indians and whites alike, when necessary.[1] Other doctors came with the Canadian Pacific or other railway construction gangs,[2] or as farmers or ranchers.[3] Dr. A. E. Porter, the first registered physician in the Territories apart from police doctors, went to Prince Albert as a private practitioner in response to the persuasions of Charles Mair, and the offer of a $2,000 bonus—which remained an offer only.[4] There were, however, various official appointments to supplement meagre professional earnings, such as hospital and jail appointments and appointments to Indian Reserves.[5]

Whatever might have brought them in the first place, early doctors, like other pioneers, learned to turn their hands to anything. Dr. J. D. Lafferty, later registrar of the College of Physicians and Surgeons, started a chain of private banks which appear to have suffered the usual fate of private banks in frontier districts. Dr. Jukes was the first registrar of land titles in Regina and had some share in securing appropriation legislation on the subject.[6] Dr. R. G. Brett was second lieutenant governor of Alberta, and the municipal and political activities of doctors in territorial days are well known. An exciting incident was the special enlistment of local doctors in the rebellion of 1885.[7]

A public activity more strictly professional in its nature was service as coroner. It is worth while to give a little space to the problems of the pioneer doctor as coroner, for there is probably no better illustration of the empiric method necessarily employed in setting up a rather advanced system of administration in an extremely primitive community. The problem was complicated by those early conflicts of jurisdiction which foreshadowed the later highly capitalized problem of dominion-provincial relations.

At first there was some hesitation about the policy to be pursued in the appointment of coroners. It was, of course, necessary to appoint many coroners who were not medical men, but was it desirable that the coroner should be a doctor? In August 1886 the lieutenant governor informed a would-be coroner (a superintendent of the Mounted Police at Lethbridge) that coroners' appointments were to be confined in future to members of the medical profession; but in January 1888 Dr. C. E. Carthew of Qu'Appelle Station was informed that "you are in error in supposing that Doctors are considered specially qualified for the appointment of Coroners as it is rather the other way."[8] Dewdney's later opinion is echoed in a letter of the attorney-general of Saskatchewan as late as 1920, in which it is pointed out that the appointment of a doctor as coroner might, in districts where medical men were scarce, prevent the admission of medical evidence at the trial, since the coroner, as judge, could not offer evidence.[9]

A coroner once anticipated the lieutenant governor by appointing himself. In July of 1883 return of an inquest was sent in by Dr. Henry Dodd of Broadview. Forget, clerk of the Council, replied that his zeal and efficiency were appreciated, but that coroners could not be self-appointed. Dodd answered with an apology and, implying that thanks to his experience as police surgeon at Newcastle-on-Tyne he would make a very good coroner, suggested that the lieutenant governor regularize his position in the obvious way. This was eventually done.[10] Coroners' fees ran to about $10 a case; the post mortem fee was also $10,[11] but the coroner presumably could not perform the post mortem. However, even a small sum in cash was probably very welcome.

A curious incident arising from inexperienced coroners and a divided jurisdiction occurred at Edmonton in 1899. A young man who died of strychnine poisoning stated before his death that he and his fiancée had arranged a double suicide. The coroner for some reason decided that an inquest was unnecessary. Later it appeared that there were strong grounds for suspecting that the young man had murdered his fiancée before committing suicide. The matter was the more serious as the girl, who was a Roman Catholic, had been buried in unconsecrated ground. The coroner, a doctor, wired the minister of justice for instructions and was told that he was under territorial jurisdiction; he then wired Haultain, and was told that inquests were a purely federal matter. The sequel was a very brisk exchange of letters between Haultain and the minister of justice, Haultain insisting that inquests were a criminal matter and therefore under the Dominion, his opponent arguing that as it was the Territorial government which "hired and fired" them, that government should issue instructions. The records suggest that Haultain won the debate, a fact which probably did nothing to increase his popularity at Ottawa.[12]

During the 1880s and 1890s doctors were coming in in slowly increasing numbers and were playing an important role professionally and in various aspects of community life. The very reputation that they built up emphasized, to the public and to the members of the profession, the necessity of some sort of public control, and particularly of a public registration to maintain adequate professional standards. The legislature attempted to meet this need by legislation in 1885.[13] Thereafter the right to practise for money was confined to four classes of people: (1) those at that time residing in the Territories and possessing a medical degree from any university or other duly authorized body in His Majesty's Dominions; (2) those British subjects at that time residing in the Territories who had been in actual practice for one year and who possessed a medical degree in the United States, granted according to law, and representing at least two years' institutional study; (3) those at that time residing in the Territories who had practised there for at least a year and who within a year should pass an examination before two medical practitioners on scientific and medical subjects as laid down in the ordinance; (4) future residents of the Territories, possessing a British medical degree as in (1). Registration was made compulsory for all practitioners. The first two classes (those duly qualified and in actual practice) could register by presenting evidence of the required qualifications and paying a fee of $5.00; those in the third class (in actual practice, but required to take an examination) were to pay a fee of $25; the others (those who might in future reside and practise) must pay a fee of $50. For illegal practice fines up to $100 might be imposed.

The ordinance required registration by 1 March 1886, but it would seem that this was a pious hope, rather than rigid requirement. By 1 March two doctors only had registered[14] and those who had refrained seem to have experienced no ill effects. However, applications for registration did come trickling in, accompanied by the $5.00 fee, and the necessary diplomas from various universities, including a number from the University of Toronto. By the end of 1886 twenty-two had registered, but these certainly did not include all qualified practitioners in the Territories. Applications for registration with the $5.00 fee—indicating practice in the Territories in 1885—continued to come in until the end of 1888, although there is evidence that at least some of those who registered as late as 1888 were required to produce special evidence of the duration of their residence and practice in order to avoid the $50 fee exacted from newcomers.[15] One doctor, who had urged that the ordinance be strict and definite, registered as late as 7 December 1888, and then sent an instalment of $2.00 on his $5.00 fee—indicating, perhaps, that he was more to be pitied than blamed.[16]

Although properly qualified doctors might procrastinate over the duty of registration, many of them probably supported the principle, not only in the public interest, but as a necessary protection for their financial interests and professional pride. Legislation should "exact proper medical education and such other qualifications as will ensure properly qualified medical men in meeting their expenses on an equal footing," wrote Dr. J. D. Lafferty to the lieutenant governor. He stated that many now practising were "utterly unfitted" for such an office; he cited an example in Calgary, a former veterinary surgeon of the North-West Mounted Police, adding firmly, "I should not like to be placed on the same footing with such persons."[17] At least where professional interests were at stake, doctors reported unlicensed practitioners. A rather prominent Edmonton doctor wrote the lieutenant governor in April 1886, inquiring whether a certain man was registered: "He is at present attending the police, and has, as far as I know, no qualifications at all, but is a pet of the Supt here."[18] The offending practitioner later passed an examination and was duly registered.[19]

On the other hand, there was some objection from the public at any restrictions which might deprive an area so poorly provided with doctors of any medical knowledge that might be available. The *Edmonton Bulletin* complained:

> The Medical Ordinance, as it now stands, is a one-sided affair, having no regard whatever for the peculiar circumstances of this North-West country. As in the case of the legal Ordinance, no one would object to a duly qualified physician being allowed a large percentage of advantage over a quack; much greater even than should be allowed the lawyer over the pettifogger, for in his case life itself, not merely money, is at stake. But that in a country such as this, where for instance, the three

hundred miles between Edmonton and Battleford, and for two hundred miles between Edmonton and Calgary [*sic*] there is no qualified physician, nor is there likely to be for years, it should be made a punishable offence for a person to receive pay for doing some necessary act of medicine or surgery, it is an outrage.[20]

This view receives some support from a letter to the lieutenant governor from one who was presumably a doctor living in Russell, Manitoba. As there was no doctor in the Territories nearer than Moosomin he was often called by those near the border, but had to work "in an illegal manner" for want of a licence to practise. He would, he said, have been able "to stamp out at once a fatal epidemic of measles" had he been armed with "magisterial or medical powers."[21] While the reader of the letter must remain more or less unconvinced, it must sometimes have been difficult to decide how far the public interest required a really strict application of the law.

The acceptance, with barely a rebuke, of very late registrations,[22] indicates that Lieutenant Governor Dewdney did not make a practice of seeking out offenders, but when a doubtful case came before him, he applied the law rather rigidly. In June 1886 he appointed Dr. Augustus Jukes and Dr. Henry Dodd examiners under the ordinance.[23] All those who wished to practise and who could not produce adequate diplomas were required to take an examination. This requirement was somewhat resented by two members of the medical service of the Mounted Police. These men, coming with partial medical training, had been for years employed as hospital staff sergeants. Sergeant John C. Holme of Maple Creek represented that he had practised medicine for seven years among police, Indians, and half-breeds, often with little or no professional supervision, and that his experience, his service, and the recognition of qualified medical men justified his registration. Although he was strongly supported by Dr. Jukes, the lieutenant governor insisted on an examination.[24] He was equally firm in the much more trying case of Sergeant A. B. MacKay who, having taken an "examination" before two Mounted Police doctors in Battleford, bombarded the lieutenant governor with requests for registration for fifteen months. Although he enlisted the supposedly powerful support of Lord Boyle of Macleod, he failed to move Dewdney.[25] Eventually he set up a drug store (there being no law about druggists at the time) and there, it was generally supposed, he not only filled prescriptions, but wrote them.

It may have been that Dewdney, weary of presiding over the medical profession, suggested to his successor that doctors could best be controlled by other doctors. At any rate, in 1888, the year of his retirement and of the inauguration of the fully elected Legislative Assembly, an ordinance[26] was passed creating the College of Physicians and Surgeons of the North-West Territories as a corporate body, to be composed of those already registered under the ordinance of 1885, and, of course, of future registrants under the new ordinance. The college was to be governed by a council of five, elected by all registered practitioners, to hold office for two years.[27] The council was to elect its own officers, such as president, vice-president, and registrar, the last-named being responsible for all elections after the first. A register was to be kept open to the public and published from time to time.[28] All those then registered in the Lieutenant Governor's Office were entitled to free registration; others were to pay a fee of $20.[29] The council was to register any member of any incorporated College of Physicians and Surgeons or of any similarly organized body in the Dominion of Canada; or anyone with such qualifications as would entitle him to be registered by such a body.[30] Those presenting a diploma representing a four-year course in medicine were also to be registered after an examination "if deemed necessary."[31] Unregistered practitioners could be fined from $25 to $100 on a suit before a justice of the peace instituted by any private person. All those registered must pay the fee of the college—not less than $1.00 or more than $2.00 a year—which was recoverable in court.

To the newly organized College of Physicians and Surgeons this ordinance entrusted the important task of promoting the interests of the profession and protecting those of the public. It was not an easy one. Excessively high professional standards and too rigid an application of the law against unlicensed practitioners would be injurious to the public, besides defeating their own end. It is significant that the ordinance actually gave the college power to stay private proceedings against unregistered practitioners. Evidently, in some places, their services were considered indispensable, and it was felt possible to entrust the newly created professional body with powers unfit to be exercised by the lieutenant governor. On the other hand, too lax an administration of the law in response to the needs of the moment would tend to discourage well-qualified men from settling in the Territories. In the exercise of this important trust the council of the college needed the interest and support of all its members. Unfortunately, this was not forthcoming. No doubt most doctors were too busy struggling to establish themselves in new communities to have much time or energy for wider professional obligations; and it is pretty certain that even the $2.00 fee was not unimportant to many of them. As late as 1898 the registrar reported that, out of eighty-nine men in active practice, only fourteen had voted in the recent elections and only nineteen were qualified to vote, the rest being more or less deeply in arrears for their fees.[32]

It was fortunate, under such conditions, that there were a few competent men who promoted the interests of the profession with energy, and with at least a very fair comprehension of the interests of the public as a whole.[33] The first elections to the council, held, after some unexplained delay, in February 1890, returned Dr. O. C. Edwards, Qu'Appelle Station; Dr. J. D. Lafferty, Calgary; Dr. R. B. Cotton, Regina; Dr. R. G. Brett, Banff; and Dr. H. C. Wilson, Edmonton.[34] Of these five men, three served on the council continuously for some ten years and two of them for almost the entire territorial period.[35] There was a similar useful continuity in the office of the registrar. The first registrar held office from 1890 to 1893. Although a well-known and popular doctor, and a man undeniably possessed of many admirable traits, it must be admitted that as registrar he was not a success. A fire in his house in 1893[36] destroyed all records except the register, which was most fortunately preserved. It is impossible to help suspecting that the fire may have been at least beneficial in simplifying a hopeless confusion. At any rate the minute book records a long series of attempts to clarify and liquidate various indiscretions, financial and otherwise, efforts still going on in 1904, a year and a half after the death of the unlucky official.[37]

His successor, Dr. Hugh U. Bain of Prince Albert, was a very different type. He held office from October 1893 until his sudden death in 1901. Always neat and precise, his entries in the minute book show an interesting development and improvement of method as the business of the council increased. His annual reports give a very clear impression of events from year to year, and his firm but tactful recommendations suggest that his influence was considerable and useful. The enthusiastic eulogy contained in the letter of condolence to Mrs. Bain was probably completely sincere, although expressed in the rather flowery language characteristic of the age and of Dr. Lafferty.[38]

Dr. J. D. Lafferty succeeded Dr. Bain. He has already been mentioned as a pioneer doctor of many interests. The pages of the minute book seem to reveal, as might be expected from his name, a man much less precise and methodical than Dr. Bain, but full of energy and enthusiasm, affectionate to his colleagues and loyal to his profession. They certainly reveal a decided Irish accent.[39] On Dr. Bain's death, Dr. Lafferty conveyed the various records from Prince Albert to Calgary, where they remained until the creation of the provinces, and then passed into the possession of the College of Physicians and Surgeons of Alberta.

The council thus was able to maintain with fair efficiency a pretty continuous membership and policy through a critical period in the Territories, when new problems were constantly arising and taking on urgency with a very rapidly increasing population. Finances caused some anxiety in the early years, as very little could be achieved on a $2.00 fee that few people paid. This difficulty was removed with the arrival of new doctors in growing numbers, as each one paid a registration fee of $50, and many paid the same amount in examination fees. When the accounts were balanced in 1893 (after the fire), the total cash accounted for was $574 with a balance of $103. Less than six years later, cash accounted for was $3,894.01 with $2,064.37 on hand.[40]

Such prosperity warranted increased expenditure. The allowance for attendance at council meetings was increased from $5.00 to $10 a day with expenses.[41] Council meetings were held every year (except in 1896) and often twice a year, generally at Banff, Calgary, or Regina. The registrar's salary went up from $50 a year in 1895 to $100 in 1899; the next year it was raised to $300, in 1904 to $500, and in 1905 to $700 a year.[42] These last rather rapid increases may have been due to the persuasive tongue of Dr. Lafferty, whose duties were increasing. Certainly, it was Dr. Lafferty who induced the council to add to the office furniture of a safe (secured by Dr. Bain), a typewriter and an office desk. As he attained proficiency on the typewriter, Dr. Lafferty assured the council, they would all wish the purchase had been made long ago, suggesting that the expenditure of $125 had not been authorized without some effort on his part.[43]

The increased expenditure was justified not only by the rapidly increasing number of registered practitioners (957 in 1906), but by a corresponding increase and variety of responsibilities. The College of Physicians and Surgeons added to its original duties of registration and examination many other interesting activities which deserve some consideration.

The conditions under which the council was authorized and required by law to register medical men have already been explained. It was suggested that members of recognized Colleges of Physicians and Surgeons in the Dominion be registered without examination. This seemed reasonable enough, but the council of the College in the Territories immediately took the position that it was also reasonable that other colleges should grant a like privilege to doctors received by examination in the Territories. Such reciprocal registration was requested, and supported with evidence on the standards exacted in the Territories. Medical bodies elsewhere, however, remained unimpressed and apparently refused to grant the privilege. To make matters worse, the Territorial Legislature in 1900 insisted on granting the privilege outright to members of Dominion colleges without asking anything in return. This measure, taken without consulting the council, illustrates the problem of an apparent clash between the interests of the profession and the needs of the community. It seems quite likely that the need of more doctors caused the assembly to insist on giving every encouragement to qualified men to come to the Territories, regardless of the quite legitimate desire of the council to secure proper recognition of its members throughout the Dominion.[44] In 1903, apparently feeling that the council was being over-rigid in the matter of registration, an ordinance was passed allowing a rejected applicant to appeal to the courts. Such an appeal was made by a member of the Manitoba College of Physicians and Surgeons, refused on the ground that this body required no examination. The appeal was sustained. Dr. Lafferty as registrar made the bitter comment that the decision made the Territories "the dumping ground for the overflow of the rest of the Dominion," but there was no redress.[45] In the cause of a general Dominion registration the council worked seriously and perseveringly, but without complete success by 1906.[46]

A very important responsibility of the council connected with registration was the examination of all applicants, other than those from Great Britain and Ireland, who were not already members of a recognized College of Physicians and Surgeons. Examinations were generally held twice a year (the exact dates were changed rather frequently) at first at Calgary, then for a year or two at Regina, then for several years at both Calgary and Indian Head—two areas of fairly dense population at the turn of the century. There was authority to hold examinations at Prince Albert, the home of the registrar, until 1901, but apparently none were held there. In 1903 Regina was substituted for Indian Head as a centre, along with Calgary.[47]

The subjects of examination in 1894 were presumably those usual in that day—chemistry, physiology and histology, materia medica and therapeutics, jurisprudence and toxicology, anatomy, obstetrics and diseases of women, practice of medicine, pathology.[48] Some changes were made in subject grouping, but no important ones in subject matter beyond the interesting addition of "sanitary medicine." Arrangements were made for homeopaths to have special papers on certain subjects,[49] and for translation of the papers of candidates who wrote in French.[50]

The original marking arrangement of 33 percent as a minimum on every subject with a 60 percent average on the whole was gradually changed as certain presumably key subjects in medical practice were "weighted" more heavily than others. Eventually the pass marks varied from twenty-five on a subject like chemistry to sixty on the practice of medicine.[51] One very early examination, perhaps the earliest, was written in 1893 by a man and his wife, among others. She passed, but he failed and had to write a supplemental. However she failed to pay her fee, and her name figures in a number of severe and even wrathful entries in the minute book.[52] She was one of nine women doctors registered before 1906.[53]

It appears from the records that medical examiners in the Territories were guilty of crimes, probably common to examiners of every time and place. In spite of exhortations from the registrar, their papers were seldom turned in punctually. The examiner in surgery, it was stated in 1901, had never turned in a paper, so that apparently the registrar and the presiding examiner were always obliged to devise something hastily at the last moment. Nor were marks returned promptly. Such procedures elicited complaints from candidates and registrar alike. Presiding examiners also were criticized for their habit of absent-mindedly pocketing the fees, and making no return either of fees or of expenses, a proceeding which might have been very profitable could it have been carried through with success.[54]

Complaints on all these matters were made by Dr. Bain in 1899 and 1900. Apparently they were not without effect, for Dr. Lafferty gave examiners an excellent character in his first report as registrar in 1902.[55] His report of 1903 contains a rather different kind of complaint in the following emphatic, if confusing, passage:

> Reverting again to the supply of medical men being greatly in excess of the demand, I would ask the opinion of the Council if it would not be wise to issue a circular to examiners to be careful in the preparation of their papers and to exercise their best judgment in marking them. To make their questions searching and practical and only such as any candidate ought to be able to make a pass on and mark close.
>
> Speaking from experience and observation of the examinations of the Council for many years I think I am justified in saying that the preparation of many of the papers from year to year bear on their faces the evidence of little thought and hasty preparation, and not always calculated to be a fair test. I have seen papers which were severe enough for candidates for the Fellowship of London and marked up to 85 and 90. I think gross errors in an answer ought not to be overlooked, but debited against the assessed value of the paper. There is no doubt our papers from year to year as a class have been sufficiently searching and comprehensive and will bear comparison with examinations of a like class anywhere, but I think the marking has been too generous in many instances.[56]

Dr. Lafferty probably had the dangerous gift of writing as he spoke. He was obviously trying to say that standards should be raised, without admitting that in the past they had been too low, a delicate undertaking in which he was not unsuccessful. He also points out, and truly, that a fair examination, rigidly marked, is a more severe test than a paper so difficult that the examiner is compelled to overlook glaring errors. Dr. Lafferty's recommendations were made at a time when the council was inclined to restrict registrations a little and to criticize the Legislature for too hospitable a policy towards new doctors.[57] Formerly it seems that, although maintaining their standards to the extent of a fairly high ratio of failures, they did try to keep the public viewpoint in mind. One doctor who failed in 1899 was allowed to register as a successful candidate because he did well in "practical subjects" and because of his "age, length of time in practice, and present location, where he does not come into competition with other medical men."[58]

This regard for the public interest and public opinion was important in governing the policy of the council towards unlicensed practitioners who seem to have been pretty numerous through the entire territorial period. Even the Mounted Police in the Yukon had to be admonished for employing as surgeon an unregistered doctor.[59] It was all very well to maintain high standards of registration and agree to tolerate the unlicensed practitioner in special cases; but the prevention of any illegal practice constituted a most difficult problem. As has been said, the ordinance left prosecution to private persons, the fines being paid to the council. In this, as in so many other matters where there is general sympathy or toleration for the law-breaker, there was little likelihood of action from private non-professional people. Registered doctors living in the neighbourhood might wish to do so, but they, like others, would be deterred by the fear of social disapproval—a very serious matter in a thinly settled area.

The council soon decided that it must provide funds for prosecutions to be initiated by its own members. In 1895 a prosecution was instituted at Calgary. By 1898 the prevention of illegal practice was becoming almost routine business at every council meeting. Those known to be practising ille-

gally had already been circularized.[60] At the August meeting
the registrar was authorized to have printed a list of the
registered members of the college, along with the medical
ordinances, examination regulations, and copies of the last
examination papers. He was then to write again to all illegal
practitioners warning that, unless they registered on or before
1 October, proceedings would be taken against them.[61] These
measures did bring results. By February of 1899 the registrar
was able to report that most of the offenders had registered.[62]
At this meeting it was further agreed to circularize all registered doctors, asking their cooperation. Doctors in one area
were particularly asked to send in reports on a man who was
practising after having been refused registration. This man
had failed in his examination. He was convicted shortly after
and fined $20 on information secured by a solicitor from an
unstated source. He tried the council examination, failed, and
was convicted again in 1901.[63]

Meanwhile, the council was initiating its regular procedure
for prosecutions. In August 1898 it was agreed that every
council member should accept some responsibility for securing evidence which might lead to convictions. The sum of
$50 was put at the disposal of each member for preliminary
measures, such as the employment of detectives.[64] By 1901,
the council's finances being in a prosperous condition, the
amount was increased to $150 with a general agreement to
press the matter regardless of expense.[65] A number of convictions were secured,[66] but the difficulties were great. Council
members complained that people would not report offenders,
or worse still, having done so, failed to produce adequate
evidence.[67] That there was little official sympathy was shown
by the coolness of the Mounted Police when asked to cooper-
ate,[68] and the imposition of fines so light as to be no serious
deterrent. Fines were as low as $5.00; they seem never to have
gone above $50, although the ordinance allowed $100. On
the other hand, legal expenses alone might run close to $50,
to say nothing of the expense of securing information for
which the council had made such generous provision.[69] In

spite of this, encouraged by the zeal and energy of Dr. Lafferty, the prosecution policy was continued throughout the period. An effort in 1901 to collect evidence in the neighbourhood of Edmonton through a regular agent (paid $1.00 a day) ended in failure.[70] By 1903, however, arrangements had been made for a law student, having been instructed by the Calgary solicitor and no doubt by Dr. Lafferty, to go along the Calgary–Edmonton line, interview all registered men, and institute prosecutions where needed. He was to be paid $3.00 a day. Described as a man of "integrity, tact and ability," he shortly came to be referred to as the "Council's prosecutor" and did work in Assiniboia as well as in the western area.[71]

The problem of illegal practitioners came up in a special way in connection with the gold rush to the Yukon at the end of the century. At the council meeting of January 1898, the registrar reported much correspondence on medical practice there. It was agreed that Dr. N.J. Lindsay, a member of the council, who was planning to go to the Yukon, whether in a professional or other capacity is not clear, should be empowered to conduct examinations and accept registrations in order that what was later termed "the very deplorable state of affairs" might be remedied. Dr. Lindsay paid his visit during 1898. He was unable to conduct examinations as the papers did not arrive. He did accept thirteen registrations, four of which were later invalidated. He also organized some sort of body, termed by him a college of physicians and surgeons, later referred to as the "Yukon Medical Council," about which nothing is very clear except that it seems to have been a kind of step-child to the college of the Territories. It seems fair to assume from the addresses in the register that, in addition to nine fees from the Yukon, the council collected at least fifteen others from men planning to go there, a total of $1,200. Dr. Lindsay's expenses amounted to something over $100. Yet when the Yukon organization requested, through Dr. Lindsay, financial aid in conducting prosecutions, the answer was that such fines as came in from the Yukon would be turned over to them, but that, as Dr. Lindsay had already contributed $10, nothing more should be asked! Such an attitude seems grasping, if not avaricious; it is possible that Dr. Lindsay brought back such glowing accounts of medical fees in the Yukon that the council felt itself entitled to some share in the gold mine.[72]

A difficult and delicate duty imposed, quite rightly, on the council was that of supervising the professional conduct of all registered members of the college. In 1892 the council was authorized to erase from the register the name of any doctor convicted of felony or found "guilty of infamous conduct in any professional respect."[73] Perhaps because it was thought desirable to regularize the enforcement of discipline, the ordinance of 1898[74] required the council to institute an inquiry on an infamous conduct charge if requested to do so by any three registered practitioners, but, it was prudently added, not "for adopting or refraining from adopting any particular theory of medicine or surgery." A special committee, later called the Committee on Discipline, was required, and was authorized to take evidence on oath and to procure subpoenas by application to a judge of the Supreme Court.

The first Committee on Discipline was organized in 1899.[75] Only three cases of discipline are recorded. The first, in 1903, was rather serious. The culprit, resident in Regina, had not a desirable record. He had failed twice in his council examinations before finally being accepted in 1899.[76] In 1902 he garnisheed the wages of an apparently very poor man for the remainder ($84) of what looks like an inflated account of $133.[77] The offence with which he was charged was that, when covered with a rash from an illness that he should have known as smallpox, he attended a patient and also went to a meeting at Qu'Appelle Station. The committee, after asking information from three government officials, one at Winnipeg and two at Regina, and receiving the slightest possible cooperation, found the doctor guilty of "very unprofessional" conduct, which they "strongly censured." While hoping that publicity would be given to the censure, they did not feel that his name should be removed from the register.[78] In 1905 a

Calgary doctor was accused of not taking proper steps to prevent a nurse engaged on a septic case from attending a confinement. It was decided that the doctor "might have gone a little further" than the advice which he did offer, but that no action was required.[79] Another case in 1905, of which no details are given, concerned a doctor at Macleod. The committee agreed that his conduct had been unbecoming to a member of the medical profession, but confined itself to giving a certain publicity to this opinion without further action.[80] There seems to have been a feeling that the cause of discipline suffered somewhat from the fact that the only punishment authorized was the extremely severe one of expulsion from the profession. No doubt, however, official censures were sufficient to warn those members of the public who were willing to be warned.

Apart from the training, organization, and discipline of members of the college, the council did make important contributions to public health, a matter rather neglected in territorial days.[81] In 1899 the Public Health Ordinance was referred to the council for recommendations on proposed amendments. The members of the college were circularized for information and advice, and although their replies were regrettably few, the council examined carefully legislation of other countries, consulted with the territorial executive, and made recommendations for the ordinance of 1902.[82]

An extremely interesting project closely connected with public health was the initiation of the "Bacteriological Laboratory," whose successor still operates in Regina. The members of the council brought the need of a laboratory to the attention of Premier Haultain. After full discussion Haultain agreed that the Territorial government would provide the accommodation and pay the salaries, on condition that the laboratory should be located in Regina and that the council provide all primary equipment. Members of the medical profession were to have free service. The laboratory was equipped by the council at a total cost of $3,795.68, and Dr. G. A. Charlton was placed in charge. His salary was paid by the Territorial government on a scale which seems to have been generous for those days. The council could afford to be proud of its success in a very important undertaking.[83]

The establishment of the Regina laboratory was one of the last projects of the Territorial College of Physicians and Surgeons. The creation of the provinces of Alberta and Saskatchewan in 1905 gave it the final task of winding up its own affairs and drafting legislation for the creation of two new provincial colleges. For the latter task the registrar received the handsome fee of $500.[84] The final winding up of the business and division of funds was complicated by the fact that, although the Alberta legislature passed its medical act in 1906, the Saskatchewan act was for some reason delayed until 1908. Therefore, in 1908 Saskatchewan, having registered many more doctors than Alberta in the past two years, objected to the exactly equal division of funds originally accepted. The matter was amicably settled, the total funds, when the books were wound up, amounting to $41,683.16, a strange contrast to the tiny budgets of less than fifteen years previously. Regret at the conclusion of official connections by men who had worked cordially together for many years was recorded by the registrar with what seems to be genuine warmth and sincerity.

The limited sources available make it very difficult to pass any judgment on the activities of the early leaders of the medical profession on the prairies. Like other newcomers they had to establish themselves and their families; and in order to do so, they had to exploit the professional training and the professional monopoly that was theirs. They were impatient at opposition, and they may sometimes too narrowly have assumed that what benefited the profession would benefit the public. But the Legislative Assembly and public opinion were well able to correct this tendency, and the constant stress on professional privileges of these able and energetic men was invaluable in modern pioneer communities whose insistence on medical services of some kind could make them an easy prey to any glib practitioner.

Notes

The writer is indebted to Dr. W. Bramley-Moore, registrar of the College of Physicians and Surgeons of Alberta, for the use of two valuable sources: the Medical Register and the Minute Book of the Council of the Territorial College of Physicians and Surgeons, both now in the custody of the Alberta College; and to Dr. G. G. Ferguson, registrar of the College of Physicians and Surgeons of Saskatchewan, and to Dr. J. A. Valens for making available Dr. Valens' collection of letters and notes on early doctors in Saskatchewan. Other sources used in preparing this article are in the Saskatchewan Archives at Saskatoon or in the Archives Division of the Legislative Library, Regina.

1. Valens File, "Early Doctors," pp. 49–54; Reports of North-West Mounted Police, Appendices by Medical Officers, in Canada, *Sessional Papers*; Jukes to Lt. Gov. E. Dewdney, 16 June 1886, Lieutenant Governor's Office, NWT, file relating to registration of medical practitioners (hereafter cited as LGO).
2. Valens File, "Early Doctors," pp. 15–16, 55; H. J. Clarke to Dewdney, 4 May 1886, LGO, p. 15.
3. Valens File, "Early Doctors," pp. 11–12, 28–31.
4. Ibid., p. 110.
5. Ibid., p. 15; H. J. Clarke to Lieutenant Governor, 25 May 1886, LGO, p. 25.
6. Attorney General's Department, NWT, G Series (hereafter cited as AG), 62 L, 95 L, 110 L, 114 L.
7. AG, 251 L.
8. A. E. Forget (clerk of Council) to Supt. P. R. Neale, 20 August 1886, Territorial Secretary's Department, file 25/4 "Coroners"; Forget to Carthew, 28 January 1888, LGO, p. 81.
9. W. F. A. Turgeon Papers, Box 40, pp. 332–33.
10. AG, 82 L; Proclamations and Orders of the Lieutenant Governor of the North-West Territories, 173, 24 June 1884.
11. Asst. territorial secretary to J. W. Jackson, 8 October 1898, Territorial Secretary's Department.
12. AG, 994.
13. *Ordinances of the North-West Territories*, 1885, no. 11.
14. Medical Register of the College of Physicians and Surgeons of the North-West Territories, 1886–1908, p. 1.
15. *Public Accounts of the North-West Territories for the ten months ended 30th June, 1889*, p. 6; AG, 274 L; LGO, p. 26.
16. AG, 264 L; Medical Register, p. 2; *Public Accounts*, 1889, p. 6.
17. AG, 264 L; Heber C. Jamieson, *The Early Medical History of Edmonton*, Edmonton, 1933 (Reprint from *Canadian Medical*

Association Journal 29 (1933): 431), p. 4. This doctor was invited to Edmonton to practise in 1881, but declined as the citizens refused to guarantee him $2,000 a year. Ibid.

18. LGO, p. 9.
19. Medical Register, no. 23, p. 2.
20. Editorial quoted (without date) in H. C. Jamieson, *Early Medicine in Alberta* (Edmonton, 1947), p. 43.
21. LGO, p. 69.
22. Ibid., p. 81.
23. Ibid., pp. 37-39.
24. Ibid., pp. 30-36, 44-48.
25. Ibid., pp. 50-52, 54, 56-57, 64, 70-71, 74, 75-77, 82-83.
26. *Ordinances of the North-West Territories*, 1888, no. 5.
27. Later extended to four years, *Ordinances*, 1898, no. 22.
28. Although the minutes indicate that a number of registers were printed, only one has come to light. It was published in Prince Albert in 1894 and contains, in addition to the register, the rules and regulations for conducting proceedings of the Medical Council and the code of ethics adopted by the Medical Association. This copy is in the Legislative Library, Regina.
29. This was a reduction of the $50 fee then charged. In 1892 the fee was again raised to $50. *Ordinances*, 1892, no. 12.
30. This clause seems to have been intended to enable qualified men from Great Britain to register without examination. This right was granted them specifically in 1890. *Ordinances*, 1890, no. 14.
31. Amendments to the registration rule were made in 1890, 1891-92, 1894, 1900, 1903. In this, as in other matters, the legislature evidently had to feel its way. Examinations seem to have been made obligatory in 1894 for all those presenting diplomas except men from Great Britain and Ireland. *Ordinances*, 1894, no. 34.
32. Seventy defaulters practising in the Territories owed $456 in fees. Minute Book of Council of the College of Physicians and Surgeons, North-West Territories, 1893-1908, pp. 83-84.
33. There is evidence that some of the leading doctors, regarding their professional training, quite rightly, as personal property, were inclined to be perhaps over-careful of their property interests. A statement on behalf of a Regina doctor, seeking an appointment as jail physician, that "it would be wrong to send another here to compete with those who as pioneers have borne the brunt," although probably sound, does suggest a somewhat personal approach. John Secord to........, 14 October 1885, AG, 297 L.

34. *The Qu'Appelle Progress*, 14 February 1890.
35. Dr. J. D. Lafferty and Dr. R. G. Brett. Dr. Brett seems to have missed one two-year term.
36. Minute Book, pp. 2-3.
37. Ibid., pp. 3, 42, 50, 63, 72, 88-89, 106-7, 168-69, 185, 260; Auditor's Report on the Estates administered by...Public Administrator for the Judicial District of Western Assiniboia, 8 July 1908, p. 11, in Turgeon Papers, Miscellaneous File.
38. Minute Book, pp. 181-82.
39. Ibid., pp. 206, 212, 262.
40. Ibid., pp. 45-46, 144.
41. Ibid., p. 154.
42. Ibid., pp. 60-61, 101, 154, 273, 279.
43. Ibid., pp. 235, 243, 248.
44. *Ordinances*, 1900, cap. 15; Minute Book, pp. 114, 130, 142, 151-52, 160, 168.
45. *Ordinances*, 1903 (2nd session), cap. 15; Minute Book, pp. 263-66 and typewritten insert at page 266.
46. Minute Book, pp. 153, 159-160, 200, 222.
47. Ibid., pp. 47-49, 101-2, 107, 133, 245.
48. Ibid., pp. 31-32.
49. Ibid., pp. 109, 131-32.
50. There is only one instance recorded. In 1902 a candidate wrote in French and his papers were translated for a fee of $20. Ibid., pp. 188, 196.
51. Ibid., pp. 40, 225, 263.
52. Ibid., pp. 47-177, passim.
53. Three of these are mentioned in Heber C. Jamieson, *Early Medicine in Alberta*, p. 138. Another was Dr. Elizabeth Matheson, a Church of England missionary of Onion Lake, whose remarkable career has recently been sketched by her daughter, Ruth M. Buck, in an article in *Saturday Night*, 23 October 1948.
54. Minute Book, pp. 115-16, 141, 158-59, 163.
55. Ibid., p. 188.
56. Ibid., p. 244. As no examinations papers have been found, it is impossible to get a modern opinion of these strictures.
57. See above, p. 176.
58. Minute Book, p. 120.
59. Ibid., p. 94.
60. Ibid., p. 108.
61. Ibid., p. 109.
62. Ibid., p. 117.
63. Ibid., pp. 127, 147, 161.

64. Ibid., p. 108.
65. Ibid., pp. 169–70. It will be recalled that the council was already provoked at the "open door" policy of the legislature with respect to registration.
66. Ibid., pp. 161, 183, 197–98.
67. Ibid., p. 207.
68. Ibid., pp. 201–2.
69. Ibid., pp. 161, 165, 183, 187, 197–98, 206.
70. Ibid., pp. 176–77.
71. Ibid., pp. 211, 242–43.
72. Medical Register, pp. 14–20; Minute Book, pp. 85, 101, 122–23, 125–26, 140–41, 160–61, 167–68.
73. *Ordinances*, 1892, no. 24. Only one name was erased, in 1897. This doctor was later reinstated, apparently on the advice of the council solicitor, who questioned the legality of the erasure, Minute Book, p. 177. The council was ready to order the erasure of another name, but desisted, again on the advice of its solicitor, ibid., pp. 106–7.
74. *Ordinances*, 1898, no. 22.
75. Minute Book, p. 138.
76. Ibid., pp. 120, 121, 147.
77. AG, 1388. The evidence is not sufficient for any conclusion. The account is almost entirely for house visits during two illnesses. The visits were generally once a day but often twice, and occasionally three times, and were charged at $2.00 each. The partial payment had been made in cash, $25, and three tons of hay valued at $24. The garnishee yielded only $4.00 as the man was a part-time employee.
78. Minute Book, pp. 224, 241–43, 256–57.
79. Ibid., pp. 275–77.
80. Ibid., pp. 289–91.
81. It was placed under the Department of Agriculture, apparently because the problem first arose in connection with plant and animal diseases.
82. Minute Book, pp. 151, 167, 185, 196, 198–99, 202–3.
83. *Annual Reports of the Department of Agriculture of the Province of Saskatchewan*, 1905, p. 45; ibid., 1906, pp. 138–39; Minute Book, pp. 262, 277–78, 281.
84. Minute Book, p. 286.

American and Canadian Medical Institutions, 1800–1870

JOSEPH F. KETT

Samuel Eliot Morison has said that the United States and British North America were as dissimilar in some respects in the first half of the nineteenth century "as if on a separate continent." The generally oligarchic character of Canadian society at a time of swelling democratic sentiment in the United States indicates the extent to which conservative government policy could put a check on potentially atomistic social conditions.

Hector St. John de Crèvecoeur once noted that while in Europe work was wanting for the hands, in America hands were wanting for the work. Free land, the manifold needs of a burgeoning society, and a tailing off of immigration between 1800 and 1840 created in the United States a labour scarcity whose corollaries were high wages, lofty aspirations, and demands for equality from the labouring classes. Oddly enough, the first two conditions, an abundance of land and a pioneer phase of development existed in Canada. Canada

Reprinted by permission from the *Journal of the History of Medicine and Allied Sciences* 22, no. 4 (1967): 343-56.

did have a higher rate of immigration, but this factor alone could not account for her conservative character and, considering that many immigrants to Canada after 1800 were dissenters from the Church of England, the effect of immigration was potentially divisive. In all these respects, then, Canada seemed fitted to embrace the democratic tone of the United States in the 1830s. In retrospect, however, the uprisings of 1837, led by Louis-Joseph Papineau in Lower Canada, and William Lyon Mackenzie in Upper Canada, were most notable for their abortiveness. Their occurrence is less significant than their futility. As Donald Creighton has observed: "The radicals in both provinces sought to persuade a people whose grandfathers had rejected the gospel of Thomas Jefferson, to accept the revised version of Andrew Jackson. They tried to induce the Canadians to re-enact the American Revolution sixty years after their ancestors had failed to take part in the original performance."[1] The year 1837 marked an interesting episode in Canadian history, but no more.

The different path followed by Canadian society in the nineteenth century can be studied in microcosm through an analysis of medical institutions in the provinces of Upper and Lower Canada (after 1840, Canada West and Canada East). At the same time a comparison with American medical institutions might yield insights into the significance of Canadian trends. As in any such comparison there are complicating factors. The ethnic issue between French- and English-speaking elements which dominated politics in Lower Canada had no precise counterpart in the United States. There were, moreover, obvious differences in size. Upper Canada in 1840 had about the same population as Maryland. One is not dealing with two nations of comparable size but with a dwarf and an emerging giant. Nevertheless, both the United States and the two Canadas made significant efforts with varying results to impose a system of professional regulation after the European model on frontier societies, efforts embracing the fields of licensure, education, and organization.

These three areas, separable in theory, had always been interrelated in activity. None existed in a vacuum. Any policy of encouraging formal medical education automatically affected entry into the profession; medical organization in the form of private or semi-public societies also impinged on the domain of licensure. Taken together, the three fields of concern constituted regulation of the profession.

In the United States, while consistent patterns emerged, no consistent policy of professional regulation was pursued during the early nineteenth century. Practice varied from state to state and, temporally, within each state. The determining factor generally was the level of social organization. In older and more settled sections regulation grew out of the efforts of semi-public societies or colleges loosely modelled on the royal colleges in London. These societies in turn emanated from small private clubs that existed for fraternal purposes in the major seaboard cities in the eighteenth century. Developments after 1760 affected the American profession in significant ways. First in time came the appearance of formal medical education at Pennsylvania in 1765. The older clubs had disintegrated as members died or retired. The presence of a guaranteed supply of doctors of medicine meant that professional organizations could become self-perpetuating. The American Revolution reinforced this tendency by creating a circle of military surgeons whose official designation and valuable experience gave a sense of importance and prestige. Moreover, war-time inflation and social dislocation opened the eyes of scattered American practitioners to the necessity of cooperation.[2] The result was the appearance in a number of states of medical societies to control entry to the profession.[3]

In newer areas of the country the primary impetus for professional organization came from outside the profession. Nervous legislatures in frontier states all but decreed a profession into existence, designating the membership, functions, and even meeting days of local societies. Some states, however, withheld licensing power from medical societies, preferring instead to work through official licensing boards staffed by delegates from private societies and non-medical officials.

Whatever approach was taken, however, difficulties between medical societies and medical schools were evident from the start. Part of the problem was technical. Was a medical degree a licence to practise? Tradition provided mixed answers. In Britain and especially in Scotland (where so many Americans had studied in the eighteenth century) the sundry licensing societies and faculties had long haggled with the universities over this issue.[4] When Americans sought an answer, necessity more than tradition governed their actions. The demands of an embryonic profession dictated the encouragement of formal education and hence increased the incentives to make the medical degree a licence. The trend was clear; state after state exempted medical graduates from the examinations of licensing boards within a few years of the latter's creation.

The decision to recognize the degree as a licence was harmless enough in itself. At least some elements in tradition sanctioned it—Oxford and Cambridge degrees had always been licences—and common sense demanded it. Had some control over the quality of medical education been possible, allowing doctors of medicine to bypass licensing boards would have had more good effects than bad. But medical schools in the early republic quickly took on molecular characteristics, breaking down into smaller particles, bouncing about at random, and forming chance alliances. The critical problem was the blurred line between private and degree-granting schools. In Britain a private school like Great Windmill was not a degree-granting institution. Its function was that of an ancillary to university education. Since government policy kept down the number of universities, some kind of ceiling could be put on the number of medical degrees. But in America incorporated degree-granting medical schools generally arose out of private instruction classes. Any relation the latter had to existing universities was at best a marriage of convenience, and quite often there was no connection.

The only way to limit the number of medical schools, consequently, was through restriction on the legislative level. In the eighteenth century when a charter was viewed as a grant of exclusive prerogative, this would have served the purpose. But by the 1820s the original meaning of a charter had changed and within a decade most states had accepted the principle of general incorporation.[5] The primary cause for the change had little to do with medical education, relating instead to the economic pressures of an expanding society and the religious denominationalism of a pluralistic society. Regardless of the causes, the effects on medical education were profound and long lasting. Since medical schools lacked effective outside control, factional disputes within an institution could not be readily resolved. Inevitably, such disputes were legion. Given the retarded state of pathology and therapy in the early nineteenth century, medical scientists rose to eminence not by scientific accomplishment so much as by force of personality, and professional rivalries took on the proportions of gladiatorial contests. Schisms in medical schools were frequent and acerbic. In the absence of outside arbitration minority factions had little choice but secession and the formation of a new medical school, a course invited by the lax nature of incorporation laws.

The pretensions of local or state medical societies formed another source of proliferation. With no medical schools before 1760, America had a score by 1830.[6] These schools were occasionally staffed by distinguished graduates of European universities but more often by quick-thinking and fast-moving local practitioners who saw professorships as passports to prestige and an increased private practice.[7] Few of the early professors had impeccable scientific credentials and some had none at all. Rivals of comparable background appeared on the scene, usually using their official positions in incorporated medical societies as springboards to chairs.[8] What ensued was a weird game blending the principles of king of the mountain and musical chairs as challengers sought to dethrone and displace the first-comers. The ultimate result was the creation of more medical schools under the control of medical societies or factions within those societies.

Since degrees were generally recognized as licences, proliferation undermined the functions of the medical societies.

Personality conflicts automatically became institutional conflicts. No effective regulation was possible in this situation though the attempt was made in a serious way until the 1830s. The final blow to professional regulation was the appearance of irregular sects like Thomsonianism, neo-Thomsonianism, and homeopathy, sects that for one reason or another did not conform to inherited notions about charlatanism and quackery. The Thomsonians were obviously sincere; the homeopathists usually as well educated as orthodox physicians. By the 1850s the very terms "regular" and "orthodox" were creating confusion and consternation. How could any true believer in Brown or Broussais label a homeopathist "irregular" because the latter subscribed to a dogmatic system of therapy? "Orthodox" physicians had no convincing answer and usually acquiesced when state legislatures, hung up on the same problem and weary of years of contention within the official profession, removed penalties on unlicensed practice in the thirties and early 1840s.

Even a casual glance at the medical history of Upper and Lower Canada reveals notable similarities to American patterns. Both Canadas had long confronted quackery, doubtless intensified by pioneer social conditions. Communication was difficult and the charlatan could skip from province to province with impunity.[9] Irregular sects, botanic and homeopathic, made their appearance and stubbornly resisted extermination. Professional rivalries were as rife as in the United States.

The end result, however, was surprisingly different. In both Upper and Lower Canada the formal structure of medical institutions weathered a series of challenges. Licensing boards composed of designated physicians were created in both Canadas after 1790 and despite frequent alterations in form they continued to function effectively down to the establishment of the Dominion of Canada.[10] There was no repetition of the total collapse that struck the American profession in the 1840s. Moreover, the numerous professional feuds in the Canadas did not produce the uncontrollable multiplication of licensing agencies that marked American experience.

The causes were partly institutional and partly psychological. Canadian nationalism then as now contained a dose of anti-Americanism. Especially in the politically troubled 1830s, there were widespread and not unjustified fears that lax enforcement of licensing laws would invite a descent on Canada by battalions of American quacks armed with republicanism as well as charlatanism.[11] Regulation, then, always had a political as well as a purely professional goal. It meant not only safeguards for health but guarantees of stability. Here the reverse was true in the United States. Amidst the democratic agitation of the 1830s, attempts by the profession to secure enforcement of licensing laws had the rubric of monopoly and were given the kiss of death, a comparison to the Bank of the United States. Medical institutions in America seemed out of step with triumphant egalitarianism; in Canada they appeared to be guarantors of triumphant paternalism.

Despite the presence of a psychological disposition to efficient organs of control, institutional regulation of the Canadian profession was a perilous business, made more so by conflicting and often contradictory national goals. Long before the formal establishment of the Dominion of Canada in 1867, Canadians had been torn by divisive issues. One, coming to a head in 1837, was the question of hierarchy versus democracy. After the abortive rebellions the Canadas entered on a "reformist" period of paternalism modified by reasonableness. A related issue, also played out but not settled in 1837, was a growing conflict between nationalism and Crown government. Finally, in Lower Canada there was racial friction between the French- and English-speaking peoples. The history of Canadian medical institutions in the nineteenth century reflected all three issues.

Crown policy generally discouraged the formation of local centres of political responsibility.[12] While the United States was actively undermining the vestiges of tight regulation of charters, the Canadas were experiencing a paralysis of every aspect of self-government. The medical effects of this were significant. Despite rapid influx of population after 1790 the Canadas made virtually no provision for medical education. What did appear was more the product of accident and unofficial local initiative than Crown design. The celebrated medical school of McGill University owed its origin to an odd stipulation in the will of James McGill voiding his bequest if teaching facilities were not established within a set period. With time running out, the authorities of McGill readily accepted the offer of a proprietary school, the Montreal Medical Institute, to affiliate with the university as a medical faculty. In Upper Canada the earliest medical education was offered privately by John Rolph, an exuberant polymath whose sympathy for the rebels in 1837 led to his temporary exile. Neither school was the product of government planning, and Rolph's led the peripatetic existence common to proprietary schools, affiliating at random with distant universities in order to secure degrees for its graduates.[13]

Rolph's school illustrated an enduring characteristic of Canadian medical education. In the United States medical schools without university connections could usually grant degrees. Daniel Drake's Medical College of Ohio was perhaps the best example but there were scores of others. But the Canadas followed British practice in sharply distinguishing private schools from degree-granting faculties affiliated with universities. Hence on his return in 1843 Rolph established a connection with the Methodist Victoria University in Cobourg. Following the accepted practice for proprietary schools, instruction was given at Toronto, not Cobourg, and there was "but slight oversight of either the curriculum or the rather troubled business affairs of the Faculty."[14] In 1856 Rolph's colleagues quarrelled with him and resigned. They began to call themselves the Toronto School of Medicine, the name Rolph had used before affiliation with Victoria. Rolph remained at Victoria until 1870.[15]

Rolph was also instrumental in frustrating the major official attempt to centralize Canadian medical education. The passage in 1849 of the Baldwin educational bill was aimed at checking the proliferation of universities along sectarian lines by replacing the hitherto Anglican-dominated King's College with a secularized University of Toronto. The Baldwin bill achieved, on paper at least, a unification of denominational colleges at one outstanding university. From Rolph's standpoint this was a calamity. Always an outsider, he had long resented the eminence of a clique of Toronto physicians, led by Christopher Widmer and including William Gwynne, William Nicol, and George Herrick, that controlled the Upper Canada licensing board and the medical faculty of King's College. Founded in 1843, the latter school had been Rolph's principal rival throughout the later forties. With the passage of the Baldwin bill the clique appeared to have received a new buttress, but Rolph, who had never lost his interest in politics, now turned it to good advantage. Holding a portfolio in the liberal ministry of Francis Hincks he used his influence to have state support withdrawn from the medical faculty of the university in 1853. Hincks, convinced that the Baldwin act had gone too far in the direction of centralization and secularization, readily acquiesced. Between 1853 and 1880 the liberal arts University College dominated affairs of the University of Toronto; no professional education was carried on.[16] With some justification Heagerty has called these years the age of the proprietary schools.[17] Rolph continued his affiliation with Victoria while his former colleagues operated the Toronto School of Medicine. Even before 1853 the Anglican leader, Bishop Strachan, had effected the establishment of a Church of England medical school, the medical faculty of Trinity University, and dissident Presbyterians started a medical faculty at Queen's University. Fragmentation had replaced centralization.[18]

The failure of centralization also had repercussions in Lower Canada, though there the occasion of trouble was antagonism between French- and English-speaking physicians. With McGill under English domination, French-speaking students in Montreal had little opportunity to obtain medical instruction. Further, the ascendancy of McGill's medical faculty touched off resentment among English-speaking physicians who aspired to teaching posts. The product of these cross currents was the Montreal School of Medicine and Surgery, founded in 1843 and run on a bilingual basis. This institution had a career as checkered as that of the Toronto School of Medicine. The Montreal school was essentially proprietary, with fees paid directly to the professors who then deposited them with the treasurer. At the year's end the latter returned the fees minus a percentage for expenses to the professors. For the first few years of its existence certificates of the Montreal school were valid licences to practise but this privilege, unique in the Canadas, was revoked in 1847. Between 1847 and 1850 the school maintained a tenuous connection with McGill; its students spent their final year at the latter institution in return for the medical degree. This connection was severed in 1850, probably because the Montreal school had fallen totally under French-Canadian dominance. From 1847 to 1867 it sought repeatedly and fruitlessly to have its certificates recognized as licences. In 1867 it began a new affiliation with Victoria University, thereafter being known as the Medical Faculty of Victoria University in Montreal.[19]

The history of proprietary schools is replete with exotic titles. Such institutions frequently sought affiliation with distant universities when no proximate university would respond to its appeals. The Medical Faculty of Victoria University in Montreal was in the same tradition as that byproduct of the New York medical wars of the 1820s and 1830s, the Rutgers Medical Faculty of Geneva College.[20] The parent university did not exercise any real control in either case. The methods used by Canadian proprietary schools were not significantly different from those of their American counterparts.

Despite the flourishing of proprietary schools in Canada after 1850 no precise similarity to American practice marked the development of Canadian medical institutions. Canada never experienced anything like the proliferation that plagued American medical education in the nineteenth century. The quick retreat that Canada made from the proprietary experiment indicated the shallowness of the roots of proprietary education in Canadian soil. Between 1887 and 1910 Canada moved rapidly in the direction of centralization with the establishment of major university schools at Montreal and Toronto. In pronouncing his sentence of execution on American proprietary schools in the latter year Abraham Flexner paused long enough in Canada to make an evaluation. Of the Quebec and Ontario schools only the medical department of Western University (founded in 1881 with a nominal university affiliation) and the Montreal branch of Laval (founded in 1878) merited contempt. The medical department of Queen's University and Laval at Quebec City were moving in the right direction. Toronto and McGill had arrived. Canada flirted with the proprietary school but the marriage was never consummated.[21]

Canadian attempts to keep down the number of medical schools were successful largely because the proprietary schools generally were not allowed to grant degrees. Though university affiliations were easily come by, the number of proprietary schools was automatically limited by the number of universities. In the United States, where by 1860 nearly every denomination and every offshoot of every denomination could boast a number of colleges or universities, this would not have made a dramatic difference. But in Canada the pattern was one major university per denomination. Whether the cause was Crown policy in Upper Canada or Crown policy reinforced by Vatican decrees in Lower Canada, the result was largely the same, a ceiling on the number of medical schools.[22]

Ironically, the very abundance of medical schools in the United States contributed to their restriction in Canada. With formal education readily available across the border, Canadian universities had less incentive actively to subsidize medical schools. One might well ask whether this was a beneficial tendency, whether in effect Canada should have had more medical schools in the nineteenth century. No quick answer can be given and any reply would depend on a number of unexplored factors: the kind of qualification possessed by rural Canadian practitioners, the comparative costs of education in the two countries, and the type and quality of medical education sought by Canadians who migrated to the United States. For all its imperfections the American proprietary system had its points. It provided a quick, cheap education to practitioners who otherwise would not have taken any formal qualification. It made medical education responsive to rural needs and prevented an overstocking of physicians in urban centres. Anomalous by twentieth-century thinking, it seemed normal and desirable in the nineteenth century. We know too little about the development of medicine in nineteenth-century Canada, but the questions are worth asking.

The most important chapters in the development of Canadian medical education focus on Montreal and Toronto. There too the most significant occurrences in the area of medical organization took place. During the late eighteenth and early nineteenth centuries licensing was the responsibility of official boards. There was virtually no organization of the profession; none of the incorporated medical societies or colleges which played so vital a role in the formation of the American profession existed in the Canadas.[23] The essential quality of such societies was capacity to make rules governing professional behaviour with a guarantee of enforcement by civil authorities. They were semi-public in function and goal. Their absence in the Canadas was the result of two factors; a government policy of discouraging decentralization of authority and difficulties arising from the presence of large numbers of practitioners with a variety of British qualifications.

Canadian students prior to 1840 could seek qualification either at McGill, in the United States, at a British or continental university, or from one of the numerous British licensing corporations like the Faculty of Physicians and Surgeons of Glasgow, the Royal College of Surgeons of Edinburgh, or the royal colleges in London. Rivalry between the licensing corporations and the universities had sharpened in early nineteenth-century Britain, making all parties unduly jealous of their prerogatives and quick to assail fancied slights.

Sensitivity of this sort destroyed the first major attempt to organize the profession in Upper Canada. In 1839 a group of Toronto physicians, including some members of the licensing boards and a large number of practitioners with Irish or Scottish qualifications, were incorporated as the College of Physicians and Surgeons of Upper Canada.[24] In form and purpose the college resembled the British licensing corporations, with the distinction between fellows and licentiates, authority to conduct examinations, and the right to initiate prosecutions. In all likelihood the college had other goals as well. Some of its fellows had long been calling for the commencement of formal medical lectures at King's College. Even a casual acquaintance with American practice would have opened their eyes to the ease with which incorporated medical societies could move into the field of education. Further, since 1827, members of the London College of Surgeons had been classed with graduates of the universities and exempted from the Upper Canada licensing examinations. This rankled licentiates of the various Scottish corporations who had long petitioned for equal treatment, and the 1839 act met their desires by extending the privileges of members of the London colleges to licentiates of every college or faculty in the United Kingdom. But more than fair play was at stake; the statute actually reduced the status of licentiates of the London College of Surgeons, hitherto allowed to practise both branches in the Canadas but now restricted to surgery. Tinged with partisanship and unacceptable to the powerful London corporations, the College of Physicians and Surgeons of Upper Canada had no real chance of success and its incorporating act was disallowed in 1840.[25]

The college's collapse was an episode but did not set a permanent trend. The licensing board continued to function until 1865 when it was re-christened the "General Council of Medical Education and Registration of Upper Canada." In

1869 a new College of Physicians and Surgeons of Ontario was incorporated and empowered to examine all would-be practitioners, including university graduates. This was far-sighted legislation, at once more sophisticated and more radical than the 1839 attempt. The new college met all the wishes of the licensing corporations and, since it provided for ample university representation on the examining board, headed off opposition from that quarter.[26] In the United States relations between the medical schools and medical societies had degenerated to the point where such a central licensing agency was impractical and in fact was not seriously considered until much later. Canada overcame the vexatious university-corporation issue with less confusion and acrimony than had either Great Britain or the United States. The Canadian universities proved less jealous of their prerogatives than the older and prouder British universities, while Canada's previous reluctance to charter medical corporations with axes to grind paid a handsome dividend. Unlike the British universities, the Canadian universities were not prepared to fight a holy war in defence of the validity of medical degrees as licences. Unlike the American medical societies, the College of Physicians and Surgeons of Ontario was not a threat to the incumbent administrations of Canadian medical schools.

Lower Canada witnessed a similar trend. The College of Physicians and Surgeons of Lower Canada was incorporated in 1847 after a long controversy which brought out the same issues as in Upper Canada. The college could grant licences in all branches, though medical graduates were exempted from examination, and fix rules regulating the length and content of preliminary education of candidates. As in Upper Canada, the original purposes of the Quebec corporation went beyond a concern for licensing. The earliest versions of the incorporating bill fitted the wishes of the French-speaking and younger English-speaking physicians. The grantees included the faculties of the Montreal School of Medicine and Surgery and another proprietary school, the St. Lawrence School of Medicine, founded in 1851 as an English rival to McGill.

After 1850 students of the Montreal School of Medicine and Surgery took their qualification from the college. Moreover, the original thinking of the framers of the college was to exclude from membership all practitioners whose licences dated back less than twenty years, a provision recognized as "an insult to the graduates of the British Universities and to Fellows, Members and Licentiates of the British Colleges of Surgeons practising in this Province." Opposition forced deletion of this clause in the final bill. The faculty of McGill still viewed the college as a threat and in 1849 the incorporating act was amended to provide automatic membership in the college to those engaged in practice in 1847 in place of a four-year waiting period originally stipulated. Vested interests, unable to prevent the formation of the college, thus forced upon it an inclusive membership policy, hindering it from becoming an organ of special interests.[27]

In the field of professional organization, then, the Canadas did not repeat American experience. Instead of a plethora of competing local and state medical societies perpetually tilting with medical schools, there were in the Canadas only three major attempts at incorporating provincial societies before 1870. One failed; the others succeeded but in a form unlikely to create chaos or bitterness. Government policy drew a clear line between a number of private and inconsequential medical societies and a few carefully supervised corporations with public functions. The movements of professional organizations and medical schools were complementary, and in the end the removal of potential sources of discord relieved pressure on the licensing structure.

Notes

1. Donald G. Creighton, *Dominion of the North: A History of Canada* (Boston, 1944), p. 237.
2. Joseph F. Kett, "Regulation of the Medical Profession in America, 1780–1860" (Ph.D. thesis, Harvard, 1964), ch. 1.
3. William F. Norwood, *Medical Education in the United States before the Civil War* (Philadelphia, 1944), pp. 30–31.

4. James A. Lawrie, *Letters on the Charters of Scottish Universities and Medical Corporations and Medical Reform in Scotland* (Glasgow, 1856), pp. 9–13; Alexander Duncan, *Memorials of the Faculty of Physicians and Surgeons of Glasgow, 1599-1850* (Glasgow, 1896), pp. 165–70; John Chapman, *The Medical Institutions of the United Kingdom: A History Exemplifying the Evils of Over-Legislation* (London, 1870), p. 23.

5. Oscar and Mary F. Handlin, *Commonwealth: A Study of the Role of Government in the American Economy, Massachusetts, 1774-1861* (New York, 1947).

6. Norwood, *Medical Education*, passim.

7. Recognized medical hierarchies existed in some but not all of the seaboard states, in Massachusetts and New York, for example, but not in Maryland and South Carolina.

8. Kett, "Regulation of the Medical Profession," ch. 2.

9. William Canniff, *The Medical Profession in Upper Canada, 1783-1850* (Toronto, 1894), pp. 63–64; M. Charlton, "Outlines of the History of Medicine in Lower Canada under the English Regime," *Annals of Medical History* 6 (1924): 223.

10. A licensing board was established at York (Toronto) in 1795 and modified in form in 1815 and 1818; the first serious legislation in the province of Quebec was passed in 1788, designating district boards for Quebec City and Montreal; John Joseph Heagerty, *Four Centuries of Medical History in Canada*, 2 vols. (Toronto, 1928), 1: 317–23; Charlton, "Outlines of the History of Medicine," p. 226.

11. Canniff, *Medical Profession in Upper Canada*, p. 111.

12. Creighton, *Dominion of the North*, ch. 5.

13. Heagerty, *Four Centuries of Medical History*, vol. 2, ch. 45; Edwin Seaborn, *The March of Medicine in Western Ontario* (Toronto, 1944), p. 262; F. Arnold Clarkson, "The History of Canadian Medical Schools. IV. The Medical Faculty of the University of Toronto," Calgary Associate Clinic, *Historical Bulletin* 13 (1948): 21–22.

14. Charles B. Sissons, *A History of Victoria University* (Toronto, 1952), p. 98.

15. Ibid., pp. 102, 124–25, 142.

16. Kenneth Bell, "Education, Secondary and University," in *The Province of Ontario*, 2 (vol. 18 in Adam Shortt and Arthur G. Doughty, eds., *A History of the Canadian People and Their Institutions by One Hundred Associates*, 23 vols., Edinburgh, 1913-1917): 384–85; Clarkson, "The History of Canadian Medical Schools," p. 22; Heagerty, *Four Centuries of Medical History*, vol. 2, ch. 45.

17. Heagerty, ibid.
18. Ibid., ch. 49; W. T. Connell, "The History of Canadian Medical Schools. V. The Medical Faculty of Queen's University," Calgary Associate Clinic, *Historical Bulletin* 13 (1948): 45–50.
19. Heagerty, *Four Centuries of Medical History*, vol. 2, ch. 46.
20. Norwood, *Medical Education*, p. 132.
21. Abraham Flexner, *Medical Education in the United States and Canada: A Report to the Carnegie Foundation for the Advancement of Teaching* (New York, 1910), pp. 322–26. The Montreal branch of Laval ceased to exist as such. The medical school of the renamed University of Western Ontario was upgraded.
22. An interesting example of the role of the Vatican was the controversy over the right of Laval University of Quebec City to establish a branch in Montreal; see Heagerty, *Four Centuries of Medical History*, vol. 2, ch. 46.
23. There were a few private societies in both Canadas before 1850, but they existed mainly for fraternal purposes and had little influence on professional regulation; ibid., vol. 1, ch. 14.
24. *Statutes of Upper Canada*, 13 parl., 4 sess. (1839), ch. 38.
25. In the mid-thirties popular pressure forced the York licensing board to abandon its English bias and include in its membership a number of physicians with Irish and Scottish qualifications; Canniff, *Medical Profession in Upper Canada*, pp. 87–88; the legal arguments for and against the college are recounted in ibid., pp. 154–57.
26. *Ontario Statutes*, 1 parl., 2 sess. (1869), ch. 45; the act also provided representation for homeopathic and eclectic practitioners on the Board of Examiners.
27. *Provincial Statutes of Canada*, 2 parl., 2 sess. (1847), ch. 26; ibid., 3 parl., 1 sess. (1849), ch. 52; Maude E. Abbott, *A History of Medicine in the Province of Quebec* (Montreal, 1931), pp. 71–72; Herbert Birkett, "A Short Account of the History of Medicine in Lower Canada," *Annals of Medical History*, 3rd ser. 1 (1939): 320–21.

Canada's Women Doctors: Feminism Constrained

VERONICA STRONG-BOAG

Professional women have long been feminism's prize exhibits. Hailed as heroines, they are cherished as the well-spring of future feminist victories. Historians have largely accepted this flattering assessment when dealing with the early women's movement. Yet an examination of the background and record of doctors trained in the Kingston Women's Medical College and the Toronto Woman's Medical College between 1883 and 1905 challenges the untempered optimism of the traditional account.

The struggle for medical training in Canada was hard and courageously fought. Almost without exception the first women students pledged themselves to the assistance of their sex and the improvement of their world. Despite the prominence of several female physicians in Canada's first women's movement, however, these women did not guarantee continuing feminist advance. The triumph and disappointment

Reprinted by permission from Linda Kealey, ed., *A Not Unreasonable Claim: Women and Reform in Canada, 1880–1920* (Toronto: Women's Press, 1979), pp. 109–29.

of their achievement has helped to shape the course of Canadian feminism.

In the nineteenth century neither Canadian universities nor professions were wholly happy with the prospect of female recruits. Opponents of higher education for women were legion. Their prophecies painted gloomy pictures of desexed, enfeebled, and arrogant female students. The coed, much the worse for her efforts to win a university diploma, would not take her "proper place" in the social order. Ill-suited to her primary tasks, she threatened the sanctity of the domestic circle. In place of the "suitable" occupation of wife and mother, "the professions and employments of public life" would be hers, a "consummation devoutly to be deprecated." Rejecting such dire forecasts, women began to win entry to the nation's universities by the 1850s; by the 1880s they were installed in institutions across the country. But acceptance by the universities did not always include the right to enrol in professional faculties on the same basis as males. Medicine, law and theology had their own traditions, which were rarely generous to women. Even when female students won the formal privilege of registration, difficulties with male professional monopolies were by no means over.[1]

Like lawyers and ministers, many doctors were determined to close their ranks to female candidates. Their resistance was a complex combination of sentiment and practicality. Male antagonism originated on the one hand from the conservatives' defence of an idealized womanhood. According to this faith, women were both the Almighty's special creations and beings uniquely susceptible to a multitude of emotional and nervous disorders. Under any rigorous program of study such as medicine, female students must, almost inevitably, collapse. Success could be won only at the unacceptable cost of a coarsened sensibility. The few masculinized and repulsive survivors would forfeit "the noblest quality a woman can possess...modesty." Potential female students were cautioned that it "would be far better for women to devote their energies to that which they are so much suited...bearing children and nursing children." Medicine was not for women because the world itself was not for them. Men alone were capable of combating its stresses. In order to "fight the good fight," however, these men needed good women at home to reassure them, to purify them, and to put up with them.[2]

Women doctors were not suspect on account of their sex alone. Male opposition stemmed also from a transformation in the nature of the medical profession itself. In the late nineteenth century the occupation was undergoing an intense period of professionalization, a process which required a tightening up of qualifications and restrictions on accreditation. Professional prestige and power depended on the assertion and maintenance of a readily identifiable orthodoxy in personnel and opinion. To achieve this, the curriculum and standards of medical schools were increasingly subject to the authority of such ruling bodies as the College of Physicians and Surgeons of Ontario. Deviance of any kind was suspect lest it raise doubts about hard-won professional standards. The association of some female doctors, excluded from most orthodox schools in North America, with controversial remedies such as electrotherapy, hydropathy, and homeopathy linked the entire sex with just the kind of questionable practices the orthodox were attempting to eliminate. One suspects too that women's particular identification with healing cults, like Mary Baker Eddy's Christian Science, provided further justification for anti-female prejudices.[3]

The growing insistence on formal and standardized qualifications for acceptance by recognized medical schools and provincial licensing bodies was one especially effective means of excluding the deviant. Stricter requirements weeded out not only the poor, as the radical Patrons of Industry in Ontario foresaw, but also female candidates. As a group, girls were offered less rigorous and less scientific training at every educational level. The Latin requirement, for instance, was especially onerous because girls were routinely discouraged

from attempting this "university" subject. Too often the ele-
vation of medicine to the status of a scientific and educated
discipline meant a renewed emphasis on masculinity.[4]

Women not only posed a potential risk to standards and
status, they also presented an economic threat in an occupation which was thought to be overcrowded. An abundance
of male rivals was serious enough but female physicians
were a special hazard. What if pregnant women preferred
their own sex for obstetrical matters? Childbirth was often
the occasion which initiated a doctor's association with a
family and its illnesses. Without such contact male practices
could decline precipitately. In view of medical men's hostility
to the ancient trade of midwifery and their reluctance to
license midwives, it is not unlikely that medical education for
women in Canada, as in Great Britain, was viewed as the
Trojan horse by which midwives might enter the kingdom of
"legitimate" medicine.[5]

Even after women wrung reluctant acceptance from medical schools, opponents had not shed their sexist assumptions.
Internships and residencies in Canadian hospitals were commonly denied women. Male physicians often were reluctant
to consult with female colleagues. Such resistance continued
far into the twentieth century, in the form of female quotas in
medical faculties and discouragement at every stage of a
woman's life.

Despite their frosty reception by the medical profession,
Canadian women were not to be put off. By mid-century
they had cause for optimism. American and British medical
schools were slowly beginning to graduate women. Many of
the early institutions were restricted to women, founded as
they were only after established programs had refused female
applicants. The Woman's Medical College of Philadelphia
(1850), the New York Medical College for Women (1863),
and the London School of Medicine for Women (1874) were
leading examples of the separatist impulse. There were many
others. Between 1850 and 1895, for instance, Americans
founded nineteen medical colleges for women. After mid-

century, opportunities for coeducational training were also increasingly available at Western Reserve College (1850s), the University of Michigan (1869), Boston University Homeopathic College (1874), and Johns Hopkins Medical School (1893). The acknowledged ability of such pioneers as Doctors Sophie Jex Blake, Elizabeth Blackwell, Elizabeth Garrett Anderson, and Mary Putnam Jacobi in Great Britain and the United States further justified the struggles of Canadian admirers.[6]

Admiration soon led to imitation. By the 1860s at the latest, Canadian women were making their way south for further education. With the notable exception of Augusta Stowe-Gullen, who completed the requirements in Toronto in 1883, all of the female physicians practising in the Dominion before 1884 had trained with doctors or in schools outside Canada, generally in the United States or Great Britain. Among their number there were such outstanding feminists as Doctors Emily Howard Stowe (New York Medical College for Women, 1867), Jennie Kidd Trout (Women's Medical College of Philadelphia, 1875), Leonora Howard King (University of Michigan, 1876), and Amelia LeSueur Yeomans (University of Michigan, 1883).

By the late 1870s advocates of "made-in-Canada" training were armed with the knowledge that opposition everywhere was retreating. The development of the Canadian women's movement in this decade gave further cause for good cheer. The emergence of the first branches of the Young Women's Christian Association, the Women's Christian Temperance Union, and various foreign missionary societies, together with a host of more local associations, raised up new sympathizers for female initiatives. Medical education was a particular beneficiary of this more receptive environment. More easily than law or theology it could be justified as a "natural" outlet for women's nurturing instincts. Support was all the more likely when medical pioneers like Emily Howard Stowe and Jennie Kidd Trout became leaders of groups such as the Toronto Women's Literary Society, later the Women's Suffrage Club. Organized women, imbued with a roused sense of sisterhood, formed a natural clientele for female doctors. Benefits were not one-sided. Female health professionals would give other women's efforts at reform new authority and stature. Doctors were after all "living proof" that women could succeed in demanding occupations and testimonials to the value of liberal reforms in general.

Inspired by advances elsewhere and reassured by growing support at home, advocates of female medical education set forth their case. First, like feminists on so many other issues, they submitted women's claim to equality before the law and justice within all institutions. Few speakers failed to acknowledge the larger principle for which they fought. Repeated emphasis on practical benefits suggested, however, that it was on these grounds that they anticipated widespread support. Women's champions reminded listeners that women often urgently needed wage employment. The unmarried, the deserted, and the widowed were frequently without any economic assistance whatsoever. To those who characterized medicine as essentially unwomanly, they retorted that "this objection is not raised when a women toils all day at chain-making or the heavy sewing machine, both more exhausting and less remunerative than professional work." Nor for that matter had women always been considered unsuited to the doctor's task. Feminists insisted on countless occasions that in former times the "ancient office of healer" had been women's, in their role as family nurse. Male jealousy had caused women to be driven from their natural field of labour. As Dr. Alice McGillivray, the first valedictorian at the Kingston College, concluded, "Woman's sphere has hitherto been chiefly defined by the half of creation, not woman, and therefore by her open to criticism." It was high time for female citizens to set the parameters of their own lives.[7]

Supporters also foresaw that female physicians would rectify shortcomings in the profession itself. So long as only male assistance was available, the female population would remain inadequately attended. As one advocate observed, "it is well

known that there are many female complaints which cannot
be properly treated for the simple reason that the medical
man does not and cannot fully understand them.') Nor was
masculine ignorance the only difficulty. Modesty's rigorous
code made women embarrassed and prudish patients. The
widespread acceptance of a lower level of personal morality
for males—the double standard—added to the unhappy pre-
dicament of timid patients. Either modesty or health seemed
at stake; there was no easy way to reconcile the two. Nor were
adults the only sufferers. Youngsters could also be intimi-
dated by an aggressive male presence in the sickroom. In contrast, female assistance was familiar and unthreatening. The
suspicion that male attendants were somehow inadequate
recurred constantly in the pleas for women doctors. Women
and children were commonly acknowledged as the special
patients of the new practitioners. According to some observers
at least, female treatment of adult males was also somewhat
improper. Underlying these sentiments there lay, if not a basic
antagonism between the sexes, at least a fundamental mis-
trust. Many women, like many men, believed that the male
sex was particularly contaminated by urban industrial society.
By comparison, women, less wedded to the business world,
seemed purer and finer. With such a viewpoint it was easy for
women to distrust male doctors.[8]

Since men were at best uncertain custodians of civilization's highest values, it was essential that women, particularly
those of the middle class, assume active guardianship. Feminists believed that female doctors would initiate and inform
women's work for their sex and their community. Their
example would inspire others with similar zeal and convince
the sceptical of women's essential contribution to the world
outside the home.

The first women licensed to practise medicine in Canada,
Jennie Kidd Trout and Emily Howard Stowe, insisted that
young women be given opportunities to study in the Dominion. Their own arbitrary treatment by the Toronto School of
Medicine lent these women the strength of bitter resentment.

Both employed a combination of practical and egalitarian points to justify the innovation. Stowe inspired her own daughter, Augusta, to take up medicine, but she also had a wider impact through her leadership of the Toronto Women's Literary Society and later of the Dominion Women's Enfranchisement Association. In the 1880s, Trout, originally a prodigy of Stowe's, was at least as influential. It appears, however, that Trout's deep religious faith, in contrast to Stowe's mounting scepticism, made her not only somewhat more conservative but also, in a religious age, more influential. This contrast may help to explain the apparent antagonism of some women students to Stowe and perhaps even the slow growth of the Women's Suffrage Club. More research needs to be done in this area before we will know for sure.[9]

One of those who chose to come to Trout for guidance was Elizabeth Smith of Winona, Ontario. She left "resolved to go through my profession and do in what measure I may be able the work that she has done." Consecrated to medicine, Elizabeth successfully wrote the matriculation exams for the College of Physicians and Surgeons of Ontario which she had previously failed. Toronto newspapers soon published the following advertisement:

> Ladies wishing to study medicine in
> Canada will hear something to their
> advantage by communicating with Box
> 31, Winona, Ontario, P.O.

With the exception of a few cranks, the replies were encouraging. Particularly heart-lifting was praise from a father whose fourteen-year-old daughter intended to take up medicine as soon as she was older. Smith forwarded all favourable inquiries to Queen's University, which had expressed interest in the admission of women.[10]

Augusta Stowe was one of those who answered the advertisement but she did not go to Queen's. Although the Kingston school offered to create a summer program equivalent to

and distinct from the men's winter course in 1880, Emily
Howard Stowe rejected this possibility for her daughter,
noting:

> There is every objection to "summer courses."...No
> person can study as well then as in cold weather, they
> cannot dissect, and by the profession generally they
> would never be recognized as of equal value with the
> winter courses. There is never the same hospital advan-
> tages in summer as winter. With regard to the excessive
> value of a Canadian degree, it is more imaginary than
> real, and if obtained from separate or summer courses its
> value would fall.

Instead she proposed that Elizabeth Smith apply either to
schools in the United States or chance the storm at Toronto as
Augusta had chosen to do. This rejection, the beginning of
Stowe's hostility to Queen's programs did not, however, deter
Elizabeth, who found her Kingston choice confirmed by
Jennie Trout.[11]

In April 1880, she joined three other candidates, Alice
McGillivray, Elizabeth Beatty, and Annie Dickson for the
first session at Queen's. All four graduated; three in 1884 and
Dickson, who was forced to leave school for a time, in 1886.

The first summer term brought the excitement of new
knowledge and self-discovery. By the close of classes the
women were united and confident. The outspoken McGillivray spoke for all of them when she outlined plans to spread
the message of women's medical opportunities.

> Now my dear, we must awaken Ontario this winter to a
> sense of the needs of her younger daughters. We must
> hurl the "Fiery Cross" through hill and dale, and startle
> something to life, either dissent or assent, the first better
> than nothing, because then we can have the satisfaction
> of exposing the meanness and small-mindedness of some
> of our *modest* fellow-creatures.

The concept of the essentially religious "mission" of female doctors was influential and very few of the new physicians seriously questioned its validity.[12]

In April 1881, Smith, McGillivray, and Beatty returned to Kingston, only to be turned away. The faculty had decreed that because few new students had applied, the course would be postponed until the following winter. That session was conducted partly with male students and partly independently. Although there were occasional problems with ribald remarks, the women generally suffered little harassment. Their optimism was such that Smith could exclaim:

> I just feel as tho I were really living these days, what with so much interesting study, so much knowledge presented to us, such labyrinths of thought, excited [by] so much to do[,] so little done and such splendid company, really life is active, life is real.[13]

High spirits did not survive the arrival of new scholars in the fall of 1882. Less sympathetic students and unexpected antagonism from one lecturer jeopardized the women's entire program. By November, Smith was driven to write:

> And then to know — *they dare* to judge me immodest — indelicate — unwomanly — to know how we are misunderstood, misjudged by most. Oh, it is enough to rouse such contending — such violent emotions as to make [the] load too heavy — that *any* should misjudge — that *any* should have other than sympathy for the great sacrifices we make.... Injustice — injustice — injustice rings in my ears and rouses me to bitter thoughts that sometimes I would dearly like to repay them fourfold what they make me suffer now.... I never think of giving up without completing the course.

Such courage attracted its champions. By the beginning of 1883 Dr. Trout was negotiating with Toronto doctors to establish a separate medical school for women. Together with Stowe she pledged $10,000. The sole stipulation was that women be admitted to the governing board and faculty of the new institution. When the Toronto male doctors proved obdurate, she turned to Kingston as an alternate site. There, sympathetic citizens, led by the prominent Liberal Sir Richard Cartwright and Queen's Principal George Grant, were more receptive. An audience gathered in June 1883 to applaud speakers hailing the unimpeachable record of female doctors, the cruelty of denying the women the full use of their education, and the possibility of trained women improving domestic hygiene. Kingston's support was confirmed when Grant, probably the nation's foremost educator, concluded that "the study of medicine was one of the things for which woman was specially adapted, and as in England and the United States, every facility should be given to her to gratify her reasonable ambitions." No woman's name appeared on the fundraising committee, but Trout led the list of subscribers with a pledge of $200 a year for five years.[14]

Unhappily for the long-term prospects of the Kingston endeavour, the same month saw a hearing sponsored by the Toronto Women's Suffrage Club. Here Emily Howard Stowe joined with male notables to plan a female college in Toronto. Unlike the Kingston Assembly, the majority attending this inaugural meeting were women. The stronger feminist movement of the provincial capital, reflected in the makeup of the audience, would be a mainstay of the young college and its successor institution, the Women's College Hospital. Trout herself, mindful of the resistance to her own very similar proposal a few months previously and perhaps jealous of Stowe's prominence, denounced the Toronto plans as a betrayal of Kingston. Her hostility to Stowe's project was influential, discouraging those like Smith, who had been tempted by Toronto's richer resources, from leaving Queen's. The extent to which the character of the medical pioneers became an issue is suggested by one Kingstonian's rejection of the Toronto initiative: "I do not care to be a student where Mrs. Stowe has any interest directly or indirectly."[15]

Such assessments set the stage for the October 1883 opening of the Women's Medical College, affiliated with Queen's,
and the Woman's Medical College, affiliated with the University of Toronto and the University of Trinity College.
Neither institution was entitled to offer degrees but only to
offer the requisite course work. Students wrote the exams of
the affiliated universities and graduated with those degrees.
After 1895, students of the Ontario Medical College for
Women, the successor to the Toronto school, could take the
examination of any medical school they chose.

By the last decade of the nineteenth century other universities were also offering women medical training. Dalhousie
University (1890), Bishop's University (1890), the University of Western Ontario (1890s), and the University of Manitoba (1891) followed the path which the Kingston and
Toronto pioneers had mapped out. The majority of female
students now trained in the Dominion but some, like Dr.
Eleanore Lennox (Homeopathic Hospital College, Cleveland,
1893), continued to go elsewhere, often for special programs.

Kingston offered separate courses until 1893, when its
years of financial difficulty and faltering enrolment exacted
their price, and it fell victim to the superior resources of its
Toronto rival. The Queen's Medical Faculty did not admit
women again until 1943. Toronto, now the only female institution in the country, enlisted the support of all who preferred
separate education. Even with this enlarged constituency, its
position was not sufficiently powerful to resist pressures to
shut down in 1905-6 when the University of Toronto agreed
to permit female candidates in its own medical courses. With
the closing of the Ontario Medical College for Women, a
unique experiment in Canadian medicine and feminism
ended.

Before that date, however, the schools produced 146 students, 34 from Kingston and 112 from Toronto. In addition
there were others, like Octavia Ritchie England (Bishop's,
1891), who took courses at the Ontario schools but chose to
finish their programs elsewhere. Most graduates cannot be

traced in any great detail. A few, however, achieved considerable prominence and their lives are well documented. Despite shortcomings in the evidence, it is possible to identify certain general trends. The majority of students, for instance, appear to have hailed from small Ontario towns like Smiths Falls, Merrickville, Brockville, Chatham, and Port Elgin or farms in their immediate vicinity. The prevalence of consciousness-raising WCTUs in rural areas and small towns is one possible explanation of such origins. At least five families sent two of their daughters, and there are a number of instances of a close female relative in nursing. Most of the scholars seemed to be daughters of ministers, doctors, teachers, or farmers, a relationship which placed them, if sometimes precariously, in the middle class. The marginality of that status in some cases is suggested by the considerable number, including Helen Reynolds Ryan (Queen's, 1885), Eliza Gray (Trinity, 1892), Margaret Blair Gordon (Trinity, 1898), and Margaret Wallace Sterling (Trinity, 1898), who financed their medical studies with some years of teaching. It is impossible to know at this time whether Elizabeth Smith's preliminary decision to use teaching as a stepping stone to medicine was typical or whether others arrived at that choice only after first selecting the more common teaching career. Although most students were single, eleven can be definitely identified as having married either before or during their programs. Eventually more than sixty-six chose marriage, some to other doctors, as did Alice McGillivray (Queen's, 1884). As far as can be judged, most married women such as McGillivray continued with their careers. Even the arrival of children was not an absolute prohibition to employment, a reflection of the flexibility of a medical practice. In contrast, married females were expected or forced to leave employment in nursing, teaching, and the civil service. At least twenty-four former students chose to take up their work in the United States, where a larger number of female institutions—asylums, hospitals, and medical schools, for instance—offered greater opportunity for women doctors. Twenty-five graduates went still further afield to missionary work in India and China. This latter choice reflected the deep religious faith and sometimes the British imperialist sentiments which characterized students. With very few exceptions they were Protestants, especially Presbyterians, Anglicans, and Methodists; in addition, many of them seem to have been evangelically inclined, as student branches of the Young Women's Christian Association suggested. Although the majority remained in Canada, the women doctors were generally "missionary minded" wherever they practised. Religious faith armoured and comforted them as "servants of God" in strange lands and as apostles of hygiene in the Dominion. In both arenas they advanced their claim, as women, to a special nurturing role.

Canadians' membership in the expanding British Empire brought with it moral as well as military and economic responsibilities. From the outset of women's entry into medical programs the mission field was considered an unparalleled "opportunity for the female graduates of our Canadian colleges." By the mid-nineteenth century the Protestant churches were finding themselves at a serious disadvantage in evangelization. The Catholics reaped considerable benefit from the medical and educational services of their religious orders while Protestants lacked these essential labour resources. The Methodist *Christian Guardian* observed,

> We see more clearly than ever before how next to impossible it is for men to have access, in their Christianizing efforts, to the female population of heathen countries; and how strong is the necessity that Christian women should go.

Increasingly sensitive to such shortcomings, the churches were equally responsive to the demands of middle-class women for a more prominent and meaningful involvement in religious life. Although leading Protestant denominations remained unwilling to accept female preachers, they were eager sponsors of female teachers, nurses, and doctors in mis-

sion fields. Since the majority of students at the medical colleges were conscientious church-goers, they were receptive to
the message that "the possibilities of medical work for opening the homes and hearts of the women of China, in the
hands of fully qualified women doctors and nurses cannot be
overestimated." Branches of such evangelical associations as
the Young Women's Christian Association and the Foreign
Missionary Society of the Presbyterian Church supplied constant reminders of the possibility, even the obligation, of a
foreign field of labour. The Kingston institution acknowledged its religious responsibilities by offering reduced fees to
potential missionaries. Its Toronto rival was equally anxious
to attract the same type of medical student, advertising that:

Ladies preparing to undertake the arduous duties connected with missionary work, will find her [*sic*] special
inducements in the study of disease. Too[,] being in a
central position and connected by so many lines of railway and steamboats, its hospitals often receive foreigners
suffering from disease, indigenous to their respective
countries, thus affording to Students a wide field for the
study of rare and peculiar forms of disease.[16]

Feminist sympathies strengthened Christian faith in motivating women to seek missionary work. Doubly armoured,
then, these women became influential agents of British cultural and political imperialism. However imperfect British
traditions and institutions, they remained, in the minds of
Canadian physicians, sufficiently superior to justify wholesale
subversion of other cultures in Asia and Africa. Women of
the non-Christian and non-European world were especially
pitied as suffering from the familiar male domination in its
most accentuated form. Footbinding, female infanticide,
concubinage, and purdah were the disabilities which most
often scandalized western feminists examining India and
China. They made attentive listeners to sermons and missionary letters which depicted "poor down-trodden sisters in the

East" crying out for assistance. These appeals encouraged feminists to carry the message, "The World is Made for Women Too," from their own lands to nations across the sea.[17]

Educated Christian physicians would transform heathen lands and uplift their women through example and service. Two graduates of Queen's testified:

> Believing as we do that no better opportunity can be given us teaching our sisters in this country [India] than when they come to us as in-patients, we have made these our first care....

> We have sought to have individual talks with our in-patients on life and death, eternity and salvation.

It was essential to reach the native women; without their co-operation nations would not escape the superstition of eastern faiths. Just as in North America, women and the family unit were the surest guardians of morality. Missionary women claimed that Christianity would give women the authority to fulfil a purifying role within their community. Thus female conversion was the best way of liberating heathens from misogynist traditions and "backward" practices. As one Toronto woman based in Canton, China, urged, "Think of 200,000,000 women! And then think of the potential power and the budding leadership...which lies in those strong brown hands and eager, agile minds! These are the women of China today."[18]

India was the first foreign mission field to attract medical graduates. Only in the 1890s did China emerge as a rival. There was an early tendency for former classmates or graduates of one institution to work in the same location, frequently in the same hosptial or dispensary. This was true, for instance, of Elizabeth Beatty (Queen's, 1884), Marion Oliver (Queen's, 1886), Margaret O'Hara (Queen's, 1891), and Agnes Turnbull (Queen's, 1892), all of whom laboured for some time in Indore, India. Common destinations were not all that surprising as denominations had their own particular missionary zones, but they also reflected the friendships which had grown up between classmates. Just as in North America, these ties would be important in bolstering faltering wills and encouraging further initiatives.

Not unexpectedly, in view of their middle-class upbringing, the first response of such women to their new homes and neighbours was often sheer horror. Margaret O'Hara, who eventually spent thirty-five happy and productive years on the subcontinent, wrote of her initial revulsion in 1892:

> There is no home life—no *real* home life, I mean—and we are surrounded by sin, suffering and superstition in filthiest and grossest forms. The first few days I was in India seemed dreadful to me.

Nevertheless, like Susanna Carson Rijnhart in Tibet and Pearl Smith Chute in China, O'Hara was quickly drawn to the people she had come to serve. Although she was never completely uncritical of local traditions she did develop respect for them. Her adoption of three Indian children reflected these sympathies. Her response to dolls sent from Canada as a lesson in neatness was also instructive. She rejected their European dress with the observation, "I firmly believe that Indians should hold to Indian dress; it is far more suitable and graceful than an European dress." For O'Hara, as for the others, her feminist inclinations played a role in helping her to identify with her adopted land. We do not yet know, however, these women's impact on indigenous feminism.[19]

Doctors were eager to train Indian and Chinese women to minister to their people just as Canadians had chosen to do. In Indore, India, Elizabeth Beatty and Marion Oliver promoted Lady Dufferin's scheme for the medical education of native women. In China, Alfretta Gifford Kilborn (Victoria, 1891) campaigned vigorously for the right of women to enter the

Medical School of the West China University. Others, like Jean Hoyles Haslam (Toronto, 1903), Jessie Allyn (Trinity, 1904), and Jessie McBean (Toronto, 1905) were founders and operators of special hospitals for women and children in India and China. In their crusades to establish new institutions and to win entry into older ones, the Canadians must often have recalled their own pioneering experiences. Campaigns against footbinding, child marriage, and widow immolation also appeared as regular, if less familiar, additions to their work. The doctors believed that with the elimination of such injustices women would play their essential social role. The full force of womanhood, at last freed of custom's chains, would purify and, incidentally, westernize "backward" cultures.[20]

The tasks of liberating and reforming other women were not easily undertaken even by adventuresome and earnest Canadians. Elizabeth Beatty, Minnie Fraser Stuart (Queen's, 1890), and Margaret O'Hara were among many to suffer repeated bouts with local diseases. Susanna Carson Rijnhart lost her first husband and child in a futile attempt to convert Tibet. Lucinda Graham (Trinity, 1891) died in Honan. Difficult as it was to endure such hardships, the doctors were certain of the benefits they brought. At a less altruistic level they no doubt appreciated the fact that in foreign fields they were afforded a level of power and authority they could never have had at home.

The careers of other graduates did not usually unfold in such exotic locales, but they too were often dedicated to feminist and reform causes. Medical workers in North America agreed that "true womanhood" had remained "dormant" too long. "Awakened" women should repudiate the senseless frivolity that engaged middle-class women in particular. A distinctly feminine point of view, nurturant, benevolent, and moral, must be brought to bear on the problems of the day.[21]

Sensitive alike to the shortcomings of their male colleagues and to the special responsibilities of female healers, new doctors gravitated to the service of women and children in Canada and the United States. Marjorie Ward (Trinity,

1894), for instance, became superintendent of the Montreal Foundling and Sick Baby Hospital; Anna McFee (Trinity, 1897) worked as resident physician to the Infant's Hospital, Randall's Island, New York. Both Jean Willson McDonald (Toronto, 1897) and Jean Cruikshank Bailey (Toronto, 1898) were associated with the New England Hospital for Women in Boston. In Toronto, Emma Skinner Gordon (Toronto, 1896) organized "incorrigible" boys into a religious and educational association. After 1898, students and graduates laboured in a medical dispensary associated with the Ontario Medical College for Women. It had been founded two years earlier as a separate institution by student Anna McFee. Here female and young patients received the more understanding treatment which was supposedly the prerogative of female physicians. At the same time the clinics maintained by the dispensary gave college students and faculty valuable experience they were frequently denied in city hospitals. The later emergence of the Women's College Hospital from the dispensary was intended to meet the same needs.

Doctors like Elizabeth Matheson Scott (Trinity, 1898) and Mary Crawford (Trinity, 1900), both of Winnipeg, also followed healthier children into the nation's schools. Their appointments as school medical inspectors reflected not only women's own interests but also society's sense of what was appropriate for "doctors in skirts." Such prejudices assisted employment in certain restricted fields. Unfortunately there was almost no female penetration of most medical specialities — such as surgery — or institutions — such as the McGill Medical School — where "maternal" qualities were believed of little importance.

Some women did, however, manage to base powerful careers on their faith in a distinctive female temperament. One leading preacher of this dogma, Dr. Helen MacMurchy (Toronto, 1900) became chief of the new federal Division of Child Welfare in 1919. Although single and childless herself, MacMurchy confessed that "the dearest wish of a true woman is to be a mother." Allied with her sister physicians,

MacMurchy used her position to educate women in the 1920s to their essential responsibility in reproduction. Her widely circulated "Little Blue Books" for Canadian mothers set out to inspire and reform their readers. Motherhood was above all the highest form of patriotism, for "No Baby—No Nation." Only a dedicated womanhood or better still, motherhood, could make up the losses suffered during the First World War.[22]

Elizabeth Smith Shortt was another influential apostle of the maternal cause. Like MacMurchy, she was not content to limit women's role to childbirth alone. In speeches across the country she argued that "the mother with the highest sense of her responsibility toward her own children is pre-eminently the woman whose interest, whose 'mothering' extends to the welfare of other children and thus becomes inevitably a student of civic conditions." Smith Shortt and the majority of her classmates divided women into two groups, the competent and the responsible and the incompetent and the irresponsible. More often than not the first corresponded to the middle class and the second to the working class. Not unexpectedly, the "larger mothering" was the particular trust of middle-class women. They alone had the time, the training, and the will to set the world right. Under their direction Canada would be reshaped according to maternally inspired objectives. In her work with the National Council of Women of Canada, the Young Women's Christian Association, and the Mother's Allowances' Commission of Ontario, Smith Shortt laboured to fulfil the stern duty she had set the fortunate of her sex.[23]

Concern for Canadian mothers and the health of the nation in general also led some physicians to examine the advantages of birth control and sterilization. Fewer births would mean better babies, healthier mothers, and a stronger country. The precise method of restraint was extremely controversial. Abstinence from intercourse probably had more public advocates, if not private practitioners, than any other means of control. It certainly appealed to those like MacMurchy and

Smith Shortt, who believed women to be essentially purer and less sensual than men. According to this viewpoint, abstinence, except when children were desired, was not extremely difficult for normal, that is maternally minded, women. In fact it could protect them from aggressive male lust. There was an additional dilemma in that birth control was too often adopted by those best-equipped, economically, psychologically, and physically, to have children. Legalization of birth control would help bring about "race suicide." The influential MacMurchy further argued in her *Sterilization? Birth Control?* (1934) that easy access to birth control would result in sexual promiscuity and debased marriages. At most it should be employed "in exceptional cases only."[24]

Some women doctors, however, were more positive about the results of birth control procedures. In Hamilton, Rowena Hume Douglas (Trinity, 1899) and Elizabeth Bagshaw (Trinity, 1905) established Canada's first Planned Parenthood Association in 1930 and encouraged the creation of similar bodies elsewhere in Ontario. Such initiatives suggest a greater willingness to recognize an active female sexuality. Unfortunately, as yet we know far too little about the history of birth control in Canada.

Some groups were considered particularly good candidates for birth control or even sterilization. Investigations of the mentally retarded by MacMurchy, Marjorie War (Trinity, 1894), Smith Shortt, and Mary Crawford created their own special concern about the unregulated propagation of the "unfit." In 1906, MacMurchy, for instance, prepared an Ontario census of the "feeble-minded" which condemned existing custodial arrangements and described the crime and immorality which were so regularly linked to retardation. Twenty years later another doctor reported that the situation had deteriorated: "The toll of war took so many of superior stock.... The burden on the superior stock—the so-called normal—is tremendous." Smith Shortt and MacMurchy saw surgical sterilization as one way of preventing the unwanted proliferation of society's misfits. There was no consensus on this "final solution" among medical women. The 1930 convenor of the National Council of Women's Committee on Mental Hygiene, Mabel Mannington (Toronto, 1900), reminded listeners that:

> Sterilization of the feeble-minded youth cannot take the place of the training and supervision needed....
>
> Again, the worst type of psychopathic heredity is often the border-line case, which would not be in an institution, nor available for surgical procedures.[25]

Female doctors pitied mothers with unwanted pregnancies, but many also feared the social problems resulting from the unregulated "breeding" of the inferior. Sympathy for their own sex went hand in hand with more conservative considerations. As members of a professional elite, doctors shared middle-class hopes for a reformed order in which efficient and rational use of human and material resources would improve, and also control, social development. Sometimes, as in the cases of Smith Shortt and MacMurchy, their views closely resembled eugenics, or the belief that human beings can and should be selectively bred for intellectual and physical improvement. Movements in favour of such programs did exist in the United States, for example, where they were often associated with middle-class fears of social degeneration. The passage of legislation permitting sterilization of the "unfit" in Alberta (1928) and British Columbia (1933), together with the formation of the Eugenics Society of Canada, revealed similar anxiety in the Dominion. However, no consensus on eugenic policies emerged among the female physicians in Canada.

Female doctors also joined other women in efforts to rectify social conditions and to advance feminist causes. To these ends they enlisted in a multitude of associations, including the Local Councils of Women, the WCTU, the YWCA, the Dominion Order of King's Daughters, the Civic Improvement League, and the Dominion Women's Enfranchisement Association. Within these bodies physicians often gave technical and scientific advice. Documenting the need for TB testing of cattle, slum clearance, water purification, and free vaccinations, they helped the women's movement keep up-to-date in a rapidly changing society. Their skills identified and eliminated some of the abuses of industrial capitalism. Not surprisingly, the expertise of these middle-class professionals also enabled the same privileged group to maintain control of the emerging welfare state. In this they acted little differently from other reform-minded male physicians.

Mindful of their own experience with male chauvinism and confident of women's equal but distinctive nature, women doctors demanded greater economic and legal rights for their sex. Like other feminists they were divided over the question of equality or protection for the female worker. Many, and probably most, decided, as did Smith Shortt, that women's potential as mothers necessitated somewhat different legislative treatment in the field of business and industry. They did demand, however, that equal effort bring equal reward regardless of sex. They were also unanimous in seeking the removal of all barriers to women in the professions. There middle-class women could presumably take care of themselves.

The franchise issue sparked the same agreement. Female doctors sided with Dr. Mary Crawford (Trinity, 1900) when she catalogued the abuses the vote would cure in her *Legal Status of Women in Manitoba* (1913). Smith Shortt, Helen Reynolds Ryan (Queen's, 1885), Lelia Davis (Toronto, 1889), Bertha Dymond (Trinity, 1892), and Margaret Blair Gordon became leaders with Crawford in the cause of female enfranchisement. Many more were foot soldiers in the same campaign. Smith Shortt supplied a vivid picture of the conditions enfranchised women would have to face:

I see as in a dream a giant working in a swampy farm. The name of that giant is Humanity, and as ever he works on in the higher levels of his swampy field, the noxious odours and miasmic vapors rise around him and lessen his vitality. As I see drains have been made on the upper edges of the swamp, and I ask, "Why does he not drain it thoroughly from, and through, its cause and centre?" I am told he cannot, that two giants greater than he control the place and will not let him do it. And as I look I see on the edges of the swampy lane, two giants greater than Humanity, and the name of one is Commercial Interests and the name of the other is Political Expediency.

It was the need for just such "giant killing" that inspired Blair Gordon to propose the suffrage referendum in Toronto's 1914 municipal election. Clean government, like new legal rights for women, would come with enfranchisement of female voters.[26]

Once the vote had been won, most doctors, like most other feminists, failed to take up roles as active politicians. Caroline Brown (Toronto, 1900) and Minerva Reid (Toronto, 1905) were two exceptions. Brown became president of the Liberal-Conservative Women's Association in Toronto's Ward Five and a city school trustee in the 1920s. Reid, the chief surgeon at Women's College Hospital between 1915 and 1925, ran unsuccessfully as a Conservative candidate in the 1926 federal contest and served on the Toronto Board of Education from 1926 to 1932. These women were exceptions. Most college alumnae appear to have devoted themselves to their practices or local community concerns at most.[27]

Former students of the college did not achieve extensive recognition even in medicine. The first 100 years of the Canadian Medical Association (1867–1967), for instance, saw no woman assume the chief posts of president or general secretary. Nor was any female doctor chairman or honorary treasurer of the Executive Committee and General Council. Nor was any woman editor of the CMA *Journal* or an honorary member during the same period. A survey of other medical/health associations in the years to 1930 also turns up very few female officers. Relatively small numbers, male antagonism, and suspicion from the male establishment seem likely explanations for women's absence from leading positions in their profession. They may have attained recognition and status in the course of their private practices, but these roles were much more limited than those envisioned by medical pioneers.[28]

The separate medical colleges offered women advantages difficult to find elsewhere. Their classes provided encouragement which male-dominated programs only rarely matched; their faculties supplied graduates with opportunities for employment, research, and influence. Memory of student years fortified female doctors in their subsequent careers, but discrimination existed everywhere outside college walls. Not surprisingly, a large number of students from Kingston and Toronto went on to Europe, Britain, and the United States where more numerous institutions offered greater opportunity. Some students, like Elizabeth Hurdon (Trinity, 1895), the author of *Gynaecology and Pathology*, stayed on in the foreign country, in her case as associate professor of gynaecology at Johns Hopkins University. Such losses can be attributed in good part to the conservatism of Canada's medical profession.

The closing of the Ontario Medical College for Women in 1906 deprived female doctors of an important stronghold of psychological reassurance and practical reinforcement. The loss could be offset only in part by the creation, in 1915, of Women's College Hospital, which soon offered residencies and specialist opportunities to women doctors. Inspiration and a reminder of old feminist ideals were also found in the Federation of Medical Women of Canada, created in 1924 by six women, including four graduates of the medical colleges. Dr. Helen MacMurchy became its first president. The federation was not, however, representative of the earlier outward-looking feminism of female physicians. Its primary aim was to serve as a means of communication between women doctors, not to agitate for new rights. It could not, nor did it intend to act as a substitute for educational institutions which championed the preservation and promotion of women's place in a male-dominated profession. The trend in the number of female physicians as a percentage of all doctors in Canada reveals the marginality of their position. The decline between 1911 and 1921 from 2.7 percent to 1.8 percent was not unrelated to the closing of the Ontario Medical College for Women. Although Abraham Flexner's influential report, *Medical Education in the United States and Canada* (1910), concluded that "women's choice is free and varied" in medicine, the situation was anything but promising. Not until much later, for instance, did the universities of McGill, Laval, and Montreal open their medical schools to female candidates. Even where women faced no overt discrimination in regulations they rarely encountered positive reinforcement. This failure went beyond the universities themselves. Nowhere in Canada's education system were girls encouraged to consider high status professional, especially scientific, employments.[29]

The establishment of a professional medical role for women was dependent on the vitality of Canadian feminism. When this faith faltered so did the cause of female physicians. Ironically enough, medical pioneers, by stressing women's unique nurturing "instinct," contributed to unfavourable trends. Like other feminists, they had no substantial critique of the "cult of domesticity" which overwhelmed war-weary Canadians by the 1920s. A renewed emphasis on family life and full-time mothering went hand in hand with a wave of Freudian-influenced popular psychology which emphasized sexuality and female irrationality. Despite the innovative aspects of their individual and collective experience, most female doctors interpreted their lives in terms of unique female qualities. At the same time their indoctrination as medical experts confirmed their membership in a middle-class professional elite. For all their battles with male doctors, the majority finally shared that group's essentially conservative approach to radical social change. A maternalist ideology and a professional orientation are hardly the best guarantees of a feminist revolution.[30]

Notes

1. "Sweet Girl Graduates," *Queen's College Journal*, 16 December 1876, reprinted in *The Proper Sphere*, ed. W. Mitchinson and R. Cook (Toronto: Oxford University Press, 1976), p. 123.
2. See the typically critical assessment of female ability to withstand pressure, "Higher Education for Women," *The Canadian Practitioner* 17 (1 June 1892): 257-60; "Female Physicians," *Canadian Medical Journal* 6 (June 1870): 570; "Co-education," *Canada Medical Record* 18 (February 1890): 119.
3. See Elizabeth MacNab, *A Legal History of Health Professions in Ontario*, A Study for the Committee on the Healing Arts (Toronto: Queen's Printer, 1970), pp. 17-41, ch. 2.
4. Ibid., pp. 29-30. For a further discussion of the Patrons of Industry, see S. E. D. Shortt, "Social Change and Radical Crisis in Rural Ontario: The Patrons of Industry, 1889-1896," in *Oliver Mowat's Ontario*, ed. D. Swainson (Toronto: Macmillan, 1972), pp. 192-235, and M. V. Royce, "Arguments over the Education of Girls—Their Admission to Grammar Schools in this Province," *Ontario History* 67 (December 1975): 1-13.
5. See, for example, "Medicus," "Over-production of Medical Men," *Canada Lancet* 24 (December 1892) and "Overcrowded Professions," *Canada Medical Record* 23 (1894-95): 142-43. See medical suspicion of midwives and their identification with female doctors in Noel and José Parry, *The Rise of the Medical Profession* (London: Croom Helm, 1976), ch. 8.
6. For a useful survey of such pioneers, see E. P. Lovejoy, *Women Doctors of the World* (New York: Macmillan, 1957). For a more analytical consideration of the situation of females in American medicine, see the important R. H. Shyrock, *Medicine in America* (Baltimore: Johns Hopkins Press, 1966), ch. 9.
7. See Mrs. J. Harvie, "The Medical Education of Women," *Educational Monthly of Canada* 5 (December 1883): 472-77; Mrs. Ashley Carus-Wilson, *The Medical Education of Women* (Montreal, 1895), p. 14; "Fidelis," "Women's Work," *The Canadian Monthly* 14 (August 1878): 30; "A Woman's Address," *British Whig* (Kingston, 4 May 1884).
8. *Queen's College Journal* (7 May 1881), p. 147; see Carus-Wilson, *The Medical Education of Women*, pp. 19-20. Stephen Leacock, Andrew Macphail, Goldwin Smith, and Henri Bourassa were among the most prominent critics of the effects of urban-industrial society on males. This criticism gave added weight to their fears about the influence of feminism; see G. Decarie,

"Something Old, Something New...Aspects of Prohibition-ism in Ontario in the 1890s," in *Oliver Mowat's Ontario*, p. 169, for one aspect of this antagonism.

9. For a useful survey of their activities, see C. Hacker, *The Indomitable Lady Doctors* (Toronto & Vancouver: Clarke, Irwin & Co., Ltd., 1974), chs. 2, 3.

10. Elizabeth Smith Shortt Papers, *Diary*, 22 April 1879, University of Waterloo; Adam Shortt Papers, Box 9, Douglas Library, Queen's University. Two of Carson's daughters did in fact complete the program at Toronto Woman's Medical College: Susanna Carson Rijnhart (Trinity, 1888) and Jennie Carson (Trinity, 1889).

11. A. Shortt Papers, Box 9, E. Stowe to E. Smith, 2 July 1879.

12. Smith Shortt Papers, A. McGillivray to Smith, 24 October 1880.

13. Smith Shortt Papers, *Diary*, 28 October 1881.

14. Ibid., 12 November 1882; *British Whig* (Kingston), 9 June 1883.

15. Smith Shortt Papers, M. Oliver to Smith, 20 June 1883.

16. "Medical Aid to Women in India," *Canada Lancet* 18 (October 1883): 51; "Women's Work in the Church," *Christian Guardian* (25 June 1879), p. 1; A. Kilborn, "The Needs and Possibilities of Medical Work for Women in China," *Missionary Outlook* (May 1899), p. 115; *Sixth General Announcement of the Women's Medical College* (Toronto, 1888-89), p. 7.

17. "Miss Oliver's Valedictory," *Queen's College Journal* (14 May 1886), p. 16; Rev. M. L. Orchard, K. S. McLaurin, *The Enterprise: The Jubilee Story of the Canadian Baptist Mission in India, 1874-1924* (Toronto: Canadian Baptist Foreign Mission Board, 1924), ch. 2.

18. Dr. Oliver and Dr. O'Hara, "Report of the Foreign Missionary Committee," *Acts and Proceedings of the Presbyterian Church in Canada* 1893-94, p. lxxv; "Harnessing Power of Chinese Women," *Globe and Mail*, 17 April 1937.

19. M. O'Hara, *Leaf of the Lotus* (Toronto: John M. Poole, 1931), p. 22; S. Carson Rijnhart, *With the Tibetans in Tent and Temple* (1901), and Hacker, *The Indomitable Lady Doctors*, ch. 6; Wilhelmina Gordon, *Four Servants of God* [n.d.], p. 134.

20. See "Reports of the Foreign Missionary Committee," *Acts and Proceedings of the Presbyterian Church in Canada*, 1888-89, p. xxxviii.

21. See the ambitions of the valedictorian, A. McGillivray, "Women's Medical College," *British Whig*, 13 October 1884.

22. H. MacMurchy, *The Canadian Mother's Book* (Ottawa: Queen's Printer), pp. 8–9.

23. See Smith Shortt, "Women in Municipal Life," Smith Shortt Papers.

24. H. MacMurchy, *Sterilization? Birth Control?* (Toronto: Macmillan, 1934), p. 150; see also MacMurchy, *The Almosts: A Study of the Feeble-Minded* (Boston & New York: Houghton Mifflin Co., 1920).

25. M. Mannington, "Mental Hygiene," National Council of Women of Canada *Yearbook* (1930), p. 94.

26. Smith Shortt, "Some Social Aspects of Tuberculosis," *12th Annual Report of the Canadian Association for the Prevention of Tuberculosis* (1912), p. 117.

27. See Brown's appeal to the feminist tradition in "Bosses Would Sway Women Voters," *Star Weekly* (Toronto) 31 May 1924.

28. See Appendix, H. E. MacDermot, *One Hundred Years of Medicine in Canada* (Toronto & Montreal: McClelland & Stewart, 1967).

29.

	Number of Women Doctors in Canada	Women as a Percentage of All Doctors in Canada
1891	76	1.7
1911	196	2.7
1921	152	1.8
1941	384	3.7

(Canada *Census*, 1891, 1911, 1921, 1941; percentages compiled by the author; no data for 1931). See A. Flexner, *Medical Education in the United States and Canada*, A Report to the Carnegie Foundation for the Advancement of Teaching (New York: 1910, 1950), p. 178.

30. See Jill Conway's provocative and enlightening discussion of the failure of professional women in the United States to understand their experience other than as an expression of "traditional" maternal femininity: "Women Reformers and American Culture, 1870–1930," *Journal of Social History* 5, no. 2 (Winter 1971–72): 164–77.

The Early Years of
Antiseptic Surgery in Canada

CHARLES G. ROLAND

Just one hundred years ago Joseph Lister publicly announced
his theory of antisepsis.[1] Subsequent biographies of Lister and
studies of his work have made it clear that relatively few surgeons grasped this philosophical concept on first exposure,
although many applied some or all of the recommended
techniques and agents. Complete acceptance and successful
use of antisepsis required an abundant supply of apostles to
train a new "generation" of surgeons. And this required time.
In Canada the understanding, use, and acceptance of Lister's
concept provide sufficient similarities with the situation elsewhere so that we can consider the Canadian history a microcosm.

First Reports

Canadian journals began to carry accounts of "Listerism"
within a few months of Lister's original publication in March
1867. Initially these journals reprinted articles and excerpts

Reprinted by permission from the *Journal of the History
of Medicine and Allied Sciences* 22, no. 4 (1967): 380–91.

from the British periodicals. By mid-1868 dozens of separate items appeared, and no Canadian physician who made any attempt to read the literature can have been ignorant of the new ideas. How many of these physicians attempted antiseptic surgery we do not know. In March 1868, a regimental surgeon, D. S. E. Bain, was the first to publish in a Canadian journal an account of antisepsis undertaken in Canada.[2]

Bain's letter, dated from Quebec, 12 February 1868, contains cursory remarks on his treatment of two patients and vaguely mentions the use of carbolic acid in an unspecified number of other patients. One patient received treatment for:

> a case of carbuncle, only remarkable for the method of treatment. It occurred in the ordinary situation, viz, the nape of the neck, free incisions were made, and a pledget of lint saturated with carbolic acid was inserted in the wound, over which a solution of the acid in glycerine...was used as the ordinary dressing. Within 48 hours the slough separated, leaving a clean healthy surface which healed rapidly under the daily application of the acid in glycerine.

The first Canadian report I have found of an elective operation (excluding the opening of abscesses) where carbolic acid was used as a dressing took place in Toronto on 17 October 1868. A 59-year-old woman, a patient of Dr. E. M. Hodder, had a large tumour removed from the left side of her face. After the surgeons had completed their work,

> the cut surfaces were wiped over with carbolic acid and oil, and the edges brought together by several points of suture and a strip of lint soaked in carbolic acid and oil laid over the cut edges and kept in its place by a few strips of plaster and a bandage.[3]

One week after the operation Hodder could report that "there has not been any suppuration, even in the course of the ligatures." The patient left the hospital, apparently cured, one month after her operation. Dr. Hodder reported the case because of the nature of the tumour, not because he used carbolic acid in dressing the wound. This aspect of the treatment appears in the case report quite naturally and casually, suggesting that by October 1868 carbolic acid was no novelty in the operating rooms of the Toronto General Hospital.

On 6 February 1869, at the Montreal General Hospital, Dr. Robert Craik performed ovariotomy on "Miss L., a tall and remarkably well-formed young lady." Craik commented:

> I had taken the precaution to soak all the sponges and ligatures in a concentrated solution of carbolic acid, and had a large quantity of the acid ready with which to impregnate all the water used during the operation, and to be applied in other ways which might suggest themselves as the operation proceeded.[4]

The patient survived the operation and removal of 31 pounds of tumour. According to Craik's account she did remarkably well. Healing occurred entirely by first intention, the sutures were removed in fifteen days, and "in a few weeks she was as strong and active as ever." The carbolic acid, not used according to Lister's recommendations, likely had little to do with the successful outcome.

J. Algernon Temple, a Toronto physician, published an essay in 1869 in which he clearly describes the philosophical ramifications of Lister's discovery and its relation to Pasteur's germ theory. In his essay Temple acknowledges his own lack of experience with the method, though he mentions Hodder's experience. Temple concludes his paper by stating that: "As far as I am concerned, myself, I have implicit confidence in it [carbolic acid], and in all cases of compound fractures that may fall to my lot, I purpose to employ it."[5] However, I have found no later paper relating his experiences.

The indiscriminate use of carbolic acid in a wide variety of unrelated conditions offended many critics. This abuse, not unexpected in an agent which proved so successful in treating conditions such as compound fractures, occurred especially often during the first decade of "Listerism." Canadian physicians experimented quite as much as those from any other country. Early in 1868 Dr. Horatio Yates of Kingston, Ontario, reported on his use of carbolic acid in an ointment to prevent scarring after smallpox. This ointment consisted in "carbolic acid, two drachms; mutton suet, two ounces, and coloured with lamp-black. This ointment was spread thickly upon black cotton wadding, which was applied over the face and forehead, holes being cut for eyes, nostrils, and mouth."[6] When the dressing was removed for the last time, Yates discovered to his delight that "not a single pit had been produced." So in this instance at least the treatment may have been helpful.

Obviously many Canadian physicians used carbolic acid, and attempted to produce antisepsis, during the two years after Lister's first publication on the subject. Yet these were isolated reports. We do not know how many Canadian surgeons had read Lister's articles or how many used carbolic acid. Many did not. The next important step, after mere awareness of the technique, was the spread of Lister's teaching by a pupil. And this process began in 1869.

Archibald Edward Malloch (1844-1919) was born in Brockville, Ontario, received an Arts degree from Queen's University, Kingston, and graduated in medicine at Glasgow in 1867. Lister was professor of surgery there and chose Malloch to be one of his house surgeons in 1868. The following year Malloch returned to Canada, destined to be a pioneer in antiseptic surgery in that country and one of the protagonists in a battle of words which resounded in Canadian medical journals for several years.

Malloch's opponent was William Canniff (1830-1910), physician, historian, and essayist of Belleville and Toronto, Ontario. In outline the source of contention was simple; Malloch was an earnest disciple of his master, and Canniff believed that Lister had accomplished little that merited the praise and attention he was then receiving.

Malloch vs. Canniff

The battle began innocently enough with an article Malloch wrote for both the *Glasgow Medical Journal* and the *Dominion Medical Journal* of Canada. In it he presented the clinical history of a young man troubled with a large fragment of articular cartilage in the right knee joint; Lister operated and removed the cartilage, using the antiseptic system before, during, and after the surgery. Six weeks after operation the patient had resumed work. In concluding his report, Malloch remarked that

> ...though a large incised wound of the knee joint may sometimes do well under ordinary treatment, if carefully stitched with a view to primary union, to leave such a wound as this wide open would, without antiseptic management, necessarily involve suppuration of the articulation. Hence, this was a good example of the antiseptic system, enabling the surgeon to adopt, with perfect safety, a course which would otherwise be certainly disastrous.[7]

Canniff did not reply directly, but in the next issue of the *Dominion Medical Journal* he published a letter referring to an earlier paper upon the subject of belladonna as a local application in surgical affections. Referring to his book *Principles of Surgery*, which will be discussed later, Canniff closed his letter with a paragraph worth quoting extensively, since it not only outlines several beliefs to which he would cling tenaciously for years but also gives a clue to the personality of the man.

> ...I claim to have first used it [belladonna] in connection with surgical diseases, especially as a local application.

Since I first used and recommended it, I have continued to employ it with a degree of success that nothing else has afforded. It is infinitely preferable to carbolic acid about which so many are excited at the present time. I do not recommend any medicated lotion in a healthy wound or ulcer, knowing that nature will invariably heal if not interfered with; and am convinced that pure air possesses no element to retard the work. It is only when there is disease that carbolic acid is found useful; but belladonna is much better.[8]

Six months after this communication Malloch presented another case report, that of a baby treated at Hamilton, Ontario, where Malloch lived the remainder of his life. It is obvious, on reading this paper, that Malloch learned his lessons well in Glasgow. Lister's recommended technique appears here complete.[9]

Three months later Canniff began a serious attempt to undermine the spread of "Listerism." Canniff could see no merit or logic in the germ theory.

... why is it necessary to summon the aid of minute germs to account for degeneration and death and decomposition of organic matter in connection with bruised and lacerated tissues? Is it possible to arrive at any other conclusion than this, that decay, degeneration, or death of organic matter, both in severe injuries and when a whole body is dead, are the result of natural processes entirely independent of influences due to air germs?[10]

Canniff's article contained a long section on the history of carbolic acid, in which he quite correctly points out that carbolic or phenic acid was in use by surgeons as a disinfectant long before Lister's publications. Lister, of course, never claimed priority in the use of carbolic acid—the principles of antisepsis were Lister's important contribution. Canniff seems never to have grasped this general philosophy, a fact which would have been less surprising had he been seventy-three years old in 1867, instead of thirty-seven. By that date Canniff had had extensive surgical experience, including several months caring for wounded soldiers in Washington, D.C., during the Civil War. It is especially surprising to find someone with this experience, who must have seen nature's many failures, asserting that "I take it to be an established fact that nature has made due provision whereby extraordinary repair of tissue may be accomplished even without the aid of surgical art." Canniff concluded his critical essay with these words:

> I would humbly submit that if he [Lister] would still further dilute until the amount of carbolic acid is quite infinitessimal [*sic*], but continue faithfully to apply the *wash* (for it is the washing that does good) he will find even greater success.

Canniff's ridicule probably assured Malloch's defence of his hero. In the next issue of the *Canada Medical Journal* Archie Malloch responded: "from a perusal of this paper ... I am led to believe that Prof. Lister's antiseptic system and its application are not fully understood."[11] Malloch's rebuttal—repeated quotations from Canniff, with comments and refutations— was the only method possible for him, because Canniff offered no original observations. No evidence appears, in any of the cited articles or in any later papers by Canniff, suggesting that he ever tried carbolic acid, much less the complete antiseptic system. After disposing of Canniff's remark that Listerism consists solely in "washing of the parts," Malloch discusses the germ theory. Despite Canniff's contention otherwise, "the most determined advocates of the germ theory have never summoned 'the aid of minute germs' to account for degeneration and death of tissues, but only for their decomposition, which, with exceedingly rare and doubtful exception, as in the case of perineal abscess, always occurs in, and is hastened by the presence of the atmosphere."

Being told that he was in error did not improve the temper of Dr. Canniff, who seems an over-proud and stubborn gentleman. His talent for sarcasm appears early in his rejoinder, in the March issue of the *Canada Medical Journal*, where he piously says:

> I humbly hope that I correctly state the question; that I do not misunderstand Dr. Malloch's words. It has been the misfortune of every one in Great Britain, who has publicly expressed his disbelief in the theory urged by Prof. Lister, to be charged either with jealousy or entire misconception of the plan pursued by that gentleman.[12]

Perhaps the best quotation to indicate that Canniff's medical generation was an earlier one than Malloch's or Lister's comes from this essay. Canniff has struggled to find some explanation, plausible to himself at least, to explain any benefits of carbolic acid while still denying the germ theory. One sentence, replete with fine-sounding abstract ideas, epitomizes Canniff's approach.

> Dr. Malloch's mind is so intently fixed upon the germ theory that he cannot discover my meaning—that the fibrin poured out for repair may be deficient in vitality, so that it rapidly degenerates into pus; and that carbolic acid applied to the tissue from which fibrin is poured, will have the effect of increasing the vitality of fibrin by which it becomes more plastic, and capable of acting its part as a healing agent.

Canniff also received a well-reasoned argument in rebuttal by Dr. W. S. Muir, from Truro, Nova Scotia. Writing to the *Canada Lancet* in response to one of Canniff's articles, Muir disposed of what was perhaps the most common argument against Lister's method.

> Dr. Canniff had no necessity to trouble himself, to fill the columns of your paper with cases treated *without*

Lister's method, and doing well, as the majority of cases treated surgically before Lister was known, as well as those now treated by other methods than his, do well....
The cases prove nothing *against* Lister, but if good, may be better, and if Lister's method insures this, why not follow it?...Dr. Canniff need not envy Dr. Lister's well earned glory. I do not wish to hurt any man's feelings, but I would ask any surgeon to take a course in Lister's clinics, and if after six months he did not change his mind I should suspect he had none.[13]

Although the battle in public print ended here, Canniff made sporadic skirmishes for years. There is no need to pursue the matter here in detail; I have found no published statement by Canniff to indicate that he ever accepted the principles of antiseptic surgery. As late as 1879 Canniff reported on a youthful patient upon whom he operated to remove a bullet. He concluded his brief paper by stating:

The wound healed without a drop of pus forming and with but little watery discharge. This would have been a striking proof of the astonishing value of antiseptic gauze, and application of germicides, had I not omitted to employ them.[14]

Here, then, is a man bitterly and resolutely opposed to the antiseptic philosophy. Can we determine why? None of Canniff's correspondence seems to have survived, so we receive no help from this source. Aside from his journal publications, however, there is one other work which may provide information. In 1866 Canniff published the first textbook of medical science written by a Canadian — *A Manual of the Principles of Surgery, Based on Pathology for Students.*[15] He began the work as a handbook for his students at the University of Victoria College in Toronto, where he was professor of general pathology and the principles and practice of surgery. Canniff's section on inflammation epitomizes pre-Listerism writings on the subject. Briefly, the *liquor sanguinis,* the normal product of inflammation, contains serum and fibrin. Fibrin contains a fibrinous element and a corpuscular element. If the former is in excess, the *liquor sanguinis*, or lymph, tends to organize; if the corpuscular elements exist in excess, the lymph degenerates into pus. These two processes are normal, expected consequences whenever inflammation occurs.

I believe Canniff was overimpressed by his undoubted intelligence and his rapid advancement in Canadian medicine,[16] partly a consequence of his publication of the manual. Only thirty-six when his book was published, Canniff may have felt himself bound to his own ideas and interpretations as he expressed them in 1866.[17] He was also a vigorously chauvinistic Canadian who wrote, for example, a strong though mawkish essay glorying in the establishment of the Canadian nation on 1 July 1867; possibly the fact that he authored a pioneering Canadian textbook made Canniff feel that he should defend himself at all costs. In this respect he resembled many other, usually older, critics of Lister and antisepsis.

Malloch, on the other hand, actually was not a vociferous disciple. After these few exchanges with Canniff he published very little on any subject. Following a visit to his old master, in 1873, Malloch did report on the current techniques in antiseptic surgery, including the carbolic acid spray.[18] From this date he published little. Nor did he achieve high rank in the medical world. This, though, did not prevent others from appreciating his qualities. For example, he was associated with William Osler and Joseph Workman, among others, as examiners in medicine for the University of Toronto, 1880–81.

Antisepsis in the 1870s

While Malloch and Canniff conducted their argument, others were using antiseptic techniques. Of course Malloch himself practised antiseptic surgery and, as we have seen, so did a few physicians in all the large cities. Yet in all these places Lister's techniques were probably applied by one or two surgeons; in the next operating room the old methods continued. Antisepsis had as yet made only random converts.

Typical of the time, perhaps, is the paper published by Dr. George Keator of St. John in 1873.[19] I have found no biographical data on Keator, but believe from his article that he was, in 1873, an older and experienced practitioner. He recommended such standbys of the nineteenth century armamentarium as leeches and antiphlogistic measures; later in his paper Keator comments on the usefulness of carbolic acid solution and explains his omission of this agent in the cases he had previously described on the completely justifiable grounds that they occurred at a time when the solution "had not then reached this part of the world." But Keator considered carbolic acid "a very valuable remedial agent" and had no understanding of the principle that carbolic acid was simply one part of a whole program designed to *prevent* suppuration.

Even less judicious was the practice of Dr. J. F. Macdonald of Hopewell, Nova Scotia. In a letter to the editor of the *Canadian Medical Times*,[20] Macdonald cited his successful use of carbolic acid in treating inflammatory sore throat, tonsillitis, diphtheria, toothache, scabies, herpes, eczema, tinea, psoriasis, acne, and eczema infantilis. The author concludes modestly by admitting that "internally I have used carbolic acid, but cannot say that I have seen any benefit from its use. In nausea and vomiting of pregnancy, in my hands, it has been a failure."

In 1874 Dr. Halford Walker, in Dundas, Ontario, used a weak solution of carbolic acid to flush out the bladder and the entrance wound after removing four calculi by lateral lithotomy.[21] A few months later the pioneering Canadian surgeon, Abraham Groves, performed ovariotomy using antiseptic methods. Groves' career was based in rural Ontario, and this case was no exception, for the patient lived in the hamlet of Douglas, Ontario. Yet Groves, despite relatively primitive conditions, practised excellent medicine; his thoughtful approach to surgery is apparent in the concluding paragraphs of this case report.

> There was one point of detail in this case which I think of considerable importance in any serious operation but which is not mentioned by the authors so far as I know. It is this—that I had all the water used during the operation boiled and allowed to cool, and then slightly disinfected. By taking these precautions all risk of introducing the seeds of after trouble by means of the water necessarily used, is avoided. This risk might by some be looked upon as quite chimerical, but surely when the germs of Typhoid Fever and other diseases are introduced very often with the water we drink, and those germs are so tenacious of life as to pass through the stomach uninjured, there may be some danger in introducing water which may be impure into the peritoneal cavity.
>
> This is a point which appears to me to be worthy of at least as much consideration as the disinfection of sponges, ligatures, etc., and one which does not seem to have, hitherto, received the attention its importance merits.[22]

Although some Canadian physicians supported Lister and used antiseptic principles, there were also many detractors. Typically, none of these men seems to have based his objections on experimental evidence but rather on emotion or on "common sense" unaided by any deep understanding of the discoveries of Pasteur. Dr. William Hales Hingston, a distinguished surgeon, in his address on surgery before the Canadian Medical Association in 1873, characterized carbolic acid's "appropriate niche of usefulness — not, in killing germs, hatched by enthusiasts for the nonce that they *might* be killed, but in diminishing suppuration and in opposing septicemia."[23] Clearly one of Hingston's personal characteristics was that he was unyielding; eleven years after delivering his address before the Canadian Medical Association, Hingston was quoted, in discussing a paper on abdominal surgery, as congratulating "Mr. (Lawson) Tait on his and Dr. Keith's disuse of Listerism in abdominal surgery, and thought the splendid results they had obtained were largely due to it."[24]

Thomas Roddick (1846-1923)

Roddick's name is justly renowned in Canadian medicine. He was a fine surgeon, active in military medical matters, and a distinguished politician and medical educator. Particularly noteworthy is Roddick's lengthy struggle, consummated in 1911, to have parliament enact a dominion-wide system of common examinations for medical graduates. Roddick often has received credit also for playing a major role in introducing antiseptic surgery into Canada. One source relates: "So it was that his foresight first introduced the use of antiseptics to the hospital wards of Montreal, and indeed to those of America."[25] Other accounts are less extreme, although Roddick tempered his own claim only slightly in a paper published in 1879. In September 1878 he read before the Canadian Medical Association a paper on "Listerism" which began as follows:

> By a somewhat singular coincidence, it was exactly twelve months yesterday since the antiseptic system of Lister, or "Listerism" as the Germans have chosen to term it, was first introduced into the practice of the Montreal General Hospital, and if I mistake not (although in this I am open to correction) into Canada.[26]

The question of priority for introducing the antiseptic system of Lister into Canada is an interesting one, as such debates always are. Roddick's biographer, MacDermot,[27] never confronts the question directly. He does point out, quite correctly, that "the mere use of carbolic acid did not mean that Lister's methods were being followed."[28] Yet it is obvious from the references already selected and quoted that while some Canadian surgeons did not believe at all in the germ theory or in antiseptic surgery, and while others were merely applying carbolic acid without any real understanding of the principles underlying the method, several practitioners made regular use of Lister's prescribed therapy many years before Roddick did so in Montreal.

The use of the carbolic spray cannot be a criterion for determining whether or not an individual subscribed to the philosophy of antisepsis. Lister did not publicly advocate the use of the spray until 1871.[29] Thus surgeons like Malloch, Hodder, and Craik cannot be faulted if their work did not include use of the spray. They were as true advocates of antiseptic surgery as the later workers who laboured enveloped in the choking mists of dilute carbolic acid. Furthermore, we know that Malloch used the steam spray in Hamilton beginning in 1873, four years before Roddick's efforts in Montreal.

If Roddick did not introduce antiseptic surgery into Canada, what credit does he deserve? There seems little doubt that his enthusiasm, vigour, and success in using the method, plus his frequent articles extolling the virtues of Listerism, combined to provide compelling advocacy of antisepsis for his colleagues. Beginning in 1877 numerous articles appeared with his signature, or that of his resident, giving detailed instructions in antiseptic technique and careful case descriptions.[30] Yet, in fairness to his predecessors, I think that Roddick's name belongs at the end of a list of pioneers, not the beginning. Roddick did not himself introduce antisepsis, although his influence may have been strong in convincing the doubtful and the hesitant. But the way he travelled was already marked by many thoughtful, critically minded surgeons in Canada who began the painful and slow process of carrying Lister's principles to the general population of Canadian physicians.

Notes

1. Throughout this essay I have used the terms "antisepsis," "antiseptic surgery," "Listerism," "antiseptic system," etc. synonymously. Some of Lister's critics during the last part of the nineteenth century used "Listerism" in a pejorative sense to indicate their disdain. Even believers in antisepsis sometimes referred slightingly to "Listerism" during the years Lister used the steam spray; these surgeons felt that all the paraphernalia were unnecessary to sound antiseptic practice. But Lister unvaryingly based his practice on the germ theory, aiming to destroy germs already present in contaminated wounds and to prevent their entry into clean wounds. I believe this definition covers all the terms I have mentioned.

2. D. S. E. Bain, "On the Use of Carbolic Acid in Surgery," *Canada Medical Journal* (hereafter *CMJ*) 4 (1868): 388.

3. E. M. Hodder, "Large Fibro Cystic Tumor," *Dominion Medical Journal* (hereafter *DMJ*) 1 (1869): 137-38.

4. R. Craik, "Two Cases of Ovariotomy: One Unsuccessful and One Successful," *CMJ* 6 (1869): 1-10. I have been unable to obtain any definite evidence of the early use of antisepsis by the French-speaking physicians of Canada. Although Michael Joseph Ahern is proposed by some, he apparently did not practise Listerism until about 1885 (personal communication from Dr. Sylvio Leblond, 2 August 1967).

5. J. A. Temple, "Carbolic Acid, and its Uses in Medicine and Surgery," *DMJ* 1 (1869): 163-67.

6. H. Yates, "Carbolic Acid in Small-Pox," *Lancet* 1 (1868): 151.

7. A. E. Malloch, "Case of Unusually Large Loose Cartilage in the Knee-Joint," *DMJ* 1 (1869): 104-6.

8. W. Canniff, Letter to the Editor, *DMJ* 1 (1869): 142.

9. A. E. Malloch, "Reports of Cases Read before the Hamilton Medical & Surgical Society," *CMJ* 6 (1869): 154-57.

10. W. Canniff, "An Examination of the Merits of Carbolic Acid as a Remedial Agent in the Practice of Surgery, with a Glance at its History," *CMJ* 6 (1870): 295-304.

11. A. E. Malloch, "The Antiseptic Theory and Proper Application of Carbolic Acid," *CMJ* 6 (1870): 337-40.

12. W. Canniff, "Carbolic Acid, and the Germ Theory," *CMJ* 6 (1870): 406-9.

13. W. S. Muir, To the Editor, *Canada Lancet* 12 (1880): 137-38.

14. W. Canniff, "Bullet Wound of the Face: Antiseptic Surgery," *Canada Lancet* 11 (1879): 353-54.

15. W. Canniff, *A Manual of the Principles of Surgery, Based on Pathology for Students* (Philadelphia, 1866). A few medical monographs, published by Canadians, appeared before 1866. These include Robert Jones' *Remarks on the Distemper Generally Known by the Name of the Molbay Disease* (Montreal, 1786) and *A Dissertation on the Puerperal Fever*, by Peter de Sales la Terrière (Boston, 1789). These, however, seem quite distinct from a textbook which is devoted to a broader area of knowledge than a single disease or condition.

    One book written by Canniff remains current and important today, and deserves mention. This is his extraordinary volume *The Medical Profession in Upper Canada, 1783-1850* (Toronto, 1894). Canniff collected here a mass of information about medical practice and medical licensure in Upper Canada (Ontario) and also preserved biographical material about scores of the early practitioners.

16. Canniff was a founding member of the Canadian Medical Association in 1867, secretary of the association in 1869, and president in 1880. Among his many other appointments, one of particular interest is his long service as the first medical officer of the City of Toronto (1883–90).

17. He demanded credit for originality in some portions of the manual and responded to a slighting review of the book with an eight-page letter to the editor, detailing those sections he believed new. *CMJ* 3 (1867): 245–52.

18. A. Malloch, "Reports of Societies: Hamilton Medical and Surgical Society," *Canada Lancet* 6 (1873): 123–28.

19. G. E. S. Keator, "Conservative Surgery in Connection with Serious Injuries," *Canada Lancet* 6 (1873): 13–18.

20. J. F. Macdonald, "Uses of Carbolic Acid," *Canadian Medical Times* 1 (1873): 18. Both Keator and Macdonald practised in Canada's maritime provinces. One other physician from this area, John Stewart (1848–1933), deserves mention. He was Lister's pupil at Edinburgh and London and played a major role in the teaching and practice of surgery in Canada's east coast region. However, he did not actually pioneer in the use of Listerism in Canada, since he remained in London until late 1878, and began practice in Nova Scotia in 1879.

21. A. Halford Walker, "Operation of Lithotomy," *Canada Lancet* 6 (1874): 180–81.

22. A. Groves, "A Case of Ovariotomy," *Canada Lancet* 6 (1874): 345–47.

23. W. H. Hingston, "Address in Surgery," *Canada Lancet* 6 (1873): 47-56.
24. Account of the Canadian Medical Association Meeting, Tuesday, 26 August 1884, *Canada Medical and Surgical Journal* 13 (1884): 119-24.
25. "Sir Thomas George Roddick," in C. G. D. Roberts and A. L. Tunnell, *A Standard Dictionary of Canadian Biography* (Toronto, 1934).
26. T. G. Roddick, "Listerism," *Canada Medical and Surgical Journal* 7 (1879): 289-301.
27. H. E. MacDermot, *Sir Thomas Roddick: His Work in Medicine and Public Life* (Toronto, 1938).
28. Ibid., p. 25.
29. R. Godlee, *Lord Lister* (London, 1917).
30. T. G. Roddick, "Correspondence," *Canada Medical and Surgical Journal* 6 (1877): 69-73; "Antiseptic Dressing in Surgery," ibid., pp. 242-48; "Listerism," ibid. 7 (1879): 289-301; J. A. McArthur, "Case of Compound Comminuted Fracture of Leg," ibid., pp. 358-60; T. Gray, "Case of Malignant Epulis," ibid., pp. 360-62; W. H. Burland, "Case of Compound Fracture of Rudisand Ulna Treated Antiseptically," ibid.

"Pure Books on Avoided Subjects": Pre-Freudian Sexual Ideas in Canada

MICHAEL BLISS

Books purporting to contain facts and wisdom about human sexuality were common in North America long before Dr. Reuben, *Human Sexual Response*, the Kinsey Reports, or even the Freudian revolution. The best-selling sex "manuals in Canada between about 1900 and 1915 were the eight volumes in the 'Self and Sex Series,'" published in Philadelphia and distributed in Canada by William Briggs, official publisher for the Methodist Church. The Self and Sex books for males were *What a Young Boy Ought to Know, What a Young Man Ought to Know, What a Young Husband Ought to Know*, and *What a Man of 45 Ought to Know*. Their author and publisher was the Rev. Sylvanus Stall, a Lutheran minister. Dr. Mary Wood-Allen, a popular lecturer and writer on sex education, contributed *What a Young Girl Ought to Know*, and *What a Young Woman Ought to Know* to the series; and Dr. Emma F. Angell Drake completed the symmetry with *What a Young Wife Ought to Know* and *What a Woman of 45 Ought to*

Reprinted by permission of the author from the Canadian Historical Association, *Historical Papers*, 1970, pp. 89–108

Know. The first "ought to know" book was issued in 1897; by 1908 the publisher claimed sales of one million copies of the series in English and the books had been translated into the leading European as well as eight Asian languages. No Canadian circulation figures have been recorded, only the claim that they outsold all other books of their kind. The individual volumes, all in common format, were accompanied by glowing commendations from prominent clergymen, medical experts (including, in later editions, the Canadian Dr. Amelia Yeomans of Winnipeg), popular writers such as Charles M. Sheldon and Margaret Warner Morley, and other public figures including Josiah Strong, W. T. Stead, Elizabeth Cady Stanton, and Anthony Comstock. Advertisements for the series in Canada were headed "Pure Books on Avoided Subjects."[1]

The Self and Sex books are a compendium of orthodox sexual knowledge and precept in late-Victorian and Edwardian Canada. It is true that they are American sex manuals. But the few works by Canadians that do exist on the subject are both derivative from and in complete agreement with foreign writers. In this field, as in so many others, Canadians initially relied on a kind of cross-fertilization from the United States. Assuming, then, the relevance of the Self and Sex series for the study of sexual thought in Canada, I will try to do three things in this paper: outline the fundamental ideas expressed in the Self and Sex books, attempt to explain the background of some of these ideas in North American medical and popular thought, and finally note some additional evidence of the spread of this approach to sexuality in Canada as well as suggest directions for further research.

I

There was no rejection of sex *per se* in the Self and Sex series. On the contrary, Sylvanus Stall advised his readers that "Sexuality has been strongly marked in all the great men who have risen to eminence in all departments of life. Without it man would be mean, selfish, sordid and ungracious to his fellow-men and uncivil to womankind. ... No other part of his being so much assists him in the development of that which is highest, noblest and best in his nature."[2] He argued that the sex act itself was meant to bring "pleasure and a sense of satisfaction," and criticized those women who proclaimed utter indifference to marital intercourse.[3] Similarly, Dr. Wood-Allen told young women that their womanhood was "the mental, moral and physical expression of sex, ... a glorious, divine gift, to be received with solemn thankfulness."[4]

The major theme of every book in the series, however, was the difficulty that the fact of sexuality created for boys, girls, men, women, husbands, wives, and the elderly.

By far the most persistent and pernicious difficulty for the unmarried was the temptation to indulge in the habit of the secret vice, the solitary vice, self-pollution, self-abuse, onanism, or masturbation. After a few pages on plants and fishes, the Self and Sex books for boys and girls became little more than anti-masturbation tracts. The subject was introduced as a misuse of sexual parts that could be learned innocently enough by sliding down banisters, climbing trees, and wearing tight clothes, or not so innocently from other children and nurses. However commenced, the act rapidly led to a grim series of consequences:

> The health declines. The eyes lose their lustre. The skin becomes sallow. The muscles become flabby. There is an unnatural languor. Every little effort is followed by weariness. There is a great indifference to exertion. ... [The victim] complains of pain in the back; of headache and dizziness. The hands become cold and clammy. The digestion becomes poor, the appetite fitful. The heart palpitates. He sits in a stooping posture, becomes hollow-chested, and the entire body, instead of enlarging into a strong, manly frame, becomes wasted, and many signs give promise of early decline and death. ...

If persisted in, masturbation will not only undermine, but completely overthrow the health. If the body is naturally strong, the mind may give way first, and in extreme cases imbecility and insanity may, and often do come as the inevitable result. Where the body is not naturally strong, a general wasting may be followed by consumption, or life may be terminated by any one of many diseases.[5]

Boys were told of how parents often resorted to drastic measures to stop the insidious habit, including tying children's hands behind their backs, to bed posts, or to rings in a wall, or simply wrapping the whole child in a strait-jacket.[6] The books for mothers and fathers did not actually advise any of these methods; but in *What a Young Wife Ought to Know* Dr. Drake called on mothers to be "Argus-eyed" in watching their babies, to keep young children from sleeping in the same bed or playing together without an adult's presence, and to teach them right attitudes at the earliest possible age.

While yet very young, they can be taught that the organs are to be used by them only for throwing off the waste water of the system, but that they are so closely related to other parts of the body that handling them at all will hurt them and make them sick. Tell them that little children, sometimes when they do not know this, form the habit of handling themselves and as a result they become listless and sick, and many times idiotic and insane, or develop epileptic fits. This will so impress them that they will not fall easily into the bad habit.[7]

Single young men who avoided the curse of self-pollution (the results of which in their book also included "the dwarfing and wasting of the organ itself"[8]) were nevertheless bedevilled with the problem of nocturnal emissions or "wet dreams." The Rev. Stall rejected the views of those experts who taught that any and all sexual emissions were indications

of coming imbecility—discounting in passing the old story
that Newton had never lost a drop of semen in his life—and
reassured his readers that even the most continent men often
experienced emissions every ten or fourteen days as a "safety-
valve." Nevertheless, it was "relatively" true that nocturnal
emissions were debilitating to the system, and "few men can
suffer emissions more frequently than once in two weeks
without serious physical loss." With proper physical and
mental habits it should be possible to avoid nocturnal emissions entirely.[9]

Resorting to sexual intercourse outside of marriage was not
an acceptable substitute for onanism. Chapters 4, 5, and 6 of
What a Young Man Ought to Know were each entitled "Evils to
be Shunned and Consequences to be Dreaded" and composed
a sixty-one page warning of the horrors of venereal disease. It
was claimed that more than 25 percent of the population was
infected with this "leprosy of lust," a sad comment on a society which inoculated its cattle against contagious diseases, but
left its own young men and women in total ignorance "to be
crushed beneath the Juggernaut of lust, disease and death, as
its gory wheels roll from ocean to ocean ... in the rising dawn
of the Twentieth Century."[10] Even the young woman of good
social standing who had innocently allowed a young man of
dubious reputation to kiss her one night on the doorstep had
fallen prey to syphilis; today she bore the loathsome dis-
figurement in consequence. "I do not need to multiply such
cases," Dr. Wood-Allen wrote. "You can be warned by one as
well as by a hundred."[11]

The chaste young couple who had enjoyed a quiet wedding
and wisely foregone an exhausting bridal tour were now
legally and morally free to indulge themselves, but not
exactly physiologically free. For they now had to deal with
the major sexual problem of married life—excess.

> Do not wait [Stall warned] until you have the pro-
> nounced effects of backache, lassitude, giddiness, dim-
> ness of sight, noises in the ears, numbness of fingers and

paralysis. Note your own condition for the next day very carefully. If you observe a lack of normal, physical power, a loss of intellectual quickness or mental grip, if you are sensitive and irritable, if you are less kind and considerate of your wife, if you are morose and less companionable, or in any way fall below your best standard of excellence, it would be well for you to think seriously and proceed cautiously.[12]

It was not entirely clear how frequently sexual intercourse could be enjoyed with safety. Some physicians were inclined to recommend once a month, but the Rev. Stall was slightly more permissive, suggesting that a couple in average health who stayed within the bounds of once a week would not be in danger of having entered upon "a life of excess."[13] On the other hand, the theory that absolute continence except for the purpose of reproduction was the ideal married state had some "very strong arguments" in its favour. Unfortunately, it required a degree of self-denial "far beyond the possession of the great mass of humanity."[14]

Nature had, however, placed a beneficial check on the natural sexual aggressiveness of males by making women sexually passive, in fact rather disinclined to participate in sexual relations at all. Husbands were to understand this diffidence in their wives, and above all to respect it. Far too many marriages were little more than legalized prostitution or arrangements by which husbands turned the right to enjoy sexual intercourse into a form of legalized rape.[15] "Be guarded, O husband!" Dr. Drake warned lustful men. "It is woman's nature to forgive,...but there comes a time when love and forgiveness have reached their limit, and love struggles vainly to rise above disgust and loathing." At the same time, though, she advised wives not to allow "little carelessnesses and thoughtless acts" to "invite attentions" which they would afterward repel. Best to preserve "womanly modesty" and "innate dignity" at all times.[16]

When men and women reached approximately age forty-five, the activity of the sexual organs would cease. Accordingly, two volumes in the Self and Sex series were designed to explain to the aging the impact of the menopause. Its main effect on sexual behaviour was flatly to rule out any further intercourse. The increased lassitude or weariness that a man of forty-five would feel after the act was a warning from nature to avoid any further use of a secretion "which can now ill be spared." Sexual indulgence from now on would merely be throwing so many pellets of earth upon his coffin. Women, too, would find that sexual relations during and after the menopause would be positively harmful, and they also had to be particularly careful during this period not to arouse their husbands.[17] But in both cases nature offered returns that fully compensated for what had been lost. Not the least of these was "the grateful sense of relief" that "the stress of the sexual impulse is gradually passing away."[18]

Before the menopause men and women of all ages could take special measures to reduce the "stress of the sexual impulse," and thereby stave off the urge to fall into one of the several kinds of sexual excess. Physical exercise was recommended for everyone, particularly bicycling, horseback riding, and calisthenics, as well as the use of dumbbells and Indian clubs by males. Cold baths or showers every morning, followed by a brisk rub-down with a course towel, were always helpful, especially for young men worried about excessive nocturnal emissions. A right diet throughout one's life was an essential complement of this regime, one which minimized the consumption of stimulating foods, such as spices, and animal foods, particularly meat. Regular evacuation of the bowels also seemed to reduce sexual propensities and contributed to general physical well-being. Further, the Rev. Stall advised that no young man troubled with sexual weakness could hope to attain entire relief while sleeping on or under bedclothes stuffed with feathers.[19] If none of this worked for a troubled young man, he could try tying a towel around his waist with a hard knot opposite the spine; by preventing him from lying on his back it would inhibit nocturnal emissions. If that failed, a footnote in *What a Young Man Ought to Know* advised that the Sax Company, 105 South Broad St., Philadelphia, offered for 50 cents "An effective and satisfactory device, to prevent lying on the back and its attendant evils."[20]

More important, sexual propensities could only ultimately be reduced by a rigid avoidance of stimulating thoughts. "No man can look upon obscene pictures without the danger of photographing upon his mind that which he might subsequently be willing to give thousands of dollars to obliterate," Stall advised young men, after earlier warning them that "The appeal to the amative and sexual nature is so universal in novels that ... no young man or young woman should be permitted to read a novel before they arrive at the age of twenty-five."[21] The Roman Catholic confessional had revealed that nineteen out of every twenty fallen women confessed the beginning of their sad state to the modern dance, and the "debasing influences" of the theatre plunged more young men into vice and sin "than it would be possible accurately to imagine."[22] The more direct carnal temptations of the married state could and should be reduced by the use of separate beds, preferably separate bedrooms, and by avoiding "the sexual excitement which comes daily by the twice-repeated exposure of dressing and undressing in each other's presence."[23] Alcohol and tobacco were condemned throughout the series as both unhealthy in general and as sexual stimulants in particular.

Many other problems peripherally related to sexual behaviour were considered in the Self and Sex books, including the need for women's dress reform to avoid the destructive effects of the "corset curse" on feminine reproductive organs, the desirability of taking a healthy and normal view of both menstruation and the curious side-effects of the menopause in women,[24] the six- to eight-week period of total confinement necessary for mothers after giving birth, and methods of caring for prostate trouble in older men (a problem on which Stall advised from his own experience). Various theories of the sex determination of children were considered, the authors leaning to the belief that children conceived early in the menstrual cycle were girls, later in the cycle, boys.[25] Abortion was condemned as infanticide, the mere desire for which might cause the birth of a monstrosity or a potential murderer.[26] Too frequent child-bearing was recognized as a problem, but the use of birth-control devices was both ineffective and injurious. The authors did delineate the "safe" period of the menstrual cycle when conception was unlikely, but generally felt that continence was the surest contraceptive (we may hope that concerned readers followed the latter advice because the recommended timing for the "safe" was exactly wrong). Marriage was a divine institution; divorce was sanctioned only for adultery and on the condition that divorcees never remarry.[27]

The most important and most emphasized of the subsidiary themes was the role of heredity in human reproduction and development. The "Law of Heredity" doomed men and women to inherit both their physical structure and all their character traits from their ancestors. All physical deformities, most kinds of insanity, venereal diseases, proclivities to sexual excess, and potential addictions to alcohol, nicotine, and masturbation passed from parent to child. So, too, did the mental impressions felt by the pregnant women, thus making it possible for women to shape the characters of their unborn children by thinking beautiful and uplifting thoughts during pregnancy, and also making it necessary for mothers to avoid upsetting experiences such as the sight of the physically deformed for fear of transmitting the same deformity to the infant in the womb.

Fortunately, the Law of Heredity was meliorated by the "Gospel of Heredity," the divine provision by which humans could overcome many, if not all, of the less fortunate effects of heredity and then transmit better qualities to succeeding generations. The Gospel of Heredity indeed held out the promise of infinitely improving the species through right physical and sexual living. In fact it was this fundamental duty to conserve and improve one's health for the sake of future generations that the authors of the "ought to know" books for women, both doctors, returned to repeatedly as the ultimate moral imperative that should bind their readers. By contrast, the Rev. Sylvanus Stall, in his books for men, was more concerned with salvation and the afterlife.[28]

Before attempting to place the ideas of the Self and Sex series in the context of North American thought on these subjects it may bear repeating that in 1915 the Methodist Church publishing house claimed these had been the best-selling books of their kind in Canada.

II

The Self and Sex series was reviewed in the *Canadian Journal of Medicine and Surgery* by Dr. B. E. McKenzie, surgeon to the Toronto Orthopedic Hospital, surgeon to the out-patient department, Toronto General Hospital, and assistant professor of clinical surgery, Ontario Medical College for Women. He found that while the books had been written for non-medical readers, "yet they throw much needed light upon subjects that the medical practitioner is called to deal with constantly, and upon which he may profitably consult this excellent series." He took issue with the question of whether conception during a state of intoxication would produce alcoholic offspring, but without further quibbling concluded that "Every book of the series may be confidently recommended...as containing the very best statement of the important information which should be supplied to every young man and woman, every boy and girl, entering upon the duties and responsibilities of life."[29]

This is not a surprising review, inasmuch as "Leading Canadian Medical Men" were at approximately the same time supplying exactly similar information on sexual problems to the Canadian public in the pages of one of the few native-Canadian home medical encyclopaedias, *The Family Physician, Or, Every Man His Own Doctor*. Here, too, masturbation destroyed beauty and manhood, leading to "absolute idiocy or a premature and most horrible death"; frequent nocturnal emissions were very harmful; children had to be shielded from late hours, sensational novels, questionable pictorial illustrations, love stories, the drama and the ball-room, all to avoid unnaturally hastening puberty; and engaged couples were commanded to exercise "caution and reserve" in their ordinary embraces because "one impure, indelicate, or low word uttered in the ear of a truly chaste and virtuous woman may be destructive of her true happiness for all time to come."[30]

Clearly, then, there was little in the complex of sexual beliefs and maxims popularized by the Self and Sex series that Canadian doctors found objectionable.

On the simplest level much of this ready medical acceptance of what now seems to be quaint, ludicrous, and/or harmful can be explained by reference to the state of medical and scientific research in the late nineteenth century. Doctrines of prenatal influence or "maternal impressions," for example, rested in large part on medical confusion about the physiological bond between mother and foetus during gestation. Doctors did not know the extent to which mental and physical shocks to a mother's system were transferred along with food and oxygen through the wall of the placenta. Lacking this basic physiological knowledge they had to pay attention to the many current stories about monstrosities and geniuses being the products of maternal impressions. Nineteenth-century medical journals are laced with reports of such cases.[31] Similarly, the key problem in the field of evolutionary thought—the question of the inheritance of acquired characteristics—would only be finally clarified at the beginning of the twentieth century by the discovery of the mechanism of genetic transmission. Until then there was no basic contradiction between Darwinian thought and the "Law" and "Gospel" of Heredity.[32]

On the crucial issue of masturbation the medical profession had long been aware of the seemingly empirically based conclusions of the first medical personnel to observe uncontrolled masturbation among large groups of people—the superintendents of asylums for the mentally ill. In a classic application of the *post hoc propter hoc* fallacy, these well-intentioned doctors (influenced as well by eighteenth-century preconceptions) concluded that as much as 50 percent of mental illness stemmed from masturbation. In their concern they penned horrifying descriptions of the effects of the practice that were often copied from their reports by the authors of popular sex manuals. Two Canadian doctors, Joseph Workman and Daniel Clarke, successive superintendents of the Toronto Asylum for the Insane, contributed mightily to the nineteenth-century masturbation scare in their respective 1865 and 1877 annual reports, anticipating everything that would be said about masturbation in the Self and Sex books. In fact, Workman's 1865 observations about the secret vice found a prominent place in one of the most popular post-Civil War American sex manuals, and were being reprinted in popular literature at least as late as 1911.[33] Although Canadian medical attitudes towards masturbation began to change gradually by the mid-1880s,[34] the up-to-date medical student of 1909 would still find in the seventh edition of William Osler's *The Principles and Practice of Medicine* that "sexual excess, particularly masturbation," was an important causal factor in hysteria, and that sexual excesses were in a number of instances responsible for neurasthenia or nervous exhaustion.[35]

By far the most influential factor shaping medical and popular attitudes towards sexuality was the persistence of vitalist concepts in physiological thought throughout the nineteenth century. Until late in the century any systematic theory of the human organism almost by definition implied the belief in some vital force or vital principle uniting its parts and enervating it in its totality. This could be just simple "vital force" or "life force," or in some of the more esoteric medical systems it could be any or all of magnetism, electricity, galvanism, animal heat, nervous energy, or nerve force. Sexual activity was the function of the human system most obviously connected with transmitting forces vital to human existence—it was the activity that transmitted life itself. Accordingly, the identification of vital energy with sexual energy was made by virtually all writers on sexual problems in the nineteenth century.[36]

This was done in two basic ways. Those writers who followed the system of the Swiss doctor S. A. Tissot (whose 1758 book on onanism was a classic in the field) taught that male semen was pure condensed vital energy, secreted from the blood for the purpose of creating a new life—a concept summarized in the engaging phrase *totus homo semen est*. The other system, first popularized in North America by Sylvester Graham in the 1830s, saw the sex act as involving an enormous release of nervous energy, a force akin to electricity. This latter view, a variation of which became physiological orthodoxy in the last third of the century, had among other things the merit of restoring the idea of some sexual sensitivity to women. Most sex manuals, however, including the Self and Sex books, mixed the two theories indiscriminately, and were generally muddled, usually dubious, about female sexuality.[37]

Whether male semen was pure vital force or whether sexual energy was simply another form of nervous energy, its expenditure was obviously a drain on the limited amount of vital energy in the human system. This is the heart of the matter. All the prohibitions and restrictions on sexual activity follow. Masturbation, nocturnal emissions, sexual intercourse itself, all represented outpourings of vital energy, the preservation of which was absolutely essential to the well-being of the human organism. As Sylvanus Stall told young men with emphasis, "Nature has provided us not only with the sacs for the retention of seminal fluid, but *its retention is necessary in*

*order that this vitalizing and life-giving fluid may be reabsorbed
into the system, and become the vitalizing and strength-giving source
of added physical and intellectual power.*"[38]

Here, then, is what might be called the doctrine of creative
sexual repression. Because sexual energy is vital energy, or life
force, it is too important to the whole physical economy to be
expended in autoerotism or mere sexual intercourse without
procreation! Far better to repress urges to waste the energy in
basically animal activities and instead use it for truly human,
truly creative, intellectual, and aesthetic purposes. In themselves sexual energy and man's sexual nature were good, and
the act of propagating a new life by the transmission of life
force was one of the great creative achievements open to man.
The only thing evil or harmful about sexuality was the way it
could be misused, abused, or indulged in irresponsibly, in
other words, wasted in non-creative activities.

(It appears that one of the implications of these vitalist
physiologies was the belief that the second most demanding
drain on vital energy was intellectual activity; thus the mind
suffered most when vital force was expended in sexual activity. Therefore, idiocy was thought to be an even more common consequence of masturbation than death. Further, the
idea of a competition between sex life and intellect as the
major consumers of vital force seems to have provided the
physiological underpinning for several nineteenth and twentieth century popular beliefs: that the nervous, intellectual
child or man was the most liable to have sexual problems;
that negroes, who were obviously short of mental ability,
must have enlarged sexual inclinations by way of explanation
or compensation; that as civilization grew ever more complex, requiring the expenditure of ever more intellectual
force, the stock of vital energy available for reproduction
would be diminished—hence the falling birth rate in the
most advanced western civilizations and fears that the most
advanced "races" would be swamped by simpler peoples who
had more energy available for copulation and reproduction.
A. R. M. Lower's 1943 article, "Two Ways of Life: The
Primary Antithesis of Canadian History," seems to contain a

representative expression of these latter fears in a Canadian setting, the physiological bases assumed.)[39]

The Self and Sex manuals were late products of a long North American tradition of home advice on sexual problems. Dozens of books on anatomy, physiology, marriage, parenthood, masturbation, etc., were churned out in the United States from the 1830s, most of them written by members of health cults or medical sects, including vegetarians, phrenologists, homeopaths, and hydropaths.[40] These authors and medical practitioners were stepping into a sort of medical vacuum created by the retreat of orthodox doctors into a medical eclecticism which for a time seemed to offer neither cures nor explanations of illness.[41] The new cultists were drawn to sexual problems partly because of orthodox medicine's reluctance to deal with them at all, partly because their systematic physiologies, usually throwbacks to the vitalism of earlier medical thought, seemed to lead directly to dislocations of vital energy as a basic cause of illness. Gradually, the regular medical profession stepped back into the field, but in so doing accepted and reinforced many of the ideas of the cultists. The influences of vegetarianism and the hydropathic (or "water-cure") system of medicine on sexual theories seem to have lingered on in the Self and Sex series' concern with reducing sexual passion by eliminating meat from the diet and by frequent bathing (and to this day Canadians continue to enjoy other legacies of the vegetarian-sexologists—the foods named after Sylvester Graham and the corn flakes and peanut butter invented by John Harvey Kellogg to make vegetarian dishes palatable at his Battle Creek Sanitarium. Kellogg's establishment was the great North American health-cure institute of the late nineteenth century, having enjoyed its first popularity catering to the young men and women terrified of the consequences of sexual excess portrayed in the director's best-selling sex manual, *Plain Facts for Old and Young*).[42]

The doctrine of creative sexual repression was intensely idealistic. Philosophic idealism was at the basis of the vitalist physiology that provided the foundations of the doctrine.

Practical idealism was inherent in the work of the medical sectarians whose systems appealed to those who hoped for a medical millennium at a time when the orthodox profession was wallowing in uncertainty. The whole movement for physiologic and sexual reform was in every way connected with the outpouring of idealism in the form of a secularized evangelicalism that caused the ferment of reform movements in the United States in the 1840s and 1850s. The evangelists of sexual repression had extremely close links with anti-slavery work, the public health movement, the movement to liberate women — often, indeed to liberate them from male sexual tyranny — and with utopian "perfectionists" such as the Shakers and John Humphrey Noyes' Oneida Community. As S. W. Nissenbaum has shown, even the founders of the American free love movement, the most radical product of "freedom's ferment" in the mid-nineteenth century, were imbued with the idealism of sexual repression; freedom to love, they taught, could be safely enjoyed about once every two years. In the post-Civil War years the institutionalized "Purity" movement — in which the Self and Sex authors were deeply involved — was the crystallization of this basic idealism, the determination to purify human life of everything that tempted or conduced to harmful mental and physical practices.[43] Further, it was precisely the metaphysical idealism of these new Puritans, stressing the ability of mind to manipulate matter, that led them to advocate the most rigid forms of state thought-control in order to protect young men and women from powerful ideas that would stimulate the material, animal passions of the body. Censorship was a form of idealistic reform. After all, only a good idealist would believe that a young woman really could be ruined by a book.[44]

If this account seems to be becoming a bit thin on purely Canadian sexual thought, consider the work of Alexander Milton Ross, a Belleville boy who was introduced into American reform circles in the 1840s by the exiled reformer Marshal Spring Bidwell. Ross took a medical degree in hydropathy in the United States, was led from friendship with leading abolitionists into active work in the South encouraging negroes to flee to Canada, was a close friend of reformers ranging from Garibaldi to John Brown, and was employed by Lincoln as a special agent in Canada during the Civil War. After the war he became one of the most renowned Canadian naturalists, was president of the vegetarian Food Reform Society of Canada, worked for temperance, women's suffrage, and women's dress reform, took credit for securing Garibaldi a pension from the Italian government, and led the anti-vaccination crusade in Montreal in 1885 (on the ground that vaccination for smallpox was a deadly ruse on the part of the Establishment to avoid its moral and social responsibility for public health). In the midst of all these activities Dr. Ross concluded from studies of insane asylum reports that fully "ONE-THIRD" of all the insane had brought the curse upon themselves by "indulgence in an unphysiological habit practised in ignorance of the results." Finding that no voice of alarm was being raised in Canada about this "worm eating at the core of society, and doing more injury than all other diseases combined," Ross resolved to do his duty. In the quarter century after Confederation he distributed, he claims, 600,000 pieces of literature alerting the Canadian public to the evils of masturbation.[45] Crusading for sexual enlightenment was then, as it is now, a necessary part of the work of any thorough-going reformer dedicated to the perfection of the human condition.

III

The Self and Sex books were advertised extensively through the Methodist Church publishing house for at least fifteen years. It seems reasonable to assume at a minimum that they were standard reference works for Methodist ministers concerned with their own and their congregations' sexual problems (the Methodist minister, for example, who wrote Sir

Wilfrid Laurier about the plight of a young lady whose husband had gone insane through self-abuse and abandoned her).[46] The series was also widely circulated by the ladies of the Canadian Woman's Christian Temperance Union, whose Department of Social Purity was specifically designed to promote the doctrine of sexual repression in all of its manifestations.[47] Dr. Ross's flood of anti-masturbation literature was supplemented by Dr. Daniel Clark's circulation of 600 copies of his own 1877 report on masturbation and insanity. The letters from educators and clergymen included in Ross's autobiography suggest widespread, semi-underground fears of and campaigns against the secret vice in the two generations after Confederation.[48] So, too, do the notes on new cures for onanism and nocturnal emissions routinely printed in Canadian medical journals—such as the 1869 suggestion of Dr. George Wood that the application of a strip of isinglass adhesive plaster "worked like a charm" in cases of incurable masturbation (after tying the hands, using hair gloves, croton oil linament, moral suasion, and many other methods had failed).[49] In addition, anyone who has browsed through nineteenth-century Canadian newspapers will have noticed the hundreds of brands of compounds, pills, tonics, magnetic and electrical devices offered by quack doctors, to cure, among other things, "sexual weakness," "unnatural drains," "failing manhood," and "diseases peculiar to women." The fact of these ads indicates that a large market existed; their language suggests a general belief in the basic equation of sexual energy and vital energy.[50]

Research into the activities of YMCA groups, youth movements such as the Boy Scouts, and possibly certain religious denominations like the Salvation Army would almost certainly locate more evidence of the work of purity reformers in Canada before World War I. From 1906 to at least 1915 there existed a formal purity organization, the Canadian Purity-Education Association, staffed mainly by doctors and operating out of Toronto. In 1914 it sponsored fifty-six lectures on aspects of social purity, probably largely on the evils of venereal disease and masturbation. It distributed literature across Canada and in the United States, and reported in 1915 that its speakers were in great demand for mothers', girls', and women's meetings.[51]

In his recent book of memoirs, *Never Sleep Three in a Bed*, Max Braithwaite has finally broken the tacit conspiracy of silence about sexuality in Canadian history by describing his own sex education in Saskatoon in the 1920s. It featured books like *The Young Husband's Guide to Married Sex*, a horrifying tract on *The Solitary Vice*, and an earnest drill and hygiene teacher who with "jaw out-thrust" and "eyes flashing" lectured to young boys on the dangers of losing their manhood. "'Take it out in good manly sport—such as boxing, wrestling, club-swinging and the rest'," he told his pupils. "I was so ashamed I couldn't look at him," says Braithwaite.[52] Undoubtedly, there are similar stories to be told in memoirs yet unwritten.

We also know that in Ontario between 1905 and 1911, 13,463 public school boys received the "advanced" purity lectures given by the Ontario WCTUs "Purity Agent," one Arthur W. Beall, a former missionary and teacher in Japan who had returned to Canada after suffering a nervous breakdown.[53] The main theme of these special talks was the danger involved in young boys bleeding away the "LIFE FLUID" from the "MALE PART." It had been secreted from the "LIFE GLANDS" and was needed to feed the brain and the nervous system. Repeated draining of this fluid would occasionally lead to death, but usually to something "ten thousand times worse than dying"—the fate of Henry, the farm boy from Perth County whose evil habits had led to hospitalization in the insane asylum. Nevertheless, Henry continued to bleed away the precious "LIFE FLUID," "until one day the doctors came along and cut off the two LIFE GLANDS just to keep the miserable dregs of a miserable existence from all being frittered away." The Henry incident was told in Lesson Nine of Mr. Beall's trail-breaking classes in sex education. The same lesson ended a few moments later with the boys all repeating after him, "The more you use the penis muscle, the weaker it becomes; but the less you use the penis muscle, the stronger it becomes."[54]

In 1911 the WCTU arranged to have the Ontario Department of Education take over this work and appoint Beall as a special lecturer.[55] He continued to lecture to Ontario pupils all through the 1920s and well on into the 1930s. The department took no official notice of his work in its reports. But acquaintances of mine remember with no little vividness this little white-haired man, dressed in a flowing red-and-blue cloak, the expression on his face of a "benign Hindenburg," striding about their classrooms delivering what he now called his "eugenics" lectures in the 1930s — interesting young boys, it is thought, in masturbation for the first time in their lives.[56] When Arthur Beall died in 1939 the *Globe and Mail* hailed him as "one of the best informed men on educational matters in Canada."[57]

The doctrine of creative sexual repression represented the orthodox, even the "enlightened" sexual attitudes of those English-speaking Canadians who read about such problems before World War I. Indeed it was sexual orthodoxy throughout much of the Western world, and therefore I would be very surprised to find any significant variation of these attitudes in whatever literature in the French language on these questions that may have circulated in Canada.[58] In this paper I have tried to explain the doctrine of creative sexual repression and explore its paternity in medical and popular thought. This has been only a discussion of the *ideas* of sexuality held by well-informed Canadians of the period. It will be up to future research to correlate these ideas with the actual sexual *behaviour* of all Canadians. Such research might include studies of prostitution through police records, court cases, and army records, as well as analyses of illegitimacy rates, birth rates, and the time-lag between marriage and the birth of a first child. Probably Canadian sexual behaviour will be shown to be related to social class, and historians should be able to apply psychological and sociological tools to explain why some classes accepted extremely repressive ideas of sexuality both in theory and practice while others did not. When we finally know who believed what and which groups acted on their beliefs, then perhaps psychologists can explore the effects of various sexual attitudes on the people who held them or were exposed to them. As a preliminary observation I think we can safely say that the doctrine of sexual repression added somewhat to the anxieties of middle class Canadians.[59]

Whatever emerges from more sophisticated and detailed future studies, I would like to urge Canadian historians to take this esoteric form of social history seriously. It has been ignored in our literature to the point where our readers might well conclude that sex simply hasn't been a factor in Canadian life. Yet who can deny that the problem of coming to terms with the fact of sex has caused Canadians more concern than the activities of all their politicians combined?

Notes

I would like to record my debt for support in this and other work to my brother, the late Dr. James Quartus Bliss.

1. For further biographical information on Stall and Wood-Allen, see *Who's Who in America*, 2 (Chicago, 1901–2): 1072, 1260; on Drake, *Woman's Who's Who of America*, 1914–15 (New York, 1914), p. 258. The circulation claim is contained in the frontispiece of the 1908 revised edition of *What a Young Wife Ought to Know*. The best-selling claim is contained in the Briggs advertisement in *The Canadian Woman's Annual and Social Service Directory* (Toronto, 1915), p. 325. The series was also regularly advertised in the *Christian Guardian* beginning in 1902. About 1908 most of the books in the series were slightly revised; in the late 1920s they were considerably rewritten and watered down. The Ryerson Press still distributed the series in Canada in the 1930s. All quotations are from the first edition.
2. Sylvanus Stall, *What a Young Man Ought to Know* (Philadelphia, 1897), p. 23.
3. Sylvanus Stall, *What a Young Husband Ought to Know* (Philadelphia, 1897), pp. 125, 127.

4. Mary Wood-Allen, M.D., *What a Young Woman Ought to Know* (Philadelphia, 1898), p. 116.

5. Sylvanus Stall, *What a Young Boy Ought to Know* (Philadelphia, 1897), pp. 104-5.

6. Ibid., p. 107.

7. Emma F. Angell Drake, M.D., *What a Young Wife Ought to Know* (Philadelphia, 1901), p. 239.

8. Stall, *Young Man*, pp. 56-57.

9. Ibid., pp. 72-77.

10. Ibid., pp. 98, 140. Also p. 121: "It has for years been a serious question in our mind whether, for the protection of the pure, the government should not brand upon the forehead those who have this disease, so that they could always be recognized."

11. Wood-Allen, *Young Woman*, p. 230.

12. Stall, *Young Husband*, pp. 95-96.

13. Ibid., p. 95.

14. Ibid., pp. 87-88

15. Ibid., chs. 2, 3, 9, 10. Especially p. 49: "With rare exceptions, both of person and of instances, in married life all the sexual aggressiveness is with the male. Wives seldom seek the closer embraces of their husbands. They are generally indifferent; often absolutely averse. With the husband, while in perfect health, the conditions are quite the opposite; and the wisdom of the Creator is manifest in the fact that were the wife equally quickened by the same amative tendencies, the male nature would be called into such frequent and continuous exercise that the power of reproduction would be either totally destroyed or so impaired that the race would degenerate into moral, intellectual and physical pigmies. God has made the passivity of the wife the protection of her husband and a source of manifold blessing to her children.

    "Upon the other hand, her uninterrupted and entire neglect of the sexual relation is wisely overcome, to the advantage of the wife, by her husband's greater sexual activity."

16. Drake, *Young Wife*, pp. 84-85.

17. Sylvanus Stall, *What a Man of 45 Ought to Know* (Philadelphia, 1901), pp. 78, 84; Emma F. Angell Drake, *What a Woman of 45 Ought to Know* (Philadelphia, 1902), pp. 148, 157-58.

18. Stall, *Man of 45*, p. 60.

19. Stall, *Young Boy*, part 4; Stall, *Young Man*, ch. 3; Wood-Allen, *Young Women*, chs. 3, 8, 9; feather beds, *Young Man*, p. 54.

20. Stall, *Young Man*, p. 89.
21. Ibid., pp. 241, 33.
22. Ibid., pp. 243, 245.
23. Stall, *Young Husband*, p. 100; Drake, *Young Wife*, p. 85.
24. Women were thought to exhibit such extraordinary behaviour during the menopause — dim vision, loss of voice, spitting of blood, hysteria, melancholia, loss of religious interest, etc. — that Stall took pains to convince their spouses not to have such women removed to insane asylums. *Man of 45*, chs. 16-18.
25. Stall, *Young Husband*, p. 288. Discussing "signs of fruitful conjunction," i.e., conception, Stall noted that "with some women the act of conception is attended with great emotion, a sense of unusual pleasure, and even of a tremor, in which all parts of the body may participate. Sometimes it is followed by a sense of weakness." Ibid., p. 95. This is the only hint that the authors of the series were aware of the female orgasm.
26. Ibid., p. 159.
27. All of Stall's thought was permeated with Christian verbiage. Early in his book for husbands he pleaded with his readers to practise Christianity, outlining in passing his remarkable sociology: one should divide society into two classes, "and then the result is seen at a glance. In the one class you have the profane, the vicious, the intemperate, the dishonest, the law-breakers, and the defiers of God and man. To this class belongs every man who staggers, reels and falls into the gutter, every tramp who walks the road, and nine-tenths of all persons who fill our almshouses. It includes, with scarcely an exception, every man and woman who fill our prisons and reformatory institutions; those who crowd the great tenements and live in filth and squalor in the slums of our cities; those whose bodies reek with physical and moral rottenness — these, and many others, constitute the class of the ungodly, and no attentive person can fail to observe that this is the character of that portion which the ungodly have in this world.

    "Now, turn to the other class. Walk up and down the streets where you find the most comfortable homes, the largest dwellings, and abodes of the most affluent and respectable in any city, and then answer the question, whether or no the wealth of the nation is not to-day largely in the hands of Christian men and Christian women? These are the people who have the best credit, who can draw checks for the largest amounts. Among this class you will find the most influential in business, the owners of our largest mercantile establishments. Men who direct and control the commerce of the world. Men who are at the head of our largest banking institutions, railroad and other corporations. But not only so. These are the people who dwell in the best homes, who eat the best food, who have the largest amount of material comforts. They are the people who enjoy the best health, who have the brightest minds, who produce the best books, the most helpful literature. They have the brightest eyes and the strongest bodies, and when cholera and plague come and sweep away men and women by the thousands, it scarcely ever crosses the line which separates these from the intemperate and the vicious, who go down before these scourges like grass before the sickle. Truly, my dear friend, if you are to look at it only from this lowest plane of present good and material comfort, godly living will bring to you the promise of life that *now* is, and in addition you will also have the promise of the life that is *to come.*" Stall, *Young Husband*, pp. 71–73. This passage was reprinted without alteration in the 1933 revision of the book.

28. On heredity, see Stall, *Young Husband*, ch. 17; Wood-Allen, *Young Woman*, chs. 28–30; Drake, *Young Wife*, ch. 11. On maternal impressions, Stall, *Young Husband*, ch. 18; Drake, *Young Wife*, ch. 8.

29. *Canadian Journal of Medicine and Surgery* 12, no. 2 (August 1902): 147–48.

30. *The Family Physician* (Toronto: Musson, n.d.), pp. 328, 164, 319, 332. Medical librarians have been unable to date this book; internal evidence suggests 1890–1905. The publishers deliberately left it undated to maintain the aura of up-to-date authority.

31. In *Ædæology, A Treatise on Generative Life* (New York, 1892), Dr. Sydney Barrington Elliott includes a list of several hundred articles on prenatal influences. For Canada, see J. Draewieki, "The Influence of Maternal Impressions Upon the Foetus," *Canada Lancet* 24 (December 1891): 110–13, in which it is concluded, "I am thoroughly convinced that different psychical and physical defects...are in most instances the results of moral impressions derived from the surroundings of the mother."

32. Mark H. Haller, *Eugenics, Hereditarian Attitudes in American Thought* (New Brunswick, N.J., 1963), pp. 59–61. Haller notes that the new theories denying the inheritance of acquired characteristics seriously distressed social reformers, who were now told that the achievements of one generation would not

be passed on to the next. For this reason the Self and Sex authors also rejected the new doctrine that had just been proclaimed. See Stall, *Young Man*, pp. 236-37.

33. *Report of the Inspectors and the Medical Superintendent of the Provincial Lunatic Asylum, Toronto, for the Year 1865* (Toronto, 1866), pp. 35-43; *Report of the Medical Superintendent of the Asylum for the Insane, Toronto, 1877* (Toronto, 1878), pp. 18-26. Workman's report was initially reprinted in John Cowan, M.D., *The Science of a New Life* (New York, 1869) and as part of the excerpts from Cowan in *The Education of Sex, a Compilation from the writings and teachings of many eminent physicians and authorities...forming a textbook on the Physiology of Marriage, the Phenomena of Life, Existing Social Evils and their Needed Reforms* (Philadelphia, 1911). For a definitive account of medical attitudes towards masturbation see E. H. Hare, "Masturbatory Insanity: The History of an Idea," *Journal of Mental Science* 108, (January 1962): 1-25.

34. Stephen Lett, "The Relationship of Insanity to Masturbation," *Canada Lancet* 19 (August, 1887): 360-63, argued that masturbation was more a symptom than a cause of mental disorder; the practice was so widespread that it could not possibly cause insanity. See also Hare, "Masturbatory Insanity." As Prof. Frank MacKinnon pointed out in the discussion at the initial presentation of this paper, other doctors seem to have held similar common-sense attitudes to the phenomenon.

35. (New York, 1909), pp. 1077, 1087.

36. Among numerous other sex manuals that have been consulted the most representative are John Cowan, *The Science of a New Life* (New York, 1869); J. H. Kellogg, *Plain Facts for Old and Young* (Burlington, Iowa, 1879; rev. ed. 1886); Diocletian Lewis, *Chastity, or Our Secret Sins* (Philadelphia, New York, Boston, Cincinnati, Chicago, 1875); George H. Napheys, *The Transmission of Life* (Philadelphia, 1870). At an indeterminate later date the Hunter, Rose Co. of Toronto published an "Enlarged and Revised" edition of Napheys. It is slightly more technical and moderate than the Self and Sex books, but not significantly different. The Cowan book, copies of which circulated in Canada, represents the extreme of nineteenth-century sexology: it calls for total vegetarianism to repress sexual desires and marital intercourse no more frequently than every two years—for the sole purpose of conception.

37. On Graham and Tissot, see S. W. Nissenbaum, "Careful Love: Sylvester Graham and the Emergence of Victorian Sexual

Theory in America, 1830–1840" (Ph.D. thesis, Wisconsin, 1968), esp. ch. 6. The Latin phrase is quoted in Lewis, *Chastity*, p. 245. For more orthodox concepts of nervous energy, neurasthenia, and the belief in the conservation of energy, see Charles E. Rosenberg, "The Place of George M. Beard in Nineteenth-Century Psychiatry," *Bulletin of the History of Medicine* 36, no. 3 (1962): 245–59; Rosenberg, "Science and American Social Thought," in David Van Tassel and Michael G. Hall, eds., *Science and Society in the United States* (Homewood, Ill., 1966).

38. Stall, *Young Man*, p. 75. Also Cowan, *Science of a New Life*, p. 91-92; Lewis, *Chastity*, pp. 25, 245–46; Kellogg, *Plain Facts*, p. 277.

39. This concept also seems to have been popularized by Tissot. In *De La Santé Des Gens de Lettres* (Lausanne, 1770) he claimed that excessive mental activity resulted in the same disorders as masturbation. On the later idea of industrial society as consumer of nervous energy, see Rosenberg, "The Place of George M. Beard in Nineteenth-Century Psychiatry," and John Duffy, "Mental Strain and 'Overpressure' in the Schools: A Nineteenth-Century Viewpoint," *Journal of the History of Medicine and Allied Sciences* 23, no. 1 (June 1968): 63–79. For fears of the impact of education on reproduction see Arthur Wallace Calhoun, *A Social History of the American Family* (Cleveland, 1919), 3: 92-93. There is a clear statement of the myth of negro sexuality in Eugene S. Talbot, *Degeneracy, Its Causes, Signs, and Results* (London, 1898), p. 60. The best statement of the general concept of the problem is in W. H. Walling, *Sexology* (Philadelphia, 1904), p. 97: "A learned author has said that one must choose between leaving to posterity works of genius or children." The Lower article is reprinted in C. C. Berger, ed., *Approaches to Canadian History* (Toronto, 1967).

40. American historians are just beginning to investigate this body of literature. Nissenbaum, "Careful Love," is invaluable—and includes a comprehensive bibliography of primary sources. See also Sidney Ditzion, *Marriage, Morals and Sex in America* (New York, 1953), and Eric John Dingwall, *The American Woman, A Historical Study* (London, 1956). Gerald Carson, *The Cornflake Crusade* (New York, 1957), ostensibly a study of the breakfast food industry, is an excellent survey of the health cults, unfortunately omitting the sexual emphasis.

41. Richard H. Shryock, *The Development of Modern Medicine* (Philadelphia, 1936), chs. 9–13; Joseph F. Kett, *The Formation*

of the American Medical Profession, The Role of Institutions, 1780-1860 (New Haven, 1968), pp. 65ff.

42. On the Kelloggs and Battle Creek, see Carson, *Cornflake Crusade*; Ronald M. Deutsch, *The Nuts Among the Berries* (New York, 1961); and Horace B. Powell, *The Original Has This Signature—"W. K. Kellogg"* (Englewood Cliffs, N.J., 1956). Although these authors ignore Kellogg's sex manuals, the inference about the growth of the sanitarium is reasonable in view of Kellogg's discussion of masturbation and his work with its victims in *Plain Facts*. His methods of treatment ranged from circumcision and the use of metal cages through suturing the male foreskin shut and applying pure carbonic acid to the female clitoris. *Plain Facts*, pp. 294-96. Kellogg also argued that nocturnal emissions in males were no more necessary than vomiting. Consistent with his theories he remained continent throughout his life although he was married and adopted several dozen children; Mrs. Kellogg was active in purity work with the WCTU.

43. Nissenbaum, "Careful Love"; on the purity movement, see David J. Pivar, "The New Abolitionism; The Quest for Social Purity, 1876-1900" (Ph.D. thesis, University of Pennsylvania, 1965). The best published discussion and interpretation of "freedom's ferment" is still Gilbert Seldes, *The Stammering Century* (New York, 1928, reissued, 1964). See also Carson, *Cornflake Crusade*, and the discussion of the Shakers and the Oneida Community in Lewis, *Chastity*.

Noyes' doctrine of "male continence" involved complete *coitus reservatus*; male incontinence, or sexual intercourse to orgasm, was nothing more than masturbation. Vital forces would only be expended for the purpose of procreation. Although conservative sexologists were repelled by the Oneida community's adoption of communal marriage and distrusted the idea of male continence, the doctrine lived on and ultimately came to Canada in the form of Dr. Alice Stockham's book on *Karezza* (orign. pub., 1896, rev. ed., 1905) or "a controlled sexual relation." When properly practised Karezza represented sexual "expression" rather than "repression" and was also an effective method of contraception. *Karezza* was given a most enthusiastic review at the 1896 Dominion Convention of the Canadian WCTU by the superintendent of the Department of Purity in Literature, Arts and Fashion, who recommended that it "should be put into the hands of every young man before marriage." *Report of the Ninth Convention of the Dominion Woman's Christian Temperance Union, 1896* (Montreal, 1897), p. 63. In 1911 McClelland & Goodchild published a Canadian edition of Dr. Stockham's earlier *Tokology* (first edition, 1883), a book on the "science of midwifery" which advocated painless child-birth through dress reform and vegetarian dietetics. *Tokology* is also one of the clearest demonstrations of the link between the women's rights movement and the doctrine of sexual repression.

44. Popular idealism, the belief in the supremacy of mind over matter, permeated North American popular culture in the late nineteenth century. See, for example, Donald Meyer, *The Positive Thinkers* (New York, 1965), and Richard Weiss, *The American Myth of Success* (New York, 1969). Doctrines of "thought power" and the "mind cure" reached their apogee in Christian Science. Their sexual implications came to their logical culmination in 1890 when Josephine Curtis Woodbury, a Christian Scientist, announced that she had had a virginal conception (the child was named "Prince of Peace"). The Self and Sex books for women stressed thought power to the point where denials had to be made that they were preaching Christian Science doctrine.

45. Alexander Milton Ross, *Memoirs of a Reformer* (Toronto, 1893); for his anti-masturbation work see pp. 215–18, 261–65. Further biographical data is in H.J. Morgan, *The Canadian Men and Women of the Time* (Toronto, 1898), pp. 883–84.

46. PAC, Laurier Papers, 62267–9, Rev. W. J. Waddell to Laurier, 1 February 1902.

47. See the *Reports* of Dominion WCTU Conventions, 1890–1911.

48. Ross, *Memoirs of a Reformer*, pp. 261–65.

49. "A Prevention for Priapism, due to Onanism," *Canada Medical Journal* (November 1869): 246–47. This suggestion was reprinted in Napheys, *The Transmission of Life*. For a suggestion of suturing with silver wire see "The Prevention of Masturbation," *Canadian Journal of Medical Science* (November 1876): 394. On the application of blisters and tonics to cure seminal emissions see "The Treatment of Seminal Emissions," *Canada Lancet* 21 (July 1889): 340.

50. Phrases taken from advertisements in the Toronto *Globe*, 1, 6, 9 September 1899. The quacks did their best business playing on fears of venereal disease ("blood poisoning"), impotence, and sterility. One of the curious implications of the doctrine of sexual repression was that too much sexual activity led to the

inability to perform at all, vital energy having been exhausted. Accordingly, the less one performed the better one performed. The Self and Sex books repeatedly warned their readers against falling into the hands of quacks, particularly those who offered to cure venereal disease. To some extent, of course, the sex writers were competing in the same market with the quacks.

51. *The Canadian Woman's Annual and Social Service Directory*, p. 273.

52. Max Braithwaite, *Never Sleep Three in a Bed* (Toronto, 1969), p. 148.

53. Figures compiled from *Reports* of Ontario WCTU Conventions, 1902–12. For biographical data on Beall, see the Toronto *Globe and Mail*, 11 November 1939, and H. J. Morgan, *Canadian Men and Women of the Time* (Toronto, 1912), p. 72.

54. Arthur W. Beall, *The Living Temple, A Manual on Eugenics for Parents and Teachers* (Whitby, 1933), pp. 62–65, 67. This little book is a word by word account of Beall's lessons.

55. *Report of the Minister of Education, Province of Ontario, for the Year 1911* (Toronto, 1912), p. 269.

56. Interview with the Rev. Harold Hendershot, April 1970.

57. 11 November 1939.

58. Particularly because of the affinity of the doctrine with Roman Catholic sexual thought and ultimately the ideas of St. Paul. Although nineteenth-century science challenged Christian ideology in many fields, in the area of sexual thought it obviously reinforced Christian beliefs. This is probably the chief reason why liberalism came to sex so much later than to other fields of human activity.

59. In chapter 1 of *The Other Victorians* (New York, 1966) Stephen Marcus attempts a general explanation of nineteenth-century sexual orthodoxy (as mirrored in Dr. William Acton's popular writings) as functions of an "essentially mechanical," "primitive form of materialism," that relied heavily on an economic model of scarcity, specifically the equation of male semen with money. This is largely incorrect. The doctrine of sexual repression was permeated with idealism. While the analogy with capitalism does hold, there is no evidence of a causal relationship. The economics of sexual scarcity arose out of the Newtonian concept of the universe and the second law of thermodynamics and were thus independent of the economics of capital scarcity.

Birth Control and Abortion in Canada, 1870-1920

ANGUS MCLAREN

In the spring of 1908 the congregation of Toronto's St. James' Cathedral was informed by the Reverend C. Ensor Sharp that the Almighty interested himself directly in the demographic details of Canada's declining birth rate: "God abhors the spirit so prevalent nowadays which contemns [*sic*] motherhood. How it must grieve Him when He sees what we call race suicide; when He sees the problem of married life approached lightly and wantonly; based on nothing higher and nobler than mere luxury and gratification of passion."[1] This fear of "race suicide" to which Sharp referred had been popularized in North America by President Theodore Roosevelt whose statement, "The woman who flinches from childbirth stands on a par with the soldier who drops his rifle and runs in battle," was only the most famous remark to be made by a generation of social observers who attributed the shrinking size of the Anglo-Saxon family to the "selfishness" of

Reprinted by permission of the author and University of Toronto Press from *Canadian Historical Review* 59, no. 3 (1978): 319-40.

women. By the turn of the century Canadians were well acquainted with such concerns. In the Canadian edition of Sylvanus Stall's *What a Young Man Ought to Know* (1897), the author expressed his horror that many women married, not to bear children, but "for the purpose of practically leading a life of legalized prostitution."[2] Crown Attorney J. W. Curry, KC, addressing the city pastors of Toronto in 1901, claimed that employment opportunities permitted women to avoid marriage or to fall back on "crime" which led to a "low birth rate."[3] According to Professor H. E. Armstrong, speaking at the 1909 Winnipeg meeting of the British Association, all attempts to bring women into competition with men were dangerous, "...for she will inevitably cease to exercise her specific womanly functions with effect, so delicate is the adjustment of her mechanism."[4] A contributor to the *Canadian Churchman* (1900) went so far as to assert that even the pressures of existing society encouraged, "to put it bluntly, in nine cases out of ten, women to murder their unborn children."[5]

What exercised the imaginations of these writers was the belief that women were responsible for the fall in marital fertility. In fact this fall was only a symptom of the major social and economic transformations Canada was undergoing at the turn of the century. Later commentators would speak of the confidence and optimism of the age, but when one examines the population discussion one uncovers many expressions of fear and foreboding. What had been a rural, agrarian society was becoming an urbanized, increasingly industrialized community. These shifts, though only partly understood at the time, were seen as posing major dangers. The population increased from 4.3 million in 1881 to 8.5 in 1920 but much of this growth was due to foreign migration. In 1871 60 percent of the population had been of British stock, in 1921 only 40 percent could claim this heritage. Could the new arrivals be Canadianized or would they overwhelm the young nation? The population was, moreover, increasingly drawn to the cities. By 1921 the dividing line was reached when over half of all Canadians were urban dwellers. It was a common-place that city life was inherently anonymous and immoral and the question was posed if it would succeed in under-mining the virtues of rural newcomers. And it was the virtue of young women which was felt to be particularly at risk. By 1921 there were 58,000 more women than men in the cities. The largest contingent of these "surplus" women were in the fifteen to twenty-nine age group. This imbalance was due in part to the new employment opportunities offered women in textile mills, tobacco companies, food processing plants, retail stores, and domestic service. In 1896 women made up 20 per-cent of the active work force, by 1931 25 percent.[6] The vast majority of these women would eventually leave their jobs, marry, and raise families, but the anxious expressed their con-cern that they would have already formed tastes and habits of independence which would render them unfit to raise the traditionally large family. Middle-class women, on the other hand, were accused of restricting family size simply out of a desire for greater luxury and self-indulgence.

The same fears of race suicide were expressed in Britain and the United States, but in Canada the anxieties of the middle-class English were exacerbated at the beginning of our period by both the fertility of the Irish and Quebec's suc-cessful "revanche des berceaux," and later by the influx of non-British migration. In an article on "The Canadian Immi-gration Policy," W. S. Wallace, a future editor of the *Cana-dian Historical Review*, warned: "The native-born population, in the struggle to keep up appearances in the face of the increasing competition, fails to propagate itself, commits race suicide, in short, whereas the immigrant population, being inferior, and having no appearances to keep up, propagates itself like the fish of the sea."[7] And turning to the threat of eventual Catholic domination, the *Canadian Churchman* be-moaned the fact that, "As France is to Germany, so seemingly is Ontario to Quebec." Such attempts by the protestant churches in Canada to wake the populace to the perils of the situation won the applause of Lydia Kingsmill Commander in *The American Idea: Does the National Tendency Toward a Small Family Point to Race Suicide or Race Degeneration?* (1907). "The French Canadians alone," she informed her readers, "being devout Roman Catholics, primitive and simple-minded, and given to agricultural pursuits are extremely prolific."[8]

As bizarre as these outbursts might first appear, they are nevertheless worthy of note because they point to one of the major social phenomena of Canadian history which has yet to be carefully examined—the late nineteenth-century decline of the birth rate. The most dramatic aspect of the decline took place in Ontario (falling by 44 percent between 1871 and 1901), so that from 1881 to 1911 it had the lowest fertility of any province. Even Quebec's general fertility rate dropped by 21 percent between 1851 and 1921, while that of Canada as a whole fell by 41 percent[9] (see Table 1).

Given the fact that despite relatively stable marriage rates and improving fecundity the birth rate of English-speaking families fell, some form of birth control must have been employed. Discovering exactly what form of control is a problem.[10] Traditional histories of birth control assume that the decline of fertility in the late nineteenth century in Europe and North America was due to the diffusion of some new knowledge or technique. It has to be recalled, however, that there were several traditional methods already available. To space births Canadian families had long relied on simple continence and the margin of safety from conception provided when a woman was nursing.[11] In addition there were two major methods of family restriction which were to be used right into the twentieth century—coitus interruptus and self-induced abortion.

Abortion was to be of special importance. At a time when withdrawal was the most widely used method of contraception—and all studies show that this was the case in Europe and North America until at least the 1930s—numerous couples would discover that a "mistake" had been made.[12] What then? Clearly those who were intent on limiting family

TABLE 1
General fertility rates, Canada and selected provinces, 1871-1931
Annual number of births per 1000 women aged 15-49 years

Year	Canada	N.S.	Quebec	Ontario	Manitoba	Sask.	B.C.
1871	189	174	180	191			
1881	160	148	173	149	366		202
1891	144	138	163	121	242		204
1901	145	132	160	108	209	550	184
1911	144	128	161	112	167	229	149
1921	120	105	155	98	125	135	84
1931	94	98	116	79	81	100	62

SOURCE: Jacques Henripin, *Trends and Factors of Fertility in Canada* (Ottawa, 1972), p. 21

size would have to contemplate the option of abortion as a second line of defence against an unwanted pregnancy. An examination of the history of abortion is, moreover, of special interest to the historian in that more references were made to it by medical and legal observers than to employment of contraceptives. By studying this "back-up method" of birth control which was called into play when other means failed, it is possible to cast a fresh light on the general question of family limitation. In what follows I will review the means of contraception available to Canadians at the turn of the century and then proceed with an examination of the abortion issue.

How would young Canadian couples of the 1890s seek to control their family size? The information available to them in published form on means of contraception was limited. Section 179c of the 1892 Criminal Code (substituted with section 207 in 1900) restricted writing on the subject: "Everyone is guilty of an indictable offense and liable to two years' imprisonment who knowingly, without lawful excuse or justification, offers to sell, advertises, publishes an advertisement of or has for sale or disposal any medicine, drug or article intended or represented as a means of preventing conception or causing abortion." The English draft code on which the Canadian law was based had only a general section on "obscene libel"; in making the sale or advertisement of contraceptives and abortifacients a specific offence, the Canadian government was following the more stringent line of the American Comstock laws.[13] Partly as a result of the law there was no organized birth control movement in Canada until the 1930s, by which time the birth rate had already reached a low level and, indeed, was about to turn upwards.

Discussion of family limitation was restricted but it did take place. It is clear from the mass-produced medical and self-help literature, mostly of American origin, which circulated widely in Canada that doctors and popular practitioners recognized the growing desire of the public to avoid overly-large families.[14] Although respectable physicians would not countenance the use of "mechanical" contraceptives, they would on occasion advise the use of certain "natural" means of control. The first means were simple continence—Emma F. Angell Drake in *What a Young Wife Ought to Know* (1908) recommended twin beds—and prolonged nursing, which was widely believed to provide protection against a subsequent conception.[15] The second advised natural method was restriction of intercourse to what was thought to be the "safe period" in the woman's ovulation cycle. Unfortunately the cycle was completely misunderstood and the so-called "safe period" was mistakenly calculated to fall at mid-month. The correct cycle was not established until the 1920s, but in the meantime several generations of physicians vaunted the reliability of their schedule. Augustus K. Gardner, for example, in *Conjugal Sins Against the Laws of Life and Health* (1874) advised waiting twelve days after the menses: "This act of continence is healthy, moral and irreproachable. Then there need be no imperfection in the conjugal act, no fears, no shame, no disgust, no drawback to the joys which legitimately belong to a true married life. Thus excess is avoided, diseases diminished, and such a desirable limitation to the number of children, as is consistent with the peculiar nature of the individuals concerned, is effected."[16] Canadian readers received similar advice in John Cowan, *The Science of the New Life* (1869), George H. Napheys, *The Physical Life of Women* (1873?), and Winfield Scott Hall, *Sexual Knowledge* (1916).[17] The information was not always consistent. H. W. Long in *Sane Sex Life and Sane Sex Living* (1919) claimed that ten days after the period a woman entered her "free time"; B. G. Jefferis and J. L. Nichols in *Searchlights on Health: Light on Dark Corners* (1894) asserted that from mid-month to within three days of the menses one enjoyed "almost absolute safety."[18] For women with short, regular cycles the suggested schedules might have offered some protection but for most they would have been disastrous.

A third natural method, but one which was not as well supported, was the practice of coitus reservatus or intercourse without ejaculation. This method met with some success in John Humphrey Noyes' Oneida Community in upstate New York and its benefits were proclaimed by Alice B. Stockham in *Karezza: Ethics of Marriage* (1896) and in *Tokology: A Book for Every Woman* (1916). The former book was so highly thought of by some Canadian women that it was enthusiastically reviewed by the superintendent of the Department of Purity in Literature, Arts and Fashion of the Women's Christian Temperance Union.[19] The problem with this form of contraception was that although its advocates claimed it raised the sexual relation to a higher spiritual level, it demanded a degree of self-control available to few Canadian males.

But what of the most reliable forms of contraception known of in the nineteenth century—the sheath, douche, and pessary?[20] Doctors would not discuss their use because such appliances were associated in their minds with the libertine, the prostitute, and the midwife, and were thus outside the realm of respectable medicine. The importance of the rhythm method and the reason why it was greeted by physicians with enthusiasm was that it was not tainted with such associations; it had been "scientifically" determined and so offered a means by which the medical profession could claim to extend its expertise into the most intimate area of human life.

When one looks for references to "mechanical" means of contraception one finds, because of both legal restrictions and medical distaste for the subject, little direct information. Women who did know about the prophylatic benefits of douching would, however, have been able to read between the lines in the advertisements for the "Every Woman Marvel Whirling Spray" which offered, according to its producer, the Windsor Supply Company, the advantages of "vaginal hygiene." The company's advertisements appeared in such diverse publications as the T. Eaton Company catalogue, Jefferis and Nichols, *Searchlights on Health*, the Toronto *Daily Mail and Empire*, and even in the staid pages of the *Dominion Medical Monthly*.[21] Of course, to be fully effective, a douche would have to be used in conjunction with a pessary. A recipe for a home-made one concocted of cocoa butter, boric acid, and tannic acid found in the papers of the feminist Violet McNaughton suggests that Canadian women were not slow in producing their own protective devices.[22]

For men the most effective contraceptive was the sheath or condom. By the 1890s they were being mass produced in Britain and the United States and distributed by druggists in Canadian urban centres. A sensational report on their easy availability was made in 1898 by the purity campaigner C. S. Clark in *Of Toronto the Good*: "I saw a druggist's advertisement a short time ago in a Toronto paper with this significant line: *Rubber Goods of ALL KINDS For Sale*. There is not a boy in Toronto, I dare say, who does not know what that means.... A young fellow of sixteen once handed me a pasteboard coin, silvered over. When I mentioned to him that I saw nothing in the possession of such a coin, he laughed and told me to tear off the outside layer. I did so, and discovered one of the articles I have endeavoured to describe."[23] What is noteworthy in Clark's report, however, is that such contraceptives were assumed to be employed, not so much to control marital fertility, as to permit extra or premarital liaisons. They were no doubt used by some to control family size but their relatively high price, their association with venereal disease and prostitution, and the claims of doctors that they caused dangerous inflammation all restricted their employment. This left then coitus interruptus as the simplest and most widespread form of contraception. Doctors might condemn it as "mutual masturbation," or "conjugal onanism," but until well into the twentieth century it was the main way in which Canadian couples sought to "cheat nature."[24]

Canadian couples had a fairly wide variety of contraceptive measures available to them by 1900 but they were all to a greater or lesser extent lacking in reliability.[25] If they failed, those who were adamant in their desire to limit family size would then have to face the serious decision of whether or not to seek an abortion. The necessary linkage of abortion with contraception was recognized by Gardner who warned his readers: "You have no right 'to take precautions,' or failing in this, to resort to murder."[26] He recognized that the very fact that a couple used other methods could prepare them psychologically, when necessary, to fall back on abortion. As the use of contraceptive measures in general increased at the turn of the century, so too would the recourse to inducement of miscarriage.

Abortion is often left out of the histories of birth control but the issue raises a number of vital questions: women's responses to their physical functions, the medical profession's views of women's health, and male and female attitudes towards sexuality. If women resorted to such dangerous remedies it was because legal and medical authorities were withholding from them information necessary for the safe control of their fertility. The fact that significant numbers of women (including working-class women) sought abortion is, moreover, strong evidence that they were not, as was frequently assumed, passive in relation to their own fertility: they wanted to control it and were willing to go to considerable lengths to do so. And, finally, the issue reveals that the development of new methods of birth control and the controversy over their use at the turn of the century took place in the presence of a reality not yet fully perceived by historians—a widespread tradition of abortion based on folk remedies.[27]

The abortion question was brought forcefully to the Canadian public's attention in 1908 by "Kit," the writer of the "Women's Kingdom" column in the Toronto *Daily Mail and Empire*.[28] In an article of 21 March entitled "Race Suicide," she noted that though one was inclined to say hard things "of married women trying by every desperate means to avoid motherhood," the real scoundrels were the doctors. "Some fashionable physician living in a grand house, driving his motor, commits—every time he gets the price—a sordid murder, and goes scot free."[29] On the previous 16 March Dr. A. G. Ashton Fletcher, graduate of the University of Toronto and surgeon to the Queen's Own Regiment, was charged along with Harry Saunders, electrician, with the death of Jessie Helen Gould. Gould, a waitress at the Cadillac Hotel, had, it was later reported in court, paid twenty dollars to Ashton Fletcher to induce a miscarriage and died shortly afterwards of acute septic peritonitis.[30] The inquest sparked a series of articles and letters to the editor. One writer to the *Daily Mail* quoted the coroner to the effect that, "for every physician arrested for the crime there are 50 going 'scot free,' and for every physician there are 500 women guilty without the physician's aid."[31]

The Jessie Gould case was not an isolated affair. A perusal of the newspaper advertisements of the time reveals the widespread advertisement and sale of abortifacients and abortionists' offers of aid. Amongst the pills and potions of quacks surreptitiously claiming to have abortive powers were Radway's Pills for "female irregularities"; "The New French Remedy: Therapion"; Sir James Clarke's Female Pills; Madame Duvont's French Female Pills; Dr. Cowling's English Periodic Pills; Chichester's English Diamond Brand Pennyroyal Pills; Dr. Davis' Pennyroyal and Steel Pills; Old Dr. Gordon's "Pearls of Health" which, according to its producer, the Queen Medical Company of Montreal, "Never fails in curing all suppressions and irregularities ... used monthly";

the "Ladies Safe Remedy: Apioline" of Lyman and Sons of Montreal who asserted that it was superior to such traditional remedies as apiol, tansy, or pennyroyal; Cook's Cotton Root Compound: "Is successfully used monthly by over 10,000 ladies," claimed Cooks of Windsor, Ontario;[32] and finally Karn's "Celebrated German Female Treatment." We know quite a bit about F. E. Karn of 132 Victoria Street, Toronto, because in 1901 he was tried under section 179c. His advertisements contained such statements as: "Thousands of married ladies are using these tablets monthly. Ladies who have reason to suspect pregnancy are cautioned against using these tablets.... They will speedily restore the menstrual secretions when all other remedies fail.... No name is ever divulged, and your private affairs, your health, are sacred to us." Did such claims, which accompanied in this case what Karn was advertising as "Friar's French Female Regulator," amount to an announcement that the product was an abortifacient? The lower court judge was taken in by the warning against pregnant women using the product; the appeal court justices recognized that this was in fact the best way to vaunt the efficacy of the product.[33]

These advertisements of abortifacients are important for two reasons. First, they reveal that women seeking an abortion could obtain drugs and potions without directly involving themselves with an abortionist. Secondly, these announcements in their assertions that they are superior to traditional methods indicate that quacks were competing with and borrowing from traditional medical lore. In the *Physiology of Marriage* (1856) William Alcott wrote: "True it is that many who find themselves pregnant resort to tradition and household practice for what they call relief. Some field, or swamp, or grove contains the needful poison; and forthwith it is swallowed."[34] A woman would first seek to "put herself right" by drinking an infusion of one of the traditional abortifacients such as tansy, quinine, pennyroyal, rue, black hellebore, ergot of rye, savin, or cotton root. Ergot of rye was long used by midwives to induce labour and today in the form of ergometrine is still employed by obstetricians. Savin was as early as 1879 "well known as a popular abortive" in Toronto.[35] The effectiveness of these drugs is hard to determine but since they were employed generation after generation it must be assumed that they could on occasion induce miscarriage.[36]

If the drugs failed, a woman might try bleedings, hot baths, violent exercises, and consumption of large quantities of gin. After this would come the riskier step of attempting a dilation of the cervix with slippery elm, a sponge tent, or catheter. It would only be as a last resort, and if it were still not beyond the sixteenth week when the quickening of the foetus caused an abandonment of all attempts, that the woman would turn to the abortionist. How would one find the help required? It was only necessary to glance at the advertisements in the personal and medical columns of the local paper. In the Toronto *Daily Mail* for 21 March 1908, there were five advertisements for "Ladies Home Before and During Confinement" and one for a Mrs. M. Summers who offered to cure "uterine tumours" and "irregularity" and in addition would send a "Women's Own Medical Adviser."[37] In the *Manitoba Free Press* for 1909 one finds similar announcements: "Ladies Avoid Unnecessary Delay and Disappointment," "Notice to Women — Have You Ever Used our Female Regulator?" with the guarantee that all information provided will remain confidential.[38] And finally the papers carried the advertisements of physicians and surgeons who by referring to their specialization in "sexual disorders" could attract the attention of the desperate.[39]

In 1908 Judge Winchester of Toronto complained that scarcely a week went by without a doctor being named in a criminal abortion and asked that the Medical Association take some action.[40] In the circumstances the timid reply made by the medical profession was revealing. The editor of the *Canadian Practitioner and Review* admitted that in Toronto alone there were probably half a dozen doctors practising abortion but he insisted that they were practically ostracized by their colleagues and at least kept out of the Toronto Academy of Medicine. They should be deprived of their licences, he conceded, but how could that be done?[41] In the following year the *Dominion Medical Monthly* went further in an article entitled, "When a doctor is accused of criminal abortion..." The author declared, "All doctors in a great city have probably been approached some time or other in this respect."[42] If some gave in to the temptation of a large fee it was because the "open door policy" in medical education had resulted in an oversupply of poor young doctors. The obvious remedy was to improve the lot of practitioners by restricting entry to the profession. What was good for doctors would eventually be good for society at large.

As far as abortion itself was concerned the medical profession took the illegality of the operation as reason enough to continue to support the notion that it was both medically and morally wrong. There were of course individual doctors who in the privacy of their consulting rooms alluded to birth control and even helped induce miscarriages. But in public doctors would only condone the termination of pregnancy by a surgeon if a mother's life was in grave danger and full medical consultation took place. What was ignored was the fact that many women had to rely on self-induced abortions as a form of fertility control because the profession, though it might advise the restriction of family size, failed to provide the information on contraception which would make this safely possible. Earlier in the century doctors might have opposed abortion because of the dangers it posed to the mother's health, but by 1900 hospital abortions could be performed with relative safety. As early as the 1840s Dr. Alfred A. Andrews of Windsor was successfully carrying out therapeutic abortions.[43] By the 1890s the processes of dilation and curettage were well advanced but such operations were refused to all but a few.[44]

What was most striking in the medical discussion of abortion was the fear voiced by numerous doctors that they could be "victimized" by women seeking help. The medical journals carried numerous articles warning physicians to turn a deaf ear to the pleas of patients. Dr. Andrews estimated in the 1870s that in Windsor there were fifty criminal abortions a year. He called on his colleagues to steel themselves against the heart-rending tales of seduced young girls, but assumed that married women could be more easily dealt with: "As for cases of married women, who, in order to shirk the responsibilities of maternity, seek to make you accomplices in a felony, you can have no difficulty. I have hundreds of such applications. The crime of foeticide is fearfully prevalent, and rapidly increasing, and corrupting and debasing the country both morally and physically."[45] The same line was followed by an editorial in the 1889 *Canada Lancet*: "What physician, in practice for any length of time, has not had many applications, often accompanied by a considerable bribe, to relieve the victim of the seducer from the social disgrace attached to her sin, or the selfish and degraded married female from the care and trouble naturally devolving on her?"[46] To spurn such pleas was to put one at the possible mercy of a vengeful woman, the editor warned, to assist her was of course out of the question, but even to see her, if she had already attempted to induce her own miscarriage, could put the physician in a position in which he could be held responsible for the consequences. Under such pressures, claimed the writer, some doctors committed suicide. But who were they? The editor gave no examples and the lack of evidence suggests that such scenes of entrapment were only to occur in the fervid imaginations of medical journalists.

When it came to explaining the apparent rise in abortion, physicians attributed the blame to the greater education of women and their declining interest in maternity, the advertisements of abortifacients, and the presence of quacks and popular practitioners.[47] The remedies suggested by the medical press included a call for the closer supervision of druggists, a more thorough registration of births and miscarriages, a restriction of medical advertising, and the reportage of all requests for abortion to "some competent executor of the law."[48]

Doctors saw the usefulness of drugstores and newspapers being kept under surveillance but they did not accept the notion that their own profession, though it too contributed to the ranks of the abortionists, should be interfered with. Doctors sought to maintain the privilege of the secrecy of the consulting room which was as sacred as that of the confessional. In fact they saw themselves as rivalling priests in upholding the moral values of society against the onslaught of abortion: "I had for many years noted and wondered at the fact [wrote Dr. Andrews] that of the married women who sought my co-operation, nearly all were Protestants...the Roman Catholic priesthood, have in their confessional an opportunity of instructing and warning their flock. Protestant women do not go there, but we, and we only, have the private ear of the whole sex, and it is, I conceive our duty, to lose no opportunity of diffusing the information we possess in this regard."[49] Similarly a contributor to the *Canadian Practitioner and Review* would assert in 1908: "It is probable that the two classes who are fighting against the evils of race suicide in all civilized countries are practitioners of medicine and priests in the Roman Catholic Church."[50] Doctors thus turned the abortion issue to their own purposes in advancing their claim to be the counsellors and confessors of protestant Canada.

Who were the women seeking abortion and what was their view of their right to do so? Mrs. Mary Wood-Allen in *What a Young Woman Ought to Know* (1898) cautioned that a woman who married but sought to limit family size inevitably would have to face the question of abortion. "If she proposes deliberately to avoid motherhood she puts herself in a position of moral peril, for such immunity is not often secured except at the risk of criminality."[51] The approach which the woman would make to the doctor was described by Emma F. Angell Drake, herself a physician. To her came many a young wife who asked to be "helped out of her difficulty." "Again they say, 'There is no harm until there is life.' 'Doctor I have missed my monthly period and have come in to have you give me something to set me right.'"[52] McFadden referred to such women as having "many ways of hiding the actual facts from themselves."[53] Thus women did not say they sought an "abortion," but rather wanted to be "made regular" or to "bring on a period." Doctors accused such patients of using euphemisms and circumlocutions, but what is clear is that many women did not consider what they were doing to be wrong. This was brought out in all the testimony on the subject. They assumed that abortion was permissible before the third month or quickening and when not induced by another person. It was this absence of guilt which most enraged and confused male physicians. Hugh L. Hodge complained: "And when such individuals are informed of the [illegal] nature of the transaction, there is an expression of real or pretended surprise that any one should deem the act improper — much more guilty."[54] Dr. E. L. Tompkins expressed the same concern in the *American Journal of Obstetrics* (1896): "There seems to be no incompatibility between high moral and religious views on other subjects and utter lack of the same in regard to abortion. I have been asked recently by a lady who is a typical Christian and a woman of the highest honor and integrity in all other matters, to produce an abortion for a young married friend whom she thought too poor to raise children."[55]

Women and doctors took different views of antenatal life. Women remained true to the traditional idea that until the mother felt the foetus "quicken" it was permissible to take what measures were necessary to make herself "regular." Dr. Ballock asserted that "I am not able to recall one who was ever particularly distressed over such an act, especially if it happened in the early months of pregnancy."[56] The thought that women rather than doctors should decide on whether life was present was what raised the ire of men such as Hodge. "What it may be asked, have the sensations of the mother to do with the vitality of the child? Is it not alive because the mother does not feel it?"[57] Many women would have answered it was not. What one finds in examining the nineteenth-century abortion issue is that doctors were seeking to instil in the public a new belief in the vitality of foetal life from the moment of conception. It is important to note how new this concept was. Abortion had not been made a statutory crime in British law until 1803 and even then the concept of quickening was retained, as it was in the revised statute of 1828, and only removed in 1837. In a similar fashion the Offenses Against the Person Act of 1861 made it a crime for the woman to abort herself whereas the acts of 1803, 1828, and 1837 had all been aimed at the abortionist.[58] In short, the notion that a woman less than three months pregnant who sought to "put herself right" was committing a crime was a recent development and had not yet been fully forced on the public conscience. In 1922 O. A. Cannon could still write in the *Canadian Medical Association Journal*: "The moral conscience of the public, including that of some physicians, needs educating, and it should be some one's business to make it known that from conception the unborn child is a human creature whose destruction is equivalent to murder."[59]

Doctors were never to be totally successful in convincing women of the immorality of abortion. For many it was to remain an essential method of fertility control. This group included single women seeking to avoid an illegitimate pregnancy and the hardships that such a birth would entail. We know more about these women than the married because their names appeared frequently in court cases.[60] There was, for example, Jessie Gould, a waitress at the Cadillac Hotel in Toronto who died of acute septic peritonitis in 1908, Mary Ellen Janes of Victoria who died of blood poisoning in 1895, Kate Hutchinson Gardener, a chambermaid of the Tecumseh Hotel in London who died of an overdose of chloroform in 1878.[61] Doctors could sympathize with the plight of the seduced young girl who was a victim of male lust. But by the beginning of the twentieth century there were reports that some women were seeking abortion, not because they could not marry, but because they wanted to retain their independence. "As one of this sort pithily put it," reported Dr. Edward A. Ballock, "she was not going to give up a hundred-dollar place for a fifty-dollar man."[62] For whatever reasons single women sought abortion, the odds are that the relative number of their attempts would be exaggerated simply because they would more likely be found out. Dr. J. F. Scott noted that married women who already had borne children recognized the signs of pregnancy earlier than the single and could thus take more effective action.[63] Moreover, a married woman who miscarried raised few suspicions; with a single woman there was the chance of the doctor, neighbours, or even the police investigating. In a time of trouble a single woman would have fewer resources at her disposal, she would have fewer people to whom she could turn, and the likelihood of dangerous complications was therefore all the greater.

The evidence suggests that most women seeking abortion were married but the numbers involved are difficult to determine. The number of arrests for abortion would be of some interest but such figures would bear no necessary relationship to the actual numbers of women seeking to terminate their own pregnancies. An abortion only came to the authorities' attention if something went seriously wrong and the figures of the police indicate, if they indicate anything at all, only the *unsuccessful* attempts. In a popular self-help medical manual such as J. H. Kellogg's *The Home Hand-Book of Domestic Hygiene and Rational Medicine* (1906) one was told that though abortion was fifteen times more dangerous than birth, only one woman in a thousand was ever punished. Where Kellogg drew his figures is not known but some credence could be given to a report in the *Canadian Practitioner and Review* of 1916 entitled "Race Suicide":

> Mrs. McKerron died in the Toronto General Hospital December 19, 1915, after a short illness. An Inquest was held, and the jury brought in a verdict that death was due to blood poisoning caused by an illegal operation performed by Mrs. Cull. In his address to the jury the coroner, Dr. Millen Cotton, said: "The question of race

suicide is growing to alarming proportions in this city." He also said there were between three and four hundred cases in the hospitals last year as a direct result of illegal operations, and in addition to these there were many cases in private houses which were not discovered.[64]

Such claims were further substantiated when the activities of professional abortionists were brought to light. The Toronto *Evening Telegram* reported that the police investigations of the activities of a Dr. Andrews gave some idea of the extent of the practice:

> Inspector Stark took possession of all the correspondence in the house, which consisted of between 200 and 350 letters, involving beyond doubt a number of criminal operations, performed on both married and single females, all over the country. Some of these letters are couched in the plainest language by educated as well as ignorant women, written confidentially but confessing to the greatest acts of shame and seduction, and offering to pay large sums of money for advice and successful treatment. Some contained grateful acknowledgement of what the doctor had done for them, and begging him to keep their secrets from the world. Others asked for immediate advice, and suggest secret interviews, when the would-be patients would be the least likely observed.[65]

The danger of abortion is hard to establish. Doctors frequently spoke as though it was inevitably followed by death but their own figures did not bear this out. It is also evident that complications arising from instrument-induced miscarriages declined as women turned to their own purposes the antiseptic lessons of Pasteur.[66] Here would be yet another reason why the number of discovered abortions would have less and less relevance to the number of undiscovered. Yet even with these qualifications some idea of the social significance of abortion can be gained if the figures on maternal mortality are viewed as the "tip of the iceberg" of all attempts at induced miscarriage. Though the infant mortality rate declined in the first decades of the twentieth century, maternal mortality remained high.[67] Studies carried out in the 1930s revealed that in the previous twenty-five years the rate remained at 5.1 to 5.5 per 1000. A contributing cause could have been the fact that as families became smaller a higher percent of all births became the more dangerous first births. But even with the large percentage of primiparous births, the lower age of mothers and the improvement in medical care should have led to a decline in maternal mortality. Bungled abortions kept the rate high. In a study of 334 maternal deaths in one year in Ontario it was discovered that fifty-nine or 17 percent were due to abortion, thirteen were deaths of unmarried women, and of the abortions one-third had been self-induced.[68] Again these figures could only represent a small fraction of the number of successful abortions.

It is of course impossible to determine exactly the rate of abortion in Canada but all reports indicated that here as in the United States it was to play a major role in lowering the birth rate. In 1896 Scott cited a "Report of the Special Committee on Criminal Abortion" of the Michigan State Board of Health which estimated, on the basis of 100 doctors' reports, that 17 to 34 percent of all pregnancies were aborted.[69] In 1922 Dr. O. A. Cannon wrote in the *Canadian Medical Association Journal* that of the 314 women he had attended during pregnancy, fifty-one had aborted. "Of fifty-one women attended by me during abortion, twenty-two admitted criminal interference. This percentage of forty-three would have been materially increased if all the patients had been equally frank."[70] Cannon placed the abortion rate at somewhere between 7 and 14 percent of living births — a figure remarkably close to that established once the practice was legalized and reliable statistics made available.

Before concluding this brief overview of the early history of birth control and abortion in Canada it is necessary to reiterate that the concern for the "slaughter of the innocents" at the turn of the century was sparked not so much by the fall of English Canadians' birth rate *per se* but by its decline relative to that of the French Canadians and the immigrant population. It was a cruel irony that many of the eugenically minded doctors who opposed the family limitation of the "fit" were clamouring in the decade before the First World War for the forced sterilization of the "unfit." In such works as A. B. Atherton's "The Causes of the Degeneracy of the Human Race," R. W. Bruce Smith's "Mental Sanitation, with Suggestions for the Care of the Degenerate, and Means for Preventing the Propagating of the Species," and James B. Watson's *Who Are the Producers of Human Damaged Goods?* (1913), doctors calmly took it upon themselves to decide who should and who should not be allowed to breed.[71] Though they claimed to be protecting "quality" of race, their own criterion of "fitness," namely high socio-economic status, predisposed them to categorize those of a lower class or different culture as genetically inferior.[72] But this eugenic concern for fit stock was, despite the reactionary premises on which it was based, eventually to provide a rationalization for tolerance of family planning. As it was made ever more obvious that women could not be prevented from seeking to control their fertility, the argument began to be voiced that safe contraception might be the lesser of two evils. In the *Canadian Medical Monthly* of 1920 A. T. Bond would argue that more reliable mechanical means of birth control would have to be accepted if only to lower the abortion rate.[73] In the same year the government demonstrated its preoccupation with the unacceptably high levels of infant and maternal mortality by establishing the Council on Child and Family Welfare.[74] Abortion and the deaths it entailed had slowly forced upon the state and the medical profession the acknowledgment that if they were seriously concerned with the bearing of healthy children they would have to take some steps in easing the burden of motherhood.

At this preliminary stage of investigation of the history of abortion in Canada it must be admitted that a large number of questions remain to be answered. We would like to know more about the dangers of self-induced miscarriages, the techniques employed, and changes of practices over time. This paper will have served some purpose if it has shown that these problems deserve further enquiry. The importance of the evidence that we have garnered is that it reveals, despite the assumption of women's passivity in relation to their fertility, the extraordinary risks they would run to control it. That they had to continue to resort to old-fashioned and frequently dangerous remedies was a consequence of the medical profession's refusal to provide them with adequate information on contraception. An examination of what was frequently simply a second line of defence against unwanted pregnancies in addition indicates the strength of the desire of couples to limit family size. Finally, if this review of the recourse to quack potions, home remedies, and back street abortions teaches us anything, it is that there was at the turn of the century — as there is today — a demand for abortion and if that demand is not met by the medical profession it will be met by others.

Notes

I would like to thank Alan Brookes, Michael Bliss, Michael and Anita Fellman, Phyllis Sherrin, Edward Shorter, and Veronica Strong-Boag for their comments and suggestions, and Basil Stubbs, chief librarian of the University of British Columbia, for making available to me his private collection of late nineteenth-century medical and marriage manuals.

1. Toronto *Evening Telegram*, 26 March 1908, p. 9.
2. *What a Young Man Ought to Know* (Toronto, 1897), p. 198.
3. Toronto *Globe*, 17 December 1901, p. 8.
4. *Manitoba Free Press*, 30 August 1909, p. 3.
5. "Childless Marriages," *Canadian Churchman*, 29 November 1900, p. 724. In 1908 the Lambeth Conference of the Anglican church officially condemned "…the practice of resorting to artificial means for the avoidance or prevention of child bearing." E. R. Norman, *Church and Society in England, 1770-1970* (Oxford, 1976), p. 270; and see *Canadian Churchman*, July-August 1908.

6. M. C. Urquhart and K. A. H. Buckley, *Historical Statistics of Canada* (Cambridge, 1965), pp. 14-18, 38-42; Terry Copp, *The Anatomy of Poverty: The Condition of the Working Class in Montreal, 1897-1929* (Toronto, 1974), pp. 29, 44-45.

7. "The Canadian Immigration Policy," *Canadian Magazine* 30 (1907-8): 360.

8. *The American Idea, Does the National Tendency Toward a Small Family Point to Race Suicide or Race Degeneration?* (New York, 1907), cited in O. C. Beall, *Racial Decay: A Compilation of Evidence from World Sources* (London, 1911), p. 89. *Canadian Churchman*, 29 November 1900, p. 724; and see also 17 January 1901, p. 37. On French-Canadian pressure in the Eastern Townships see Robert Sellar, *The Tragedy of Quebec: The Expulsion of its Protestant Farmers* (Toronto, 1907; and 1974 with introduction by Robert Hill); Henri Lemay, "The Future of the French Canadian Race," *Canadian Magazine* 37 (1911): 11-17; P. Louis Lalande, "La revanche des berceaux," *Action française* 2 (1918): 98. For fears expressed by the Québécois about their own birth rate, see R. P. Henri Martin, OP, "La dépopulation," in *Semaine Sociale du Canada, quatrième session, Montreal, 1923*, "La Famille," *Compte rendu des cours et conférences* (Montréal, 1924), pp. 140-61; and Susan Trofimenkoff, *Action Française: French Canadian Nationalism in the Twenties* (Toronto, 1975), pp. 74-75.

9. Jacques Henripin, *Trends and Factors of Fertility in Canada* (Ottawa, 1972), p. 21, and see also John Davidson, "The Census of Canada," *Economic Journal* 11 (1901): 595-602; W. J. A. Donald, "The Growth and Distribution of Canadian Population," *Journal of Political Economy* 21 (1913): 296-312.

10. On statistical evidence that such controls were employed by the upper middle class from the 1850s see Michael Katz, *The People of Hamilton, Canada West: Family and Class in a Mid-Nineteenth Century City* (Cambridge, Mass., 1975), p. 35; and see also Lorne Tepperman, "Ethnic Variations in Marriage and Fertility: Canada in 1871," *Canadian Review of Sociology and Anthropology* 11 (1974): 287-307.

11. See L. F. Bouvier, "The Spacing of Births Among French Canadian Families: An Historical Approach," *Canadian Review of Sociology and Anthropology* 5 (1968): 17-26, and Jacques Henripin, *La Population canadienne au début du XVIIIe siècle* (Paris, 1954), pp. 86-87.

12. On the prevalence of coitus interruptus, see E. Lewis Faning, *Report on an Enquiry into Family Limitation and its Influence on*

Human Fertility During the Past Fifty Years. Papers on the Royal Commission on Population, 1 (London, 1949): 7–10; Earl Lomon Koos, "Class Differences in Employment of Contraceptive Measures," *Human Fertility* 12 (1947): 97–101.

13. On the attempt to use section 207 against Dorothea Palmer of the Parents' Information Bureau of Kitchener, Ontario, see *R v Palmer* (1937), *Ontario Weekly Notes*, 371; *R v Palmer* (1937), *Canadian Criminal Cases*, 20. On the American experience, see Linda Gordon, *Women's Body, Women's Right: A Social History of Birth Control in America* (New York, 1976).

14. With a tabooed subject such as the artificial limitation of family size, the historian is faced with the inherent limitations of public sources and the fact that such sources as they exist deal primarily with urban conditions. On the problem of such sources and in particular the use of American tracts that circulated in Canada, see Michael Bliss, "Pure Books on Avoided Subjects: Pre-Freudian Sexual Ideas in Canada," above, pp. 255–83. For a specific example of the way in which information on "sex hygiene" was brought from America to Canada, see Beatrice Brigden, "One Woman's Campaign for Social Purity and Social Reform," in Richard Allen, ed., *The Social Gospel in Canada*, National Museum of Man Mercury Series (Ottawa, 1975), pp. 36–62. The full story of birth control in Canada can only be known after the completion of the number of women's oral history projects currently under way. For work done elsewhere see "Family History Issue," *Oral History* 3 (1975): 1–64, and Sherna Gluck, "Recovering Our Past Through Oral History Interviews," cited in Susan J. Kleinberg, "The Systematic Study of Urban Women," in Milton Cantor and Bruce Laurie, eds., *Class, Sex and the Woman Worker* (Westport, Conn., 1977), p. 35.

15. Emma F. Angell Drake, *What a Young Wife Ought to Know* (Toronto, 1908), pp. 131ff.

16. *Conjugal Sins Against the Law of Life and Health* (New York, 1874), pp. 182–83. An additional reason for doctors' enthusiasm for the "safe period" was the Vatican's tacit acceptance from the 1880s of this "natural" form of control. See John T. Noonan, *Contraception: A History of its Treatment by Catholic Theologians and Canonists* (Cambridge, Mass. 1965), pp. 441–42.

17. Cowan, *The Science of the New Life* (New York, 1869), pp. 110ff; Napheys, *The Physical Life of Women* (Toronto, n.d.), pp. 92–96; Hall, *Sexual Knowledge* (Toronto, 1916), p. 215.

18. Long, *Sane Sex and Sane Sex Living* (New York, 1919); Jefferis and Nichols, *Searchlights on Health: Light on Dark Corners*

(Toronto, 1897), p. 248; and see also Anon, *Nature's Secrets Revealed* (Marietta, Ohio, 1917), pp. 197ff.

19. There were Canadian editions of both *Karezza* and *Tokology*. For Stockham, see Bliss, "Pure Books on Avoided Subjects," above, p. 281n43. On coitus reservatus see also Long, *Sane Sex*, p. 128.

20. For the development of contraceptives in the nineteenth century, see the notes in Angus McLaren, "Contraception and the Working Classes: The Social Ideology of the English Birth Control Movement in its Early Years," *Comparative Studies in Society and History* 18 (1976): 236–51.

21. *T. Eaton Co. Catalogue—Spring and Summer* (no. 46) (Toronto, 1901), 1920; Toronto *Daily Mail and Empire*, 21 March 1908, p. 21; *Dominion Medical Monthly*, July 1916; and see *Woodward Catalogue* (Vancouver, 1912), p. 143.

22. Linda Rasmussen et al., *A Harvest Yet to Reap* (Toronto, 1976), p. 72, and see also G. Kolischer, "The Prevention of Conception," *Dominion Medical Monthly* 19 (1902): 116–19.

23. C. S. Clark, *Of Toronto the Good* (Montreal, 1898), p. 127. As examples of what Clark was talking about, see the advertisements of "rubber goods" placed by F. E. Karn Ltd, "The People's Popular Drug Store," in the Toronto *Daily Star* and Cyrus H. Bowes in the Victoria *Daily Colonist* of 1906.

24. For attacks on withdrawal, see Napheys, *Physical Life*, p. 97; Jefferis and Nichols, *Searchlights*, pp. 244ff; J. H. Kellogg, *Man, the Masterpiece* (London, 1903), p. 426. That medical warnings against coitus interruptus were not taken seriously, at least by Canadians of Scottish ancestry, is suggested by the fact that the practice was jocularly referred to as "Getting off at Kilmarnock," that is, the last train stop before Glasgow (personal communication).

25. See C. Tietze, "The Use-Effectiveness of Contraceptive Methods," in C. V. Kiser, ed., *Research in Family Planning* (Princeton, 1962), p. 367.

26. Gardner, *Conjugal Sins*, pp. 180–81. The readers of the *Canada Lancet* were informed: "Married men and women are either refusing [to bear children] or limiting their output to two or three. This is the fruitful source of prostitutionism, abortionism, onanism and mental and moral degeneracy," 27 (1895): 337. See also the warnings in Jefferis and Nichols, *Searchlights*, p. 244.

27. On the practice in England, see Angus McLaren, "Abortion in England, 1890–1914," *Victorian Studies* 20 (1977): 379–400, and "Women's Work and Regulation of Family Size: The

Question of Abortion in the Nineteenth Century," *History Workshop Journal* 4 (Autumn 1977): 70-81; and for New Zealand, André Lévesque, "Grandmother Took Ergot: An Historical Perspective on Abortion in New Zealand, 1897-1937," *Broadsheet* 44 (1976): 18-31.

28. In the United States where the birth rate decline had preceded that of Canada, the first surge of protests against abortion came in the 1860s and 1870s. See Horatio Storer, *On Criminal Abortion* (Boston, 1860): John Todd, *Serpents in the Dove's Nest* (Boston, 1867); R. Sauer, "Attitudes Towards Abortion in America 1800-1973," *Population Studies* 28 (1974): 53-67.

29. *Daily Mail and Empire*, 21 March 1908, p. 21. "Kit," the pioneer woman journalist Kathleen Blake Watkins, knew more than most about the medical profession as she was married to a physician, Dr. Theodore Coleman.

30. Ibid., 16 March 1908, p. 4. An equally prominent physician, Dr. Archibald Lawson, lecturer on the principles and practices of medicine at Halifax, had been implicated in a similar affair in 1883. See *Canada Medical and Surgical Journal* 12 (1883-84): 252.

31. *Daily Mail and Empire*, 4 April 1908, p. 21; and see also the *Evening Telegram*, 18, 20 March 1908.

32. Advertisements taken at random from the Toronto *Globe*, November 1901; *Daily Mail and Empire*, October 1892, Toronto *World*, November 1900; *Dominion Illustrated Monthly*, September 1898. Cook's Cotton Root Compound appears to have been the most widely advertised product, being puffed as early as 1892 and as late as 1906 in papers as far apart as the Vancouver *Semi-Weekly World*, December 1900, and the Halifax *Herald*, January 1906. On the use of cotton root as a popular abortifacient in the southern United States, see Herbert Gutman, *The Black Family in Slavery and Freedom*, 1750-1925 (New York, 1976), pp. 80-82.

33. On the Karn case see *R v Karn* (1903) 5 *Ontario Law Reports*, 704 (CA); *R v Karn* 5 *Canadian Criminal Cases*, 479; *R v Karn* 6 *Canadian Criminal Cases*, 543. On other abortives see *R v Scott* (1912) 3, *Ontario Weekly Notes*, 1167 (CA). Some women might have taken such pills simply to ease menstrual pains, but there is little doubt that the intent of the advertisers was to suggest that their products could be put to less innocent uses.

34. *Physiology of Marriage* (Boston, 1856), p. 185.

35. See *R v Stitt* (1879) 30, *Upper Canada Common Pleas*, p. 30.

36. Pennyroyal and tansy are irritant drugs with a toxic action; ergot of rye, cotton root, and quinine are oxytocic agents that stimulate the mobility of the uterus. On home remedies, see *Canadian Practitioner and Review* 39 (1914): 668, and C. J. Polson and R. N. Tattersall, *Clinical Toxicology* (London, 1959), pp. 545-49.
37. *Daily Mail and Empire*, 21 March 1908.
38. *Manitoba Free Press*, 30 August 1909.
39. Canadian papers also carried the advertisements of American druggists and physicians, and some Canadian women, to protect their anonymity, sought abortions in nearby American cities such as Chicago, Rochester, and Detroit. See, for example, *R* v *Backrack* (1913) 28, *Ontario Law Reports*, 32 (CA) in which the question was posed if the crime committed by Canadians while in America could be prosecuted in Canadian courts.
40. *Daily Mail and Empire*, 6 April 1908, p. 4.
41. *Canadian Practitioner and Review* 33 (1908): 253.
42. *Dominion Medical Monthly* 32 (1909): 121.
43. Alfred A. Andrews, "On Abortion," *Canada Lancet* 7 (1875): 289.
44. On therapeutic abortion, see *Canada Lancet* 13 (1881): 342-43; 32 (1899): 113; *Canadian Practitioner and Review* 25 (1900): 331, 334-36, 401.
45. Andrews, "On Abortion," p. 291.
46. "Abortionists," *Canada Lancet* 21 (1889): 217. See also "Does Abortion Pay?" ibid., 42 (1908-9): 648-49; John T. Winter, "Criminal Abortion," *American Journal of Obstetrics* 38 (1898): 85-92.
47. See, for example, *Canada Lancet* 26 (1894): 76; 38 (1905): 88-89. A few sex reformers asserted that men, because of their lack of self-control, so burdened women with pregnancies that their seeking abortion was really the fault of males. See Kellogg, *Man*, p. 423; James C. Jackson, *American Womanhood: Its Peculiarities and Necessities* (Dansville, NY, 1870), pp. 89-90.
48. *Lancet* 21 (1889): 217. On the problem of registration, see R. E. Mill, "Birth Registration and Public Health," *Canadian Journal of Public Health* 6 (1915): 135-36.
49. Andrews, "On Abortion," p. 291.
50. *Canadian Practitioner and Review* 33 (1908): 253.
51. Mary Wood-Allen, *What a Young Woman Ought to Know* (Toronto, 1898), p. 241.
52. Drake, *Young Wife*, pp. 125, 129, 130.

53. Bernarr McFadden, *Womanhood and Marriage* (New York, 1918), p. 139
54. Hodge, *Foeticide or Criminal Abortion* (Philadelphia, 1869), pp. 32-33; see also Ely van de Warker, *The Detection of Criminal Abortion* (Boston, 1872), p. 42.
55. *American Journal of Obstetrics* 33 (1896): 130-31.
56. Ibid., 45 (1902): 237.
57. Hodge, *Foeticide*, pp. 21-22; and see also Andrew Nebinger, *Criminal Abortion: Its Extent and Prevention* (Philadelphia, 1870), p. 16; "A physician," *Satan in Society* (New York, 1872), p. 119.
58. See L. A. Parry, *Criminal Abortion* (London, 1931).
59. "Septic Abortion," *Canadian Medical Association Journal* 12 (1922): 166.
60. See *R v Cook* (1909) 19, *Ontario Law Reports*, 174 (CA); *R v Garrow and Creech* (1896) 5, *British Columbia Reports*, 61; *R v Pettibone* (1918) 2, *Western Weekly Reports*, 806.
61. Gardener was in fact purposely murdered by Dr. Thomas Neill Cream, a madman who, claiming to provide abortifacients, administered poison to and killed at least two Canadian and four English women. On the career of this Canadian "Jack the Ripper," see W. Teighnmouth Shore, *The Trial of Thomas Neill* (London, 1923).
62. Ballock, *American Journal of Obstetrics* 45 (1902): 238.
63. Scott estimated that 75 to 90 percent of all abortions were carried out by married women; "Criminal Abortions," *American Journal of Obstetrics* 33 (1896): 80.
64. *Canadian Practitioner and Review* 41 (1916): 120-21; and see Kellogg, *The Home Hand-Book of Domestic Hygiene and Rational Medicine* (London, 1906), pp. 356-57.
65. *Evening Telegram*, cited by Clark, *Of Toronto the Good*, p. 124.
66. Cannon, "Septic Abortions," pp. 163-64.
67. See *Canada Lancet* 40 (1923): 84-87; National Baby Week Council, *Some Maternity and Child Welfare Problems* (London, 1925), p. 39; Helen MacMurchy, *Maternal Mortality in Canada* (Toronto, 1928); Suzann Buckley, "Efforts to Reduce Infant Mortality in Canada Between the Two World Wars," *Atlantis* 2 (1977): 76-84; Neil Sutherland, *Children in English-Canadian Society: Framing the Twentieth Century Consensus* (Toronto, 1976), pp. 56-70; Veronica Strong-Boag, *The Parliament of Women: The National Council of Women in Canada, 1893-1929* (Ottawa, 1976), pp. 206, 265.
68. J. T. Phair and A. H. Sellers, "A Study of Maternal Deaths in the Province of Ontario," *Canadian Public Health Journal* 35

(1934): 563-79; and see also F. W. Jackson and R. D. Jeffries, "A Five Year Study of Maternal Mortality in Manitoba, 1928-1932," ibid., p. 105; Helen MacMurchy, *Sterilization? Birth Control? A Book for Family Welfare and Safety* (Toronto, 1934), p. 97.

69. Scott, "Criminal Abortions," p. 78.
70. Cannon, "Septic Abortions," pp. 163-65.
71. Atherton, *Canada Lancet* 41 (1907-8): 97-101; Smith, ibid., 40 (1906-7): 969-76; Watson, *Who Are the Producers of Human Damaged Goods?* (Toronto, 1913). See also Zlata Godler, "Doctors and the New Immigrants," *Canadian Ethnic Studies* 9 (1977): 6-17, and Terry L. Chapman, "Early Eugenics Movement in Western Canada," *Alberta History* 25 (1977): 9-17.
72. On the relationship of eugenics to contraception, see my study, *Birth Control in Nineteenth Century England* (London, 1978).
73. Bond, "The Birth Rate," *Canadian Medical Monthly* (1920): 258. See also Bernarr McFadden, *Manhood and Marriage* (New York, 1916), pp. 87ff.
74. R. D. Defries, *The Development of Public Health in Canada* (Toronto, 1940), p. 78. The argument that a lower birth rate would reduce infant mortality was not accepted by all. Detecting this line of thought in the report of the City Improvement League of Montreal, a Catholic journalist replied: "Catholic mothers hold that to be born and baptised is a good compared with which the duration of mortal life is insignificant, for it means eternal life in heaven. Of course all wish to see infant mortality reduced as far as possible: but we do not want to see male and female professors of eugenics corrupting the morals of Catholic Canadian women, and we are sure the clergy of Montreal will know how to silence them." *America: A Catholic Review of the Week* 2 (19 February 1910): 515.

Dr. Ernest Jones, Psychoanalysis, and the Canadian Medical Profession, 1908-1913

THOMAS E. BROWN

Dr. Ernest Jones is best remembered today as the biographer of Sigmund Freud, the father of psychoanalysis.[1] It is often forgotten that Jones was himself a highly gifted analyst, author of a number of minor classics of the psychoanalytic canon, including *Rationalization in Everyday Life*, *Hamlet and Oedipus*, and *On the Nightmare*, and, perhaps most important, the man who almost singlehandedly forced a hearing for Freud's theories, first in North America, and later in England.

The impact of Jones' Freudian evangelizing mission on the American medical profession has recently been succinctly examined by Nathan Hale, Jr., as part of his book *Freud and the Americans: The Beginnings of Psychoanalysis in the United States, 1876-1917*.[2] Hale, however, gives little attention to the fact that Jones' brief five-year stay in North America from 1908 to 1913 was spent in Toronto as pathologist to the Toronto Hospital for the Insane, first director of the Psychiatric Out-Patient Clinic, and associate professor of psychiatry in the University of Toronto, and that Jones conducted an equally vigorous propagation of the Freudian gospel among his Canadian colleagues. Cyril Greenland has examined Jones' career in Toronto but his account fails to rise above the level of narrative history and offers no adequate analysis of a number of important questions that must be answered.[3] First, what "version" or "interpretation" of psychoanalysis was presented to Canadian medical men by Ernest Jones? Did Jones in his numerous articles and lectures accurately present the central ideas of his master, Freud? Second, how did Canadian physicians react to these new ideas, and to the man who espoused them so forcefully? And third, why did they respond to psychoanalysis as they did? This essay attempts to answer these questions and to assess the stormy career of Ernest Jones in Toronto and the reception accorded psychoanalysis in Canada on the eve of the First Great War.

The path that led twenty-nine-year-old Ernest Jones to Toronto in the fall of 1908 had not been an uneventful one. Jones was born on 1 January 1879, in the village of Rhosfelyn, Wales, "the first child and only son" of Thomas and Mary Ann Jones. Jones enjoyed a solid middle-class Victorian upbringing. His father, Thomas, was a qualified colliery engineer and for most of his career was "general secretary" of a large steel-making concern in Wales. He was, as Jones recalled, "altogether a typical Samuel Smiles hero, and one of the better products of the 'liberal' industrial era of good Queen Victoria." Mary Jones was also a typical Victorian matriarch—as Jones remembered her, "the most thoroughly and yet unostentatiously self-effacing woman I have known, devoted to the interests of her husband, her children, relatives, neighbours, house, and garden."[4]

Ernest himself was a rather precocious youngster if his autobiography, *Free Associations: Memories of a Psycho-analyst*, is to be believed. Noting that "psycho-analysts and other investigators have repeatedly deplored the absence of data concerning childhood sexuality," Jones assures his readers that "the practice of coitus was familiar to me at the ages of six and seven, after which," he drily notes, "I suspended it and did not resume it till I was twenty-four." Jones' intellectual development was equally rapid. At the age of nine he was sent to the Swansea Grammar School, obtained a scholarship to Llandovery College, "*the* leading public school in Wales," at the age of thirteen, and began his medical studies at the University College of South Wales, Cardiff, in 1895, at "the early age of sixteen." The young Jones found university life "a heartening experience." He decisively cast off his already faltering religious faith, embraced "Socialist doctrines," and perhaps most important discovered "a predilection for neurology" from among his medical courses.[5]

In the fall of 1898 Jones left Cardiff for London to pursue a twenty-month clerkship at University College Hospital. He records that he worked "hard and successfully, feeling very happy that I had so definitely found my *métier*." And in 1900, at the age of twenty-one, he completed his clerkship and became a "qualified medical man."[6]

For the next three years he enjoyed "the magic of glittering success: success enough to satisfy the most ambitious young doctor." He remained for a while at University College Hospital, first as house-physician in neurology, and then as house-surgeon to the great neurosurgeon Victor Horsley. He then went as house-physician to the Brompton Chest Hospital, and at the beginning of 1903 he became resident medical officer to the North-Eastern Hospital for Children. It was here that things started to go sour, that suddenly, as Jones put it, "fate hammered one hard blow after another in rapid succession, until all the dizzy early success and promise crumbled to dust." He was forced to resign from the North-Eastern Hospital for the grave offence of spending the night away from the hospital without obtaining permission from the proper authorities. Shaken, but obviously not daunted, Jones tackled the difficult Doctor of Medicine examinations, gaining first place and "a heavy gold medal worth £20." Soon after he took his MRCP "only a fortnight after reaching the necessary age, and thus attained the rank of a consulting physician."[7]

It was well for Jones that he had. He was to find all the usual doors to rapid advancement closed to him. The appointment of resident in neurology at the prestigious National Hospital, Queen's Square, which Jones both coveted and expected, went to another, less qualified man. He came to see himself, perhaps correctly, as "a marked man, a *mauvais sujet*, among the powers-that-be."[8]

There followed four years of disappointment, anger, and frustration, four years of minor second-rate appointments and a little consulting work. And yet these four years from 1903 to 1907 were to be decisive in terms of Jones' intellectual development. Freed from the necessity of compliance to the dictates of orthodox medical enquiry, Jones' imagination took off and soared into unknown territory.

He became increasingly intrigued with the functional neuroses, that is, the psychoneuroses, which, as Jones noted, "constituted one of the most puzzling sets of phenomena in the purview of the neurologist" of the day. He quickly came to dismiss the dominant materialist view that the body could influence the mind, "but not the mind the body," and he recounts that he "used to ask neurologists why mental processes were to be excluded from their field of daily work and from nowhere else in their lives." When he received no satisfactory answer, he began to read widely but "assiduously" in "the immense French literature on hypnotism, hysteria, and double personality."[9] He also studied with growing interest the work of Americans William James and Morton Prince and that of the Englishman Frederic Myers, founder of the Society for Psychical Research. By 1905 Jones was well versed in the newer psychotherapeutic methods of treatment, especially hypnosis.

In that year he had his first chance to try out their effectiveness for himself. He had, as he relates, "the good fortune to come across a case of exceptional interest," that of a man named Tom Ellen. Following a train collision in which he sustained no obvious physical injury, Ellen had become "stone-blind,... had lost the sense of taste and smell, had extensive memory disturbances, and suffered from severe pain and various mental attacks." However, "most striking of all was the remarkable symptom of feeling that his body was folded over on itself, so that he consisted only of one side" (a condition called allochira). Jones saw the unfortunate Ellen for over two years and through the use of hypnosis and "persuasion therapy" was able to restore his sight totally. Jones found Ellen "a museum of material" that quickly confirmed his suspicions that the standard physiological explanations of afflictions like Ellen's were completely inadequate.[10] He clearly saw that the symptoms were of psychological origin and could be alleviated only by psychotherapeutic means.

While working with Tom Ellen, Jones was also investigating another intriguing neurological mystery of the time, that of aphasia. In this instance, however, his efforts were to end, not in success, but in scandal. Two young mentally defective children whom Jones was testing in his research accused him of behaving "indecently" during a speech test, a charge the authorities seemed only too willing to believe. Jones actually spent a night in jail, and then, "for two dreadful months, lived on the edge of an abyss" before the magistrate dismissed the case. He saw that "personal respectability would not be enough in the future; only the most rigid medical orthodoxy" would do. This, of course, was the one thing of which Jones was incapable. Pursuing his new interest in psychotherapy he had discovered the writings of Freud and, as he put it, "had to go to school again."[11]

Jones had first heard of Freud in 1903 when, at the urging of his close friend Wilfred Trotter, he had read Mitchell Clarke's review of the *Studies in Hysteria* which had been published originally in *Brain* in 1898. He then poured through "the much fuller account of the *Studies*" in Frederic Myers' *Human Personality* and Havelock Ellis' "discussion of the new findings," which appeared in 1904 in the first volume of his celebrated *Studies in the Psychology of Sex*.[12] Jones next turned to the writings of Freud himself, beginning with the famous "Dora analysis." And although his German "was not good enough to follow it closely," Jones "came away with a deep impression of there being a man in Vienna who actually lis-

tened with attention to every word his patients said to him."
Jones became an immediate and enthusiastic Freudian convert and records simply that he "began practising his method
at the end of 1906."[13]

In September 1907, Jones journeyed to Amsterdam to
deliver a paper at the International Congress of Neurology.
There he had his first personal encounter with a practising
Freudian analyst in the person of Dr. Carl Jung of the Burg-
hölzli Asylum in Zurich. Jones arranged to visit Jung at the
end of November on his way back to England after attending
"a special post-graduate course in psychiatry at Kraepelin's
Clinic in Munich." He found Jung "a breezy personality. He
had a restlessly active and quick brain, was forceful and
even domineering in temperament, and exuded vitality and
laughter; he was certainly a very attractive person."[14] Jung,
initially at least, was equally impressed with Jones. He informed Freud:

> Dr. Jones of London, an extremely gifted and active
> young man, was with me for the last 5 days, chiefly to
> talk with me about your researches. Because of his
> "splendid isolation" in London he has not yet penetrated
> very deeply into your problems but is convinced of the
> theoretical necessity of your views. He will be a staunch
> supporter of our cause, for besides his intellectual gifts
> he is full of enthusiasm.[15]

Freud, ever eager for new converts beyond the confines of
Vienna, replied, "Your Englishman appeals to me because of
his nationality; I believe that once the English have become
acquainted with our ideas they will never let them go."[16] Freud
could not have been more wrong. The English medical establishment was to display a great and long-lasting antipathy to
his ideas, as the hapless Jones was only too soon to discover.

In February 1908, Jones found himself once again surrounded by the opprobrium of scandal. At the West End
Hospital for Nervous Diseases, Jones had encountered a ten-
year-old girl "with an hysterical paralysis of the left arm"

and a colleague challenged him to see if he could discover "any sexual basis for the symptom." He perhaps unwisely accepted. He felt there could be little harm in asking the girl a few questions, but was aware enough of the explosiveness of the situation to interview the child "in the operating theatre with the door open and nurses moving in and out." He discovered that "the girl had been in the habit of going early to school to have a few minutes 'play' with a slightly older boy, and one day he tried to seduce her. She turned on one side and warded him off with the opposite arm, but at the critical moment this went numb and weak and remained paralysed." The child later boasted that "the doctor had been talking to her about sexual topics." The girl's parents were naturally outraged, complained to the hospital authorities, and Jones was immediately called upon to resign. This meant, as Jones well knew, that "all hope [had] vanished of ever getting on to the staff of any neurological hospital in London."[17] His London career was effectively at an end.

Almost fortuitously, an avenue of escape from the "peculiarly arid soil provided by the medical profession in London" soon presented itself in the form of a self-imposed exile to one of the distant outposts of the Empire. Jones learned that Dr. C. K. Clarke, superintendent of the Toronto Hospital for the Insane, professor of psychiatry and dean of medicine in the University of Toronto, was looking for a bright young man to head up his new psychiatric clinic which he intended to model on that of Kraepelin's famous Munich clinic. Armed with testimonials from such eminent physicians as Sir William Osler, Sir Frederick Mott, and Sir Victor Horsley, Jones secured the appointment.[18] Just how much Clarke knew of Jones' checkered past is a moot point. At the time, Clarke wrote to the provincial secretary of Ontario, "I find him just the sort of an inspiration the younger men of the staff need. He is quite young, quiet, unobtrusive and a devoted student."[19] Young and devoted, yes, but quiet and unobtrusive! No one was ever to accuse Jones of being these things, as Clarke was only too quickly to find out, undoubtedly much to his own chagrin.

Jones arrived in Toronto at the beginning of October 1908, and while he was to find "life in Toronto... in many ways very pleasant," it is clear that he was never to be really happy there. He had two "serious" complaints about the city. One was the climate and the other was

> the intellectual atmosphere. It was not merely that I found myself back in the Biblical and Victorian atmosphere of my boyhood—that would have been bad enough to someone bent on emancipation—but it was the dead uniformity that I found so tedious: one knew beforehand everyone's opinion on every subject, so there was a complete absence of mental stimulation or exchange of thought.[20]

It is not surprising, therefore, that at least initially, Jones directed almost all his energies on behalf of the Freudian cause south of the border at his colleagues in the American medical profession. He quite correctly assumed that they, unlike their Canadian counterparts, would be more receptive to psychoanalysis.

In December 1908, Jones accepted an invitation from Dr. Morton Prince, a leading American psychotherapist, to come to Boston to discuss some of the "newer aspects of clinical psychology." Jones scored a major triumph at the Boston gathering when he won over Dr. James J. Putnam, professor of neurology at Harvard and one of the most distinguished physicians in the United States.[21] Jones and he became "excellent friends" and Putnam ably supported Jones when he publicly "opened the campaign for psycho-analysis" at the first American Symposium on Psychotherapy held in New Haven in May 1909. And in September, Jones was in Worcester, Massachusetts, to hear Freud, who was making his first and last American visit, deliver his lectures on psychoanalysis at Clark University.

It was at the Clark University conference that Jones, for the first time, was made abruptly aware that he did not enjoy

Freud's full confidence and trust. In his autobiography Jones relates that after their first meeting at the Salzburg Congress in April 1908, Freud "told Jung he found me 'very clever'; so our first impression of each other, like all subsequent ones, had been favourable."[22] The recently published *Freud-Jung Letters*, however, reveal that Freud's initial reaction to Jones was anything but "favourable," and that, indeed, until after the Clark University meeting Freud was deeply suspicious of Jones' motives and his loyalty to the movement.

When Jones visited Freud in Vienna in May 1908, Freud informed his new confidant, Jung, that:

> Jones is undoubtedly a very interesting and worthy man, but he gives me a feeling of, I was almost going to say racial strangeness. He is a fanatic and doesn't eat enough. "Let me have men about me that are fat," says Caesar, etc. He almost reminds me of the lean and hungry Cassius. He denies all heredity; to his mind even I am reactionary. How, with your moderation, were you able to get on with him?[23]

Jung, too, had begun to have his doubts about Jones. In a letter to Freud on 12 July 1908, he noted that:

> Jones is an enigma to me. He is so incomprehensible that it's quite uncanny. Is there more in him than meets the eye, or nothing at all? At any rate he is far from simple; an intellectual liar (no moral judgement intended!) hammered by the vicissitudes of fate and circumstance into many facets. But the result? Too much adulation on one side, too much opportunism on the other?[24]

Freud immediately replied:

> I thought you knew more than I about Jones. I saw him as a fanatic who smiles at my faint-heartedness and is affectionately indulgent with you over your vacillations.

How true the picture is, I don't know. But I tend to think that he lies to the others, not to us. I find the racial mixture of our group most interesting; he is a Celt and consequently not quite accessible to us, the Teuton and the Mediterranean man.[25]

The inaccessible and inscrutable Jones became an increasing worry to both Freud and Jung as news of his activities in North America began to filter back to them at the beginning of 1909. Both men believed that American "prudery" might prove an insurmountable obstacle to the widespread acceptance of psychoanalysis in the United States. In November 1908, Jung wrote to Freud that:

For some time now I have noticed the gentle zephyrs of prudery blowing across from America, for which Morton Prince seems to have quite a special organ. Everyone is terribly afraid of his practice, everyone is waiting to play a dirty trick on someone else. That is why we hear so little of the people who have worked with me and visited you. In America they are simply pushed to the wall.[26]

Freud agreed, telling Jung in January 1909:

There is a good deal to be said about America. Jones and Brill write often, Jones' observations are shrewd and pessimistic, Brill sees everything through rose-coloured spectacles. I am inclined to agree with Jones. I also think that once they discover the sexual core of our psychological theories they will drop us. Their prudery and their material dependence on the public are too great.[27]

They were determined, however, that psychoanalysis be presented to the Americans with the "sexual core" of the theory intact and undiluted. As Jung commented on 19 January 1909:

Our little circle is thriving [in Zurich].... The Americans are a horse of a different colour.... We have noticed this prudishness, which used to be worse than it is now; now I can stomach it. I don't water down the sexuality any more.[28]

But this, they began to suspect, was exactly what Jones was doing. Freud therefore attempted to bolster Jones' resolve in a letter on 2 February 1909.

As for your diplomacy I know you are excellently fitted for it and will do it masterly. But I am afraid it is easy to do too much in this way. Consider it a piece of psychoanalysis you are performing on your countrymen. You are not to say too much at once or at too early a moment, but the resistance cannot be avoided; it must come sooner or later, and it is best to provoke it slowly and designedly.[29]

On 24 February, however, Freud was writing Jung: "From Jones and about him I have received very strange news."[30] The exact nature of this news remains uncertain but it appears to have centred on Jones' support of Morton Prince. In *The Life and Work of Sigmund Freud*, Jones records:

A slight disagreement between us arose over the personality of Morton Prince, a man whom I had known through correspondence in London days years before and with whom I always stayed on my visits to Boston. He had been the first American pioneer in psychopathology, a fact which I felt deserved some recognition. Furthermore he freely opened his periodical, *The Journal of Abnormal Psychology*, to papers on psychoanalysis, almost the only one then available for that purpose. He was a thorough gentleman, a man of the world, and a very pleasant colleague, as I found in cooperation with him for some years in editing his *Journal*. But he had one serious failing. He was rather stupid, which to Freud was always the unpardonable sin. When he rejected an abstract of Brill's on the quite legitimate ground that its language was too unseemly for his lay audience, which included many clergymen and old ladies, Freud was very angry, and wanted me to disassociate myself from him. He insisted that Prince was a man with whom one had to be prepared for "bad intentions veiled by friendly speaking" (February 22, 1909), and nothing I could say would shake his opinion.[31]

It seems, then, that in Freud's eyes, Jones' willingness to acquiesce in Prince's ignoble attempt to "water down the sexuality" for the American audience was clear proof of his wavering loyalty to the Freudian cause. And to Freud disloyalty, not stupidity, as Jones contended, was *the* "unpardonable sin." Jung, for his part, shared Freud's diagnosis of Jones. He saw Jones as a "compromiser," reluctant to speak out forcefully on the "sexual core" of Freud's theories. He wrote to Freud on 7 March:

I still can't figure out the news about Jones. In any case he is a canny fellow. I don't understand him too well. I had a good and sensible letter from him recently. He displays great affection not only for me but for my family. To be sure, he is very nervous about the emphasis placed on sexuality in our propaganda, a point that plays a big role in our relations with Brill. By nature he is not a prophet, nor a herald of the truth, but a compromiser with occasional bendings of conscience that can put off his friends. Whether he is any worse than that I don't know but hardly think so, though the interior of Africa is better known to me than his sexuality.[32]

Freud continued to be "put off" by Jones as he began to make plans to attend the Clark University conference at Worcester in September 1909. In June he wrote to Jung: "I should very much like to talk to you about America and have your suggestions. Jones threatens me, not without ulterior motives, with the absence of all the leading psychiatrists. I expect nothing of the moguls."[33] At the Worcester meeting, therefore, Freud confronted Jones with his growing doubts about his loyalty. As Jones records the incident:

> During the Worcester time, Freud formed an exaggerated idea of my independence and feared, quite unwarrantably, that I might not become a close adherent. So he made the special gesture of coming to the station to see me off to Toronto at the end of the stay and expressing the warm hope I would keep together with them. His last words were "You will find it worthwhile." Naturally I was able to give him full assurance and he never doubted me again.[34]

Jones was properly chastened, as the completely different tone of Freud's letters to Jung after the conference clearly reveal. On his return to Europe Freud received "a nice contrite letter from Jones."[35] And at the beginning of 1910 he told Jung: "The other day I had a letter from Jones, more contrite than necessary. 'I'll be good from now on,' he says. His resistance seems to have broken down for good."[36] And on 13 January 1910: "Jones is so sincerely contrite in his letters that I vote for taking him back into our favour. He is doing good work."[37] By May Jones was clearly back in Freud's good graces. He informed Jung:

> This morning I found a long letter from Jones in Washington waiting for me. He reports on the exciting events at the American Psychopathological Association on 2 May. By and large they were favourable to us. Since he must have written you the same thing, I won't dwell on it. As usual, Putnam seems to have done very well

and Jones himself is making up for last year's ambiguities with indefatigable zeal, great skill, and I was going
to say, humility. Which is most gratifying.[38]

Freud's new-found trust in Jones was not misplaced and was to
be amply repaid. Jones threw himself back into the struggle to
win acceptance for psychoanalysis in North America with a
passionate intensity obviously born of the need to prove
beyond all doubt his devotion and loyalty to Freud. It was
Jones, not surprisingly, who in the summer of 1912 proposed
the formation of "a small group of trust-worthy analysts as a
sort of 'Old Guard' around Freud."[39] As the creator of the
famous "Committee" Jones was clearly demonstrating to
Freud that he was the most loyal of the loyal.

It was with Freud's stinging rebuke at the Clark University
conference just behind him that Jones finally launched the
crusade for psychoanalysis among his Canadian medical colleagues. He began by publishing his New Haven address
"Psycho-Analysis in Psycho-Therapy" in the November
1909 issue of the *Bulletin of the Ontario Hospitals for the Insane*,
the house journal of the Ontario asylums' system. It was
probably the first introduction that many Ontario psychiatrists and neurologists had had to Freud's ideas. Jones began
the article by saying that he and other physicians engaged in
the struggle against nervous and mental disease had clearly
come to recognize that they had "secured a new therapeutic
weapon of the utmost value," which might be described "as
the capacity to alleviate certain complaints by purely mental
measures, in other words as psycho-therapy in its broadest
sense." Most psychotherapy, however, Jones continued, was
"employed in a quite empiric way" and often unsuccessfully.
Psychoanalysis, on the other hand, "a second stage in the evolution of psycho-therapy" offered "a deeper insight...into
the essential nature and origin of the morbid phenomena."
He then outlined Freud's "deeper insight" that "the symptoms in the psycho-neuroses owe their origin to the fact
that...certain processes, particularly strivings, desires, and

impulses" which "if they are not absorbed in the main stream of the personality are apt to manifest an independent activity out of control of the will. This activity is usually of a low order, of an automatic and almost reflex kind" and "is generally an unconscious activity, that is to say, it operates without the subjects being aware of it." Put simply, Jones said, "every psycho-neurotic symptom is to be regarded as the symbolic expression of a submerged mental complex of the nature of a wish." "The central aim of the psycho-analytic method," Jones continued, is to enable "the patient to discover and appreciate the significance of the mental process that manifests itself as a symptom."

Jones then briefly outlined the psychoanalytic method which relied on the word-reaction association tests of Jung, the "free association" technique, and "the analysis of the patient's dreams by means of a special technique introduced by Freud." These techniques, Jones argued, enabled the analyst to bring the repressed wish from the unconscious into the conscious with the result that the patient was able "to free his personality from the constraining force of these complexes, and, by taking up an independent attitude towards them, to gain a degree of self-control over his aberrant thoughts and wishes that was previously impossible." The psychoanalytic method, Jones assured his readers, had been used successfully in treating "practically all forms of psycho-neuroses, the different types of hysteria, the phobias, obsessions, anxiety neuroses, and even certain kinds of sexual perversions." He then concluded by attributing this success to the fact that other psychotherapeutic methods such as hypnosis or "persuasion therapy" merely blocked "the outward manifestation of the underlying pathogenic idea," whereas psychoanalysis effectively removed the outward symptom by ferreting out and thus removing the underlying pathogenic idea itself.[40]

The striking omission in Jones' presentation, of course, is the lack of any reference to the sexual nature of the unconscious wishes buried in the neurotic personality. The article, however, had been presented originally to an American audience in May 1909, when, as Freud and Jung had so clearly recognized, Jones was still "very nervous about the emphasis placed on sexuality in our propaganda." Jones displayed no such nervousness in "The Psycho-analytic Method of Treatment," an address he delivered before the Niagara District Association in St. Catharines, Ontario, on 24 November 1909. He insisted that:

> Investigation by Freud's methods discloses the fact that every psychoneurotic symptom is the distorted expression of a repressed wish-complex.... As to the nature of the pathogenic factors two general remarks may be made, namely that the complexes usually arise in infantile life, and that they are most often of a sexual character. These two remarks may seem rather to contradict each other, but that the sexual life of early childhood is far richer and more complex than is generally supposed is one of the matters that Freud has most illuminatingly demonstrated.[41]

Clearly Jones was no longer troubled by the "ambiguities" that earlier had so alarmed Freud. Canadian physicians were to get their Freud pure and undiluted, with the "sexual core" perhaps all too prominently displayed.

In April 1910, Jones continued his campaign by publishing two articles in the *Bulletin of the Ontario Hospitals for the Insane.* "Freud's Theory of Dreams," which Jones had already read before the American Psychological Association in the previous December, presented a detailed and straightforward review of Freud's pioneering work in the analysis of dreams. Freud had shown, Jones argued, that:

> A dream is...not a confused and haphazard congery of mental phenomena, but a distorted and disguised expression of highly significant psychical processes that have a very evident meaning, although in order to appreciate

this meaning it is first necessary to translate the manifest content of the dream into its latent content in the same way that a hieroglyphic script yields its meaning only after it has been interpreted.[42]

Jones' second article, "Psycho-analytic Notes on a Case of Hypomania," contained such explicit details of the sexual life of a psychotic patient that the storm of protest it eventually aroused was to hasten Jones' departure from Toronto. Jones was very interested in the application of psychoanalytic techniques to the treatment of the psychoses. In this respect he was following Jung, who, in his ground-breaking study *The Psychology of Dementia Praecox* (1907), had shown that some psychotic patients were indeed accessible to psychoanalytic treatment. Freud, on the other hand, believed, perhaps correctly, that the psychotic, unlike the neurotic, was too "narcissistic," too caught up in his own inner world, to permit the crucial "transference" process between patient and analyst to operate successfully.[43]

In his article Jones reported the results of what he believed was the first "psycho-analysis of a case of manic-depressive insanity." The patient was a thirty-nine-year-old woman who had been admitted to the Toronto Hospital for the Insane in 1908. She alternated between periods of depression and excitement but, Jones observed, had "none of the peculiar 'shut-offness' or loss of contact with the immediate environment that is the most constant accompaniment of dementia praecox." Jones used the Jungian word association test in an attempt, as he put it, to "actually penetrate into the patient's mind." After a very detailed presentation of the results of the test and of his conversations with the patient, Jones concluded the article with this lengthy summary.

A woman, of passionate temperament and strong religious training, had at the age of sixteen been seduced, and at the age of nineteen married another man by whom she was already pregnant. After bearing one child she had a miscarriage, which she attributed to a gonorrhaea contracted from her husband, and underwent a number of gynaecological operations and other treatment for the relief of subsequent pelvic complications; her ovaries were removed at the age of twenty-three. As the years went by, her desire to have more children was strong, and her sexual inclinations increased in intensity; at the same time her husband's capacity to gratify these grew less, and she contrasted him unfavourably in this respect with her former lover. She thus blamed her husband twice over for her lack of children. She had illicit relations with other men, which caused her much remorse. Religious appeals to forsake her evil ways and lead a new life she interpreted as a revelation indicating the error of her past sexual life and advocating a new form of sexual life. For a number of reasons this idea of a new sexual life took the form of the fellatorism perversion. She tenderly loved her husband, so there arose in her mind an intense conflict between this feeling of love and duty, and the forces impelling her to turn from him to a new kind of life. The compromise between the two sets of forces was found in identifying, for a number of reasons, the act of fellatorism with the partaking of the holy sacrament. A number of abnormal mental processes were the direct outcome of this; such were delusions of poisoning, refusal to take food, intense excitement evidently of errotic [*sic*] origin, belief that various ministers were in love with her and eager to lead her into the "new way" of sexual life, etc. These abnormal processes clinically constituted recurrent attacks of mania.[44]

Jones was convinced that he had shown that "by means of the knowledge gained by psycho-analytic methods...abnormal mental processes...[could be] rendered intelligible...in a way otherwise impossible" and that "most valuable clues into the significance and origin of the psychoses" obtained. And while he stressed that "no generalizations as to the nature of manic-depressive insanity are offered from the observation of this case," he left little doubt that he viewed repressed sexual desires as *the* major etiological factor in its formation.

The next opportunity for Jones to further the Freudian cause came at the annual meeting of the Canadian Medical Association held in 1910 in Toronto in the first week of June. Jones helped to arrange a special "symposium on Psycho-Neuroses" and he marshalled his forces well. Of the four major speakers, two besides himself were confirmed Freudians. Dr. J. J. Putnam, whom Jones had won over in December 1908, came from Boston and delivered a paper, "Etiology and Treatment of the Psychoneuroses," which Freud himself praised as "an excellent apologia for psycho-analysis."[45] Dr. August Hoch, a New York psychiatrist who had studied with Jung, spoke on "The Relation of Insanity to the Psychoneuroses," arguing that "the principles, which Freud and Jung have taught us, can no longer be overlooked in psychiatry."[46] Only Dr. W. H. Hattie, superintendent of the Nova Scotia Hospital, in a paper entitled "The Psycho-Neuroses in Asylum Practice," found himself "not sufficiently convinced" to commit himself "definitely" to the support of Freud's theories.[47] Jones' own paper, "A Modern Conception of the Psycho-Neuroses," was an able complement to Putnam's more general paper. He dealt mainly with "the question of classification of the neuroses" but did make a few rather dogmatic remarks on the etiology of the neuroses. He stated that "in the past fifteen years, thanks to the researches of Freud, we have learnt to recognize the specific cause of the neuroses, namely, some disturbance of the sexual function; in other words, one maintains that no neuroses can possibly arise with a normal sexual life." He then added even more pointedly that "The specific cause [of the neuroses] in question are various sexual experiences in early childhood, of a kind I here have no time to describe." He did find time, however, to again remind his audience that "Freud has shown that the sexual life of children, though widely differing from that of adults, is far richer and more significant than is commonly supposed."[48] On the whole, Jones deemed the symposium a victory for the psychoanalysts, although he later recalled that a "virulent" attack had been launched against him by "two American neurologists" who had "decided to attend the meeting so as to discredit me in my own home town." But Jones felt that "Putnam and I got the better of them."[49]

The symposium represented the high point in Jones' Canadian campaign for psychoanalysis. By the middle of 1910 he had presented all of the essential core ideas of the Freudian system to his Canadian medical colleagues. He had dealt with psychoanalysis both as a theoretical explanation of the origin of the psychoneuroses and as a method for their treatment. And while he continued to publish articles in Canadian medical journals until he returned to England in 1913, these served either to clarify specific points in the psychoanalytic exegesis or to answer objections to it.[50]

The initial response of the Canadian medical profession to psychoanalysis was mixed, but generally negative. It ranged from outright and violent rejection and denunciation to a rather begrudging admission that at least something of what Jones was saying was worth a closer look. But certainly no Canadian physician of the stature of Dr. J. J. Putnam in the United States became an immediate and thoroughgoing Freudian convert.

The views of Dr. C. K. Clarke, Jones' superior at the Toronto Hospital for the Insane and generally recognized as the "dean of Canadian psychiatrists," are rather representative of those who were most bitterly opposed to psychoanalysis. After reading Freud's Clark University lectures, he informed Jones in April 1910: "Any ordinary reader would gather Freud advocates free love, removal of all restraints, and a relapse into savagery."[51] Clarke seems never to have altered this, his initial reaction to psychoanalysis, and it is clear that he remained an opponent of the Freudian viewpoint to the end. In 1923, the year before his death at the age of sixty-six, Clarke was invited to deliver the prestigious

Maudsley Lecture before the Medico-Psychological Association of Great Britain. Clarke chose to assess the past problems and accomplishments, and the future prospects of psychiatry in Canada. He squarely placed the Freudian enthusiasts in the category of past problems.

> We have our outbursts of enthusiasm in certain circles over psycho-analysis, Freudian theories, and sex problems ad nauseum, but it was when the war broke out that the neo-psychiatrists, neuro-psychiatrists, near-psychiatrists, psycho-neurologists, and psychological healers of all kinds, found themselves. They grew overnight and the younger they were the more knowledge they claimed to possess.[52]

Sex problems ad nauseum! That was the crux of the opposition of Clarke and many of his colleagues to psychoanalysis. Freud's seeming preoccupation with sexual matters was not merely disgusting, but decidedly dangerous. It was bad enough that Freud argued for the ultimate sexual origin of all the psychoneuroses, but when he hypothesized the existence of an active sex life in children, he had violated accepted standards of good taste and propriety. An editorial writer in the *Canadian Journal of Medicine and Surgery* in 1913 deplored what he believed was Freud's "gross exaggeration" in both these areas.

> It would appear,...regarding the subject dispassionately, that the weight of evidence is on the side of the opponents of the theory. It is not disputed that the sexual motive plays an important part in the creation and development of the neuroses, but it is denied that it is the supreme factor.... To argue that a baby, by certain actions such as sucking the thumb, signifies that he or she is impelled by sexual instinct, is in fact neurotic, appears to the ordinary mind to pertain to gross exaggeration. Until further and more convincing proofs, if

that be possible, are brought forward, the medical profession will be content to dismiss some of his views as visionary and even pernicious.[53]

Indeed, so pernicious did some Canadian practitioners find Freud's views that Jones found himself accused of introducing sexual matters into his lectures when no mention of them in fact had been made. When he delivered a lecture on "The Relation Between Organic and Functional Nervous Diseases" to a postgraduate clinic at the Toronto Orthopedic Hospital in November 1910, a Dr. J. S. Hart asked Jones "why the element of sex predominated in functional nervous diseases." Not caught so easily, Jones neatly countered by pointing out that "the word sex had not been mentioned during the lecture" and that "it was more important to determine *whether* sexual factors predominated in the neuroses than why."[54]

The rather unequivocal rejection of Freud's theories by many Canadian medical men was matched, however, by the willingness of others who, while remaining skeptical, were prepared to give Freud's views a closer scrutiny. These men saw that there was more to Freud than "sex problems ad nauseam." As Dr. W. A. Turner of London, Ontario, put it:

> Any criticism ... of Freud's views ought to separate the hypothesis which he has enunciated, such as his conceptions of conflict, repression, and the influence of subconscious mind from the method of psycho-analysis by which he arrived at his conclusions.[55]

Freud's hypothesis that "the repressed complexes are invariably of a sexual character" might be "pernicious and visionary" but his free association method, if properly refined and adopted, was perhaps a promising therapeutic tool. As Dr. C. S. McVicar, pathologist to the Toronto Hospital for the Insane, explained in 1913:

> Investigation by psycho-analysis promises especially to bridge the gap between the so-called functional neuroses

and the definite neuroses.... If the psycho-analytic technique can be simplified, chastened and standardized, it will add to the number of workers, and more convincing data will be forthcoming on which to determine the merits of a promising means of study.[56]

But some doctors wondered whether simplifying, chastening, and standardizing Freud's method of treatment would be enough. Dr. B. E. McKenzie of Toronto asked:

Is there not the danger that the inquisitor may put into the patient's mind what he subsequently finds there? ... If there has been an unfortunate experience, a moral trauma, of which these patients are ashamed, which their better selves would shun and forget, to which they have no desire to return, and from which they wish to escape, so that the memory of it has disappeared into the limbo of the long forgotten past, is it reasonable that any good can result from tearing open the wound afresh and exposing the patient to still further humiliation and regret? Is it a humane purpose? Is it rational? Is it not better to let the dead past bury its dead, to let bygones be bygones, and to encourage the unfortunate psycho-neurotic to look upward and outward instead of compelling her to mingle with the humiliating regrets of past errors?[57]

Dr. W. H. Hattie of the Nova Scotia Hospital echoed Dr. McKenzie's concern. Freud's "method demands so exhaustive an investigation of the mental life that one feels that the investigator must be singularly free from bias and the patient singularly irresponsive to suggestion if the results are to be perfectly dependable."[58] Similarly, Dr. George Young of Toronto noted that:

Freud does not attribute his results in any way to suggestion. Nevertheless, one cannot overlook certain outstanding features of the treatment. The patient gradually learns that his malady is mental in origin and that the physician is on the right track. The latter cannot help showing his satisfaction as he approaches the cause of the trouble. This inspires hope and increases expectancy of the result. The journey has been long and fraught with pain, but Mecca is almost in sight. Once there nothing more will remain to be told and the resistance will end. At Mecca the physician expects a cure and so finally does the patient. Can suggestion be excluded as a factor in the result?[59]

What many Canadian doctors found most objectionable about the psychoanalytic method, then, was that it necessitated the dredging up of very private and painful memories from the patient's past. Not only did they suspect that many of the memories recovered were fraudulent in that they owed their origin more to "suggestion" by the analyst than to the patient's actual recall, but they clearly dreaded the acute embarrassment the airing of such memories might cause not only the patient but themselves.

There were other less serious drawbacks to psychoanalysis as well. As Dr. Young outlined them:

(1) [Psychoanalysis] demands an intimate knowledge of normal and abnormal psychology, a thorough training and exceptional personal qualifications. (2) [Psychoanalysis] establishes confidential relations between doctor and patients which may be unpleasant and a source of danger to the former. (3) The cure is tedious and the financial question cannot be overlooked. (4) The treatment is symptomatic. The predisposition remains and there is nothing to prevent the patient "breaking out in a new spot." (5) It is not applicable to all nervous troubles.[60]

Freud's therapeutic method was promising, therefore, but as it stood it was too complicated for the average practitioner, too time-consuming and perhaps too costly to the patient, too lacking in "scientific" objectivity, and most important, too capable of making the neurotic patient worse by recalling distressing memories that were best left forgotten. Psychoanalysis was not *the* long-sought panacea for the problem of neurotic illness. Rather it was just one of a number of encouraging new techniques, out of which, as Dr. Young insisted, "the future scientific psycho-therapy would grow."[61]

The skepticism, ridicule, and hostility with which many Canadian physicians first greeted psychoanalysis can be explained in a number of ways. Jones himself was certainly partly to blame. His abrasive personality and haughty manner did little to endear him, and therefore by association, the ideas he espoused to his Canadian colleagues. But Jones was only the vehicle through which many in the Canadian medical profession first learned of Freud's ideas. It was the ideas themselves that caused such consternation. Psychoanalysis insisted on raising a number of highly discomforting questions about, what Freud himself called, the "'civilized' sexual morality" of the late nineteenth-century social order.[62] Beyond that, it offered an alarming challenge to the "somatic" interpretation of nervous and mental diseases that was established orthodoxy among Canadian neurologists and psychiatrists.[63] Psychoanalysis threatened not only to undermine the whole elaborate structure of the nineteenth-century moral order, but also to destroy the scientific world view of the medical profession.

Ernest Jones was never the most tactful of men. The portrait that emerges of him during his Toronto years is that of a brash, egotistical, impudent young man, who often displayed a rather callous disregard for the shortcomings of others. In his autobiography, Jones offers an analysis of himself and of how others probably perceived him as a young doctor that cannot have been very wide of the mark. He speculated that many

> senior physicians... doubtless regarded my efforts as the ambitious and perhaps impertinent strivings of a young man who needed to be kept in his place. Added to

which...I had a tongue. And a young man may be so filled with righteousness that he can see no reason for restraining his tongue when his virtuous endeavours meet with opposition. That is my diagnosis of myself in those years, and I should not cavil if someone couched it in harsher terms—using such words as opinionated, tactless, conceited, or inconsiderate.[64]

Jones could be all of these things and more.

He was a particularly nasty and withering opponent at medical gatherings when his obviously less enlightened colleagues failed to acknowledge what were to him the self-evident truths of the psychoanalytic gospel. Here is his own account of his style at one such meeting, that of the Chicago Neurological Society in January 1911.

At the meeting all the speakers supported me, except Sidney Kuh, who made a very stupid and ill-mannered attack. "He couldn't agree with Freud's logic that because Frauenzimmer in German means woman, therefore to dream of rooms means something sexual," etc. etc. Unfortunately for himself he laid himself badly open, and as I had much pent-up Affekt that was crying for [abreaction] I let myself go, and exposed his ignorance mercilessly. It was perhaps not the most politic thing to do, but one is not always dictated by wisdom.[65]

Jones undoubtedly alienated many of his American and Canadian colleagues by such tactics.

He could be equally devastating in print, as Morton Prince, the noted American psychotherapist, found out. He and Jones had first met in December 1908 and had become close friends. Jones had even incurred Freud's displeasure in early 1909 by defending Prince's handling of the *Journal of Abnormal Psychology*. But when Prince began to express publicly his growing doubts about psychoanalysis, he quickly felt the sting of Jones' acid tongue.[66] Prince was deeply wounded, apparently

not so much by Jones' actual criticisms as by the "bitter...
offensive, not to say insolent" manner of the attack.[67] In a
letter to their mutual friend Putnam, he bitterly assailed "the
attitude" of Jones and the Freudians.

> ...Jones is a fanatic. It is the fanatic attitude—the atti-
> tude of Christian Science, Spiritualism, Suffragettism. It
> was the attitude of the Abolitionists, Martin Luther and
> reformers in general....any one with that attitude may
> not be invited into the "society of scholars" including
> scientists. It destroys the judgment. The capacity to
> weigh criticism, to see in perspective and true propor-
> tion. It is all right for a reformer in Religion or politics.
> But in science there is no common ground on which
> such a person can meet with a scientifically minded per-
> son again:
> I admire the fanatic who goes forth to fight for the
> faith, to battle nobly, but then he must be prepared to
> lay down his life without whimpering.... I am afraid
> Jones will never be a hero—poor dear.[68]

Many of Prince's colleagues who had to endure Jones' cutting
and condescending remarks in the public forum or in print
must have entertained similar unkind feelings towards him,
and it undoubtedly must have affected their receptivity to
the ideas Jones was always trying to force on them.

Nor did the unsettling rumours about Jones' private life do
anything to enhance his reputation or that of the Freudian
cause. Jones had set himself up in Toronto at 407 Brunswick
Avenue with his elder sister and his mistress, a charming
Dutch-Jewish girl named Loe, who shared "the housekeeping
responsibilities." To make matters worse, Loe, besides being
heavily addicted to morphia because of a chronic and painful
kidney complaint, was also severely neurotic and for much of
her stay in Toronto "seldom left her bed."[69] Although Jones
passed her off as his wife, Loe's odd behaviour cannot have
gone unnoticed by the wives of the good Toronto doctors.

Far more damaging to Jones' good name and character was the scandal that overtook him at the beginning of 1911. Scandal, of course, was nothing new to Jones as his earlier London career had demonstrated. This one, however, with its particularly lurid sexual undertones, had even the usually confident Jones greatly shaken and upset. He informed Putnam on 13 January 1911 that:

> You will be grieved to learn that this week very serious personal trouble has arisen here: to put it quite shortly, a woman whom I saw four times last September (medically) has accused me of having had sexual intercourse with her then, has gone to the President of the University to denounce me, is threatening legal proceedings, and has attempted to shoot me. At present I am being guarded by an armed detective.
> She is a hysterical woman, who has been divorced for adultery, and whose main complaints on coming to see me were (1) being haunted by erotic thoughts concerning a certain woman with whom she used to sleep (she is pronouncedly homosexual) and (2) general mental confusion and tension arising from fear that she might satisfy her desires by appealing to some man on the street. I did not treat her by psycho-analysis, but got her to talk, tried to calm her, etc. Unfortunately she had an acute fit of Übertragung [transference] (she was a stranger here, and I was the first man she had spoken to for months), and made unmistakeable overtures. She broke off coming, in high dudgeon at being rebuffed, and I heard nothing of her for over four months. In the meantime she got into the hands of some doctors of doubtful reputation, as well as a woman doctor of very severely strict views; the latter fell in love with her and it was reciprocated. They were people who had cooked up rumours about my "lax" views and harmful treatment (stupid stories about my prescribing adultery, illicit intercourse, etc.), and a regular incubation of delusions took place all

round. I foolishly paid the woman $500 blackmail to prevent a scandal, which would be equally harmful either way.

You may imagine I am very worried indeed, and dreadfully tired, so I cannot go further into details. I have gone to the best lawyer here, and he is hopeful of pulling the matter through all right. Still![70]

Nor was Jones' already precarious position made any more secure by the fierce opposition that suddenly surfaced over the article on "a case of hypomania, with some sexual details" which he had published in the *Bulletin* in April 1910. As he again lamented to Putnam: "The Provincial Minister to whose ears it has come had a stormy scene with Dr. Clarke about it last week, and declares he would have prevented such 'filthy stuff' going through the mails had he known of it."[71] By February, however, the besieged and beleaguered Jones could inform Putnam that "my troubles seem to be slowly settling, provided that no fresh explosion takes place."[72] Jones had been saved largely through the personal intervention of Sir Robert Falconer, president of the University of Toronto, who, as Jones put it, took a "very sensible" attitude to both affairs.

In his public and private conduct, then, Jones had shown himself to be decidedly lacking in tact and ordinary good common sense. His rather arrogant disregard for the moral and intellectual sensibilities of his colleagues did little to advance the cause of psychoanalysis in Canada. Ultimately, however, it was the psychoanalytic doctrine that was completely unacceptable to many Canadian medical men. Psychoanalysis threatened to do two things: first, to tear away the veil of reticence and secrecy that surrounded all matters of a sexual nature and to expose the shame and hypocrisy of the "civilized" sexual morality of Edwardian Canada, and second, to tear down the whole noble intellectual edifice of psychiatric and neurological theory that had been so laboriously built up since the days of Pinel and Tuke in the 1790s.[73]

At the centre of the late nineteenth-century doctrine of "civilized" sexual morality lay the belief that while the sex drive was a natural thing, it had to be carefully husbanded and controlled. Such thinking reflected the nineteenth-century preoccupation with "vitalistic" theories of the human organism. It was thought that the human body, much like an electric circuit, contained a fixed amount of energy, or "vital force," or "life force" as it was called. The maintenance of this force in proper balance was believed essential to the health of the organism. Overindulgence in any activity, whether of a physical or mental nature, could endanger that equilibrium. Particularly to be avoided was overindulgence in sexual activity, for not only would the "life force" be rapidly drained from the body, but the energy expended in such a way was unavailable for the pursuit of those higher and truly creative intellectual and aesthetic tasks that were essential for the progress of mankind.

Here, then, was the doctrine of "creative sexual repression" with a vengeance.[74] Both men and women were enjoined to chastity before marriage; self-restraint, ideally, continence, except for procreative purposes, within marriage. To secure these goals the lid of "prudish reticence" was clamped down tightly on the discussion of all sexual matters. It was argued that the less people knew or thought about sex, the less likely they were to overindulge in it. Purity of thought as well as deed, therefore, became an integral part of the code of "civilized" sexual morality. But this conspiracy of silence on sex served other far less noble purposes. It enabled the internal contradictions, in particular the "double standard," in the system to go unnoticed and unchallenged. Children were said to be "innocent" and lacking in sexual desire. Yet they were often observed to engage in the secret vice of masturbation. Anguished parents nevertheless maintained the fiction that such practices never took place. Women were carefully shielded from any knowledge of their sexual roles and it was commonly believed that they were without sexual feeling, let alone passion. But this idealization of the "virtuous woman" served only to mask and perpetuate the subordination and exploitation of women.[75] Men, on the other hand, could and were expected to "sow their wild oats" in and outside marriage so long as adultery, fornication, and prostitution were properly abhorred and never spoken of. To have spoken openly of them would have been to expose the "double standard."

The conspiracy of silence, however, could not forever prevent the surfacing of the inconsistencies and evils inherent in the code of "civilized" sexual morality. As Nathan Hale, Jr., has noted, "civilized morality was, above all, an ideal of conduct, not a description of reality. In many respects this moral system was a heroic effort to coerce a recalcitrant and hostile actuality."[76] By the 1890s the code was beginning to break down in Europe and Great Britain, exposed for the unsavoury fraud it was by the writings of Krafft-Ebing, Havelock Ellis, Edward Carpenter, and Freud himself. Certainly by 1905 when Freud published his *Three Essays on Sexual Theory*, as Henri Ellenberger has pointed out, "the zeitgeist was of extreme interest in sexual problems."[77]

Such was not the case in North America, however. Hale and others have shown that in the United States "up to about 1912 standards of purity grew more vigorous and more refined."[78] In Canada, the major tenets of the doctrine of "civilized" morality were, if anything, even more intact. Therefore, when Jones lamented in 1911 that "The attitude in Canada towards sexual topics has I should think hardly been equalled in the world's history: slime, loathing, and disgust are the only terms to express it," he was in no sense exaggerating.[79] Unfortunately for Jones, it was Canadian doctors who were among the most stalwart defenders of the code of "civilized" morality.

Michael Bliss has shown that many Canadians of the Edwardian period absorbed much of their sexual knowledge and morality from the eight volumes of the "Self and Sex Series," an American production that enjoyed "best seller" circulation in Canada between 1897 and 1914.[80] The four volumes for gentlemen included *What a Young Boy Ought to Know*, *What a Young Man Ought to Know*, *What a Young Husband Ought to Know*, and finally, *What a Man of 45 Ought to Know*, and there were similarly four volumes for the ladies. These "Pure Books on Avoided Subjects," as they were advertised in Canada, all preached the doctrine of "civilized" sexual morality, and were endorsed by a number of Canadian doctors. Dr. B. E. McKenzie of Toronto, who reviewed the series in 1902, believed that "every book of the series may be confidently recommended...as containing the very best statement of the important information which should be supplied to every young man and women, every boy and girl, entering upon the duties and responsibilities of life."[81] Other "Leading Canadian Medical Men" produced their own compendious medical encyclopaedia *The Family Physician, Or, Every Man His Own Doctor*, which simply reiterated the same prohibitions and admonitions contained in the "Self and Sex Series."[82] Before the turn of the century, Drs. Joseph Workman and Daniel Clark, both superintendents of the Toronto Asylum, had done their bit to increase the pandemic public fear of the evils of masturbation by publishing tracts on the "enshrouded moral pestilence."[83]

It is not surprising, therefore, that Ernest Jones and the Freudian ideas he stood for were greeted with hostility and incredulity by many in the Canadian medical profession. Psychoanalysis asked Canadian physicians to believe that it was the conspiracy of silence on sexual matters that was itself responsible for much of the neurotic illness of the time; that bringing human sexuality out into the light of day and openly acknowledging its existence could lead to a more genuine and just moral order than that based on the "civilized" morality of Edwardian Canada. Beyond that, psychoanalysis asked Canadian doctors to accept that children were sexually active, that indeed they were rather precocious sexual beings. Such argument flew in the face of all that the good Canadian doctors held to be most sacred. How could they be expected to welcome such repulsive speculations, for that surely was all that they could be, especially when they were expounded by a brash young upstart like Jones. Freud's ideas simply had to be dismissed as the wildest "unscientific" speculation because they threatened, if indeed true, to bring about, as Dr. C. K. Clarke so aptly put it, "a removal of all restraints, and a relapse into savagery." But psychoanalysis threatened even more. It seemed not only to make mock of the doctors' moral beliefs but also to challenge the basic intellectual premises and assumptions on which the psychiatric and neurological orthodoxy of the day rested.

In November 1909, Jones wrote to his friend, Dr. J. J. Putnam, that "Materialism (views of intestinal toxaemia, etc.) is even more rampant here than anywhere in the States, and it is a great opportunity to strike a blow at it."[84] What Jones was lamenting was the domination of both Canadian psychiatry and neurology by a thorough-going "somaticism." It was accepted dogma that nervous and mental illnesses were the symptoms or manifestations of organic brain disease. As Dr. C. K. Clarke explained in 1899: "An insane person is one in whom the normal brain function has been disturbed by actual disease, either functional or organic."[85] The neurotic patient displayed milder symptoms of mental derangement, but these also were the result of organic brain disease. As a Toronto neurologist, Dr. Campbell Meyers, noted: "That mental disorders rest upon a physical basis is well recognized, and that we may, with reasonable certainty, regard deranged function of the cells of the higher centres as the cause of all the symptoms" in neurasthenia or brain exhaustion "is assured."[86] The mind was eternal and inviolate. It was the organ of mind only, the brain, that was diseased, and every case of nervous or mental illness was the result of definite brain lesions.

Some psychiatrists and neurologists, however, admitted that these lesions could be found elsewhere in the nervous system, or because of the theory of "reflex action" in some other organ system of the body.[87] Hysteria, for example, at least until Freud showed otherwise, was widely believed to be a malady confined solely to women and resulting from some organic disease in the female reproductive organs. But most often alienists and neurologists thought in terms of marked and well-defined brain damage in the great majority of cases of nervous and mental illness. They were encouraged in this belief by the fact that in general paresis, which was perhaps the most common form of insanity found in many nineteenth-century asylums, post mortem examinations almost always did reveal gross pathological changes in the brain tissue.[88] It then became very easy and natural to extend the general paresis "paradigm" to all other categories of nervous and mental disease. When post mortem examinations failed to produce evidence of the expected brain lesions, which happened with embarrassing frequency, few alienists or neurologists thought to question the validity of the whole "somatic" approach, but simply and conveniently postulated the existence of "functional" lesions which could not be detected by existing laboratory methods. But most were certain, as Dr. David Shirres, neurologist to the Montreal General Hospital, explained, that "Some day, when we have a more perfect technique, and higher magnifying microscopes, we may be able to place some of the so-called functional diseases in the organic group."[89]

The somatic outlook also spilled over into considerations of the etiology of nervous and mental illness. Insanity and neurasthenia were organic brain diseases, but what had caused these diseases in the first place? By 1900 there was only one acceptable "predisposing" cause, and that was heredity. People became insane or neurotic because they had inherited a defective or weakened nervous constitution. Both psychiatrists and neurologists stressed the importance of the "hereditary taint" over and over again in their articles. For example, Dr. Daniel Clark, who lectured to University of Toronto medical students in the 1890s on nervous and mental diseases, stated quite emphatically that "Heredity is the most potent cause of insanity in its predisposing tendency."[90] The same thing held true for the neuroses, particularly for neurasthenia, as Dr. A. T. Hobbs, medical superintendent of the

Homewood Sanitarium in Guelph, Ontario, argued in 1909. "Heredity plays an important part in the preparation of the ground soil for the cultivation of these noxious neurotic weeds."[91] Environmental or "moral" causes were not ruled out, particularly in the production of the neuroses, but these were only the "immediate" causes, and most psychiatrists and neurologists insisted that the "hereditary taint" was undoubtedly *the* underlying causative factor. As Dr. James Russell, superintendent of the Hamilton Hospital for the Insane, put it:

> The popular opinion of the day is that the vast increase in insanity is due to the restless spirit of the age, the intense competition in business and the breakneck struggle for wealth, place and power. It is believed that the consequent exhaustion resulting from this overtax of the brain is the cause of widespread mental disorder...there is an element of truth in this opinion,...but to rank it as the great predisposing or exciting cause of insanity is nothing short of a popular fallacy.... Heredity is the chief cause of insanity, and every other form of mental degeneracy.[92]

The degree to which both the psychiatric and neurological specialties were dominated by the somatic outlook, however, is best reflected in their treatment procedures. Turning first to the psychiatric profession, it is clear that by 1900 the era of "moral treatment," of the attempt to reach the insane patient through individualized "psychological" therapy, was long a thing of the past in Canadian asylums.[93] After all, insanity was a fixed organic disease of the brain, and any attempt to reason, cajole, or indeed threaten the patient back into sanity had, of necessity, to end in failure. The alienists, therefore, increasingly saw their function to be largely custodial, not curative. As Dr. Russell stated: "our chief function is to surround this large population [the 85 percent who were 'more or less hopelessly insane'] with the comforts of life, and to make their sojourn as pleasant as possible."[94] "Active" treatment as the psychiatrists conceived it, consisted of, as Dr. J. B. Murphy of the Brockville Hospital for the Insane outlined it:

> pleasant and healthy environment, scrupuously clean and pleasant living and bedrooms, regular hours for sleeping and eating, good food, suitable clothing and amusements in the form of games, entertainments, and reading matters, . . . and employment of some kind.[95]

Few psychiatrists were content with the existing treatment methods at their disposal, and they were constantly trying out new therapeutic techniques. Unfortunately, their inability to see insanity as anything but a physical malady much like any other greatly limited the range and ultimately the effectiveness of their new treatment procedures. Some alienists experimented with the use of continuous baths, others with new drugs or combinations of drugs.[96] Dr. R. M. Bucke of the London Asylum carried out gynaecological operations on over two hundred insane women in the belief that their insanity was the result of "reflex" disturbances in the reproductive organs.[97] Dr. C. K. Clarke of the Toronto Asylum argued that no advance in treatment would ever take place until the asylums were provided with adequate pathological laboratories. He was convinced that "the morbid conditions [in insanity] must have a definite basis [in the diseased brain] and until we know what that is there must be no end of groping."[98] Much along the same lines, other psychiatrists insisted that the first priority was the proper classification of the insane. The new classification system of dementia praecox, manic-depressive insanity, and paranoia, introduced by the German psychiatrist Emil Kraepelin in the 1890s, seemed to offer the hope that at last a fairly accurate prognosis of the various insanities could be arrived at and then more successfully treated. Too many psychiatrists, unfortunately, felt they had done their jobs when they had properly classified their patients, and if anything, the new Kraepelin nosology led to less "active" treatment in the asylums instead of more. The tendency developed to label an increasing number of the more esoteric and difficult varieties of insanity as dementia praecox, that form of insanity thought to be virtually incurable and most resistant to treatment of any kind.[99] Therefore, for all their attempts to find new treatment procedures and therapies for the insane, Canadian alienists remained trapped within the parameters of the somatic orthodoxy of late nineteenth-century medicine.

Their colleagues in neurology were also trapped. While the psychiatrists confronted the most difficult cases of mental illness in the asylums, the neurologists tackled the "borderland of mental disease," the milder nervous diseases that seemed to afflict a great many people in Edwardian Canada. Most often they were called upon to treat the condition known as "neurasthenia," or "brain exhaustion," which was believed to be a disease peculiar to the North American environment, just as hysteria was a classic European malady.[100] The neurasthenic could display a bewildering array of symptoms, as Dr. Daniel Clark pointed out:

> The want of sleep, followed by a low power of thinking in the pursuit of daily business: the weakening of the power of attention and a desire to wander from necessary thought; a shrinkage from doing a business which hitherto was a delight; becoming abnormally wearied in mind when doing routine and ordinary work; not the natural facility to put ideas into words, and an unnaturalness of temper in respect to small matters and on small occasions: and change of manners and feelings to near friends and relatives without any just reason, are cardinal characteristics.[101]

And these symptoms were, of course, the result of organic brain disease brought on most typically by, as Dr. Richard Monahan of Montreal suggested, the "stress of modern life, with its strain and worry," and as always somewhere in the background, the "hereditary taint."[102] Neurasthenia was to be treated much like any other purely physical disease, by the elaborate system introduced by Dr. S. Weir Mitchell in the 1880s of isolation, absolute bed rest, overfeeding, massage, and sometimes electro or hydrotherapy.[103]

Beginning about 1900, however, some Canadian neurologists began to experiment with psychotherapy in the treatment of neurasthenia. But it is clear that the use of psychotherapy extended little beyond the attempt at moral suasion on the part of the physician. As Dr. A. T. Hobbs of Guelph told his colleagues in 1909:

> You must quietly impress upon him that he is going to get well. You may have to reassure him time and again. Do not get impatient with him. Instil into his mind the axiom that "he will not feel well until he is well." Encourage him every time you see him, and present to him always a cheerful front. Outline his treatment carefully and in detail....His case naturally takes time, tell him so.[104]

Psychotherapy remained, therefore, only an adjunct to the more orthodox Weir Mitchell "rest cure," and there was clearly little recognition of the psychological roots of neurasthenia or other neurotic illnesses.

When Ernest Jones arrived in Toronto in 1908, then, most of the Canadian psychiatrists and neurologists he was to encounter fully accepted the somatic medical orthodoxy of the times. Psychoanalysis challenged that orthodoxy on all fronts. First, Freud and his followers argued that the psychoneuroses, and probably many of the varieties of insanity, were not fixed organic diseases of the brain but rather diseases of the mind. Second, they insisted that nervous and mental illness were not caused by the "hereditary taint" but by unconscious mental conflict in the individual psyche. And finally, they insisted that the psychoneuroses and even many forms of insanity could only be treated successfully by mental means—by psychoanalysis. For Canadian doctors to have accepted all or any of these arguments would have entailed their disavowal of a medical world view that by training and experience they had come to see as unimpeachable scientific truth. This the majority of them found it impossible to do. Jones expected no more, for as he wrote in the *Dominion Medical Monthly* in July 1910:

> It is interesting to note that, with certain exceptions [the medical profession] being essentially stable, responsible and therefore conservative, tend[s] on the whole to lag behind in the general moral progress of the community; that is, [it] characteristically prefers to defend older and established conventions rather than to further the adoption of newer ones.[105]

Ernest Jones left Toronto for the last time in May 1913. Both by word and deed he had made himself something of a pariah to his Canadian colleagues. But his departure was occasioned more by the critical state of Loe's health. Both her physical and mental condition had deteriorated rapidly during her stay in Toronto. As Jones records, "in 1912 she decided to go to Vienna and place herself in Professor Freud's hands." Jones accompanied her, but hoped "to spend part of each year in England and part in Canada, since the university work could easily be got through in four or five months."[106] When the senate of the University of Toronto refused to endorse this arrangement, Jones settled permanently in London, where for the remaining forty-five years of his life he was to battle fearlessly and unceasingly in the Freudian cause.[107] As to the immediate fate of psychoanalysis in Canada, as Jones himself sadly lamented, after his departure, "the spark died out."[108]

Notes

An earlier version of this paper was read at a Department of Psychiatry Colloquium at Queen's University in February 1974.

1. Ernest Jones, *The Life and Work of Sigmund Freud*, 3 vols. (New York, 1953, 1955, 1957).
2. Nathan G. Hale, Jr., *Freud and the Americans: The Beginnings of Psychoanalysis in the United States, 1876-1917* (New York,

1971). See also John C. Burnham, "Psychoanalysis and American Medicine, 1894–1918: Medicine, Science, and Culture," *Psychological Issues* 5, no. 4 (1967), monograph 20.

3. Cyril Greenland, "Ernest Jones in Toronto, 1908–1913, a Fragment of Biography," *Canadian Psychiatric Association Journal* 6 (June 1961): 132–39, and 11 (December 1966): 512–19.

4. Ernest Jones, *Free Associations: Memories of a Psycho-analyst* (New York, 1959), pp. 31, 27, 26, 25, 11.

5. Ibid., pp. 57, 62, 51, 31.

6. Ibid., pp. 93, 90.

7. Ibid., pp. 112, 94.

8. Ibid., p. 115.

9. Ibid., pp. 125, 156, 155.

10. Ibid., pp. 158, 157.

11. Ibid., pp. 159, 148, 147.

12. Jones, *Life and Work of Sigmund Freud*, 2: 30. See also Jones, *Free Associations*, p. 159.

13. Jones, *Free Associations*, pp. 162, 159.

14. Ibid., pp. 165, 163.

15. William McGuire, ed., *The Freud-Jung Letters* (Princeton, N.J., 1974), Jung to Freud, 30 November 1907, p. 101.

16. Ibid., Freud to Jung, 8 December 1907, p. 102.

17. Jones, *Free Associations*, pp. 151, 150.

18. See Mott's letter, reproduced in Greenland, "Ernest Jones in Toronto, Part II," *Canadian Psychiatric Association Journal* 11 (December 1966): 516–17.

19. Ibid., Clarke to W. J. Hanna, 29 October 1908, p. 514. See also Clarke to Hanna, 23 October 1908, in Cyril Greenland, *Charles Kirk Clarke: A Pioneer in Canadian Psychiatry* (Toronto, 1966), pp. 18–19.

20. Jones, *Free Associations*, pp. 196–97, 193.

21. Ibid., pp. 187–90. See also Hale, *Freud and the Americans*, pp. 203–7.

22. Jones, *Free Associations*, p. 166.

23. McGuire, *Freud-Jung Letters*, Freud to Jung, 3 May 1908, p. 145.

24. Ibid., Jung to Freud, 12 July 1908, p. 164.

25. Ibid., Freud to Jung, 18 July 1908, p. 165.

26. Ibid., Jung to Freud, 11 November 1908, p. 176.

27. Ibid., Freud to Jung, 17 January 1909, p. 196.

28. Ibid., Jung to Freud, 19 January 1909, p. 198.

29. Freud to Jones, 2 February 1909, cited in Jones, *Life and Work of Sigmund Freud*, 2: 63.

30. *Freud-Jung Letters*, Freud to Jung, 24 February 1909, p. 206.
31. Jones, *Life and Work of Sigmund Freud*, 2: 61–62.
32. *Freud-Jung Letters*, Jung to Freud, 7 March 1909, p. 208. See also Freud to Jung, 9 March 1909, p. 211, and Jung to Freud, 11 March 1909, p. 212.
33. Ibid., Freud to Jung, 3 June 1909, pp. 227–28.
34. Jones, *Life and Work of Sigmund Freud*, 2: 58.
35. *Freud-Jung Letters*, Freud to Jung, 11 November 1909, p. 261.
36. Ibid., Freud to Jung, 2 January 1910, p. 283.
37. Ibid., Freud to Jung, 13 January 1910, p. 287.
38. Ibid., Freud to Jung, 17 May 1910, p. 317.
39. Jones, *Life and Work of Sigmund Freud*, 2: 152, 93. On the "Committee" see ch. 6, pp. 152–67.
40. Ernest Jones, "Psycho-Analysis in Psycho-Therapy," *Bulletin of the Ontario Hospitals for the Insane* (hereafter, *BOHI*) 2, no. 4 (November 1909): 32–43.
41. Ernest Jones, "The Psycho-analytic Method of Treatment" in Jones, *Papers on Psycho-analysis* (London, 1913), pp. 195, 202.
42. Ernest Jones, "Freud's Theory of Dreams," *BOHI* 3, no. 5 (April 1910): 96.
43. See Paul Roazen, *Freud and his Followers* (New York, 1975), pp. 140–45. See also, Ernest Jones, "Psychiatry Before and After Freud," in Jones, *Four Centenary Addresses* (New York, 1956), pp. 67–93.
44. Ernest Jones, "Psycho-analytic Notes on a Case of Hypomania," *BOHI* 3, no. 5 (April 1910): 119–20; also 104, 109, 110.
45. *Freud-Jung Letters*, Freud to Jung, 10 October 1910, p. 357. For Putnam's article see *Canada Lancet* 43 (August 1910): 893–908.
46. August Hoch, "The Relation of Insanity to the Psycho-neuroses," *Canada Lancet* 44 (October 1910): 107.
47. W. H. Hattie, "The Psycho-Neurosis in Asylum Practice," *Canada Lancet* 43 (August 1910): 920.
48. Ernest Jones "A Modern Conception of the Psycho-Neuroses," *Canada Lancet* 43 (August 1910): 909, 910, 916.
49. Jones, *Free Associations*, p. 190. One of the neurologists was Joseph Collins of New York.
50. See, for example, Ernest Jones, "Some Questions of General Ethics Arising in Relation to Psychotherapy," *The Dominion Medical Monthly* 35, no. 1 (July 1910): 17–11; Jones, "The Therapeutic Effect of Suggestion," *BOHI* 4, no. 1 (October 1910): 84–96; Jones, "The Relation Between Organic and

Functional Nervous Diseases," *The Dominion Medical Monthly* 35, no. 6 (December 1910): 202-7.

51.   Jones to Freud, 20 April 1910, cited in Jones, *Life and Work of Sigmund Freud*, 2: 57. Jones assessed Clarke in the following terms. Clarke "was a man of parts, an excellent Canadian type. He was a very kind and humane person.... He possessed little scientific knowledge, but his heart was set right in this respect and his ambition was to develop it in his sphere to the best of his abilities." *Free Associations*, p. 178.

52.   C. K. Clarke, "The 4th Maudsley Lecture," *The Public Health Journal* 14 (December 1923): 537.

53.   W. A. Y., "An Attack on Freud's Theories," *Canadian Journal of Medicine and Surgery* 33 (1913): 10.

54.   Reported in the *Canadian Journal of Medicine and Surgery* 29 (1911): 55.

55.   W. A. Turner, "Some Aspects of Neurology to General Practice," *Canada Lancet* 45 (August 1912): 925.

56.   C. S. McVicar, "Some Psychiatric Problems from the General Practitioner's Standpoint," *Canadian Medical Association Journal* 3 (November 1913): 951.

57.   B. E. McKenzie, "The Psycho-Neuroses," *Canadian Medical Association Journal* 6, no. 2 (February 1916): 134.

58.   W. H. Hattie, "Some Problems in Psychiatry," *The Maritime Medical News* 22 (May 1910): 143.

59.   G. S. Young, "Psycho-Therapeutic Treatment," *Canada Lancet* 43 (January 1910): 347-48.

60.   Ibid., 347.

61.   Ibid., 348.

62.   See "'Civilized' Sexual Morality and Modern Nervous Illness," in James Strachey, ed., *The Standard Edition of the Complete Psychological Works of Sigmund Freud*, 9 (1906-1908): 181-204.

63.   See Nathan Hale, *Freud and the Americans*, ch. 2, "American 'Civilized' Morality, 1870-1912," pp. 24-46, and ch. 3, "The Crisis of the Somatic Style, 1895-1910," pp. 71-97.

64.   Jones, *Free Associations*, p. 96. See also Jones, *Life and Work of Sigmund Freud*, 2: 162-63.

65.   Nathan G. Hale, Jr., ed., *James Jackson Putnam and Psychoanalysis* (Cambridge, 1971), Jones to Putnam, 23 January 1911, p. 254. This volume contains letters between Putnam and Jones, William James, Freud, Morton Prince, and Sandor Ferenczi.

66.   See Ernest Jones, "Remarks on Dr. Morton Prince's article: 'The Mechanism and Interpretation of Dreams,'" *Journal of Abnormal Psychology* 5 (February-March 1911): 328-36.

67. Hale, *James Jackson Putnam*, Prince to Putnam, 25 February 1911, p. 328.
68. Ibid., Prince to Putnam, 3 March 1911, pp. 332-33.
69. Jones, *Free Associations*, pp. 140, 180, 197.
70. Hale, *James Jackson Putnam*, Jones to Putnam, 13 January 1911, pp. 252-53.
71. Ibid., Jones to Putnam, 23 January 1911, p. 254. See also *Freud-Jung Letters*, Freud to Jung, 29 September 1910, p. 355, and Jones, *Freud*, pp. 109-10.
72. Ibid., Jones to Putnam, 5 February 1911, p. 255.
73. The literature on nineteenth-century psychiatric theory and practice is now extensive. See particularly Michel Foucault, *Madness and Civilization* (New York, 1965); Henri Ellenberger, *The Discovery of the Unconscious* (New York, 1970); Norman Dain, *Concepts of Insanity in the United States, 1789-1865* (New Brunswick, N.J., 1964); Gerald N. Grob, *Mental Institutions in America: Social Policy to 1875* (New York, 1973); David J. Rothman, *The Discovery of the Asylum* (Boston, 1971); Charles E. Rosenberg, *The Trial of the Assassin Guiteau* (Chicago, 1968); Kathleen Jones, *A History of the Mental Health Services* (London, 1972); and Ruth Caplan, *Psychiatry and the Community in Nineteenth Century America* (New York, 1969).
74. The phrase is borrowed from Michael Bliss, "Pure Books on Avoided Subjects: Pre-Freudian Sexual Ideas in Canada," above, p. 268.
75. See Caroll Smith-Rosenberg, "The Hysterical Woman: Sex Roles and Role Conflict in 19th-Century America," *Social Research* 39, no. 1 (Spring 1972): 652, 78. Also Charles Rosenberg, "Sexuality, Class and Role in 19th-Century America," *American Quarterly* 25, no. 2 (May 1973): 133-53.
76. Hale, *Freud and the Americans*, p. 25.
77. Henri Ellenberger, *The Discovery of the Unconscious* (New York, 1970), p. 502.
78. Hale, *Freud and the Americans*, p. 33.
79. Hale, *James Jackson Putnam*, Jones to Putnam, 23 January 1911, p. 254.
80. See Michael Bliss, "Pure Books on Avoided Subjects," above pp. 255-83.
81. B. E. McKenzie, *Canadian Journal of Medicine and Surgery* 12, no. 2 (August 1902): 147-48, cited in Bliss, "Pure Books on Avoided Subjects," above p. 264.
82. For another interesting example of the popular literature on sex, see Dr. B. G. Jefferis and J. L. Nichols, *Light on Dark*

Corners: A Complete Sexual Science (Toronto, 18th ed., 1894), "Sold only by subscription."

83. *Report of the Medical Superintendent of the Provincial Lunatic Asylum, Toronto, for the Year 1865* (Toronto, 1866), pp. 35–43, and *Report of the Medical Superintendent of the Asylum for the Insane, Toronto, 1877* (Toronto, 1878) pp. 18–26.

84. Hale, *James Jackson Putnam*, Jones to Putnam, 19 November 1909, p. 209.

85. C. K. Clarke, "The Evolution of Imbecility," *Queen's Quarterly* 6 (April 1899): 298.

86. Campbell Meyers, "Neurasthenia in Some of Its Relations to Insanity," *Canadian Journal of Medicine and Surgery* 16 (1904): 93.

87. See, for example, Daniel Clark, "Reflexes in Psychiatry," *Canadian Journal of Medicine and Surgery* 5 (1899): 86–93.

88. For an early attempt to understand the pathology of general paresis by a Canadian alienist, see Joseph Workman, "Cases of Insanity Illustrative of the Pathology of General Paralysis." *American Journal of Insanity* 13 (1856–57): 13–24.

89. D. A. Shirres, "A Plea for the Neurasthenic," *The Montreal Medical Journal* 35, no. 3 (March 1906): 161.

90. Daniel Clark, *Mental Diseases* (Toronto, 1895), p. 244.

91. A. T. Hobbs, "Some Aspects of Neurasthenia and Their Treatment," *The Canadian Practitioner* 34 (1909): 13.

92. James Russell, "Insanity, Its Causes and Remedies," *The Canadian Practitioner* 27 (1902): 628. For other examples of this stress on heredity by Canadian doctors, see Henry Howard, "The Increase of Insanity: What is the Cause?" *Canada Medical and Surgical Journal* 5 (1877): 1–8; Daniel Clark, "Heredity," *Canadian Methodist Magazine* 19 (1884): 257–67; R. M. Bucke, "The Origin of Insanity," *The Canadian Practitioner* 17 (1892): 219–24; and W. H. Hattie, "The Prevention of Insanity," *Canadian Medical Association Journal* 1 (November 1911): 1019–26.

93. For good brief surveys of "moral treatment" in the United States, see Eric T. Carlson and Norman Dain, "The Psychotherapy that was Moral Treatment," *American Journal of Psychiatry* 117 (December 1960): 519–24; and J. Sanbourne Bockoven, "Moral Treatment in American Psychiatry," *Journal of Nervous and Mental Diseases* 124 (August–September 1956): 167–94, 292–321.

94. *Report of the Medical Superintendent of the Asylum for the Insane, Hamilton, for 1895* (Toronto, 1896), p. 124.

95. *Report of the Medical Superintendent of the Brockville Asylum for the Insane for 1902* (Toronto, 1903), p. 133.
96. See J. C. Mitchell, "Hydrotherapy in the Treatment of the Insane," *BOHI* 4, no. 2 (January 1911): 35-57. Also W. A. Marshall, "The Use of Hypnotics in Acute Mania," *BOHI* 6, no. 3 (April 1913): 162-66; and Dr. Daniel Clark's experiments on himself with the drug hyoscyamine, *American Journal of Insanity* 40 (1884): 258-79.
97. See R. M. Bucke, "Surgery Among the Insane in Canada," *American Journal of Insanity* 55 (1898): 1-19. See also A. L. Smith, "Insanity in Women from the Gynaecological and Obstetrical Point of View," *Canada Lancet* 34 (1901): 655-63; and Ernest Hall, "Gynaecological Treatment in the Insane," *The Canadian Practitioner* 33 (1908): 147-51.
98. C. K. Clarke, "Dementia Praecox," *Canadian Journal of Medicine and Surgery* 21 (1907): 221.
99. See, for example, J. P. Harrison, "Dementia Praecox," *BOHI* 3, no. 5 (April 1910): 6-18.
100. See for example, W. B. Pritchard, "The American Disease: An Interpretation," *Canada Lancet* 37 (July 1905): 982-95. The term "neurasthenia" was first introduced by the American physician George M. Beard in 1869. See Charles E. Rosenberg, "The Place of George M. Beard in 19th Century Psychiatry," *Bulletin of the History of Medicine* 36 (1962): 245-59. See also John S. Haller, Jr., and Robin M. Haller, *The Physician and Sexuality in Victorian America* (Urbana, Ill., 1974), ch. 1, "The Nervous Century," pp. 3-44.
101. Daniel Clark, "Neurasthenia," *The Canadian Practitioner* 13 (1888): 210.
102. Richard Monahan, "The Neurotic: A Character Study in Medicine," *The Montreal Medical Journal* 39, no. 9 (September 1910): 588.
103. See A. H. Walker, "Rest in Neurasthenia," *The Canadian Practitioner* 12 (1888): 245-48; Campbell Meyers, "Neurasthenia," *Canada Lancet* 33 (1900): 503-6; and H. B. Anderson, "Neurasthenia in General Practice," *The Canadian Practitioner* 34 (1909): 754-67.
104. A. T. Hobbs, "Some Aspects of Neurasthenia and Their Treatment," *The Canadian Practitioner* 34 (1909): 15.
105. Ernest Jones, "Some Questions of General Ethics Arising in Relation to Psycho-therapy," *Dominion Medical Monthly* 35, no. 1 (July 1910): 17.
106. Jones, *Free Associations*, p. 197.

107. On Jones' resignation see: University of Toronto Archives, *Papers of the Presidents of the University of Toronto*, Sir Robert Falconer to Clarke, 13 and 25 October 1913; Jones to Falconer, 22 October and 15 November 1913; and Falconer to Jones, 3 and 28 November 1913. On Jones' later career see: Edward Glover, "Obituary: Ernest Jones," *British Journal of Psychology* 49, part 3 (August 1958): 177–81; D. W. Winnicott, "Obituary: Ernest Jones," *International Journal of Psycho-analysis* 39, part 5 (1958): 298–304; and Elizabeth R. Zetzel, "Ernest Jones: His Contribution to Psycho-analytic Theory," *International Journal of Psycho-analysis* 39, part 5 (1958): 311–18.

108. Jones, *Life and Work of Sigmund Freud*, 2: 77. The Canadian Psychoanalytic Society was not founded until 1952. It became part of the International Psycho-analytic Association in 1957, the year before Ernest Jones' death at the age of seventy-nine.

"To Create a Strong and Healthy Race": School Children in the Public Health Movement, 1880-1914

NEIL SUTHERLAND

Between the 1880s and the 1920s a growing band of English Canadians created and began to test a new consensus on the situation of the child in their society. In the four major dimensions of their enterprise they worked to change the nature and improve the quality of family life, to establish new systems of child and family welfare, to transform Canadian education, and to organize child and family health care.[1] Of these reform efforts the public health movement had the most immediate, the least ambiguous, and the most accurately measurable positive effects on the lives of Canadian children.

Canadians got down to public health work at a particularly auspicious time. "I recall," wrote the first secretary of the Ontario Board of Health, Peter H. Bryce, in 1910, that "three wholly remarkable events" took place in 1882; Louis Pasteur dramatically proved the effectiveness of immunization for anthrax in sheep, Robert Koch discovered the tuberculosis

Reprinted by permission from the *History of Education Quarterly* 12, no. 3 (1972): 304-33.

germ, and the provincial government established the Ontario Board of Health.[2] That Bryce joined these three events so closely together sharply illuminates the fact that Ontario established its board, the first such permanent body in Canada, at the beginning of the bacteriological era in public health. First the Ontario and then the other provincial boards of health were able to begin their work by using the knowledge that the earlier sanitary phase of the public health movement had already produced. However, because they were new institutions, not tightly tied by tradition to any particular procedures and staffed by the extremely enthusiastic workers that characterize the first generation of reform enterprises, they were also able to incorporate easily into their practices many of the dramatic and effective bacteriological discoveries of the last two decades of the nineteenth century. In fact, children and then infants became the prime beneficiaries of many of the medical discoveries made in the battle against communicable diseases. In the combination, then, of sanitation and bacteriology, public health workers gradually developed potent machinery for improving the health of children.

Canadians built what they came to call their public health movement around a professional core of public health physicians, sanitary inspectors, and public health nurses. Municipal and provincial boards of health and, to a lesser extent, school boards and provincial departments of education employed these health workers. When Ontario established its Provincial Board of Health under the provision of the Board of Health Act of 1882, Canada achieved its first permanent public health organization. Prior to this time, the provinces had set up public health boards only on a temporary basis in response to the threat of particular emergency situations. Two years later, the legislature passed a new Public Health Act, based on the English Consolidated Public Health Act of 1875, which greatly strengthened the powers of the Ontario board. The other provinces gradually followed Ontario's lead and, as Bryce explained, the 1884 Act became "practically the Public

Health Act of seven other provinces."[3] Quebec and New Brunswick set up permanent provincial health boards in 1887, as did Nova Scotia, Manitoba, and British Columbia in 1893, Alberta in 1907, Prince Edward Island in 1908, and Saskatchewan in 1909.[4] These boards, their municipal counterparts, and the other public agencies that gradually got involved in public health gave their professional employees financial and other support that ranged from grudging to enthusiastic. In their efforts to add to the range of public health services, many community, provincial, and national organizations both prodded and supported this official apparatus. In turn, the professionals and their amateur supporters gradually formed a number of specialized health groups and societies such as the Canadian St. John's Ambulance, the Canadian Red Cross Society, the National Sanitarium Association, the Canadian Association for the Prevention of Tuberculosis, the Public Health Committee of the National Council of Women, and the Canadian Public Health Association.

As their numbers grew and their public support increased, and they both generated their own knowledge and put to use that which was discovered elsewhere, those in the Canadian public health movement sharpened mightily the focus of their work. From their initial preoccupation with sanitation as a means of protecting and improving the health of Canadians as a whole, they turned to sorting out the distinct groups in the population for which they could expect more specialized public health measures to yield worthwhile results. As part of this process they gradually centred in on three aspects of child health. In the first phase of this work, which is the subject of this paper, they strove to protect and then to improve the health of school children. Next they began the difficult task of reducing mortality among infants and young children. Finally they tried very hard to come to grips with what those involved described as the "problem" of feeblemindedness. In these three endeavours, those in the public health movement failed only in the case of the feebleminded; otherwise they achieved a quite remarkable degree of success.

Not only did they bring about an undoubted improvement in the health of school-aged children but, by the end of the era, they were beginning to bite into the much more complex problems of infant mortality.

In Canada as it had elsewhere, the public health movement lighted on school children as its first clearly perceived client group among the young. In the first phase of this effort, from the 1880s to the early years of the twentieth century, health workers made sanitation the school's first line of defence against disease. In its second annual report, in 1883, the Ontario Board of Health explained that it had "good reason to believe" that many schoolrooms were "in a very unsanitary condition" and that "neglect of precautions to prevent the spread of contagious and infectious diseases, overcrowding and many other causes of diseases" were common.[5] It was, however, one thing for a board of health to set minimum sanitary standards for schools and another thing altogether to persuade local school boards to apply them. In 1891, the secretary recorded in the minutes of a local school meeting in the London area that it had been "moved and seconded, that a vote be taken of those present how they feel on ventilating the schoolhouse. Twenty-eight against it and one for it."[6] Even urban school systems only very slowly implemented the new sanitary standards. In 1897, teachers, parents, and pupils directed many complaints to the local trustees about the unsanitary conditions in Victoria schools.[7] The state of Toronto schools at the turn of the century also provoked sharp debate in that city.[8] In rural areas the battle against filth continued to be an unremitting one. As late as 1920, a rural medical health officer in Nova Scotia explained that of thirty schoolhouses he had recently visited, only one had satisfactory toilets and in no less than twenty-eight of them "urine and feces were over the seats and floors."[9]

If infectious diseases breached these modest and ineffectively enforced sanitary barriers, then regulations that excluded infected children from school supposedly formed the next line of defence for both school pupils and the wider community. After suffering through a particularly widespread diphtheria epidemic in 1886, for example, Ontario decided to compel parents, teachers, and health officials to report "the existence in any house of smallpox, cholera, scarlatina, diphtheria, whooping cough, measles, mumps, glanders or other contagious diseases." These regulations forbade both children with these diseases and their families to associate with other children and excluded them from school.[10] Since the medical profession still had not agreed on whether tuberculosis was infectious or how to treat it, this disease was not on the list. When they faced substantial outbreaks of infectious diseases, local school and health officials characteristically responded by closing schools entirely until the incidence of infection declined. In March 1885, for example, the New Westminster, B.C., school board decided "to close the public schools during the prevalence of scarlet fever."[11]

In their efforts to limit the spread and effect of contagious disease, however, public health workers initially faced even greater public apathy, reluctance, and opposition than they did in their work in improving sanitation. Over the century since Jenner's work of 1796–1800, medical workers demonstrated time and again the efficacy of vaccination against smallpox. As recently as the epidemic of 1885, Canadians saw how, by means of a well-organized and vigorously pursued effort of vaccination and quarantine, Ontario kept its deaths from smallpox to eighty-four while over the same time 3,175 people died of the disease in Montreal alone.[12] In most provinces school trustees had the power to exclude unvaccinated children from school.[13] Except when they were faced by an actual outbreak of smallpox, however, such as the one in British Columbia in 1892, trustees were extremely reluctant to enforce vaccination regulations.[14] In 1910, for example, a public health officer reported that "thanks to the 'Conscientious Scruples' as by rule permitted," 1,500 public school pupils in Halifax were not vaccinated.[15] In 1911 the Toronto School Board refused to enforce compulsory vaccination laws and the Ottawa Board of Health took the same stand in 1912.[16] As late as 1920, Saskatchewan health officials found that "very few children of school age" had been vaccinated.[17]

To back up their two main lines of defence, and to assist them in their work in other areas, public health officials also made modest forays into the field of school curriculum. They tried diligently to interest practising teachers in public health and to ensure that new teachers had proper grounding in physiology, hygiene, and public health.[18] In addition, they worked to have hygiene, physiology, and, later, physical culture included among the compulsory subjects in elementary schooling.[19] Their reason for taking this position was a simple one: the "susceptible minds of the young," argued a committee of the Ontario Board of Health, were "particularly adapted to receive and retain such instruction, which will afterwards be spread broadcast among the masses, thus preparing the way for the enforcement of sanitary laws."[20]

By the turn of the century, then, Canadian public health officials had established two sets of controls, which were by no means universally enforced, with which they tried to protect the health of children while they were at school. First, they set minimum standards of sanitation for school premises and, second, they excluded from school those children who were obviously suffering from a stated list (which omitted tuberculosis) of infectious diseases. Health workers hoped, as well, that teachers would give their pupils some instruction in hygiene and perhaps some physical training as well. So far as such youngsters were protected at all, the general provisions made for the public health of the community sheltered the health of infants and other children not attending school.

Over the next two decades a whole cluster of developments made very radical changes in preventative health work for children in Canada. Undoubtedly the most important cause of these changes was the astonishing growth in medical science, especially in bacteriology.[21] Turning laboratory discoveries into effective weapons of public health, however, was a complex matter taking place over a considerable number of years. Consider, for instance, diphtheria. Diphtheria found its main victims among school-aged children and since the public health movement campaigned against the disease with increasing vigour over these years, the fight against it provides an excellent example of the intimate connection between bacteriology and the health of the young. In 1891 and 1892, for example, the Ontario Board of Health reported that not only was diphtheria "a disease peculiarily liable to attack with malignity children under ten years," but also that there was "no single cause" that contributed "so largely to the dissemination and continuance of this pest as the introduction of its contagion in the schoolroom."[22] Since diphtheria germs lost virulence "by free exposure to sunlight, moisture and fresh air," the board explained that the main preventative was proper ventilation of schoolrooms.[23] The work against diphtheria proceeded, almost simultaneously, on a number of different fronts. While scientists and physicians explored and developed as rapidly as possible the practical potentialities of a series of laboratory discoveries, public health officials were hard at work explaining to colleagues, to physicians in private practice, and to the general public precisely what they had learned and persuading, cajoling, and occasionally coercing them to use the product of this new knowledge.

Between 1884 and 1894, French, German, and American bacteriologists—particularly Friedrich Loeffler, Emile Roux, Alexandre Yersin, Karl Fraenkel, Emil von Behring, and W. H. Park—made the central core of discoveries that gradually led to the control of diphtheria. They proved, to summarize their work very briefly, that a powerful, soluble toxin produced by the Klebs-Loeffler bacillis caused the general symptoms of diphtheria; that, in addition to the obviously ill, convalescents and even well persons could infect others with the disease; that laboratories could use the blood of animals (especially horses) to produce a powerful antitoxin; that this antitoxin was an effective agent against cases of diphtheria; and that it prevented diphtheria from developing in persons who had been exposed to the disease.[24] Three practical results flowed almost immediately from these discoveries. First, with the discovery that diphtheria was a true zymotic disease, public health officials brought it under their control. In 1891, for example, Ontario passed an order-in-council that directed health authorities to handle diphtheria as they did smallpox.[25] Second, physicians began to use laboratory tests both to diagnose accurately cases of diphtheria and to govern the quarantine period of diagnosed cases and those relatives who had unfortunately been incarcerated with them. Other places quickly copied this work that began in North America in 1893 under the leadership of the indefatigable Dr. Hermann L. Biggs of the New York City Public Health Department. Since the Ontario Board of Health had established a laboratory in 1890, it was able to conduct tests for diphtheria almost as soon as that in New York.[26] Third, doctors began to use antitoxin to treat both diagnosed cases of diphtheria and those who had been exposed to the disease. While a Berlin doctor first used antitoxin on a human patient in 1891, Roux himself made the treatment widely known through his classic paper to the Eighth International Congress of Hygiene and Demography in Budapest in September 1894.[27] Again Dr. Biggs's New York Public Health Department, which began producing antitoxin in the autumn of 1894, took the North American lead in this work.[28] Canadian public health authorities quickly followed suit and by 1899 their use of antitoxin had produced a notable decline in diphtheria deaths.[29] By 1905, the decline was clearly worldwide.[30]

As health workers and some of the general public came to realize that society had at last some means for exerting much tighter control over diphtheria, they embarked on the first arduous phase of the public health movement's efforts against the disease. Although Hamilton's medical health officer, Dr. W. F. Langrill, argued optimistically that if public health workers had "the same support in control of diphtheria as smallpox, it would be no longer prevalent," he also demonstrated that his fellow physicians were clearly one very important part of the problem.[31] "Just recently," he reported in 1901, "a child died from what the attending physician called laryngitis." Suspicious of this diagnosis, Langrill interviewed the doctor who "claimed the disease was not diphtheria, but admitted that two children in the same family had just previously had a 'sore throat with some traces of membrane.'" Meanwhile the child's family conducted a public funeral for their son with "small boys acting as pallbearers." The result of this negligence, Langrill concluded, was that "five neighbouring children were infected with diphtheria...all in a severe form."[32]

Families of infected children also stood in the way of effective control of diphtheria. Where isolation hospitals existed, as they did in most sizable centres in Ontario by 1903, medical health officers had the power to place diphtheria cases in them.[33] Families that placed their afflicted children (usually accompanied by their mothers) in such hospitals not only reduced the likelihood that the disease would spread in their households and neighbourhoods, but they also increased the chances that the children would survive the attack of the disease.[34] While some families welcomed such an opportunity to improve the odds for their children and to avoid the often severe hardships of family quarantines, when others objected, health officers were often very reluctant to use their powers. Other families avoided both quarantines and the isolation hospital by concealing cases of the disease.

Recalcitrant parents and physicians, however, were not the only problem; public health workers themselves had to learn through long experience that only if they distributed it free would physicians and families use antitoxin as early, as frequently, and as widely as was necessary to exploit its full potentiality as a means for controlling the disease. In 1914 Ontario began, for instance, to distribute biological products, such as diphtheria antitoxin, from its own laboratories at prices much below commercial ones. Eventually, in 1916 the Ontario government made these products free to everyone.[35] The Saskatchewan Bureau of Public Health made similar arrangements. Even so, the death rate from the disease remained at about 8 percent of cases because, as the bureau lamented, "the people of our country fail to recognize cases in the early stage when if antitoxin were freely used the death rate would be negligible."[36] School trustees had much to learn as well. As part of his work in dealing with a diphtheria epidemic in Oshawa in October 1920, the district medical health officer "called a meeting of the School Board and the Board of Health," but "only after much discussion" did they eventually agree that "all school children should have an immunizing dose of Anti-toxin."[37]

While the public health movement gradually implemented the results of the first round of discoveries, medical researchers continued to work on diphtheria, thereby opening up the second phase of the campaign against the disease. By using the Schick test, devised in 1913, physicians could sort out in older children those susceptible to diphtheria from those who had developed an immunity to the disease. To the former, they could then give toxin-antitoxin to build up their immunity.[38] By the early 1920s Canadian public health authorities and physicians were beginning to use both procedures fairly regularly.[39] Both phases of this campaign against diphtheria had positive, measurable effects on the disease. For the first, Ontario reported that between 1903 and 1918 the death rate for diphtheria in that province fell from thirty-one to twelve for every 100,000 population.[40] For the second, as toxin-antitoxin gradually provided children with permanent immunity, the incidence of diphtheria in the Canadian population went from 76.7 per 100,000 of population in 1926 to 57.1 in 1931 to 18.6 in 1936 to 24.9 in 1941 to 20.7 in 1946 to 1.8 in 1951, to .8 in 1956.[41]

In addition to providing new knowledge and new techniques, this great research effort on diphtheria and other diseases had other positive effects on the health of children. Since it contrasted so sharply with the plodding progression characteristic of improvements in sanitation, the very momentum with which one bacteriological discovery followed on another, and the speedy and dramatic way in which many of them displayed their effects, became in themselves important parts of the improvement process. The rapid series of discoveries seem, indeed, to have been at the root of the characteristically missionary zeal and the sometimes almost millennial expectations of many health workers. Their enthusiasm was highly infectious and quickly spilled over into the general public as well. In the early years of the century, Canadians began to raise the level of their expectations in the area of public and especially of child health.

As they had been twenty years before in the earlier emphasis on sanitation, school pupils were the first group of children to reap some benefits from this new bacteriological era in public health. In the light of the growing fund of new knowledge, public health workers and the general public began at the turn of the century to focus their attention more sharply on the health of school children. When they did so they saw two very obvious weaknesses in existing arrangements. First, while either a physician or sanitary inspector decided whether or not a particular school met minimum sanitary standards, generally the teacher had the far more difficult task of diagnosing that a pupil had an infectious disease and excluding him from school. By the time such diseases as diphtheria, or even tuberculosis, reached the point in their cycle where a teacher saw that a child was sick enough to be excluded from school, the ailment had often reached an advanced stage and may already have spread to other pupils in the schoolroom. It was obviously no longer sufficient to rely on teachers or private physicians to locate and quarantine infected children. If they were to utilize fully the improved diagnostic tests and more effective methods of treatment public health workers decided that they must screen every child for infectious diseases. But even when the teacher or family physician properly and accurately diagnosed infectious disease and kept the child out of school, there was very little assurance that his family would provide him with the necessary treatment, that they would protect themselves from the infection, or that the child would not, outside of school hours, pass the disease on to his friends and acquaintances.

To solve these problems, some people concluded, clearly public health workers should inspect and visit pupils as well as schools. In 1901, for example, the Windsor, Ontario, School Board required children who had been away for over a week be examined by their family physicians or the medical health officer before they could return to school.[42] But this step, worthwhile as it probably was (for one thing it brought a dramatic improvement in school attendance), focused on the wrong end of the problem; doctors examined children only after a disease had run, or almost run, its course. As the Ontario Board of Health stated in its report both in 1899 and 1901, in its opinion the next stage in the control of infectious diseases in children was, at least during emergencies, to have "physicians visit the schools to examine for suspects ... and to follow up the absentees to their homes."[43]

As Canadian health authorities and others interested in this work began to press seriously for such procedures, they examined carefully what was going on elsewhere. While medical inspection of school children had been discussed in France as early as the end of the eighteenth century, it was not until the last three decades of the nineteenth century that the nation made any substantial efforts to implement such ideas. And although regular medical inspection of pupils began in Brussels as early as 1874, throughout Sweden in 1878, and in Paris in 1879, the early efforts made in Britain and the United States were the major influences on Canadian developments.[44] The latter, particularly, provided the models that Canadian centres usually followed. In contrast, too, to the sanitary phase of the public health movement, when provincial, state, or national authorities generally took the initiative, in all three countries municipal authorities in urban centres took the lead in introducing school inspection work.

In 1890 the London School Board appointed the first school medical officer in Britain. In 1893 the Bradford Board copied this action and other boards gradually followed suit.[45] This early work stimulated considerable discussion and enquiry in Britain that eventually produced national legislation. In 1907 the British Parliament passed the Education (Administrative Provisions) Act that set up a School Medical Department under the Board of Education that was to encourage local school authorities to undertake regular medical inspection of school children as rapidly as possible.[46]

In the face of an epidemic of diphtheria in 1894, Boston established North America's first school medical inspection system. Philadelphia and Chicago followed suit the next year.[47] Despite these pioneering ventures, however, the New York Department of Public Health created the scheme that became the most influential model for Canadian practice. In 1897 the department appointed 150 physicians as part-time school medical inspectors. As Dr. Hermann Biggs explained to a meeting of the British Medical Association in Montreal later the same year, he directed the doctors to inspect, each day, the children that teachers excluded from class and to send home every pupil "found to be suffering from any form of general contagious disease or any contagious disease of the eye or parasitic disease of the skin."[48] In 1902 Biggs added two new steps to the procedures. First, he required school physicians to make, every seven to ten days, a routine examination of all pupils for contagious disease and minor infections of eyes or skin.[49] Second, and following the suggestion of Lillian D. Wald of the Henry Street Settlement, he appointed a corps of school nurses to follow up the work of the doctors.[50] In 1905, Biggs further broadened the scope of the school medical system when he instructed the doctors to begin examining children for non-contagious physical defects.[51] If a physician found any such problem, he notified the parent of it by post card. The department soon discovered, however, that the parents corrected only a very small proportion (it estimated 6 percent) of the defects reported to them. To deal with this situation and other problems of child health, the New York Board of Health established a separate Division of Child

Hygiene, under Dr. S. Josephine Baker, and immediately increased its staff of school nurses to 141. In September 1908, the nurses began to visit the homes of all children discovered to be suffering from physical defects in order to persuade the parents to provide the necessary treatment.[52] One year later, the department claimed that already the nurses' visits had raised the level of treatment from 6 to 83 percent.[53] By 1911 some 443 American cities had duplicated such systems.[54]

To get first-hand information about the situation in Europe and Britain, Canadians attended both the second and third medical congresses on school hygiene.[55] Canadian organizations also brought out English officials to explain their work. In April 1911, for example, Dr. George Auden, chief medical superintendent of the Birmingham schools, spoke on medical inspection to a meeting of the Ontario Education Association and other Canadian organizations.[56] More often, however, Canadians evaluated their initial efforts against those systems set up in the United States. In 1909 in her report on medical inspection in Canadian schools to the International Congress of Women, Mrs. J. N. Smillie listed Canadian efforts in terms of their being attempts "to follow in the footsteps of New York and other large American cities."[57] Addressing the first meeting of the Commission of Conservation, in 1910, Dr. Peter H. Bryce argued that in establishing and operating a school medical inspection, Canadians should copy the example of New York.[58] In outlining the aims for medical inspection in public schools in Canada, an editorial in the *Public Health Journal* used only American experience as its evidence.[59]

In the 1890s, Dr. J. G. Adams, a Toronto dentist, made the first major effort to have health professionals examine the physical condition of Canadian school children. After conducting an extensive survey of the condition of children's teeth both in Canada and elsewhere, Adams concluded that children's teeth decayed "at a much earlier period than they did formerly" and that the teeth and mouths of "a large percentage" of children were "in a very unhealthy and often disgusting condition."[60] In 1896, Adams aroused the interest of the Toronto Trades and Labor Council, the Hamilton Local Council of Women, and the Toronto Dental Society in the matter, and stirred some public discussion through newspaper reports of his conclusions.[61] In response to a number of requests, the Ontario Board of Health appointed a committee to look into the situation. In its report, the committee agreed with Adams' conclusions, and, referring to similar efforts in Germany and Britain, strongly recommended that local boards of health and school trustees appoint dental inspectors to examine the teeth of school pupils.[62] It did not, however, suggest that such inspections be made mandatory.

At this point the whole matter foundered. The Toronto School Board refused to add "three or four thousand dollars on to our already over-burdened taxpayers."[63] The provincial Department of Education completely ignored the suggestions of its sister agency. Except for the Hamilton Local Council of Women and the Toronto Trades and Labor Council, the public demonstrated at best only lukewarm support for the scheme. Some local councils of women could not agree that dental inspection was a matter of first priority, arguing instead that perhaps the state of pupils' eyes was a more serious problem. Other critics explained that the out-patients departments of some hospitals gave free care to the teeth and eyes of poor children.[64] No organizations made really vigorous efforts to persuade health or school boards to overcome their natural reluctance to venture into a new area of service. From this short-lived campaign, however, some laymen learned that sometimes one had "to step outside the ordinary routine of practice" in order to implement new standards of preventative health care and, further, that because it was "easy to investigate them with regularity and without risk of repetition," school children made excellent experimental subjects.[65]

After Adams' efforts failed, Canadians waited some years before trying again in any substantial way to introduce preventative medicine into their schools. Like Adams' plan, they directed their first efforts at only one dimension of the whole problem. In 1903 the Vancouver School Board decided that, because of the "prevalence of defective vision" amongst its charges, it should provide instruction for city teachers in the mechanics of eye testing. The board therefore arranged for two nurses from the City Hospital to give instruction to the teachers.[66] During the same year some Ontario communities began to deal with local epidemics of children's diseases by employing physicians on a temporary basis to examine school children and to visit those who were absent.

In 1906, under the aegis of the municipal Board of Health, Montreal began the first regular and systematic medical inspection of school pupils in Canada.[67] The following year the Sydney, N.S., medical health officers began to inspect school pupils on an annual basis. In the same year, the Vancouver School Board appointed a physician as full-time medical inspector of school children and the Hamilton board appointed Canada's first school nurse. In 1907, as well, Ontario passed legislation that permitted school boards, if they wanted to, to undertake school medical inspections. By the end of 1910, in addition to the four communities already noted, Halifax, Lachine, Toronto, Brantford, Winnipeg, Edmonton, and Nelson, B.C., made some form of medical inspection of their school pupils. In 1914, the *Public Health Journal* made a national survey of the work.[68] By this time, in the three maritime provinces, only four Nova Scotia communities—Amherst, Halifax, Truro, and Sydney—reported that they conducted any form of school medical inspection. In the province of Quebec, the cities of Montreal, Westmount, and Lachine inspected their pupils. In Ontario, fourteen communities—Toronto, Ottawa, Kingston, London, Brantford, Niagara Falls, Brockville, Sault Ste. Marie, Steelton, North Middlesex, Hamilton, Peterborough, Stratford, and Fort William—made school medical inspections.[69] In the prairie provinces, the cities of Winnipeg, Regina, Saskatoon, Prince Albert, Calgary, and Edmonton inspected their school children. Under the terms of British Columbia's legislation, passed in 1910, which called for an annual inspection of all school pupils, teachers, and school janitors in the province, medical inspectors worked in Victoria, Vancouver, Nelson, New Westminster, and South Vancouver.[70] Other communities across Canada reported that they were seriously considering instituting school medical inspection.

Once it entered the work, the Toronto School Board rapidly surpassed the others and erected one of the most comprehensive and widely reported school medical systems in the world. As such, it quickly became the model for many other Canadian communities. Starting about 1906, the Toronto Local Council of Women and other groups tried to persuade local health and school officials to introduce medical inspection into the city schools.[71] In this endeavour they met the very firm opposition of Dr. Charles Sheard, Toronto's chief medical officer. In response to the agitation by the council and some of its affiliated groups Sheard sampled the health of Toronto school children but "decided against appointing scores of doctors and nurses" because "there was not sufficient data to warrant it."[72] In Sheard's opinion school medical inspection was "a pure fad, instituted principally by women," who were "apt to give way to sentiment" and listened "to the talk of agitators" who wanted "easy billets for their friends, with good pay and little work."[73]

At this point, the publisher of the Toronto *Telegram*, John Ross Robertson, entered the affair. For a long time, Robertson had been extremely active in the improvement of the health of children and had been substantially responsible for the growth and development of Toronto's superb Hospital for Sick Children.[74] When, in the early part of 1910, Robertson became interested in the Council of Women's campaign for school medical inspection he entered into it with his usual journalistic flair. He investigated how New York and other places managed school nursing and medical inspection and himself wrote a series of reports on the subject for his newspaper. In addition, he offered $2,500 to the Toronto School Board to pay the costs of a school nursing experiment in the

Toronto schools for a year. By deciding early in 1910 to conduct a medical survey to discover the number of mentally defective children in the schools of Toronto, the School Board had already demonstrated its own growing interest in health matters.[75] Robertson's intervention in the affair apparently convinced the board that it would also have to begin medical inspections. Accordingly it turned down Robertson's offer but on 25 February 1910, bypassing the municipal Board of Health, it put $2,500 in the year's estimates for medical inspection. Very soon thereafter it hired Miss Lina Rogers as its first school nurse and soon-to-be director of school nursing.[76]

Once underway, the Toronto School Board rapidly expanded its school medical system. In 1913, the chief inspector of schools, James L. Hughes, stated with pride that "Toronto was spending in that year almost as much for medical care as the whole educational system had cost only ten years earlier."[77] By 1914 the School Health Department took care of the health of the 45,000 Toronto school pupils with a staff of one chief medical officer, twenty-one physicians who worked as part-time medical inspectors, one dental inspector and four dental surgeons who worked part-time, one superintendent of nurses, and thirty-seven full-time school nurses.

In 1914, when the *Public Health Journal* made its survey of medical and dental inspection in Canada, school and public health authorities could put their responses into the context of twenty years of North American and about eight years of Canadian practice in this matter. Partly because they had been able to build effectively and with little modification on American efforts, Canadian workers had accumulated a surprisingly wide range of practical experience in school inspection over a short time. One may, therefore, ask of the 1914 reports and other contemporary Canadian material three important questions: what were school and health workers trying to accomplish with school medical inspection, what means did they use to accomplish their task, and how effective were they in reaching their goals?

At first, Canadians who favoured the medical inspection of school children saw their purpose in essentially negative terms; they wanted to reduce or to eliminate the evil of disease from their communities. As they actually got into the work, however, Canadian school medical workers and their supporters, in common with their British and American counterparts, gradually shifted their goal to the much more positive one of creating a nation whose children were all in rude good health. By 1914, moreover, many urban centres in Canada had shifted the focus of their public health work in schools from premises to pupils. To control communicable disease, health professionals regularly inspected school buildings and examined pupils, teachers, and janitors. Instead of the teachers having to do so, physicians or nurses now excluded the sick pupils and readmitted those who had recovered. In Ottawa, for example, the school physician examined the children for "scarlet fever, diphtheria, tonsilitis, measles, German measles, mumps, smallpox, chicken pox, whooping cough, ring worms, contagious skin diseases and pediculosis."[78] In some places, such as Vancouver, Edmonton, Calgary, Winnipeg, Toronto, Montreal, and Halifax, physicians inspected the pupils. In others, such as Regina, Prince Albert, Kingston, and Niagara Falls, school nurses made the initial inspections.[79] Although medical inspectors in British Columbia were supposed to examine teachers and janitors for infectious diseases once a year, there and elsewhere they seem to have made such inspections only on initial appointment. In 1914, for example, the Halifax medical officer reported only that he had examined eight new teachers "with the result that four were passed as 'satisfactory', the balance being given either 'modified' or 'unsatisfactory' certificates."[80]

Since these were the years, too, when the great crusade against tuberculosis was growing "in equipment and strength," all inspectors showed particular interest in this disease.[81] In 1910 the Hamilton School Board assigned one nurse to full-time detection of tuberculosis among school pupils.[82] In that year alone she detected twenty cases, which were sent to sanitoriums. Toronto placed one assistant medical officer in charge of tuberculosis inspection and, in 1913, the city opened up a "forest" school for pretubercular and other sickly children.[83] Other centres, such as Hamilton and Vancouver, instituted "open air" classrooms for the same group.[84] In all areas, school nurses gave particular attention to locating tubercular children and those who were "contacts."[85]

In addition to searching out communicable diseases, most inspectors also looked for chronic defects. As the examiner in North Middlesex put it, "the body of the school child was considered a machine in order to answer the question, 'Is it in good running order?'"[86] In Regina, the school nurse examined "particularly for defective eyesight, defective hearing, enlarged tonsils and adenoids, carious teeth, pediculosis, for symptoms of tuberculosis, lateral curvature, goitre, and chorea."[87] Generally, as the Nelson, B.C., medical inspector explained, her duty in such cases began and ended "with recommendation for treatment" and she customarily notified parents "requesting them to take the child to the family physician."[88] No authority reported that it invited parents to be present at the inspection of their children. Indeed, at least some places, physicians conducted their examinations *en masse*. The South Vancouver medical inspector reported that pupils were "brought into the teacher's room apart from the class-rooms in groups of ten, boys and girls separate." Despite this rather wholesale procedure, the same inspector explained it was "the rarest exception to have objections made by either parent or pupil."[89]

The incidence of inspection varied greatly from place to place. Probably the most thoroughly inspected pupils were those of Toronto. Almost as well served were the 550 pupils in Steelton, Ontario. Other centres, such as Regina, Edmonton, Winnipeg, Lachine, Sydney, N.S., and certain British Columbia areas, established less frequent but systematic examination. Often the main work of the doctor was to inspect or examine those pupils referred to him by the school nurse or teacher. In Montreal, for example, physicians visited large schools every day and small schools at least twice a week to examine referrals. In Kingston, a school nurse visited each school twice each week and inspected all the pupils in their classrooms every two weeks.

Such a bewildering array of practices reflected local differences in what the school or health board knew about child health and preventative medicine, how much interest they had in the matter, and how much in the way of services they felt the local taxpayer would support. It also clearly demonstrated that the public health movement had not yet developed an optimum pattern of inspection and referral, or divided the task between physician and nurse in such a way that the skills and time of both were used effectively and efficiently. Nevertheless, by 1914 the school nurse was clearly moving into the central position in school medical programs. As she moved between school and home she found of necessity that she had to add preventative medicine, teaching, and even social welfare to her primary task of preventing the spread of communicable diseases. In the school, she did some or all of the routine inspections, examinations, readmissions, and often minor first aid work as well. She kept up the medical records of the pupils, taught health to teachers and pupils through such means as lectures, demonstrations, and "nose blowing" and "tooth brushing" drills, and ran school health clubs like the Little Nurses League in Winnipeg, or the Little Mothers classes in Regina, Vancouver, Victoria, and Stratford. In most places, however, her main task was to visit the home of the infected pupil who had been excluded from school and of the child who had an untreated chronic condition. Often, these early home visits opened the school nurse's eyes as to just how much there was to do.[90] Especially in poor homes, nurses kept a sharp eye out for cases of infectious diseases, including previously concealed cases. In Lachine, for example, the medical inspector (in this instance a physician) discovered contagious diseases in 17 percent of the 751 homes he visited over one school year.[91] When they saw how fruitful such work could be, school boards and health boards directed the nurse to exploit to the full the wider opportunities opened up by home visits.

When her powers of persuasion proved to be insufficient, the school nurse in Toronto and other cities was able to coerce the parents. If they refused to do anything for a child who was "really suffering from want of medical or surgical attention," the nurse referred the case to the Juvenile Court which took "prompt action."[92] In Toronto, the court fined some poor parents for refusing to carry out school medical officers' orders for operations "on children suffering from adenoids and enlarged tonsils." In commenting on this matter, the editor of the *Public Health Journal* argued that "parents must not be allowed to stand in the way of their children's complete recovery." To do so would "render negatory the very useful system of inspection that has been adopted in the schools."[93]

As physicians and nurses sorted out their separate roles in school health services, Canadian dentists began to argue that they too had an important place in any comprehensive program. On 22 November 1910, as the last of a series of public meetings in Ontario, Dr. John W. Dowd, formerly of Toronto and more recently inspector of schools in Toledo, Ohio, addressed a dinner held in his honour by the Toronto Dental Society. An honoured guest of the evening was the pioneer of dental inspection of school children, Dr. J. G. Adams.[94] This impressive occasion culminated a campaign by the Toronto Dental Society "to have a dental inspector appointed...to instruct teachers and pupils how to take care of their teeth and mouths to the end that length of life and happiness may be increased."[95] There was about this particular campaign and other efforts to promote dental hygiene a certain flamboyance, an excess in claims and rhetoric that sometimes brought them close to being a caricature of the whole children's health movement. In his address, for example, Dr. Dowd ingeniously argued that if one assumed that "the dental surface in the ordinary mouth is from 22 to 24 square inches" and only 8 percent of this area was properly cared for, then there was left "5 square feet of uncleaned surface in every schoolroom." If this area were visible to the naked eye, Dowd went on, "there would be a panic" but because it was not, the pupils involved were "breathing everywhere, coughing everywhere, expectorating nearly everywhere" with the result that disease "developed among the men and women in the world."[96] In 1911 an editorial in the *Public Health Journal* claimed that "fully 99 percent" of children were "in need of dental treatment."[97]

The activities of the Toronto Dental Society were the most active Canadian manifestation of what its promoters called the "oral hygiene crusade."[98] This movement, which began in Germany in the closing decades of the nineteenth century, arrived in North America early in the twentieth. It produced a great flurry of activity on this continent in the years between 1908 and World War I. This campaign had a variety of roots in contemporary dentistry. First, a new generation of better-trained dentists displayed a growing concern for preventative work. As well, some of the excitement and sense of imminent accomplishment that the bacteriological discoveries gave to medicine in these years spilled over into dentistry. Finally, dentists were anxious to demonstrate that their craft was on the rise and that in fact it was well on the way to becoming one of the important professions of the modern community.

These factors alone, however, could not account for the successes achieved by the dental movement. On one hand, behind all the exaggeration and the self-seeking quality of the campaign, there was a serious situation. As Dr. Adams had been some years earlier, the pioneers of medical inspection were appalled at the dreadful state of the teeth of the children they examined.[99] In his annual report for 1911, the Montreal health officer, Dr. J. E. Laberge, explained that 19,843 of the 59,685 children his department had examined over the year suffered from decayed teeth. While this did not necessarily mean that these children were suffering from "any serious physical disability," Laberge argued that "it was necessary to take cognizance of such matters, as defective teeth often meant that there was some deeper-seated malady, such as tuberculosis, bad digestion and so forth."[100] On the other hand, public support for the school to inspect and even to treat children's teeth, which revealed itself in the Toronto dinner, was another example in the sharp rise in the standards that Canadians were applying to the health of children. Dentists in the crusade offered no really convincing evidence that the teeth of Canadian children were then any worse than they had ever been. In contrast, however, to their response to Dr. Adams' alarms in 1896, by 1910 some Canadians were clearly willing to do something about the situation.

When the real state of their pupils' teeth was reported to them, most school or health boards decided to have medical inspectors include defective teeth among the chronic conditions they reported to parents. Despite the enthusiasm of some parts of the dental profession for a separate school dental service, and the model for one that Toronto and later Vancouver provided, however, it was the school nurse who eventually undertook most of the work for preventative dentistry in the school. She examined teeth, persuaded parents to have caries treated, demonstrated the proper use of the tooth brush, conducted tooth-brushing drills, sometimes provided children with free tooth brushes, and often arranged for free treatment for poor and indigent children.[101]

Public health workers, school officials, and school and health board members often expressed their pleasure with the early results of the medical inspection of Canadian school children. While one may ask whether the actual effects of what they did supported these generally subjective feelings on the matter, two difficulties stand in the way of a really precise and accurate answer to this question. First, as the example of diphtheria clearly showed, the vigorous pursuit of this disease by medical inspectors was perhaps only the most important of a number of factors that initiated its decline. Second, Canadian school medical workers neither subjected their early work to vigorous scientific analysis nor did they keep the kinds of records that would have permitted others to do so. In their speeches, articles, and official reports of the topic, Canadian workers generally took as given the fact that foreign and Canadian centres already inspecting their pupils had fully proved the worth of the practice. Such statements of worth as they did offer were general ones like that of British Columbia's Board of Health, which explained that there could be "no doubt of the progress...being made" by means of medical inspection.[102] Public health workers clearly saw their tasks as extending the practice to areas where it did not yet exist and expanding the scope of the service where it did. When health officers included statistics in their annual reports, they recorded without analysis such items as the number of classrooms and pupils that they had inspected over the year and the number and types of defects they had discovered in them. In 1918, the Calgary School Board reported, its medical inspector conducted 950 physical examinations, and its school nurses made 3,862 inspections and visited 969 classes and 219 homes. In addition, the board's eye, ear, nose, and throat clinic tested 4,981 pupils and treated 392 eye cases, 72 ear cases, and 52 nose and throat cases and its dental clinic treated 522 children, performing 1,041 dental operations on them.[103]

Nevertheless, public health workers, school boards, and boards of health offered a great deal of not very precise though definite evidence that medical inspection was an effective device for the improvement of public health generally and the health of children in particular. Montreal, with the longest experience in the work, made consistent though low-keyed claims as to the worth of what it did. In 1909, three years after the city began such work, Mrs. Smillie reported to the International Congress of Women that medical inspection had sharply decreased the incidence of contagious diseases in the schools. She noted particularly that "no serious epidemic of measles, scarlet fever or diphtheria" had occurred "since the installation of regular inspection."[104] In

1911 the city's health officer disclosed that although his inspectors had concluded that 27,348 of the 59,685 children examined in the year "were not in a satisfactory state of health," when he compared this situation to their findings of preceding years, he saw nonetheless "a great improvement."[105] In 1914 the Montreal Board of Health concluded that by the means of school medical inspection, "pediculosis and scabies have almost disappeared from the schools" and there had been "a great diminution of contagious diseases in the city." The board was so pleased with these and other results of its work that, in 1918, it organized a separate division of child hygiene for Montreal schools.[106]

Elsewhere, medical inspectors also reported many positive results of their work. In an entirely typical statement, the school medical inspector for Saint John, N.B., reported, four years after beginning the work in that city, that there had been "a great lessening of the number of more serious conditions found in the school." The effect of this change, he went on, was to make his work increasingly "preventative as well as curative." Of the physical defects calling for reports to parents he found that, in 70 percent of cases, they were "promptly attended to" and even in poorer districts he obtained this percentage of treatment "eventually by following up and rectifying the cases."[107] In 1919 the Vancouver school medical officer explained that in the previous year alone his department increased by 125 percent the number of treatments that it had "secured for children suffering from various physical defects."[108] In 1921 the Hamilton medical health officer boasted of the "vast improvement" that two years of dental inspection and treatment had made on the teeth of school children in Hamilton. Over this time his department's surveys and clinics had reduced from 90 percent to 70 percent the number of children whose teeth needed treatment.[109] While "parents, teachers, and medical men" testified as to the worth of medical inspection, noted the British Columbia Board of Health in the same year, they also strongly brought home to the board the need for "follow-up work."[110] By the early 1920s most health officials would probably have concurred with the conclusion on school medical inspection reached by the chief medical officer for New Brunswick, Dr. George G. Melvin. Although no public health activity in his province presented such difficulties and involved "so great a direct expenditure," Melvin wrote, yet in view of what was "possible to accomplish, and the outstanding importance of that accomplishment," the province just had to overcome the difficulties.[111]

By the time the nation went to war in 1914, public health workers and their supporters had persuaded urban Canadians of the undoubted merits of maintaining sanitary schools and of medically inspecting school children. While such reformers had taken a long time to implement sanitary standards, in only fifteen years they had popularized the idea of inspection to the extent that most urban school systems in Canada either inspected their pupils or were on the verge of doing so. In their school medical services members of the public health movement firmly believed that they had developed and demonstrated the worth of a practical and effective way of making Canada a healthier and happier nation. By this time, too, many workers were eager to take what they saw as the next obvious step in their efforts, that of extending their service to all the children in small towns and country districts. When Alan Brown observed, however, that Canadian child care materials gave him "the impression that they were not intended for use outside the city limits" he put his finger on the major flaw in the whole public health apparatus as it affected rural children.[112] As they began to tackle rural work systematically, public health workers first discovered that they had to shift their principal sphere of activity from the municipal to the provincial level of government. Next, and far more important, they found that they had to subsume the school medical inspection campaign under the until then distinctly separate crusade to protect and improve the health of infants and young children. At this point, the effort to improve the health of school children ceased to be a separate entity in the public health movement and became but one part of a much wider campaign to improve the health of all Canadian children.[113]

Notes

In an address to the Canadian Public Health Association meeting in Montreal in December 1911, James Roberts, who was the medical health officer for Hamilton, Ontario, argued: "Our chiefest concern is with the children, the rising generation. We should aim first of all to create a strong and healthy race" (James Roberts, "Insanitary Areas," *Public Health Journal* [hereafter cited as *PHJ*] 3 [April 1912]: 182). I gratefully acknowledge the help of my colleague, Professor John Calam, in the preparation of this paper.

1. I examine this reform movement as a whole in my Ph.D. dissertation, "Children in English-Canadian Society: Framing the Twentieth Century Consensus" (Minnesota, 1973). See also my article "The Urban Child," *History of Education Quarterly* 9 (Fall 1969): 305–11.

2. Peter H. Bryce, "History of Public Health in Canada," *Canadian Therapeutist and Sanitary Engineer* 1 (June 1910): 278–91.

3. Ibid., p. 290; see also Peter H. Bryce, "The Story of Public Health in Canada," in *A Half Century of Public Health: Jubilee Historical Volume of the American Public Health Association*, ed. Mazÿck P. Ravenel (New York, 1921), pp. 56–66.

4. R. D. Defries, ed., *The Development of Public Health in Canada: A Review of the History and Organization of the Public Health in the Provinces of Canada, with an Outline of the Present Organization of the National Health Section of the Department of National Pensions and National Health, Canada* (Toronto, 1940), pp. 15, 35, 49, 56, 67, 90, 101, 115, 131. For the background to the Ontario legislation, see Bryce, "History of Public Health," pp. 287–90, and R. D. Splane, *Social Welfare in Ontario, 1791–1893: A Study of Public Welfare Administration* (Toronto, 1965), p. 199. For an account of the English Public Health Act of 1875, see W. M. Frazer, *A History of English Public Health, 1834–1939* (London, 1950), pp. 114–25.

5. Ontario Board of Health, *Report*, 1883, p. xlvi.

6. Ibid., 1891, p. 38.

7. See, for example, *Victoria Colonist*, 13 April 1897, p. 8, and 14 May 1897, p. 8.
8. Ontario Board of Health, *Report*, 1898, pp. 68–75; Toronto *Globe*, 2 May 1900, p. 7, and 4 May 1900, p. 12.
9. A. C. Jost, "The Conservation of Child Life," *PHJ* 11 (November 1920): 503–12.
10. Ontario Board of Health, *Report*, 1887, pp. iii–v.
11. New Westminster *British Columbian*, 14 March 1885. See also *Victoria Colonist*, 17 October 1891, p. 1, *British Columbian*, 11 May 1894, p. 3, *Colonist*, 8 January 1900, p. 4, and Toronto *Globe*, 19 June 1900, p. 12.
12. Ontario, Board of Health, *Report*, 1885, pp. 29–34.
13. Ibid., 1887, p. v; ibid., 1888, pp. iv–vi.
14. *British Columbian*, 3 June 1892, p. 4.
15. *PHJ* 2 (April 1911): 184.
16. Ibid., 2 (May 1911): 221; ibid., 3 (May 1912): 249–55.
17. Saskatchewan Bureau of Public Health, *Report*, 1919–20, p. 8. For an account of the legal status of compulsory vaccination, see Peter Frank Bargen, *The Legal Status of the Canadian Public School Pupil* (Toronto, 1961), p. 79.
18. See, for example, Ontario Board of Health, *Report*, 1882, pp. 168–76; ibid., 1883, pp. xlv, 400–408.
19. See, for example, ibid., 1883, pp. xlvi, 242–43; ibid., 1890, pp. xiii–xvi, lxxxix–xcvii; *British Columbian*, 9 April 1892, p. 4.
20. Ontario Board of Health, *Report*, 1883, pp. 242–43.
21. George Rosen, *A History of Public Health* (New York, 1958), pp. 344–403.
22. Ontario Board of Health, *Report*, 1892, p. 19; ibid., 1891, p. 1.
23. Ibid., 1892, p. 19.
24. Privy Council, Medical Research Council, *Diphtheria: Its Bacteriology, Pathology and Immunology* (London, 1923), pp. 44–63, 126–29, 232–35; C. E. Winslow, *The Life of Hermann M. Biggs: Physician and Statesman of the Public Health* (Philadelphia, 1929), pp. 102–30; Rosen, *History of Public Health*, pp. 319–20, 333–36; and Ontario Board of Health, *Report*, 1890, pp. lvii–lxii.
25. Ontario Board of Health, *Report*, 1901, p. 8.
26. Ibid., 1890, p. lxxviii; Defries, *Development of Public Health in Canada*, pp. 77–88.
27. Medical Research Council, *Diphtheria*, pp. 61–62.
28. Hermann Biggs, "The Development of Research Laboratories," New York Department of Health, *Monthly Bulletin* 1 (March 1911): 54–56.
29. See, for example, Ontario Board of Health, *Report*, 1899, p. 12.

30. R. H. Mullin, "Recent Advances in the Control of Diphtheria," *Canadian Medical Association Journal* 14 (May 1924): 398-406.
31. Ontario Board of Health, *Report*, 1903, p. 46.
32. Ibid., 1901, p. 93.
33. Ibid., 1903, p. 48.
34. In a crude comparison of home versus hospital treatment, Bryce demonstrated this fact as early as 1903. Ibid., 1903, p. 52. See also the much more accurate confirmation of the efficacy of hospital treatment in Toronto between 1912 and 1919 in Mullin, "Recent Advances."
35. Ontario Board of Health, *Report*, 1920, pp. 37-38; Defries, *Development of Public Health in Canada*, pp. 77-88.
36. Saskatchewan Bureau of Public Health, *Report*, 1917-18, p. 17.
37. Ontario Board of Health, *Report*, 1920, p. 167.
38. Medical Research Council, *Diphtheria*, pp. 349-61.
39. See, for example, Ontario Board of Health, *Report*, 1921, p. 204.
40. Ibid., 1920, p. 37.
41. M. C. Urquhart and K. A. H. Buckley, eds., *Historical Statistics of Canada* (Toronto, 1965), p. 45.
42. Ontario Board of Health, *Report*, 1901, pp. 110-11.
43. Ibid., p. 6; see also ibid., 1899, pp. 72-74.
44. Rosen, *History of Public Health*, p. 365.
45. Frazer, *English Public Health*, p. 257.
46. Ibid., pp. 256-58, 323-24.
47. Rosen, *History of Public Health*, p. 366.
48. Winslow, *Biggs*, p. 157.
49. Ibid., p. 186.
50. Lina Rogers Struthers, *The School Nurse: A Survey of the Duties and Responsibilities of the Nurse in the Maintenance of Health and Physical Perfection and the Prevention of Disease Among School Children* (New York, 1917), pp. 17-18.
51. Winslow, *Biggs*, p. 193.
52. Ibid., pp. 214-15.
53. Ibid., p. 215; for a more detailed account of the work of the Division of Child Hygiene, see "Division of Child Hygiene," New York Department of Health *Monthly Bulletin* 1 (January 1911): 14-16, and Ernst J. Lederle, "The Needs of the Department of Health," ibid., 1 (October 1911): 236-37.
54. Russell Sage Foundation, *What American Cities are Doing for the Health of School Children: Report Covering Conditions in 1038 Cities* (New York, 1911). The report was summarized for Canadians in *PHJ* 2 (September 1911): 433.

55. Ontario, *Sessional Papers*, 1907, no. 62, pp. 23–26; James Kerr and E. W. Wallis, eds., *Transactions of the Second International Congress on School Hygiene, London, 1907*, 3 vols. (London, 1908); A. Maloine, ed., *Ille Congrès International D'Hygiène Scolaire, Paris, 2-7 Aout, 1910*, 3 (Paris, 1911): 9.

56. George A. Auden, "School Inspection and the Public Health Service," *PHJ* 2 (May 1911): 207–10. See also L. Haden Guest, "Poverty and School Clinics," ibid., 2 (July 1911): 317–19; L. Haden Guest, "School Clinics," ibid., 4 (May 1913): 272–77.

57. International Congress of Women, *Report of the International Congress of Women, held in Toronto, Canada, June 24-30, 1909*, 2 vols. (Toronto, 1910), 2: 57.

58. Commission of Conservation, *Report*, 1910, p. 132.

59. *PHJ* 2 (June 1911): 276.

60. J. G. Adams to P. H. Bryce, 10 February 1896, quoted in National Council of Women (hereafter cited as NCW), *Yearbook*, 1896, p. 463; A. E. Webster, "Status of Dentistry," *Dominion Dental Journal* (hereafter cited as *DDJ*) 22 (December 1910): 571–607.

61. NCW *Yearbook*, 1896, pp. 35, 41–42, 457–70; Ontario Board of Health, *Report*, 1896, pp. 76–82; *Colonist*, 25 July 1896, p. 8.

62. Ontario Board of Health, *Report*, 1896, pp. 80–82.

63. NCW *Yearbook*, 1896, p. 459.

64. Ibid., pp. 49–50, 457–60, 469–70.

65. Ibid., p. 467.

66. Vancouver School Board, *Report*, 1903, p. 17.

67. J. Edouard Laberge, "Inspection médicale des maisons d'éducation," *Bulletin Sanitaire* 9 (1909): 117–24.

68. *PHJ* 5 (February and March 1914): 91–98, 150–60.

69. While the *PHJ* did not list Fort William, the National Council of Women's Public Health Committee in 1911 noted it as one of a number of communities where medical inspection was under way (NCW, *Yearbook*, 1911, pp. 43–47).

70. See also Alice Ravenhill, "The Health of Public School Children in British Columbia," *The Child* 4 (June 1914): 697–99.

71. NCW, *Yearbook*, 1910, pp. i–ii.

72. Edward Miller Steven, *Medical Supervision in Schools: Being An Account of the Systems at Work in Great Britain, Canada, the United States, Germany, and Switzerland* (London, 1910), pp. 182–83.

73. Ibid.

74. Alfred Wood, "The Largest Sick Children's Hospital in the World," *Canadian Magazine* 12 (February 1899): 314–18; Toronto *Evening Telegram*, 20 December 1909, p. 18; Toronto

Globe, 1 June 1918, pp. 5, 7; "John Ross Robertson," in J. E. Middleton, *The Municipality of Toronto: A History* (Toronto and New York, 1923), pp. 57–58.

75. *Evening Telegram*, 14 January 1910, p. 18; *Globe*, 28 January 1910, p. 14.
76. *Globe*, 25 February 1910, p. 16; *Evening Telegram*, 25 February 1910, p. 10.
77. Bruce N. Carter, "James L. Hughes and the Gospel of Education: A Study of the Work and Thought of a Nineteenth-Century Canadian Educator" (Ed.D. diss., University of Toronto, 1966), p. 360.
78. *PHJ* 2 (December 1911): 588–89.
79. Jean Browne, "School Nursing in Regina," *PHJ* 5 (February 1914): 91–92; "Medical Inspection of Schools in the Middle West," ibid., pp. 94–95; "Medical Inspection of Schools in Ontario," ibid., 5 (March 1914): 159–60.
80. "Medical Inspection of Schools in Nova Scotia," *PHJ* 5 (February 1914): 98.
81. NCW *Yearbook*, 1912, p. 102; John J. Heagerty, *Four Centuries of Medical History* (Toronto, 1928), pp. 226–45.
82. Ontario Board of Health, *Report*, 1910, pp. 148–50.
83. Struthers, *The School Nurse*, pp. 132–43; see also Leonard P. Ayres, *Open Air Schools* (New York, n.d.).
84. Daniel Hockin, "The Rotary Clinic," *Twenty-fifth Anniversary of Rotary Club of Vancouver, Canada: 1913-1938* (Vancouver, 1938), pp. 14–15.
85. See, for example, Canada, Department of Health, *Handbook of Child Welfare Work in Canada for the Year, March 31, 1922* [hereafter cited as *Handbook*], ed. Helen MacMurchy (Ottawa, 1923), p. 56.
86. *PHJ* 5 (March 1914): 160.
87. Browne, "School Nursing in Regina," pp. 91–93.
88. "Medical Inspection of Schools in British Columbia," *PHJ* 5 (March 1914): 150.
89. Ibid., p. 153.
90. Struthers, *The School Nurse*, pp. 1–4.
91. "Medical Inspection in Quebec," *PHJ* 5 (March 1914): 156.
92. Struthers, *The School Nurse*, p. 40.
93. *PHJ* 4 (February 1913): 94.
94. "Complimentary dinner to John W. Dowd, by the Toronto Dental Society, Nov. 22, 1910," *DDJ* 22 (December 1910): 570–600.
95. "Editorial Notes," *DDJ* 22 (October 1910): 511–12.

96. John W. Dowd, "The Mouth and the Teeth as Factors in Public Health," *DDJ* 22 (December 1910): 573.

97. *PHJ* 2 (May 1911): 221.

98. For the origin and development of the oral hygiene crusade, see E. B. Hicks, "Free Examination of School Children's Teeth: What Oral Hygiene Means to Them," *DDJ* 22 (October 1910): 460-66; Arthur Day, "What is Being Done Outside of the Dental Office for the Improvement of the Human Mouth," *PHJ* 3 (May 1912): 235-39; Professor Dr. Dieck, "The Care of the Teeth of School Children in Germany," ibid., 4 (June 1913): 366-69, and Robert M. McCluggage, *A History of the American Dental Association: A Century of Health Service* (Chicago, 1959), pp. 248-53. For what dentists saw as the social implications of their work, see the talk by Dr. A. W. Thornton, Toronto, to the Canadian Public Health Association's 1912 meeting entitled "The Dentist as Social Worker," *PHJ* 3 (September 1912): 524; and W. D. Cowan, "Dental Caries in School Children and Dental Inspection," ibid., 4 (November 1913): 602-5.

99. See, for example, James Stuart, "Public School Medical Inspection," *Canadian Therapeutist* 1 (August 1910): 379-81.

100. *PHJ* 3 (April 1912): 222; see also, C. P. Kennedy, "Report on the Mouths and Teeth of the Children in Two Public Schools of Toronto," *DDJ* 22 (December 1910): 571-72, and A. E. Webster, "Dental Inspection of Two Schools in Toronto," ibid., pp. 600-604.

101. See, for example, Struthers, *The School Nurse*, pp. 141-42, 205-25, and Browne, "School Nursing in Regina," p. 93.

102. British Columbia Board of Health, *Report*, 1920, p. 15.

103. Canada, Dominion Bureau of Statistics, *Historical Statistical Survey of Education in Canada* (Ottawa, 1921), p. 110.

104. International Congress of Women, *Report... 1909*, 2: 58.

105. *PHJ* 3 (April 1912): 222.

106. *Handbook*, p. 153.

107. Ibid., pp. 81-82.

108. Vancouver School Board, *Report*, 1919, p. 39.

109. Ontario Board of Health, *Report*, 1921, p. 317.

110. *Handbook*, p. 40.

111. Ibid., p. 78.

112. Alan Brown, "Problems of the Rural Mother in the Feeding of Her Children," *PHJ* 9 (July 1918): 297.

113. See "Children in English-Canadian Society," pt. 2.

Public Health in
Montreal, 1870–1930

TERRY COPP

The connection between inadequate wages, poor housing conditions, and a mortality rate which marked Montreal as one of the unhealthiest cities in the western world was perfectly clear to many contemporary observers. Ames had established the very high correlation between poverty and premature death for the section of the city he studied in 1897. Mortality rates in the crowded working class wards remained at more than double the levels of higher income areas throughout the period under review. By the twentieth century medical science possessed the capacity to bring about significant reductions in mortality and morbidity rates without any change in the living conditions which created so much of the problem. But in Montreal gastro-enteritis, tuberculosis, diphtheria, typhoid, and even smallpox wreaked havoc in the lives of the working class long after such diseases

Reprinted by permission of the Canadian Publishers, McClelland and Stewart Ltd., from Terry Copp, *The Anatomy of Poverty: The Condition of the Working Class in Montreal, 1897-1929* (Toronto: 1974), pp. 88-105.

had been brought under a degree of control in other North American and European cities. Why did Montreal have such a poor record in the field of public health? Some of the reasons are revealed by tracing the history of public health work in the city.

Municipal public health services had existed in Montreal in an organized manner since 1876. The Health Bureau's designated functions were similar to those defined for local authorities under the British Public Health Act of 1875 and reflected the contemporary concentration on sanitary inspection.[1] The theoretical basis of such sanitary codes rested on the belief that disease was caused by miasmas produced from decaying animal and vegetable matter. Disease could be prevented, it was believed, if dampness was overcome, drainage and sewerage improved, and waste materials, "nuisances," removed efficiently. If a disease broke out a physical quarantine was imposed, to be lifted when the infected persons were "better." Shops, markets, abattoirs, dairies, and milk distributors were inspected to correct bad sanitary practices and condemn spoiled foodstuffs. The British public health system which evolved from these principles was something less than a complete success even within its limited concerns, because insufficient attention was paid to the appointment of competent, independent inspectors with the appropriate power to deal with violators. Still, there is considerable evidence that the improvements in public health laws were an important factor in the decline of death rates in Britain. The general mortality graph for Montreal shows a steady decline in the death rate between 1877 and 1884, and one may speculate about the possible effects of the new health system, but many other factors could account for the changes.

The concentration on sanitary inspection which marked mid-Victorian public health in Montreal as elsewhere was challenged after 1880 by the series of discoveries in bacteriology which began with the work of Robert Koch. The practice of inoculation for smallpox had been understood for some time and much work on the "germ theory" of disease

had been accomplished prior to the 1880s, but the burst of
scientific creativity associated with the names of Pasteur,
Cohn, and Koch led to a fundamental change in the medical
approach to man's most deadly enemies. The isolation of specific disease-producing organisms and the development of
therapeutic and prophylactic vaccines for the treatment of
many of them must be regarded as a truly revolutionary
change in the history of mankind.

The medical profession in Montreal was kept well abreast
of these developments. The McGill Medical Faculty, even
after the departure of Osler in 1884, was one of the better
institutions in North America and the faculty of the Laval
Medical School was equally conversant with the new discoveries and with their implications for public health. Unfortunately, none of this advanced knowledge was of much
assistance to the victims of the smallpox epidemic of 1885-86
which claimed the lives of at least twenty-five hundred
Montrealers, mainly the poor. The vaccination riots of that
winter required the use of militia units returning from the
Northwest Rebellion campaign to maintain order and act as
sanitary police. The crisis did spur the authorities to action.
The Quebec Public Health Act of 1886 was intended to serve
the same function as Disraeli's 1875 legislation. Municipalities were required to establish health boards across the
province and a provincial board charged with research and
regulatory functions was established.[2]

The Quebec Public Health Act was unfortunately a very
defective piece of legislation. The provincial board could
force a municipality to create a local health board and the act
provided legal authority for a variety of public health measures, but no municipality could be compelled to enforce the
regulations or finance an adequate program. If the reforms
which the act made possible had been implemented in Montreal and vigorously enforced, then much would have been
accomplished. As it was, even the question of smallpox vaccination was not adequately resolved for a generation. For
one thing, after compulsory smallpox vaccination had been

authorized in 1901, most municipal health boards failed to act.[3] As a result, the disease could easily spread. It was not until the epidemic of 1903 that the board ordered municipalities to undertake compulsory vaccination.[4] The Quebec government's Royal Commission on Health and Social Welfare notes in its historical summary that only one death from smallpox occurred after 1918 in Montreal.[5] This did not mean the disease was eradicated and considering that more than thirty years had passed since the 1886 epidemic, there was little cause for self-congratulation in this belated achievement.

The inadequate response to the problem of smallpox was not an isolated case. The implications of the bacteriological revolution may have been thoroughly grasped by the Quebec medical profession but institutional responses were slow in coming. The provincial Health Board did establish a bacteriological laboratory in 1894 and the Montreal Health Department included a second lab among its facilities, but neither laboratory was adequately organized or staffed.[6]

In a speech before the British Medical Association, which held its convention in Montreal in 1897, the director of the Montreal department, Dr. Louis Laberge, described the functions of the department in terms of sanitary inspection of houses and streets, meat and milk inspection, and the disinfection of contaminated buildings. Laberge had a staff of twenty sanitary inspectors, four meat inspectors, two milk inspectors who were veterinary surgeons, and one disinfector.[7] The department was clearly operating in the tradition of the sanitary ideal.

Montreal was dependent for much of its public health assistance on the work of private voluntary agencies and specialized hospital departments. Ideally, such private initiatives should have supplemented public facilities and pioneered new approaches to public health problems. It may be argued that this is precisely what happened in the long run, but such a statement would be too facile. It might be as accurate to suggest that such institutions quickly developed a stake in the public health business and instead of serving as pressure groups to encourage the adoption of vigorous, metropolitan-wide services, the tendency was to expand their individual spheres of activity without much regard for coordination or gaps in services. Large, heavily populated sections of the city were left without convenient access to public health services and the observer cannot help but be struck by the scarcity of medical and para-medical facilities in the heavily populated wards of the east end.[8]

The most important single force working for the establishment of a progressive public health system was the Quebec Board of Health. Its chairman, Dr. E. P. Lachapelle, and the permanent secretary, Dr. Elzéar Pelletier, had a clear understanding of what reforms were necessary and they conducted a vigorous campaign to accomplish their aims. The board had to concern itself with public health throughout the province but a large part of its energy was directed towards the city. Board members, and Pelletier in particular, were active participants in international public health congresses and organizations. Pelletier, for example, was made treasurer of the American Public Health Association in 1897. The annual reports of the board, as well as its monthly publication, *Bulletin Sanitaire*, contain a good deal of information about developments in Britain, France, and the United States.

The original text of the Public Health Act of 1886 was amended a number of times and major revisions were undertaken in 1901 and 1906.[9] The main reforms sought by the Quebec Board of Health, apart from those dealing with factory conditions and housing standards, were the enforcement of compulsory vaccination for smallpox, similar regulations for anti-diphtheric inoculation, the medical inspection of school children, adequate controls over the purity of milk and ultimately pasteurization, the development of treatment centres and sanitoria for tuberculosis, and water purification programs. The board did not merely talk about these reforms. Detailed plans were prepared and the by-laws of the Public Health Act amended to authorize municipal action in these areas.

The key word here is "authorize." The board had limited powers to enforce some of its recommendations during emergencies, but it could not compel municipalities to take preventive action. The reason for this is obvious enough. The provincial government was not prepared to finance capital or operating costs of public health programs. Municipalities would have to raise the money for such expenditures from their own tax resources and public health, except in time of epidemics, proved to have a low priority.

Montreal's infant mortality rate was the city's most serious public health problem. Between 1897 and 1911, approximately one out of three babies died before reaching the age of twelve months. As late as 1926, the rate was still 14 percent, a figure almost double the average for New York or Toronto. The single most important cause of infant mortality was "disease of the digestive system," usually classified as "diarrhoea and enteritis." Between 1906 and 1915 more than 42 percent of the 45,000 children under two years of age that had died were the victims of "infantile diarrhoea."[10] By 1927 the percentage of such deaths had been reduced to 33 percent of the total, but even this figure was substantially greater than in any other large North American city.

The importance of gastro-intestinal diseases in Montreal's infant mortality rate is reflected in the peculiar pattern of infant deaths in Montreal. Whereas in most cities the highest percentage of deaths occurred in the first month after birth, the crucial period for Montreal's children was from one to six months. Studies of infant mortality in other countries provide an essential framework for analysing this phenomenon. One of the standard text books on public health used in Canadian medical schools in the 1920s cited a study of infant mortality in England and Wales, where accurate statistics were available. In the conclusion of that work the author argued that:

It appears then that under the term "infant mortality" we are classing together two radically different types of causes of death.... The first type consists of deaths due

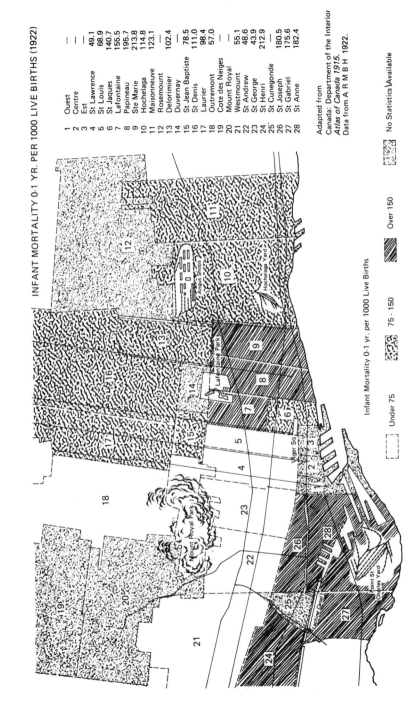

INFANT MORTALITY 0-1 YR. PER 1000 LIVE BIRTHS (1922)

1	Ouest	—
2	Centre	—
3	Est	49.1
4	St Lawrence	68.9
5	St Louis	140.7
6	St Jaques	155.5
7	Lafontaine	195.7
8	Papineau	213.8
9	Ste Marie	114.8
10	Hochelaga	123.1
11	Maisonneuve	
12	Rosemount	102.4
13	Delorimier	
14	Duvernay	78.5
15	St Jean Baptiste	111.0
16	St Denis	98.4
17	Laurier	57.0
18	Outremont	
19	Cote des Neiges	—
20	Mount Royal	55.1
21	Westmount	48.6
22	St Andrew	43.9
23	St George	212.9
24	St Henri	
25	St Cunegonde	180.5
26	St Joseph	175.6
27	St Gabriel	182.4
28	St Anne	

Adapted from
Canada: Department of the Interior
Atlas of Canada 1915.
Data from A R M B H 1922.

Infant Mortality 0-1 yr. per 1000 Live Births

Under 75   75 - 150   Over 150   No Statistics Available

to developmental factors which vary but little from place to place, year to year, and class to class, and appear to be caused by fundamental influences which we do not fully understand, and at present seem unable to control. The second type consists of deaths mainly due to respiratory diseases and enteritis caused by influences in the post-natal environment, most prevalent in crowded, smoky, industrial and mining districts, and probably entirely preventable.[11]

Montreal's high infant mortality rate was due to "influences in the post-natal environment" and such deaths were "most prevalent in crowded, smoky, industrial...districts" of the city.

The Children's Bureau of the U.S. Department of Labor expressed its views on the incidence of high infant mortality in a different way.[12] It defined a "Safety Zone" for babies which involved the following criteria:

(a) The majority of fathers earn living wages;
(b) Mothers are not employed during the year before or the year after birth;
(c) Proper maternal care is provided during the period of child birth;
(d) The father and mother are literate, i.e. able to read and write;
(e) Proper housing conditions exist.

No comparable studies of infant mortality were undertaken in Montreal but the available evidence would seem to confirm the pattern described in the British and American studies. For example, in 1921 the infant mortality rate for the well-off suburban cities of Outremont and Westmount[13] and the upper income wards in west end Montreal was less than 6 percent, while the adjacent west end working class wards had rates in excess of 20 percent. Infant deaths in the older east end wards were also around the 20 percent mark. The newer working class wards in the north-east sections of the city reported considerably lower rates, between 9 and 12 percent, but there is a high probability that this is the result of incomplete data. The city's unusually high infant mortality was clearly linked to the general problem of the condition of the working class.*

The Montreal Health Department never attempted to develop a statistical correlation between poverty and death rates, but it regularly reported the data in terms of a simple ethnic breakdown. At first three and then four categories were used: French Canadian; other; Catholic; Protestant and Jewish. Consistently throughout the thirty years under review, the statistics showed a dramatically higher mortality rate among French Canadians, particularly in regard to infant mortality.

French-Canadian doctors had long argued that the high infant mortality in Quebec was primarily due to the tendency of French-Canadian mothers to wean their infants very quickly and bottle feed them, often on a mixture of beef extract and cereal—"la bouille traditionnelle." Dr. Séverin Lachapelle had attacked this practice and argued the case for breast feeding in a series of books and lectures from 1880 onwards.[14] His theme was repeated time and time again in articles published in the *Bulletin Sanitaire* and the popular press.

Observers struck by the significantly lower infant mortality rate among the impoverished Jewish immigrant community in Montreal claimed "that Jewish mothers almost invariably feed their children at the breast."[15] It is difficult

---

* The statistics on illegitimate children born in Montreal provide one of the most stunning illustrations of infant mortality patterns. Approximately three quarters of all recorded illegitimate children died before they were one year old. In 1924, for example, there were 1,114 illegitimate births recorded and 878 died. Of this number, 542 died between the ages of one and six months, suggesting what conditions were like in the crèches and infant "boarding houses" which looked after the majority of these children. *Annual Report of the Montreal Board of Health*, 1924, pp. 21, 22.

to establish the validity of this contention and since the statistical basis for the calculation of Jewish births and mortality was recognized as inadequate, no real basis for comparison exists. In fact, the problem of the validity of the city's "vital statistics" makes comparisons between ethnic groups very difficult. The highly organized French-Canadian parish network in the older wards of the city provided a well-established mechanism for reporting births (baptism) and deaths. The same was true for at least the traditional Irish Catholic parishes. The Protestant and Jewish communities seem to have been far less systematic in registering and reporting vital statistics.

Nevertheless, it is probable that the French-Canadian infant and general mortality rates were higher than those of other ethnic groups, for it is apparent that there was a disproportionate amount of poverty among French Canadians. The predominantly French-Canadian east end of the city contained the highest proportion of low income wage earners, the highest percentage of female workers (including, it may be presumed, young mothers), and the least adequate public health facilities. It should also be noted that pasteurization of milk was begun in the city in the first years of the twentieth century, but prior to World War I only dairies in the English-speaking west end of the city were supplying pasteurized milk to their customers.[16]

The high mortality rate from gastro-intestinal diseases seemed to point to impure food and water as the direct causes. Montreal's water supply was adequately controlled by 1914 and this may help to account for the downward trend in infant mortality around that time. But the city's milk supply, which had long been singled out as the key factor in infant deaths, could not be as easily purified.

The provincial government had established a Milk Commission in 1900 and had drawn up a list of rules designed to regulate the conditions under which milk was produced. The municipal Health Department also established sanitary rules for dairies and employed several milk inspectors to visit dairy farms shipping milk to the city. The inadequacy of even this limited sanitary inspection was fully revealed in 1914 when the federal Department of Agriculture published the results of a bacteriological study of the milk supply of Montreal.

The investigators visited all of the major dairy farming districts supplying milk to Montreal and acquired samples of the milk at the point of production. In order to classify their samples, they had to create a "new" grade of milk, grade "D," which was described as "five times worse than grade 'C' milk." The "C" category was used in North America for milk which was not fit for drinking but could be used in manufactured food. Twenty percent of the 285 samples of milk sent to Montreal for ordinary consumption were classified as Grade "D" and 30 percent were listed as "C." By the time the milk reached Montreal, shipped in milk cans loaded in ordinary freight cars, 90 percent of it was unfit for human consumption by the standards used in large American cities.[17]

"Reputable" milk dealers attempted to overcome this by pasteurization, but less than a quarter of the city's milk supply was pasteurized in 1914 and, of the six large dairies investigated by the commission, only one carried out completely effective pasteurization. The most common method of milk distribution was to measure a quart with the top of a milk can and pour it into a container brought by the customer. The big dairies bottled milk, but the commission pointed out that bottling was no guarantee of purity.[18]

This report recommended careful inspection of dairy farms, a strict classification of milk, and compulsory pasteurization by controlled methods. The investigators also pointed out that New York City had cut its infant mortality rate in half by establishing pure milk depots in poorer sections of the city and suggested that Montreal should act along these lines.[19]

All of these recommendations and indeed the revelations about the city's milk supply had been publicized before. In addition to the constant warnings and recommendations put forward by health officials, popular newspapers like *Le Canada* had carried articles on New York's milk depots and the pioneering system of controls developed in Rochester.[20] A significant response had been slow in developing, but by 1911 three "Gouttes de Lait" providing free milk had been established in Laurier, Delormier, and St. Andrew's wards.[21]

In 1912 the municipal Health Department began to implement the recommendations of a report prepared by Dr. Sévérin Lachapelle of the Laval Medical Faculty, Dr. A. D. Blackader of McGill, and Dr. Elzéar Pelletier. As an interim measure, the report proposed the establishment of twelve additional "Gouttes de Lait" in the areas of highest infant mortality.[22] Six thousand dollars was appropriated to assist in creating the new milk depots and by 1914 the city was spending $17,420 on twenty-seven depots. In that year, 3,101 infants were registered with "Gouttes de Lait" and the Health Department noted that the death rate among those registered was only fifty per thousand, less than one quarter of the overall infant mortality rate.[23]

Lachapelle and Blackader had recommended the development of a permanent organization involving the appointment of a number of public health nurses and the transformation of "Gouttes de Lait" into medical and educational public health centres. The war seems to have curbed the development of this more systematic attack on infant mortality. By 1916 the civic grant to existing milk stations was reduced to just $12,000 and there was a slight decline in the number of "Gouttes de Lait."[24] In 1918 the municipal Health Department established an Infant Hygienic Division and the following year a number of municipal baby clinics, along the lines recommended in 1912, were opened. Civic action in this field had been slow in coming, but by 1927 there were twenty-seven public and private baby clinics and 41 percent of all newborn infants in the city were supervised by a clinic.[25]

The *Report* on Montreal's milk supply had suggested a number of regulatory measures. In 1914 the city's health officials had drafted a comprehensive milk by-law which provided for the grading of milk and the strict enforcement of sanitary rules. The by-law was not adopted until 1925, partly

because of doubts about its legality, partly because of controversy about compulsory pasteurization, and partly because of
City Council's inertia. However, in the intervening years,
considerable public pressure had gradually built up in favour
of pasteurization and by 1926, when the law requiring it
began to be enforced, 94 percent of the city's milk was being
pasteurized.[26]

The perennial problem of the gap between legislation and
strict enforcement was dramatically illustrated to the people
of Montreal in 1927 when an epidemic of typhoid fever
swept the city. The source of the typhoid virus, which killed
533 people, was traced to a dairy which superficially met
sanitary standards and pasteurized its milk, but the worker
who turned out to be a typhoid carrier had not been examined.[27] Yet it must be noted that the campaign against infant
mortality began to show significant results in the 1920s. An
infant mortality rate in 1927 of 113 per thousand was
nothing to be proud of and other cities had accomplished
considerably more, but at least a basis for controlling infant
mortality had finally been established.

The second most important public health problem in the
city was tuberculosis. Between 1900 and 1918, the mortality
rate from TB was always in excess of 200 deaths per 100,000
population, a figure which placed Montreal in a unique category among large North American cities. As in the case of
infant mortality, the published statistics present some problems of interpretation. The mortality rate from TB was
always much higher among French Canadians than among
other ethnic groups. In 1927, for example, the Montreal
Health Survey reported the following rates: French Canadians 167; British Canadians 95; Jews 32 (per 100,000).[28]
Again it must be pointed out that the system of reporting
mortality was so deficient that some caution must be used in
generalizing from these statistics. For example, descriptive
evidence points to a very high rate of TB among the city's
Jewish immigrant community and that is not reflected in the
statistics.[29]

When the tuberculosis statistics are broken down by ward, a familiar pattern emerges. In 1921, St. Denis Ward with 202 deaths per 100,000 had the worst record and St. Anne's Ward was second with 186. Only one-third of the population of St. Anne's Ward was French Canadian but the vast majority were poor. The rates for upper income St. Andrew and St. George Wards were fifty per 100,000.

Prior to 1909-10, when the provincial government appointed a Royal Commission on Tuberculosis, the campaign against the "white scourge" had been left entirely to private initiative. The Royal Edward Institute, modeled on Edinburgh's famous Victoria Dispensary, had been established in 1909 as a result of a gift from the Burland family.[30] The Royal Edward was as well equipped and as "progressive" as any TB clinic in the world, but its services could reach only a fraction of the infected population. Even then, the absence of adequate sanitorium facilities made it very difficult to "cure" cases which it was able to diagnose early enough for treatment.

The Royal Commission recommended the establishment of additional clinics on the basis of one for every 50,000 people, the building of a preventorium, a sanitorium, and a TB hospital.[31] The commissioners noted that the current practice was that every advanced TB patient had to be released from hospital once a satisfactory diagnosis had been made because no sanitarium space was available. Experience in other cities suggested that the TB morbidity rate was usually ten to twelve times the mortality rate. Applied to Montreal, this meant that 80 percent of those afflicted with TB, as many as eight to ten thousand persons, were not receiving any medical attention.

For the next twelve years, provincial and municipal health officials and some citizens' groups pressed for the implementation of the Royal Commission's recommendations. Dr. S. Boucher, the city's health director, was particularly concerned with the construction of a TB hospital so that the most severe cases could at least be isolated. The Sisters of Providence were prepared to operate such a hospital but the City Council, while willing to rent a building to the Order, suggested that the $150,000 required to renovate and equip the building would have to be raised by public subscription.[32] It was not until 1924 that the Sisters of Providence were able to begin construction of the Sacré Coeur Hospital in suburban Montreal.[33]

The same year witnessed the formation of a new public health organization called "The Montreal Anti-Tuberculosis and General Health League." The league was chaired by Sir Arthur Currie and was composed largely of Montreal businessmen. Lord Atholstan, the publisher of the *Montreal Star*, was a prominent member and he launched the work of the league by donating $100,000 to the Royal Edward and Bruchési institutes to open two new clinics, one in east end Hochelaga Ward and the other in St. Henri.[34]

The league rapidly became involved in a wider range of public health activities and in 1928 it financed a systematic survey of public health activities in Montreal. The report, which is discussed in more detail below, described the city's tuberculosis services in the following terms:

The skeleton of a good service is locally present and some good work is being done along most of the essential lines. For a full measure of success, however, it is necessary that the activities of all agencies, public and private, be brought together and coordinated into a unified tuberculosis programme; that funds and personnel be made available to extend the nursing, medical, sanitorium, hospital and preventive services so well begun.[35]

Fifteen specific recommendations were listed in the report and it was noted that "many of these needs" had been pointed out by the director of the Montreal Health Department in a report issued in 1914.

In 1910 the Royal Commission on Tuberculosis had noted that Montreal's mortality rate from TB was considerably higher than that of any other large North American city. Seventeen years later, the relative position of the city remained unchanged. The world-wide decline in TB death rates after 1918 (caused, it is believed, by the high death rate among TB victims during the flu epidemic of that year) was reflected in the city's statistics, but throughout the 1920s, Montreal's TB mortality rate was three times the figure for Toronto.

Between 1911 and 1921 Toronto had developed a "comprehensive plan" for dealing with tuberculosis, but as Dr. J. G. Fitzgerald noted in his review of anti-tuberculosis work in Canada,

> two or three provinces and some municipalities have lagged and their tuberculosis records indicate it. In those places where money, energy, initiative, and enthusiasm in the crusade have been expended, the results indicate definite reductions in mortality; where they have not, tuberculosis continues to take its necessary toll. Not because of social conditions, race, or any undue susceptibility to the disease but chiefly because of ignorance, and apathy, and an unwillingness to appropriate sufficient money to really cope with the menace of the great white plague. Public health in the special field of anti-tuberculosis work is purchasable as in all others and liberal appropriations will result in a reduction in the number of tuberculosis deaths.[36]

Tuberculosis continued "to take its unnecessary toll" in Montreal not only because of poverty and poor living conditions, but also because of the inadequacy of the public health system.

The city's poor record in combating tuberculosis may be partially explained by the fact that "no specific remedy against the disease" had yet been discovered. A systematic attack on tuberculosis would have involved large expenditures on clinics, preventoriums, and sanitoriums and the required expenditure seems to have been beyond the capacity of the existing political system. But what explanation can be offered for the failure of the community to take the obvious step of organizing an effective program for the control of diphtheria?

The history of diphtheria control reveals a remarkably consistent pattern for most of North America.[37] The discovery of the specific micro-organism responsible for the disease occurred in 1884. By the mid-1890s the use of diphtheria antitoxin in the treatment of cases was widespread. Diphtheria death rates dropped dramatically from around 150 deaths per 100,000 population to approximately one quarter of that figure. Montreal's experience was similar to that of other North American cities until around 1910. For the next ten years the world diphtheria death rate continued to decline generally while Montreal's rate actually increased. The continued decline in diphtheria death rates in most North American cities was facilitated by the development of the Schick test which permitted the physician to determine if the individual possessed natural immunity to diphtheria, an important consideration when systematic attempts were made to examine large numbers of children.

The Health Department of the City of Montreal did not develop a systematic program for controlling diphtheria in the period under review and it continued to present a major health hazard. By the early 1920s a new breakthrough in the treatment of the disease had occurred. A vaccine for active immunization had been developed to replace the antitoxin which conferred only temporary protection from diphtheria. Mass immunization of pre-school and school age children was now a high priority for most public health departments. It was not until 1926 that a major campaign for diphtheria immunization was launched in the city and then the agent was the Montreal Anti-Tuberculosis and General Health League, not the Health Department.[38] The death rate from diphtheria was as selective as other diseases. It had virtually disappeared from the "City Above the Hill" before the First World War but in the working class wards it continued to

take a high toll of young lives. Much the same kinds of statements could be made about the history of other contagious
diseases but such analysis would add little to the picture
already presented.

The provincial and municipal Health Boards, some newspapers, and a number of private organizations had lobbied for
improvements in public health facilities since the 1880s.
Thus, there was no dearth of information nor lack of plans to
cope with the crisis in public health. When the Montreal
Anti-Tuberculosis and General Health League commissioned
A Survey of Public Health Activities in 1927, the real purpose
was not so much to gather information as to publicize well-
known facts. The Committee on Administrative Practice of
the American Public Health Association was engaged in a
consultative capacity and the technical committee, composed
of local public health specialists, used the appraisal form for
city health work prepared by the American Public Health
Association. The appraisal system used was based on

> standards arrived at as a result of very careful and com-
> plete studies of the public health activities in cities of a
> population of over 40,000. In each phase of public
> health service the standard has been set so that 25 per
> cent of the cities studied which were carrying on such a
> service would attain a perfect rating. It is, therefore, not
> an idealistic and unobtainable goal which is set but one
> which may be closely approached by any city which has
> a well planned and properly directed public health
> programme.[39]

The general conclusion of the survey was that "Montreal's
official and voluntary services measure only about two thirds
of the best examples of such services in other cities of comparable size."[40] In fact, the results of the survey are even more
damning when the details are examined. "Milk control" was
graded at 57 percent of the standard, "Communicable Disease
Control" at 54 percent (diphtheria immunization received
one point out of a possible thirty), and "Tuberculosis Con-

trol" at 55 percent. Other grave deficiencies noted included the general failure to provide prophylactic treatment of the eyes of new-born infants to prevent ophthalmia, the cause of 25 percent of all blindness.[41]

The *Survey* chastised the "municipal authorities" for having "been slow in accepting the modern public health programme as an official responsibility." The budget of Montreal's Health Department provided for a per capita expenditure of just thirty-nine cents as compared to an average expenditure in the twelve largest American cities of seventy-eight cents per capita. Even after the expenditures of voluntary public health agencies were counted, the estimate of sixty-nine cents per capita was lower than what all but two of the American cities surveyed were spending out of public funds alone. The *Survey* suggested that the city should allocate an additional $364,000 to the Health Department and recommended that this level of expenditure, which worked out to ninety-one cents per capita, should be reached within three years.[42]

The authors of the *Survey* had firm views on the nature of public and private responsibilities in the field of public health. "The care of the public health," they wrote,

is generally accepted throughout the civilized world as a state responsibility. Under modern living conditions, community action must be taken to protect the individuals who make up the community. In addition, certain phases of public health work required legal enactment and, therefore, an organized force to carry it out....

The voluntary health agency is essentially a pioneer organization. Its main functions are to investigate new fields of work and having proven their value to create sufficient public interest to ensure continuation of the service.[43]

They had too much experience of public health work in Montreal to believe that the municipal and provincial governments would assume full responsibility. As a result, they recommended a compromise which would provide uniform standards and comprehensive planning while utilizing the existing network and voluntary health agencies. Private agencies would be financed by a system similar to that outlined in the Quebec Public Charities Act.

> The Municipality and the Province would each contribute one-third of the cost of such work carried on by private organizations provided always that it is health work which is of proven value and that it is carried on according to a standard set by the public authority.[44]

Such payments would be made to private agencies only upon the recommendation of the municipal Health Department.

The proposal to systematize public health work was not carried out and grants to private agencies continued to be discretionary. The budget of the municipal Health Department did increase steadily between 1927 and 1930. Public expenditures reached a level of sixty-one cents per capita in 1930, rose to sixty-four cents in 1931, and remained at that level throughout the Depression.[45]

Notes

1. See Fraser Brockington, *A Short History of Public Health* (London, 1966), for a survey of British public health practices.
2. See R. D. Defries, ed., *The Development of Public Health in Canada* (Toronto, 1940), for a brief review of the history of public health legislation in each province.
3. *Annual Report of the Quebec Board of Health* (hereafter *ARQBH*), 1903–4, p. 60
4. Ibid.
5. Quebec, *Royal Commission on Health and Social Welfare* (The Castonguay-Neveau Report), 1966, I: 29.
6. Montreal Health Survey Committee, *Survey of Public Health Activities* (Montreal, 1928), chapter 22, "Laboratory Service".
7. British Medical Association, *Souvenir of Montreal 1897*, p. 143.
8. See map of "Health Activities," Montreal Health Survey Committee, *Survey of Public Health Activities*, p. 17.

9. The public health by-laws introduced in 1901 and 1906 are included in *ARQBH* for those years.

10. *Annual Report of the Montreal Board of Health* (hereafter *ARMBH*), 1916, p. 46.

11. J. G. Fitzgerald, *An Introduction to the Practice of Preventive Medicine* (St. Louis, 1926), p. 539. Fitzgerald was the director of the School of Hygiene and the Connaught Laboratories, University of Toronto.

12. Cited in ibid., pp. 540–41.

13. Quebec Board of Health, *Bulletin Sanitaire*, 1926.

14. See Dr. Séverin Lachapelle's *Manuel d'Hygiène* (Montreal, 1890), *La Santé pour tous* (Montreal, 1890), and *Femme et nurse* (Ottawa, 1901).

15. *Bulletin Sanitaire*, 1926, p. 155.

16. This information on pasteurization was "confirmed" in an interview with a gentleman long active in the city's dairy industry who had better remain anonymous. The interview was not a particularly harmonious encounter.

17. J. C. Harrison, *The Milk Supply of Montreal* (Ottawa, 1914), p. 13.

18. Ibid., p. 33.

19. Ibid., p. 67.

20. For example, in 1907 *Le Canada* published a series of articles around the theme *Le lait qui tue*.

21. *ARMBH*, 1912, p. 12.

22. Ibid., pp. 12–18.

23. Ibid., 1916, p. 48.

24. Ibid.

25. Ibid., 1928, p. 44.

26. Ibid., 1926, p. 118a.

27. Ibid., 1927, pp. 28–57.

28. *Survey of Public Health Activities*, p. 62.

29. See Quebec, *Royal Commission on Tuberculosis* (Quebec, 1909), quoted in Terry Copp, *Anatomy of Poverty*, Appendix B.

30. Quebec, *Royal Commission on Tuberculosis*, p. 121.

31. Ibid., pp. 7–9.

32. *ARMBH*, 1921, p. 41.

33. Ibid., 1924, p. 43.

34. Ibid., p. 44.

35. Montreal Health Survey Committee, *Survey of Public Health Activities*, p. 70.

36. Fitzgerald, *Introduction to the Practice of Preventive Medicine*, p. 97.

37. Based on ibid., ch. 2.

38. The Montreal Health Department began to distribute small amounts of free vaccine to families who could not pay for it in 1928. A doctor's certificate stating that the family was unable to pay was required. *ARMBH*, 1928, p. 143.
39. Montreal Health Survey Committee, *Survey of Public Health Activities*, p. 16.
40. Ibid., p. 17.
41. Ibid., p. 7.
42. Ibid., 142–43.
43. Ibid., p. 24.
44. Ibid., p. 25.
45. *ARMBH*, 1927–39.

Medical Attendance in Vancouver, 1886-1920

MARGARET W. ANDREWS

In Vancouver's first thirty-four years, medical attendance there acquired the character which nearly sixty years later still typifies this most highly valued of all health services. By 1920, Vancouver had an adequate supply of well-trained and well-paid doctors whose services were normally delivered in the impersonal setting of a downtown office; their patients had a wide range of social, economic, and ethnic backgrounds; and medical care for patients who could not afford to pay was subsidized by those who could.

Although medical attendance would ideally be studied from historical documents originating with its recipients, its ordinary and private nature makes such documents rare and their discovery a matter of chance; this paper will instead use documents prepared from the practitioners' point of view. In the first section here, inferences are drawn from a collective study of Vancouver doctors; in the second, from the medical work of an individual doctor whose daily records have sur-

Reprinted by permission from *BC Studies*, no. 40 (Winter 1978-79), pp. 32-55.

vived in part. Since in this paper medical attendance is being considered as a social process, its scientific aspects (which were changing rapidly during the period studied) are not discussed in any detail here.[1]

I

The doctors studied in this section were selected thus: a doctor was selected if there was a year between 1898 and 1920 (inclusive) in which he or she was listed as resident in Vancouver in the register printed every year or two by the College of Physicians and Surgeons of British Columbia and also listed in the most complete Vancouver directory available, or if he or she was listed in the classified section of any of those directories and also registered by the college as licensed to practise in the province. The 332 doctors thus selected will be referred to as if they were all the doctors practising in Vancouver during those years, although it is unlikely they were: doctors who arrived in Vancouver after the compiling of one directory and left before that of the next are not included, nor are those who neither informed the college of their residence in Vancouver nor advertised in the classified section of the directory.

The documents used[2] for selecting the doctors are also the principal source of information about them. The College's registers list each doctor's medical licences, current place of residence, and university degrees. The directories consistently give a doctor's address or addresses; they sometimes give his or her medical specialties, medical credentials, consulting hours, employer, or partner; and they report some temporary absences.[3]

The ratio of doctors to population in Vancouver from 1898 to 1920 varied from twelve to eighteen per 10,000, with an increasing trend of about .1 per 10,000 per year. (See figure 1.) A ratio of five doctors per 10,000 of population was asserted to be desirable by Abraham Flexner in his influential

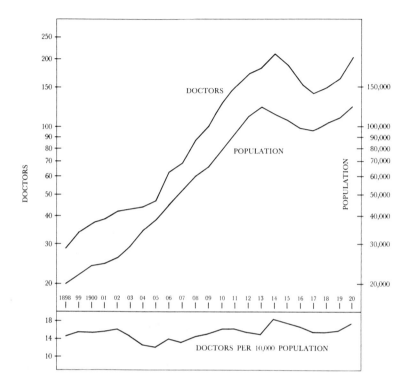

FIGURE 1

Doctors in the Population, Vancouver, 1898-1920

SOURCES FOR FIGURES

1-3. College of Physicians and Surgeons of British Columbia, Master Register of the College; College of Physicians and Surgeons of British Columbia, *Register*, 1898, 1899, 1901, 1902, 1903, 1904, 1905, 1906, 1907, 1908, 1909, 1910-11, 1912-13, 1913-14, 1914-15, 1916-17, 1918, 1919, 1920; Henderson's Publishing Co., pub., *Vancouver Directory*, 1901, 1903-1920; Henderson's Publishing Company, pub., *British Columbia Directory*, 1898, 1900, 1902; Rowland E. Green, pub., *Vancouver Directory*, 1899-1900; City of Vancouver, *Annual Report*, 1922, pp. 68-69. (The data in figure 1 refer to the beginning of the years indicated: the number of doctors cited as practising at the beginning of a year was determined from the city directory for that year indicated above; the population cited as at the beginning of a year is that given in the 1922 *Annual Report* as at the close of the preceding year.)

4. Daybooks [see note 11], 1893, 1894, 1903, and 1904, sections for Obstetrical Records.

TABLE 1
Place of Medical Training of Doctors Practising in Vancouver 1898-1920*

Degree-granting institution	Doctors who registered in B.C.:		
	before 1910	1910-1920	Total
McGill	62	38	100
Toronto	45	36	81
Manitoba	20	14	34
Queen's	14	18	32
Other Canadian institutions	10	6	16
U.S. institutions	25	16	41
British institutions†	18	14	32
Other institutions	0	4	4
Information lacking	1	1	2

* Doctors who had medical degrees from more than one institution are counted for each.

† Figures include doctors with British licences and no medical degrees.

SOURCES: College of Physicians and Surgeons of British Columbia, Master Register of the College; College of Physicians and Surgeons of British Columbia, *Register*, 1898, 1899, 1901, 1902, 1904, 1905, 1906, 1907, 1908, 1909, 1910-11, 1912-13, 1913-14, 1914-15, 1916-17, 1918, 1919, 1920; Henderson's Publishing Co., pub., *Vancouver Directory*, 1901, 1903-20; Henderson's Publishing Co., pub., *British Columbia Directory*, 1898, 1900, 1902; Rowland E. Green, pub., *Vancouver Directory*, 1899-1900.

report of 1910 on medical education in the United States and Canada,[4] and it is tempting to conclude immediately from this assertion that Vancouver had an overabundance of doctors. However, it is not reasonable to compare the actual ratio for Vancouver with Flexner's suggestion, since the latter applies to an area including both rural and urban population. Nevertheless, two observations discussed below, namely the short duration of medical practices and the willingness of doctors to give generously of their time, do lead to the conclusion that Vancouver doctors were underemployed.

It was often possible during the period of this study for a woman in Vancouver to be attended by a female doctor, and there was some feeling that this should be customary.[5] However, there were never enough female doctors in town: there was one practising in 1899 and 1900, but no others from 1898 to 1904; between 1905 and 1920 there was always at least one and sometimes as many as five.

Most of the doctors practising in Vancouver during the period of this study were trained at the McGill or Toronto medical schools, whose programs were considered "excellent" by Flexner. Nearly all the rest also had respectable training in Canada, Britain, or the United States.[6] (See table 1.) Thus, by the standards of the day, Vancouver doctors were well trained.

The 332 doctors studied here had among them 424 periods of medical practice in Vancouver; 243 doctors had one period of Vancouver practice, eighty-seven had two, one had three, and one had four; 211 of the 424 periods of practice were for one, two, or three years. (See figure 2.) Some of these periods continued to the end of the period of this study (those represented by shading in figure 2), but more were ended by a doctor's decision to go elsewhere, perhaps in the hope of greater financial success. Consider this from the patients' point of view: since the typical medical practice in Vancouver between 1898 and 1920 had continued for only a few years, the probability of a sustained relationship with a single doctor was low. Since the city's population as a whole was likely quite mobile, it is unreasonable to assume that such a relationship was expected by patients, but its absence was nevertheless a weakness in the system of medical attendance: familiarity with the medical history of patients and their families was very important when diagnosis depended almost entirely upon a doctor's personal powers of observation and deduction; geographic mobility deprived many in Vancouver of the opportunity for such familiarity to develop.

Of the 332 doctors, seventy-one (21 percent) had, before setting up practice in Vancouver, practised in British Columbia in places outside the other urban centres (Victoria and New Westminster). Experience with such non-urban practice became less common with the passage of time: among those who were licensed in British Columbia before 1910

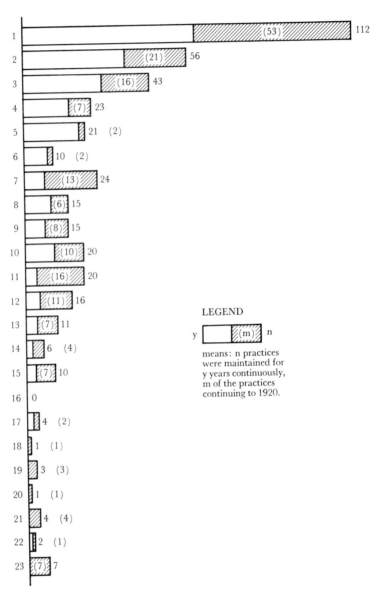

FIGURE 2

Duration of Doctors' Practices in Vancouver, 1898-1920

(189 of the 332), fifty-nine (31 percent) had had a non-urban practice in British Columbia before coming to Vancouver; among those who became licensed in British Columbia from 1910 to 1920 (143 of the 332), only twelve (8 percent) had. Doctors who knew of working-class life through the close proximity inevitable in the province's small mining and agricultural towns likely had a closer rapport with working-class patients than was possible for doctors with only urban experience.

Figure 3 shows the geographical distribution of Vancouver doctors' offices in 1902, 1911, and 1920 respectively.[7] Most of these offices were located in the vicinity of the "M" formed by Granville, Hastings and Main Streets. With the passage of time, the density of offices increased on the Granville Street leg of the "M": nearly half the doctors in Vancouver had offices in the 700 block of Granville in 1920. There were doctors' offices scattered in the outlying residential areas in all three years: in 1902, there were a few in the section of the West End between Coal Harbour and Robson Street; in 1911, there were some in the section of the West End between Robson Street and Davie Street, some across False Creek (in Kitsilano and along Broadway from Granville Street to Main Street), some in the eastern part of the city near Victoria Drive, and some outside the city boundaries in Cedar Cottage; in 1920, there were offices even farther from the centre of town, but offices in residential areas were clearly becoming less popular with doctors.

Of the twenty-nine doctors practising in Vancouver in 1898, nineteen (66 percent) lived and worked at the same place; only twenty-five (12 percent) of the 202 doctors of 1920 did so.[8] Specifically, although doctors' offices were concentrated in the central core of the city throughout the first two decades of the century, most offices located there had lost their domestic character by the end of the second decade.[9] Along with other privileged citizens, doctors had come to feel that downtown residences were undesirable and had moved to such uncongested areas as the West End, Shaughnessy, and Point Grey.[10]

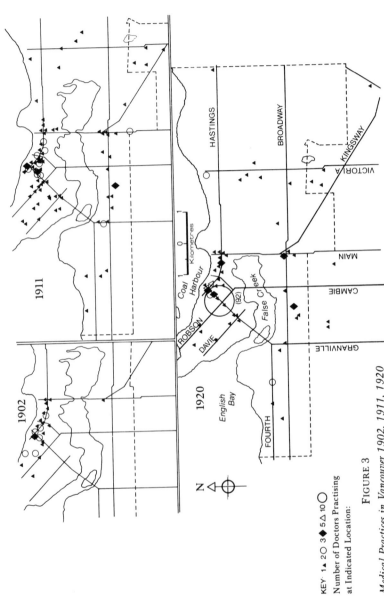

KEY: 1▲ 2○ 3◆ 5△ 10○

Number of Doctors Practising
at Indicated Location:

FIGURE 3

Medical Practices in Vancouver 1902, 1911, 1920

The combination of city growth, separation of doctors' offices from their homes, and concentration of these offices in the downtown area promoted a more formal and impersonal relationship between doctor and patient. At the turn of the century it was likely that the doctor consulted by an individual or family lived and worked nearby, was encountered frequently in everyday life, and could easily be fetched by a neighbour or family member in case of need; by the end of the second decade of the century it was more likely that people would not frequently encounter their doctors except on a professional basis and that when they needed medical attention they would either travel to a downtown office or summon a doctor by telephone.

II

The sources used in the above collective study of doctors tell nothing about the type of person who sought medical attendance, his or her reason for doing so, the kind of attention given by a doctor, or the way medical attendance was financed. For this more personal sort of information we turn to a set of nine daybooks kept from 1885 to 1904 by a Vancouver doctor, Henri Evariste Langis.[11]

A gregarious bachelor, Langis was fond of theatre, romantic verse, and evenings with friends.[12] He was born near Rimouski, Quebec, on 25 October 1857; his ancestors included men active in Quebec affairs in the seventeenth century. He attended primary school in Rimouski, then continued his formal education at the Quebec Seminary, at Laval University, and finally at the Victoria Medical College in Cobourg, Ontario (part of the Ecole de Médecine et Chirurgie of Montreal); he received the M.D. degree in 1883.

Before putting down roots in Vancouver, he moved from place to place for a number of years. After graduation, he became an employee of the Canadian Pacific Railway, working in the Ontario Lakehead and then in Yale, Port Moody, and Vancouver.[13] Perhaps in April 1886, and certainly prior to the fire which destroyed Vancouver in June of that year, he left on a trip which included Honduras and New Orleans;[14] he may have been looking for a place to set up practice. He was certainly looking for work in California in September 1886, when he travelled on foot for a day and a half to a mine fifty kilometres northeast of Sacramento; he did not get a job there, but was working later in the month, perhaps in San Francisco.[15]

Upon his return to Vancouver in 1887, he formed a medical partnership with W.J. McGuigan (another former CPR doctor), which lasted until the latter's death in 1908.[16] His integration into the anglophone community is illustrated by his appointment in 1888 to the first Medical Board of the City Hospital[17] and by his adoption of English as his preferred language.[18] He gained a reputation as an able surgeon and obstetrician.[19] His income, which increased from $2,500 in 1888 to $9,500 in 1904,[20] appears to have been remarkably good for a doctor of his day: early in the twentieth century, the average physician in Chicago charged fees comparable to his and earned from $1,500 to $3,000 per year; Chicago eye, ear, nose, and throat specialists earned from $3,000 to $6,000.[21]

He adopted a scientific approach to medicine earlier than many doctors: he bought a microscope in 1885, at which time microscopes were not yet used in course work by most American medical schools.[22]

During his years of practice in Vancouver, he lived in the downtown premises he and McGuigan shared as offices. He moved to a farm near Parksville on Vancouver Island in 1909,[23] and spent most of his remaining years there;[24] he died in 1937 at the age of seventy-nine.

Langis' patients in Vancouver included Chinese, Japanese, native Indians, and people of assorted European nationalities. In view of the second-class social status of Orientals and native Indians, it is worth noticing that members of these ethnic groups did receive treatment, sometimes even non-emergency treatment. Table 2, showing nationality of the

TABLE 2
Ethnicity of Babies Delivered by Dr. Langis

Ethnic group (categories are Langis')	1893–1894 Langis engaged		1903–1904 Langis engaged	
	Before labour	Not before	Before labour	Not before
Canadian	6	4	50	18
English	11	3	6	2
French Canadian	7	2	5	2
Jewish	5	3	3	1
German	8	1	1	—
American	1	1	3	4
Irish	1	2	2	1
Scottish	3	1	—	—
New Foundlander	2	—	2	—
Danish	3	—	1	—
Swedish	—	—	2	2
Polish	—	2	—	1
Syrian	1	—	—	—
Greek	—	—	—	1
Australian	—	—	1	—
Chinese	—	—	1	—
Japanese	—	—	—	1
French	—	—	1	—
British	—	—	1	—
American/Canadian	—	—	3	—
Irish/Canadian	—	—	3	—
English/Canadian	—	—	1	1
Greek/English	—	—	1	—
Italian/English	—	—	1	—
Belgian/American	—	—	1	—
Halfbreed	—	—	—	1
Unknown	9	6	1	1
Total	57	25	90	36

SOURCES: Daybooks [see note 11], 1893, 1894, 1903, and 1904, sections for Obstetrical Records.

babies Langis delivered during two two-year periods, gives the clearest available indication of the ethnic background of his patients.

Langis frequently attended another group of second-class citizens, the women of the city's red-light district. He attended Laura Scott and her employees from 1890 through 1904, first

TABLE 3
Occupations of Dr. Langis' Paying and Nonpaying Patients, March 1888

Occupations of paying patients (16 patients)	Occupations of nonpaying patients (11 patients)
Carpenter (2)	Farmer
Hotel Proprietor	Plasterer
Sawmill Foreman	Restauranteur
Sawmill Tallyman	Carpenter/Builder
CPR Locomotive Engineer	Clerk
Hotel Employee	CPR Engine Turner
CPR Draughtsman	Boarding House Operator
Hotel Clerk	Clothing Store Partner
Ship Captain	Hotel Partner
Storekeeper/Postmaster	Lumberman
CPR Engineer	Sawmill Boom Tender
CPR Striker	
Bartender	
Hotel Keeper	
Dry Goods/Grocery Store Partner	

NOTE: Occupations are not known for twenty-five patients; sixteen of these paid Langis' bills and nine did not.

SOURCES: Daybooks [see note 11], 1888; E. Mallandine and R. T. Williams, pub., *The British Columbia Directory*, 1887; R. T. Williams, pub., *Vancouver City Directory*, 1888.

at 54 and then at 111 Dupont Street.[25] He did not have such sustained contact with other bawdy houses, but did record visits to "Helen" at Sadie Talbot's and to "Pearl," "Thelma,"[26] and a number of other women living on Dupont Street. It is unlikely that more than a handful of Vancouver doctors attended prostitutes as regularly and extensively as Langis.

Table 3 shows the occupations of about half of Langis' patients in March 1888 (those whose occupations could be ascertained from city directories); it suggests that, although his practice included people with a wide range of occupations, unskilled workers were patients relatively infrequently. However, since the occupation of about half the patients is unknown, and since directory compilers were likely to omit people living in boarding houses or other temporary housing

TABLE 4
Sex of Dr. Langis' Patients

	1890	1891
Visits to patients known to be female	160	335
Visits to patients known to be male	549	828
Visits to patients whose sex is not known	11	43
Visits to females as a percentage of all visits	22%	28%
Visits to females as a percentage of visits to patients whose sex is known	23%	29%
Visits to males as a percentage of visits to patients whose sex is known	77%	71%

NOTE: According to the 1891 Census, the population of Vancouver was 13,709; 8,942 males (65%) and 4,767 females (35%).

SOURCES: Daybooks [see note 11], 1890 and 1891; Canada, Dept. of Trade and Commerce, *Census of Canada, 1921*, vol. 1 (Ottawa, 1924), p. 340.

(a type of accommodation favoured by unskilled workers), this conclusion is open to doubt.

Table 4 shows the sex of Langis' patients in 1890 and 1891, together with the proportion of males and females in the city according to the 1890-91 census. It seems that women received, in proportion to their number, less frequent medical care than men. Since the need for medical care due to accidents among men is presumably at least offset by that due to pregnancy among women, the discrepancy should not be attributed to a difference in need, but rather to a difference in the importance assigned by society to the two sexes' receiving medical care: men rather than women usually provided family incomes, and women who did support themselves had lower incomes than men and therefore less to spend on medical attendance.

A few occurrences of names in Langis' daybooks span several years (for example, the records of his delivery of the Pierre Tardifs' first child in 1893 and of their seventh eleven years later), but most span only a year or two. The apparently short duration of Langis' contact with most of his patients is in accordance with the geographic mobility one would expect in a population which included many immigrants seeking to better their fortunes.

Langis made himself highly available to his patients. There is no record of his stated office hours, but at least one Vancouver doctor of the period advertised morning, afternoon, and evening hours;[27] Langis attended patients on all seven days of the week and at night. On occasion, he would visit a patient several times a day, day after day.[28] He was also prepared to spend time travelling to patients outside Vancouver: he frequently went across Burrard Inlet to Moodyville, and he made calls on Lulu Island and in Port Hammond and Steveston.[29]

Langis' work load made this use of his time feasible. In 1885, he ordinarily saw from one to three patients a day, and there were frequently days when he saw no patients at all.[30] In 1888, he ordinarily saw from three to five patients a day, six or seven on a busy day, and only one on a slow day. In 1903 and 1904, he ordinarily saw from five to twelve patients a day, three on a slow day.

Although Langis' records usually do not indicate a patient's complaint, exceptions occur frequently enough to give a sense of the kind of medical work he performed; he delivered babies, treated accident victims with dislocations, fractures, and crushed limbs, treated those sick with smallpox and other infectious diseases, gave vaccinations, plugged teeth, and performed surgery ranging from circumcision and tonsillectomy to mastoid and abdominal operations.[31] As this list indicates, Langis' patients came to him for healing and sometimes for obstetrical or preventive health care.

Langis was called on to heal those who suffered from ill health which stemmed from the widespread recreational use of alcohol and sex typical of a town containing a large number of single men, many there after months in logging or mining settlements.[32] It is likely that some of the accident cases treated by Langis were the result of drunkenness,[33] and he was also asked to treat the direct effects of over-consumption of alcohol. He received the following note at 2 a.m. from the bartender of the Atlantic Saloon.[34]

Dear Sir.

Will you kindly treat Mr. Rose, he has bean Drinking hard. and need some attendance.

Kindly send bill to me and oblige

Yours truly

G. C. Dittherner

What treatment Langis gave in this case is not recorded, but he did send an alcoholic to hospital for a few days on at least one occasion.[35]

Patients came to Langis with syphilis. Although his daybooks do not indicate the nature of the treatment he gave these patients (it was presumably the approved treatment of the day—prolonged dosing with potassium iodide, mercury, or both),[36] they do reveal the psychological response of a patient to syphilis, and perhaps the disease's impoverishing effect. One Julien LeBlanc was examined by Langis in March 1887 and found to have syphilis. LeBlanc paid his bill, but did not again seek Langis' assistance until February of the following year. By then, his apparent nonchalance had changed to concern. He saw Langis six times in February and four times in March. (These visits are marked as paid.) He saw him twice in April and five times in July. (These visits are marked "n.g."—no good.) After mid-July, LeBlanc disappears from Langis' records.

Many sorts of preventive medical attendance, including prenatal care, have become increasingly accepted by the public during the course of the twentieth century. Considering which of Langis' patients arranged for prenatal care may yield some insight into the beginnings of this acceptance.

In both 1893-94 and 1903-4, 70 percent of the women Langis attended in childbirth had engaged him prior to the

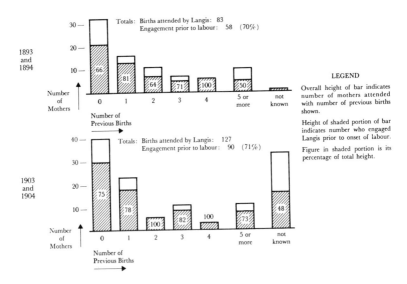

FIGURE 4

Number of Previous Births by Mothers Attended at Delivery
by Dr. Langis, with Fraction Engaging Him Prior to Labour

onset of labour, and therefore had the advantage of some prenatal care.[37] (See figure 4.) Ethnic background does not seem to determine who sought prenatal care (see table 2), nor does economic position (as indicated by occupation): the wives of a dyer, a steward, a pedlar, a tinsmith, and a watchman booked in advance; the wives of a stonemason, a paperhanger, a jeweller, and a commercial traveller did not; three labourers' wives booked in advance, five did not.[38] On the other hand, the high proportion of premature births and difficult deliveries among women who booked in advance (table 5, data for 1893 and 1894) does suggest that women who had reason to expect difficulty with their pregnancy or delivery were likely to book in advance. Figure 4 indicates that women who had already given birth (and therefore knew whether they did so easily or not) were more likely to book in advance than women pregnant for the first time.

TABLE 5
Obstetrical Problems Among Dr. Langis' Patients

	1888	1891
Deliveries	9	30
Langis engaged before labour	—	—
Miscarriages and stillbirths	1 (11%)	3 (10%)
Premature births	1 (11%)	1 (3%)
Difficult deliveries	—	—

	1893	1894
Deliveries	46	37
Langis engaged before labour	31	27
Miscarriages and stillbirths*	2 (6%)	4 (15%)
Premature births*	5 (16%)	4 (15%)
Difficult deliveries†*	7 (23%)	8 (30%)

— Data unavailable

* These data for 1893 and 1894 are only available for patients who engaged Langis before labour. Percentages here refer to that group.

† For example: shoulder presentation, hemorrhaging or use of forceps.

SOURCE: Daybooks [see note 11], 1888, 1891, 1893 and 1894, sections for Obstetrical Records.

A woman who turns to a doctor during pregnancy must believe that he can increase her comfort and the safety of herself and her child. Earlier in the nineteenth century, distrust of doctors and their methods was common on this continent.[39] That so many of Langis' patients sought his assistance before the onset of labour—not just when its pains might have made them ready to clutch at any chance of relief—suggests a high level of popular belief in the benefits of medical attendance, and presumably reflects popular awareness of the increasing effectiveness of medicine.[40] It is interesting that this awareness was not confined to ethnic and occupational groups with high social status.

Between 1894 and 1903, Langis' obstetrical patients began to arrange to have their babies in hospitals. (The first evi-

TABLE 6
Analysis of Deliveries by Dr. Langis, 1903-1904

		Total delivered	Delivered in hospital	Percent in hospital
	0	40	12	30
	1	23	1	
No. of	2	6	0	6*
previous	3	11	0	
births	4	3	1	
	5 or more	11	1	
	Not known	33	5	15
Langis engaged				
Before labour		90	10	11
Not before		37	10	27
Total		127	20	16

* This is the percentage of all deliveries known to be preceded by one or more previous births.

SOURCE: Daybooks [see note 11], 1903 and 1904, sections for Obstetrical Records.

dence of hospital delivery appears in the 1903 daybook; the preceding daybook was for 1894.) Table 6 indicates that most of Langis' obstetrical patients in 1903 and 1904 still preferred to have their babies at home, and that women having a first baby were more likely to go to hospital than those who had already given birth. (Perhaps this was because they had fewer domestic responsibilities than women with children.)

During the years covered by the nine daybooks, there were five unmarried women among Langis' obstetrical patients; one was mentioned in his records for 1893 and four in those for 1904. None of these women engaged his services in advance, two had their babies in hospital, and all five were pregnant for the first time. Langis received payment for attending two of the women—from the woman herself in one case and from a local contractor in the other. The social standing of the remaining three was likely quite low: one was a waitress, one was apparently a native Indian, and Langis indicated that the child of the third was coloured.[41] That these women, although stigmatized by pregnancy outside marriage, sought a doctor's attendance shows again the generality of expectation that his health service would be available.

In the days before periodic medical examination of the seemingly healthy became common, the life insurance medical examination was for many the only occasion when a doctor had an opportunity to identify incipient health problems and recommend treatment. Like other doctors, Langis performed many of these examinations,[42] some for large life insurance companies and some for benevolent associations.[43] The typical life-insurance medical examination of the day consisted of auscultation and percussion of the bare chest, accompanied by close questioning of the applicant about his habits and health and about the health of his family; sometimes, particularly if the policy applied for carried large benefits, the applicant's urine was also analysed.[44]

Langis received no payment for a large part of his medical work; table 7 indicates the numbers of his paid and unpaid visits in the month of March (as a sample) of some years; table 3 shows the occupations (based on information in city directories) of a number of Langis' patients in March 1888, and indicates that there was no clear difference in social or economic standing between those who paid and those who did not. Of those who did pay, the well-to-do tended to pay infrequently, while working-class patients paid at frequent intervals and often paid a large bill in instalments.[45] There is no indication that Langis neglected patients who did not pay.[46] Although medical care could be had from Langis without payment, failure to pay was not respectable; people even paid on behalf of others for whom they felt responsibility or affection—Chinese servants, employees, family members, and mistresses.[47]

TABLE 7
Amount of Medical Attendance Given by Dr. Langis
for Which He Was Paid

Period	Visits	Paid visits
March 1885	86	19 (22%)
March 1887	46	19 (41%)
March 1888	111	65 (59%)
March 1890	67	36 (54%)
March 1891	116	68 (59%)
March 1893	176	54 (31%)
March 1904	209	81 (39%)

NOTE: The number of visits which were paid for may be underestimated. Langis' monthly records of cash received sometimes show payments from patients when there is no corresponding indication of payment in his record of daily visits. This is particularly common for 1891–1904. His records for 1894 and 1903 seem so clearly inaccurate that they have been omitted from this summary.

SOURCE: Daybooks [see note 11], 1885, 1886–1888, 1888, 1890, 1891, 1893, and 1904.

Group medical insurance plans helped guarantee that medical bills would be paid. Langis' daybooks show quarterly payments from the Ancient Order of Foresters (AOF), commencing in 1891 and varying in amount only slightly from one quarter to another;[48] the consistency of amount suggests that these payments were based on the number of AOF members in Vancouver. His daybooks also show payments from the Independent Order of Foresters (IOF) and the Canadian Order of Foresters;[49] payments from these groups show no regular pattern, so it is likely that Langis provided medical care for their members on a fee-for-service basis. Group medical insurance plans were also established by companies: Langis' daily entries mention the Hastings Mill Company; the telephone company; Kelly, Douglas, and Company; and, most frequently, Ironside, Rannie and Campbell.[50] The last-named company (contractors specializing in railroads and public works) had a plan which provided both medical and hospital care for employees who contributed to one of the company Hospital Funds; these funds were administered by the company, and a company official signed the order for medical care which was presented to a doctor by a sick or injured employee.[51]

Langis appears not to have increased his fees in the years from 1888 to 1904. The increase in his income in this period was due to the growth of his practice, particularly his practice of obstetrics and surgery, which paid well.[52] With this specialization, his practice also included an increasing proportion of hospital visits. The changes in Langis' practice reflect fundamental changes in the world of medicine: there was in the years covered by Langis' daybooks such growth in medical knowledge and technology, in the number and sophistication of medical institutions and in the expertise of medical personnel that the increased likelihood that medical attention would provide cure or relief of sickness encouraged people to seek it and to submit themselves even to its specialized forms, hospitalization and surgery.[53]

III

The adequacy of medical attendance may be measured by determining whether there are enough doctors to meet the demand for that service, whether the doctors are competent, and whether the people who need the service receive it. It is clear that there were more than enough doctors to meet the demand in Vancouver during the period of this study, and that they had, for the most part, been well trained by the standards of the day. It is less clear that those who needed medical attendance received it: although Langis' practice shows that no group of people (in particular, no group determined by income, social standing, or ethnicity) was systematically excluded, and that medical attendance was available to those who could not pay for it, there were nevertheless those who did not go to doctors because of fear, superstition, ignorance, or unwillingness to receive charity.

Two patterns of change in doctors' collective behaviour during this period do point to an increase in the use of medical attendance: an increasing frequency of separation of office from residence (noted in section I) and a decreasing frequency of partnership practice[54] suggest that the affluence of doctors in Vancouver increased over these years. An increase in their fees would explain this, but it seems unlikely they would have made such an increase, given their apparent underemployment (Langis, who did in fact become more wealthy, does not seem to have increased his fees); it is more likely that incomes rose because practices increased in size. Since, as we have seen, the doctor-population ratio did not change significantly over these years, it seems clear that the fraction of the population receiving medical attendance increased—that there was an increased demand for this service.

During the period of this study, doctors' routine attendance on patients unlikely to pay their bills was the basis of a system whereby those who could afford to pay for medical care subsidized those who could not. This system worked because social attitudes which equated respectability with economic self-sufficiency motivated people to pay for medical attendance, either individually or through group plans which spread the cost of high medical bills and compelled saving. However, the system worked imperfectly: the same social attitudes led many people of limited means to fail to seek a doctor's care until their cases were desperate; moreover, the power of social opinion was not completely effective, and some who could have paid their doctor bills did not. This, and a growing sense of the social waste inherent in untreated ill health, encouraged the development of the new, less individualistic social attitudes expressed in the proposals—frequent after the end of the First World War—for a state medical service.[55]

Notes

The author wishes to acknowledge the research assistance provided by a Canada Council Doctoral Fellowship.
1. Studies of medical attendance tend to emphasize the state of medical knowledge, the role of government, the growth of medical institutions and organizations, or the contributions of great physicians. I have found the following works helpful in writing this paper—they describe medical attendance in its social setting and see it as subject to economic, philosophical, psychological, and political influences; William C. Rothstein, *American Physicians in the Nineteenth Century, From Sects to Science* (Baltimore, 1972); Ruth G. Hodgkinson, "The Social Environment of British Medical Science and Practice in the Nineteenth Century," in William C. Gibson, ed., *British Contributions to Medical Science* (London, 1971), pp. 29-53; Noel Parry and Jose Parry, *The Rise of the Medical Profession, A Study of Collective Social Mobility* (London, 1976), chs. 7 and 9. I know of no good interpretive studies of medical attendance in Canada. The following works are useful for factual information: Robert E. McKechnie II, *Strong Medicine, History of Healing on the Northwest Coast* (Vancouver, 1972); T. F. Rose, *From Shaman to Modern Medicine, A Century of the Healing Arts in British Columbia* (Vancouver, 1972); R. G. Large, *Drums and Scalpel, From Native Healers to Physicians on the North Pacific Coast* (Vancouver, 1968); H. L. Burris, *Medical Saga, The Burris Clinic and Early Pioneers* (Vancouver, 1967); Emily Carr, "Doctor and Dentist" in her *The Book of Small* (1942; rpt. Toronto, 1966), pp. 138-41 of the edition cited: Charles G. Roland, "Diary of a Canadian Country Physician: Jonathan Woolverton (1811-1883)," *Medical History* 15 (1971): 168-80; William Perkins Bull, *From Medicine Man to Medical Man, A Record of a Century and a Half of Progress in Health and Sanitation as Exemplified by Developments in Peel* (Toronto, 1934).
2. Unless otherwise indicated, the material in this section is drawn from the master register of the College of Physicians and Surgeons of British Columbia, the college's printed registers for 1898, 1899, 1901, 1902, 1903, 1904, 1905, 1906, 1907, 1908, 1909, 1910-11, 1912-13, 1913-14, 1914-15, 1916-17, 1918, 1919, 1920 (all to be found at the offices of the college in Vancouver); the Vancouver directories published by Henderson's Publishing Company for 1901 and 1903-20; the British Columbia directories published by Hen-

derson's Publishing Company for 1898, 1900, and 1902; and the Vancouver directory published by Rowland E. Green for 1899–1900.

3. The "physicians and surgeons" classified sections of city directories between 1898 and 1920 also included advertisements of fifty-four people who were not registered with the College of Physicians and Surgeons. Most of these (forty-one) advertised in only one directory; seven advertised in two; three advertised in three; two advertised in four; and one advertised in six. Five of these unlicensed "doctors" also advertised as dentists; one shared an office with a licensed doctor; the women (three in number) may have been midwives. A plentiful supply of legally qualified doctors undoubtedly limited the success of these practitioners, and their careers were liable to be curtailed by prosecution under the Medical Act. The infrequency with which an unlicensed person advertised for more than one year suggests that these or other influences were fairly effective in inhibiting their practice of medicine.

4. Abraham Flexner, *Medical Education in the United States and Canada* (1910; rpt. New York, 1960), p. 14. Canada as a whole had 9.7 doctors per 10,000 population; the United States had 17.6 per 10,000 population. In the latter country, small towns were more likely to have a superfluity of doctors than large cities (ibid., pp. 14, 320).

5. *Vancouver Daily Province*, 13 December 1916, p. 4; Vancouver City Archives, City of Vancouver, Minutes of the Board of School Trustees, vol. 6, Management Committee Minutes, 25 January 1915 and 29 January 1917.

6. Flexner considered the education given by the Manitoba and Queen's medical schools less good than that given by the Toronto or McGill medical schools, but as representing "a distinct effort toward higher ideals" (*Medical Education*, p. 325); British medical training in general was good; that given in the United States ranged from the excellent training given at Johns Hopkins to the worthless training given at "degree mills" (Flexner; *Physicians' Panel on Canadian Medical History*, a discussion held in Lac Beauport, 7 October 1966, and sponsored by Schering Corporation Ltd. and the Canadian Medical Association, published June 1967, n.p., 5th and 6th pages; F. N. L. Poynter, ed., *The Evolution of Medical Practice in Britain* [London, 1961], pp. 11–14, 31–32, 50–55).

7. Some doctors who practised in the Vancouver area outside the city boundaries are included on these maps.
8. This is inferred from the lack of separate office addresses in the directory entries for them.
9. For a description of the atmosphere of doctors' offices which were located in homes, see "The Doctor's Wife," *Canada Lancet* 20 (1888): 176-79.
10. Walter G. Hardwick, *Vancouver* (Don Mills, Ont., 1974), pp. 87-88, 105-6.
11. There is a daybook devoted to entries for each of the years 1885, 1888, 1890, 1891, 1893, 1894, 1903, and 1904. In addition, there is one containing entries for 1886, 1887, and 1888. These daybooks are in the Vancouver City Archives, catalogued as Add. Mss. 16. I will cite them here simply as "Daybooks."
12. *Port Moody Gazette*, 9 August 1884. Apart from the Daybooks, and the copy of Williams' *Directory* mentioned below, there are only three items in his docket at the Archives. Two of these are a theatre program and a letter from a young child. The following note is written in the margin of the 1891 Daybook, pages for 12-22 September: "Sarah, la divine Sarah — played last night as [illegible] play La Tosca to night Sept 22 [illegible]." The words of "Three Knights," a poem or song, are written in the (otherwise unused) June and July cash record section of the 1885 Daybook. Newspaper clippings of "The Shooting of Dan McGrew" and "Salut a l'Empereur" are inserted near the back of Langis' copy of Williams' *Vancouver City Directory* for 1888.
13. Additional biographical information on Langis may be found in the *News-Herald*, 12 June 1937, p. 1; *Daily Province*, 12 June 1937, p. 5; *Vancouver Sun*, 12 June 1937, p. 3; Letter from H. E. Langis to R. E. McKechnie in F. W. Howay and E. O. S. Scholefield, *British Columbia from the Earliest Times to the Present* (Vancouver, 1914), 1: 615-17; College of Physicians and Surgeons of British Columbia, Master Register; W. D. Keith, *St. Paul's Hospital, Vancouver, B.C., The History of the Medical Staff 1920-1940* (n.p., [1950], p. 2; "Biographies of Early British Columbia Doctors," University of British Columbia, Woodward Library Memorial Room (three unpublished volumes); Vancouver City Archives, Add. Mss. 54, vol. 13, file L-29.
14. "Biographies of Early British Columbia Doctors"; *Vancouver Advertiser*, 18 January 1887. There are no entries in the

1886-88 Daybook dated between 19 April 1886 and 6 September [1886].
15. Daybooks, 6 September [1886], the facing page, and 21 September 1886 to 4 December 1886.
16. Keith, *St. Paul's Hospital*, p. 3; "Biographies of Early British Columbia Doctors."
17. Vancouver City Archives, Vancouver General Hospital Archives Book for 1886-1901, 23 September 1888.
18. From 1888 on, the Daybook entries were written only in English. Earlier, they were written in a mixture of English and French.
19. *News-Herald*, 12 June 1937, p. 1; *Daily Province*, 12 June 1937, p. 5.
20. Daybooks, 1888 and 1904, monthly cash sections.
21. "Incomes of Physicians," *Dominion Medical Monthly and Ontario Medical Journal* 18 (1902): 220.
22. Daybooks, 1885, monthly cash account section; Rothstein, *American Physicians in the Nineteenth Century*, p. 262.
23. Keith, *St. Paul's Hospital* p. 2.
24. The Vancouver directory shows that Langis was again practising in the West Hastings Street area of Vancouver in 1919. There is no mention of him in Parksville or Vancouver directory listings for the years 1920 through 1923. He is listed as a resident of Parksville from 1924 to 1937. In 1937 he is listed in the Vancouver directory at the address of a nephew.
25. For example: "Rosa (L. Scott) [$]3" (Daybooks, 21 November 1893), and "Laura Scott, girl pd." (Daybooks, 28 August 1904).
26. Daybooks, 3 and 4 March 1904, 14 March 1893, 24 and 26 November 1904.
27. Henderson's *City of Vancouver Directory*, 1901, p. 766, listing for Herbert W. Riggs. The general practitioner of the day was expected to be available at any time. (James Gregory Mumford, *A Doctor's Table Talk* [Boston, 1912], p. 52.)
28. Daybooks, 8-16 July 1887 and 13-19 November 1904.
29. Daybooks, 8 March 1893, 6 April 1893, 17 January 1893, 19 March 1894, 8 May 1894.
30. Langis accounted for his small practice thus: "The first few years the clientele was not very big, as most of the heads of families worked for the C.P.R. and were attended by their own [CPR] surgeons." Letter from H. E. Langis to R. E. McKechnie, in Howay and Scholefield, *British Columbia*.

31. Daybooks, 13 August 1887, 23 August 1887, 6 March 1893, 2–8 October 1904, 28 November–3 December 1904, 8 April 1893, 2 June 1887, 15 September 1904, 18 September 1904, 11–14 October 1904; Daybooks, 1904, pocket inside back cover (order from the Ironside, Rannie, and Campbell company, dated 4 December 1904); *News-Herald*, 12 June 1937, p. 1.

32. For evidence of the recreational use of alcohol and sex in Vancouver during this period, see M. Allerdale Grainger, *Woodsmen of the West*, (1908; rpt. Toronto, 1964), p. 15; McKechnie, *Strong Medicine*, p. 139.

33. For evidence of accidents resulting from drunkenness, see University of British Columbia Library, Special Collections, British Columbia Electric Railway Papers, box 146, file 562, accident reports for 23 December 1914, 20 September 1913, 19 December 1913, 14 January 1914. There is no reason to believe Langis did not treat similarly caused accidents.

34. Daybooks, 1904, pocket inside back cover.

35. Daybooks, 20–22 October 1904.

36. "Treatment of Syphilis," *Canada Lancet* 20 (1888): 245–46; R. W. Taylor, "Some Practical Points in the Treatment of Syphilis," *Canada Lancet* 22 (1890): 244; "The Best Method of Administering Potassium Iodide," *Dominion Medical Monthly and Ontario Medical Journal* 25 (1905): 281–83.

37. For a description of the care recommended early in the century for pregnant women by a McGill lecturer, see David James Evans, *Obstetrics, A Manual for Students and Practitioners* (2nd ed.; Philadelphia, 1909), pp. 59–61.

38. Daybooks, 1893, 1894, 1903, 1904, sections for Obstetrical Records.

39. During the nineteenth century, the popularity of Thomsonianism, patent medicines, and, to a lesser extent, homeopathy, indicates a rejection of regular physicians and their methods. (Rothstein, *American Physicians in the Nineteenth Century*, passim.)

40. Ironically, the practice of obstetrics was slow to improve. The maternal death rate, although it declined markedly among charity patients in hospitals, improved very little among private patients in Britain and America during the years covered by Langis' daybooks (Evans, *Obstetrics*, p. 123), and Flexner complained as late as 1910 that obstetrical training of doctors was inadequate to meet the needs of mother and child (Flexner, *Medical Education*, pp. 117–18).

41. Daybooks, 1893 and 1904, sections for Obstetrical Engagements and Obstetrical Records; Daybooks, 29 January 1893 and 15 March 1904; Daybooks, 1893, section of monthly accounts, entry for 26 April.
42. "With the great growth of life and fraternal insurance during the past few years, practically every physician is engaged to some degree as examiner for some company or association." (Review of Charles Lyman Green's *The Medical Examination for Life Insurance...*, *Dominion Medical Monthly and Ontario Medical Journal* 24 [1905]: 229.)
43. For example, Daybooks, 23 June 1888, 26 July 1888, 29 November 1888, 27 November 1888.
44. Frank W. Foxworthy, ed., *Life Insurance Examination* (St. Louis, 1924), p. 40; George Wilkins, *Hints as to Medical Examination for Life Assurance*, (Montreal, [1880s?]). I am pleased to thank J. M. Champagne, underwriting supervisor of the Canadian Foresters Life Insurance Society, and Elizabeth Gibson, librarian of the Sun Life Assurance Company of Canada, for sending me copies of turn-of-the-century medical examination forms, which were also informative.
45. For example, the daybooks show that Charles Doering (a partner in a brewery) or members of his family had thirty-four visits from Langis in 1894. Doering paid Langis $62.50 on 16 January 1894 and $75.00 on 4 December 1894. In contrast, C. E. Maddams (according to Langis, a steward; according to the directory, a porter) had his eighth child delivered by Langis on 3 May 1894. Maddams paid $20 on 13 May and $5 on 14 July.
46. Patients who had not paid continued to receive care from Langis. For example, Jennie Wilson was visited by him on 11, 12, and 14 March 1888, even though a bill for $60 sent the preceding August had not been paid (Daybooks, 1886–88).
47. For example (all citations refer to Daybooks): "Mrs Dan Ross, Chinaman" (5 August 1905); "A. B. MacNeill, Chinaman" (5 and 7 October 1904); "Jas Summers [of the White Swan Hotel] (white servant) [$]10" (20 June 1891); "T. D. Cyrs [proprietor of the Granville Hotel] (H. Pinard) pd" (3 October 1893); "W. E. O'Brien pd mother" (13 October 1904); "Blanche Lewis Annie pd" [Both Blanche and Annie Lewis lived at 138 Dupont Street, in the house of Blanche Wood] (19 September 1904); "Fred Martin a lady" (10 September 1904).

48. Recorded payments received from AOF were:

10 Oct. 1891	32.25	6 Jan. 1894	41.00	6 Jul. 1903	104.50*
Jan. 1892	33.75	5 Apr. 1894	36.00	17 Oct. 1903	108.50
21 Jan. 1893	39.25	10 Jul. 1894	40.75	13 Jan. 1904	103.50
7 Apr. 1893	38.25	8 Oct. 1894	37.75	6 Apr. 1904	105.75
3 Aug. 1893	38.25	5 Jan. 1903	104.00	5 Jul. 1904	110.00
10 Oct. 1893	38.50	8 Apr. 1903	104.25	18 Dec. 1904	104.50

  * Apparently in error, this is recorded as from the IOF (Daybooks, monthly cash account sections).

49. Recorded payments received from IOF were:

8 Dec. 1891	7.50	24 Feb. 1893	21.75	9 Jun. 1894	10.00
28 Dec. 1891	25.00	2 Mar. 1894	25.00		

Recorded payments received from COF were:

15 Jan. 1894	21.00	19 Jul. 1894	10.00	23 Oct. 1894	22.50
10 May 1894	10.00				

(Daybooks, monthly cash account sections).

50. Daybooks, 28 May 1887, 2 October 1888, 30 June 1904, and 10, 15, 22, 24, 25, 29, and 31 August 1903.

51. Daybook for 1904, pocket inside back cover (orders for medical care).

52. The usual charge for a visit was $2.50, but it might be $5.00 if made during the night. Charges for a confinement varied from $15.00 to $40.00. Charges for operations ranged from $15.00 to $20.00 for minor ones to $125.00 for major ones. In practice, Langis seems to have used a sliding system of fees: he sometimes marked accounts "paid" when his cash receipts showed that the patient had paid less than the amount due.

53. For a clear discussion of the interrelationship of medical science and medical attendance, see Rothstein, *American Physicians in the Nineteenth Century*, chs. 13–15.

54. Four (14 percent) of the twenty-nine doctors identified in this study as practising in Vancouver in 1898 practised in partnership, ten (10 percent) of the 101 doctors of 1909 did, and only two (1 percent) of the 202 doctors of 1920 did.

55. For examples of such proposals, see the *Daily Province*, 20 December 1918, p. 15, 27 December 1918, p. 7, 12 February 1919, p. 5; *Vancouver Daily Sun*, 5 March 1919, p. 1.

The Impact of Epidemic Influenza: Canada, 1918-1919

JANICE P. DICKIN MCGINNIS

According to a Chinese proverb, "after war comes plague." War provides perfect conditions for the spread of disease. Soldiers are brought together from many backgrounds and forced to live in close proximity to people having different immunities from their own. They are sent out to troop across foreign territory, meanwhile suffering from lowered sanitary and nutritional standards. Exhausted and sick, they come into contact with civilians of similarly lowered resistance. Different diseases are brought together in a medium excellent for their mutation and growth. After the cessation of hostilities, armies are sent home to spread unfamiliar, and perhaps even brand new, forms of sickness among a population likely suffering from some extent of privation due to the war. In Europe during the nineteenth century and earlier the end result was usually typhus. After World War I, it was "Spanish Influenza."

Spanish influenza did not come from Spain. That country likely acquired the blame because, not involved in the war

Reprinted by permission of the Canadian Historical Association from *Historical Papers*, 1977, pp. 121–40.

and having no press censorship, its epidemic in the spring of 1918 was the only earlier one widely publicized.[1] In fact, the flu seems to have broken out in China, notably in Canton in late February 1918. The next outbreak was recorded in France, possibly imported there with a contingent of Chinese labourers. By 5 March, it was spreading among United States troops stationed at Camp Funston, Kansas. By April, it was again reported in continental Europe, Spain not being afflicted until May. During this period, the disease was not given epidemic standing, nor was it always recognized as influenza. For example, England's June epidemic in the army camps was diagnosed as botulism.[2]

Although this earlier epidemic was much milder than that which came later, it certainly adversely affected the trench warfare. A Québécois soldier, Arthur Lapointe, stationed at Agny, France, has left a record of just how quickly flu could disable a soldier and indeed, a whole company. In his diary he notes under the date of 30 June 1918 that several of the men have been seized suddenly with a violent headache, other pains, and fever. A signaller is rolling on the ground, the ser-geant-major has just been evacuated half unconscious and a runner has collapsed. Lapointe goes into his dugout for lunch, finds he cannot eat, readies his personal effects for the immi-nent relief of the company, and starts to climb the dugout stairs. "As I reach the top, my head swims with sudden nau-sea, everything around me whirls, I totter, then fainting, fall to the ground." Upon regaining consciousness he rejoins his company, many of which are in the same condition, and it embarks on a one-hour trudge through one mile of trenches to the aid post. One man, forced to crawling on hands and knees, has to be left behind till help can be secured. The com-mander, also sick, joins his company at the post and they are taken by ambulance to the rear. Lapointe is given permission to stay in billets rather than go to the hospital. After two days of being nursed by a friend, he is able to return to duty. At no point does Lapointe diagnose his own condition as flu. He suffers from it again in November while stationed at Bram-shott Camp, England. This time, it is diagnosed as the after-effects of being gassed but there can be no doubt, from the symptoms he describes, the speed with which the disease spreads, and the prevalence of flu in his area each time, that he was afflicted with Spanish influenza on both occasions.[3]

The infection invaded Canada, not surprisingly, on troop ships. The *Araguayan* left England 26 June and developed 175 cases among 763 soldiers on board. The first incident in which civilian officials took part involved the steamship *Somali* which had been granted pratique when it stopped in at the quarantine headquarters on Grosse Isle in the St. Lawrence River. However, upon arriving at Quebec City, several of its crew proved to be suffering from the flu and, after unloading, the ship was ordered back to Grosse Isle for care of the sick and general fumigation on 9 July 1918. By 11 July, forty-six crew members were in the Grosse Isle hospital. By the next morning, the number had risen to sixty-seven and by nightfall had reached seventy-two. At approximately the same date, the *Nagoya* arrived at Montreal and the *Med 1099* hospital ship at Halifax, likewise carrying the flu.[4]

However, the disease seems not to have spread very rapidly throughout the summer. The isolated cases that no doubt occurred were generally not recognized as Spanish flu. Indeed, even once the epidemic started in earnest, authorities were very reluctant to diagnose it as the real thing, sticking to descriptions of "ordinary flu" and catarrh. However, it was obvious by the end of September that Canada had a problem. On 23 September 1918, the Calgary *Herald* began regularly reporting on the flu. From these reports the routes of the infection throughout the country can be traced. The first cited 300 college students sick at Victoriaville, PQ, nine United States sailors dead from flu on ships in Quebec City harbour in the last few days, and the fifth flu-related death among the Polish infantry stationed at Niagara Camp, Ontario. The next day, new cases and deaths were reported at both Arthabaskaville and Trois Pistoles.

By this point, New York and Massachusetts were undergoing very serious epidemics, especially in the army camps, so it is likely that Canada was now being infected from overland as well as through its ports. By 28 September, the flu had not only reached Montreal where it was epidemic in the barracks but Canada was already exporting the disease back to Europe. On 28 September, the troop ship, the *City of Cairo*, sailed from Quebec City with 1057 troops. Nearly all on board contracted flu before arriving in Davenport on 11 October, with thirty-two deaths at sea. On arrival 244 cases were transferred to the hospital, 114 of these on stretchers. The *Hunstead*, which had sailed from Montreal two days before the *City of Cairo* experienced similar casualties, as did the *Victoria* sailing from Quebec City on 6 October. To protect itself from contamination from its own homeland, the Canadian army in England was forced to place all new recruits in segregation camps for twenty-eight days.[5] While protecting the training camps from infection, this move must also have provided excellent conditions for the incubation of flu among the newly arrived troops.

Meanwhile, back home the epidemic had reached the Maritimes by the end of September. Sydney and North Sydney, Nova Scotia, experienced five deaths by 30 September. The reports on Halifax seem to indicate, at first glance, that that city was not similarly afflicted. Around the beginning of October, it was sending doctors and nurses to help out the especially hard-hit city of Boston. However, since it is known that flu-ships had entered the port in the summer and again at the end of September,[6] the more likely reason for this magnanimity was the debt Halifax owed Boston for the considerable help that city had rendered at the time of the disastrous Halifax explosion in 1917. By 11 October, Halifax was certainly suffering in epidemic proportions.

Epidemics traditionally travel along the usual lines of communication; therefore, it was obviously only a matter of time before the railways would bring the infection west. However, a questionable decision by Canadian military authorities speeded up the process considerably. The quarantined barrack in Quebec City numbered among its inhabitants several seemingly-healthy soldiers due to be transferred to Vancouver. At the end of September, these men, who had certainly been in contact with the flu, were loaded onto a CPR train and sent west. As men became ill, they were handed over to health authorities at several points along the way. At 3 a.m. on 2 October, one officer and fourteen privates were dropped off in Calgary. By the time the troops reached Vancouver, the whole train had been ordered quarantined.[7] This move, however, was a little too late for the prairies. The infected soldiers soon spread disease throughout the military hospitals they were taken to, then throughout their camps and then into the surrounding civilian community. It is true these areas would have eventually been hit anyway. For example, shortly after the troop train arrived in Calgary, infection entered that city through at least three other channels.[8] But the infection via the military was by far the most significant one, introducing so large a number of sick into that most perfect medium for incubation, the army camp.

The flu next spread along the railways and highways into the remoter parts of all provinces. Smaller Ontario centres were the first to report, then those in the southern prairies. The epidemic was serious in Edmonton by 18 October and raging in the northern prairies generally by the beginning of November. Also by that date the Queen Charlotte Islands had been infected, either by Canadian or United States vessels. Newfoundland was probably infected by fishing ships from the Grand Banks. The Yukon and Northwest Territories were contaminated via Alaska and did not really suffer until the rivers opened allowing mail and flu to reach remoter areas in the spring.

It is obvious from the newspaper reports that the more isolated centres would be able to watch the dreadful disease stalk towards them and it might be thought that quarantine would be tried. As a matter of fact it was. At least three smaller prairie municipalities—Lethbridge, Taber, and Pincher Creek—ordered all CPR passenger cars sealed while passing through and set up roadblocks run by the Alberta Provincial Police on the major incoming highways.[9] None of them escaped infection. In fact, Pincher Creek suffered so dreadfully that it had to ask for the RNWMP surgeon to come over from Fort Macleod when all the town doctors went down sick at once.[10] Prince Edward Island, the only province allowed (under the terms of its entering Confederation) quarantine rights from the other provinces, tried a somewhat less stringent method. As had been done during the New Brunswick smallpox epidemic earlier that year, PEI asked that all passengers for the island be checked by a medical health officer and stopped if symptoms were present.[11] On a larger scale, an attempt was also made to quarantine the entire Yukon Territory. Indians were warned not to wander across the border into Alaska, all Yukon-bound travellers were checked by United States health authorities in Skagway, and for a while quarantine barracks were opened at Carcross and Whitehorse.[12] But none of these places escaped infection. In fact the only inhabited place on the entire globe left untouched was Tristan da Cunha, a tiny island 1500 miles south of St. Helena in the Atlantic Ocean.[13]

What was this disease with which the whole world now had to deal? Influenza was by no means a new disease. In the nineteenth century alone it had appeared in major epidemic proportions on at least six occasions—in 1800, 1830, 1843, 1857, 1874, and 1889-90. The last of these was the most virulent and affected 40 percent of the world's population. Influenza's earlier history is more difficult to chart, partly because, being an epidemic rather than an endemic disease, it was given a different name each time it made one of its periodic appearances: flu, grippe, feveret, epidemic catarrh, Spanish, Chinese, or German disease, or even *coqueluche*, a term now used for whooping-cough. It is even possible that the great epidemics of sweating sickness in the sixteenth century were actually influenza.

The name influenza comes from the Italian for influence, from influence of the stars, accepted in the fourteenth and fifteenth centuries as the cause of the disease. In the sixteenth century contaminated food was the accepted cause; in the seventeenth and eighteenth it was blamed on sudden changes in temperature. From then on, it was increasingly viewed as a contagious disease, but this did not find general acceptance until after 1890.[14]

Influenza has been, and still is, passed off as a mildly amusing disease. This is partly due to the fact that, although it generally has a high morbidity, it also usually has a very low mortality. Its importance is also masked by the fact that, although it reduces the resistance to other diseases, it is these other diseases, readily identifiable in their own right, that usually do the killing and are therefore regarded with much greater respect. Included are pneumonia, encephalitis, and meningitis.[15] Another way in which influenza may be masked is by an epidemic of a more acute, unrelated disease occurring at the same time, thereby drawing attention from the lesser disease. For example, two Canadian flu epidemics, in 1830-32 and 1847-48, were both hidden in this way, the first by cholera and the second by typhus.[16] This may be partly the reason the 1918-19 epidemic was regarded as so serious at the time. Medical authorities had learned to control most of the major communicable diseases. Throughout the war they had congratulated themselves on avoiding typhus and typhoid fever, the usual scourges affecting armies. But the importance of the 1918-19 epidemic cannot be dismissed simply by pointing out that it had no competitors. The influenza of those years was a very serious disease.

As stated, influenza generally exhibits a high morbidity but a low mortality. The 1918-19 variety was different in that it had a very high morbidity (from 15 to 50 percent in various countries) coupled with a much higher mortality rate (about 1 percent of those who contracted flu, died). It also manifested the curious feature of killing, not the very young and the very old—its usual victims—but healthy individuals in the prime of life.[17] Its symptoms ranged from mild to acute and generally started with a sudden onset complete with shivering, severe headache, pains in the back and legs, and a general feeling of prostration. Occasionally there was giddiness and collapse, a dry and sore throat, and a hacking cough. Also likely to appear were a fever, often high, a flushed face, injected eyes, heavily furred tongue, and a drowsy state complete with sensitivity to bright light. In serious cases pleurisy and pneumonia might develop, or cyanosis, a bluish discoloration of the skin and mucous membranes, due to an excessive concentration of reduced hemoglobin in the blood. This last symptom usually preceded death and added fuel to an opinion that had some popular currency that the culprit was not influenza at all but black plague.

The sudden onset, diversity of symptoms, and difference in degrees of illness led to problems in controlling the disease. Quarantine, which had not worked for whole communities, did not work for individuals or their families either. The medical health officer of Edmonton has left a cogent summary of the various difficulties militating against effective quarantine of flu sufferers. To start with, influenza was not a notifiable disease and therefore not subject to even modified quarantine by placard, of the type applicable to measles and whooping cough. This obstacle was easily overcome by most authorities early in the epidemic simply by rushing a new law onto the books. Then the perplexities began in earnest. Some cases were so mild that they were diagnosed as the common cold and therefore not placarded. Many citizens regarded quarantine as an injustice either because they did not consider the diagnosis correct or were convinced that their neighbours were cheating. Some doctors became careless or indifferent in reporting their cases because they alleged other physicians were doing the same and that the members of the health department were guilty of discrimination. At the same time, the health department had several officials down sick or recovering and the rest were overworked. The department could not hope to check up on anyone it felt was lax. Neither could it gain anything by prosecuting offending householders or physicians who did not report cases, as it was unlikely any magistrate would convict on evidence of doubtful or contradictory diagnosis. Besides there was no proof that quarantine did any good. People taking great precautions to avoid infection did not seem to be any more successful than those taking none whatsoever. The high incidence of infection among professionals combating the epidemic was more likely due to fatigue than exposure.[18] Other health officials agreed that quarantine was not worth the effort. Of fifty-two state and provincial health officers polled by the American Public Health Association, thirty-three felt that quarantine and placarding measures for flu were impracticable. Ten hedged their answers and only nine felt the measures practicable.[19]

If quarantine would not work, there were other measures that could be tried. One was the enforcement of masks. Laws to this effect were passed by various municipalities, provinces, and states. The laws varied in application, some enforcing masks only for those actually caring for the sick, some for people in contact with the public such as bank tellers and store clerks, some for anyone entering crowded places like trains or street cars, and some, for example, Alberta's, demanding that everyone wear a mask at all times while outside the home. The mask could be partly removed during meals. However, masks proved to be an even less effectual form of prevention than quarantine. Not only were they practically impossible to enforce but they were probably dangerous even when worn. The medical theory motivating the use of masks was that, since the contagion was passed from person to person through the respiratory tract, masks would both stop an early sufferer from passing it on while still at large in the community and would also stop healthy people from picking it up. It is probable that masks did exercise some control of the first problem, even if only by curtailing the activities or output of those two public villains of the epidemic, the sneezer and "the careless spitter." It is possible that well-cared-for masks also offered some degree of protection. However, this involved frequent changes of masks and disinfection of old ones, something few people appear to have done. An improperly cared-for mask was dangerous to wear. The damp, unsanitary cotton was the perfect environment for the breeding of germs. But few people likely suffered because of this. The grotesque masks were widely unpopular and the contemporary newspaper evidence is that they were generally not worn at all or just pulled into place when a policeman came in view.[20]

If people did not support quarantine or masks as means of prevention, they did look for answers in alcohol and patent medicines, chiefly those containing alcohol and/or narcotics. Such remedies relieved or masked the symptoms of more diseases than just flu. Medical science had not advanced much beyond dealing with symptoms by this point and the general public accepted pain-killing as the greatest good, or at least the greatest good possible. Prohibition in several areas and a general shortage of potable alcohol, due to the practice of filling army demands first, pretty well held consumption of alcohol in check. Doctors' prescriptions were seen as the fairest way of sharing out such supplies as were available. A good deal of the narcotics were also distributed under prescription, handed out in massive proportions. For example, during October 1918, Chicago pharmacies filled 741,825 prescriptions. Of these, 441,641 were for flu or pneumonia and of these 104,010 contained either opium, opium derivatives, cocaine, or chloral.[21] Evidence is that Canadian druggists were similarly hard pressed.[22] In addition to prescription drugs, a large quantity of patent medicines were available. Many of these contained narcotics, often with an alcohol base. Canadians had been consuming fair quantities of these commodities for several years,[23] and newspaper ads throughout the flu epidemic cashed in on the current crisis. Everything from laxatives to sweeping compounds were billed as specifics in the prevention of flu. Their effects ranged from harmful to useless. There was no drug that could prevent or cure influenza.

Neither was there an effective preventive vaccine. Various attempts were made at concocting one but almost everything militated against the successful completion of such an endeavour. For one thing, the epidemic hit too fast and too hard to allow health professionals much time for clinical experimentation. As one Canadian military physician lamented:

> I must express my regret that owing to press of work, night and day, while many medical officers were sick, I and my colleagues in the military hospital have been unable to work out this interesting problem in the scientific way it should be done.[24]

The other major problem with vaccination for flu was that the causative organism in the 1918-19 epidemic could not be identified until the introduction of a strong enough microscope in 1933. Vaccines were concocted from the variety of organisms found in the respiratory tract of sufferers. The preparations varied with parts of the world, depending on the types of organisms likely to be present in the sputa of a person whose resistance was lowered by flu. For example, in temperate zones where streptococci are prevalent, these were nearly always included in the vaccines but in Africa where they rarely occur, they were not used.[25] It is possible that these shotgun preparations did help prevent contraction of secondary diseases like pneumonia, but it is obvious that any efficacy they might have had against the actual influenza virus could only have been due to luck.

Vaccines were prepared and distributed throughout Canada in the autumn stages of the flu, but contemporary medical opinion generally agreed that while the right vaccine would be invaluable, it probably had not been found yet.[26] The matter was discussed in detail at a special meeting of the American Public Health Association called at Chicago in December 1918 to discuss the flu. The consensus was that vaccine should only be used on an experimental basis, its results being unknown and perhaps dangerous. Some Canadian health authorities were still not convinced that vaccination should be abandoned. The federal government was ambivalent about the matter. It refused to send vaccine to the Yukon and Northwest Territories in late 1918 because, in its opinion, no serum had been proved as a specific. But it did issue limited supplies to the Mounted Police for distribution to the northern Indians in the spring of 1919.[27]

Unable to prevent the spread of the disease, authorities were forced to turn their attention to the immediate problems of caring for the sick and helping as many as possible to struggle through to recovery. Canada, as a country, got off fairly lightly, although some regions, such as Labrador and the province of Quebec, suffered more than others. Statistics of the period are incomplete and those for the flu are particularly untrustworthy as the disease was not made notifiable until the epidemic was under way, the proper authorities were too busy to always report cases and deaths, some cases were so mild they never received official notice, and many cases and deaths were misdiagnosed as due to other causes. A conservative estimate is that at least one-sixth of the entire population was attacked and that 30,000 of these died. In later years the mortality estimate has been revised upwards to around 50,000, with a consequent increase in the morbidity estimate. The Canadian death rate per 100,000 for the years 1917, 1918, and 1919 shows a jump due to the epidemic: 12.7, 15.9 and 13.7, respectively. The province of Quebec alone suffered in excess of 530,000 cases and almost 9,000 deaths. Even Alberta, with a population of only 590,000 recorded over 38,000 cases and more than 4,300 deaths. Canadians also suffered overseas, the armed forces reporting 45,960 cases and 776 deaths.[28] Crude and undigested as these figures are, they do indicate at least one thing—a lot of people were sick and in trying to provide the necessary care, Canadian society would be taxed as never before.

The flu was very contagious and the onset fast. The public was made aware of the symptoms and advised to go to bed immediately. Most sufferers had little choice as the earlier symptoms were often extremely debilitating. Once in bed, they might remain there for a few days or a month, depending on the severity of the attack. Pneumonia was a frequent aftereffect, keeping the patient in bed even longer or causing death. Sufferers who were very ill had to be moved to hospitals; the moderately ill could be cared for at home if one or more adults in the family were still healthy; whole families who were ill had to be removed to hospitals or have regular help from outside the home. Someone had to look after all these people. Some place also had to be found to put them, and food to feed them, and beds and sheets and bedpans and hundreds of other significant little items.

The regular medical facilities were, of course, turned to first but they soon broke down under the strain. Hospitals had been badly under-staffed throughout the war,[29] having lost not only doctors but nurses and orderlies to the armed forces, and support staff to better paid war jobs. The flu stretched the available staffs beyond their limits. In addition, morbidity was high among the medical professions. Consequently, there were even fewer professionals to treat even more patients. The buildings, too, were soon overtaxed. Some communities, realizing from the first that it was dangerous to put flu patients into regular hospitals, set up emergency centres immediately. Eventually almost all municipalities were forced to provide some type of emergency accommodation.[30] Buildings for this purpose were not usually too hard to find: schools could always be closed in most urban areas and hotels taken over in smaller towns. Provisioning these makeshift hospitals was another matter. The armed forces had had first call on most medical material since the war began. Even beds could be an almost insuperable problem in remote areas. The Yukon territorial secretary wrote three companies in December 1918 asking about the availability of beds should the flu strike. One could lay its hands on fifteen if needed, the other two had none although one promised fifteen mattresses and twenty-five sets of blankets.[31] Officials struggled with these problems as best they could and as the epidemic peaked in some centres, now superfluous equipment and supplies could be sent further along the line to where they were most needed.[32]

Extra trained medical staff could also be found in related services. The Victorian Order of Nurses, forbidden by its charter to care for contagious cases, dropped the rule for the duration of the epidemic.[33] The Canadian Red Cross turned from rolling bandages for the war to making masks and pneumonia jackets for civilians.[34] The Voluntary Aid Detachment of the St. John Ambulance Brigade provided many qualified volunteers, many of whom had to take over completely in remoter areas.[35]

The duties of non-medical officials were also stretched to meet the crisis. In Montreal, police and firemen delivered food and fuel to those confined to their homes. Toronto postmen were given cards to fill out at each place on their rounds, asking the number of adults and children in the family, how many were ill, and who needed help. In Ottawa, the Department of the Interior sent out a circular on 12 October to all offices urging officials to persuade "your women clerks" to volunteer for home nursing chores. By 6 November, the Privy Council added incentive by offering all such volunteers leave of absence with pay and guaranteed them that this would not interfere with their annual statutory leave. In the far north, RNWMP officers covered as much as 178 miles in eight and a half days to bring isolated Indian communities serum, supplies, and general information about the impending epidemic. And in northern Alberta, they not only tried to enforce quarantine but, on at least one reserve, took over the duties of a frightened Indian agent, hauled firewood, made soup, coaxed the sick to eat, and spoon-fed them brandy. The general public also responded to the call. In addition to the thousands of women who went into the homes of the sick to care for their basic needs, others staffed soup kitchens and provided transportation. Benevolent societies and charities surveyed houses to ascertain who needed help and collected contributions of food and clothing from individuals, organizations, and even businesses.[36]

One of the main reasons that such diverse types of people were involved in the flu fight was that nobody was quite sure whose responsibility it was and if people had waited for some sort of superior organization to take hold, it would have been too late. The confusion among authorities as to what was within their legal realm is obvious. When the acting deputy minister of immigration and colonization wired the inspecting physician at Grosse Isle asking him to take care of the *Somali* problem, he received the reply: "I will act in accordance with your wishes but would kindly ask you to communicate with our department so that they might give me special authority to that effect." The acting deputy minister fired off a terse reply to the effect that Immigration and Colonization was the official's department and a memo to the head of the Public Health Branch relating the transaction and asking:

Under these circumstances, I would feel greatly obliged if you would arrange to notify the various members of your staff that the Public Health Branch is now part of the Department of Immigration and Colonization.

The offending quarantine officer contritely apologized for his lack of information. It was an unfortunate incident, especially since the quarantine service dealt admirably with an almost impossible situation. At the beginning, until a tougher law was passed, officers could not demand the quarantine of influenza cases but could only accept into their barracks anyone the captains of vessels might want to leave behind. Even after the law was changed, the officers could stop only ships from "overseas" and could do nothing about either Canadian ships from infected home ports or United States vessels. They did not even have jurisdiction over vessels that did not show their first signs of infection until in port. These were the responsibility of municipal or provincial authorities, not federal, which meant that their sick were to be taken ashore for treatment rather than to the isolation station, thereby defeating the whole purpose of coastal quarantine.[37]

Other government bodies ran into similar problems of jurisdiction and lack of information. Worriedly watching the approach of the epidemic, the commanding officer of the RNWMP post at Great Slave Lake wrote on 20 December

1918, to the commanding officer at Peace River asking that he be sent all necessary medicines to fight the impending epidemic before it hit the population in his charge. Proceeding through channels, the letter was sent to the assistant commissioner at Regina who, on 20 January 1919, enclosed it in a letter to the comptroller in Ottawa. Things were a little speedier from then on. The comptroller sent out letters regarding the matter, dated 24 January 1919, to the departments of the Interior and of Indian Affairs and to the Privy Council. Four days later the deputy minister of the interior advised the comptroller to wire Regina authorizing the RNWMP officials there to send the requested supplies, to be used according to the opinion of the officers at Slave Lake and to be paid for by Interior. A wire to that effect went to Regina that night. The Department of Indian Affairs did not reply until 4 February at which time it announced it had already sent drugs to schools and missions at Forts Smith and Simpson and had bypassed channels to inform the CO at Great Slave Lake of this directly on 31 January. As a result, these two areas got double their ration of medicines, as the CO at Peace River informed Regina on 11 February that the drugs that had come through channels had been forwarded by him to those two and to three other northern communities by registered mail. The whole process had taken almost eight weeks to transact and even then had not come off quite right. However, the expended time probably mattered little. As the CO at Peace River explained, he could not send the medicines to two other forts until navigation opened and the mails started on 1 June. If the mails could not get through until then neither in all probability could the flu.[38]

Other northern worthies also had their problems with jurisdiction. Canada having no quarantine against the United States, the medical health officer at Whitehorse had to rely on officials at Skagway to stop people with flu from getting on the train to Whitehorse. After United States objections over the expense, Canadian authorities agreed to pay half the costs in mid-January 1919. But even this gave Canada no say over how the inspections were carried out. White-horse imposed its own quarantine on travellers arriving there from Skagway in April. It dropped them in early May when Skagway announced the flu there was waning. Less than two weeks later, in a letter to his superior in Dawson, the RNWMP inspector at Whitehorse laments that he and the medical officer of health are not getting very reliable information from the United States authorities and that even though he understands he cannot send a man to check up on quarantine operations there without permission from the foreign government, he thinks it would be a good idea to at least have someone to send on accurate reports. At any rate, quarantine against Skagway had already been reimposed.[39]

Under the circumstances, people got information and help where it was available and gave them in return. The acting gold commissioner of the Yukon asked for and received posters and pamphlets relating to flu from the mayor of Vancouver. When Boston thought it had happened upon the ideal facilities in which to treat pneumonia patients, it sent out blueprints and instruction unsolicited, to many Canadian and United States health officers. Larger Ontario towns pro-vided accommodation and help for sufferers from surround-ing communities which had not had the foresight to build hospitals. Alberta cities not only cared for the sick from sur-rounding rural areas but their health departments handled requests for help and information that came in not only from within the province but even from British Columbia and Oregon. The provincial department also overstepped its responsibilities to send aid to outlying areas. Finally, things became so disorganized in the north that the provincial Health Board revoked the powers of the local boards and ran things from Edmonton.[40]

There were other attempts at reorganization. In Quebec, the Conseil Supérieur d'Hygiène was transformed into the Bureau Central d'Hygiène and given full powers to take any measures necessary to halt the spread of the flu. The Mont-real Board of Health, previously consisting of laymen, was replaced by one of physicians. Ontario passed an order-in-council granting the Board of Health summary powers to take over any land and unoccupied buildings for hospital purposes. It also gave local medical health officers full power to close public places such as schools and theatres. Regina established a central health bureau and Edmonton, because of a shortage of nurses, set up a system whereby professionals visited homes and made diagnoses but left their actual nursing care to volunteers working under their instructions.[41] The Canadian railways wanted organization on an even larger scale — viz. a central board of two doctors (advisers) and one businessman (the administrator) to collect information as to sources of infection and to standardize methods of prevention and treatment. Such a board would be given

> the authority to order whatever may be necessary to protect the country against the threatened breakdown of the industrial and transportation machinery if the disease continues at its present rate, and to take its present toll of workers.[42]

The board was never appointed.

The railways had good reason to be concerned. They were among the hardest hit of all Canadian business concerns. From late October to early December, newspaper wire services chronicled their woes. On 22 October, the Grand Trunk terminal at Toronto announced that 219 of its staff were off sick with flu and it was therefore necessary to place an embargo on all freight going east. It was two days later that the railways called for a central organization of health services, an estimated 1,373 of their Ontario employees alone being off sick by this time and the west to east embargo now applying to all rail lines. Even a small city like Calgary reported 216 CPR men sick. Fortunately, in an ironic sense, passenger demand was also off due to the flu — as much as 50 percent in the west. On 28 October, Ottawa announced that for the duration of the flu, demurrage would not be charged against those shippers unable to take railroad cars they had reserved. The train service was obviously in no position to be sticky about businesses living up to their obligations and was no doubt relieved at the release this generosity on their part gave them from their own. The next day it was announced from Montreal that as many as 10,000 railroad workers were off with flu in eastern Canada and that the only goods the War Board would allow to be shipped from west of Toronto to east of Toronto were shipments destined for overseas. On 1 November, the estimate was raised to 14,000 employees sick and, while the epidemic was abating in the east, it was only starting to take its toll in the west. In hopes of averting quite so severe a crisis there, the War Board was sending several thousand bottles of serum to inoculate free any railroad employee who was willing. By the last week in the month, rail service was still under normal and the commissioners extended the demurrage release under the provision that the shipper be able to prove that its own problems extended from the epidemic. But the end was almost nigh. Beginning 3 December, normal service was restored to prairie lines.[43]

Other concerns also suffered losses because of the flu. Some Alberta coal mines were shut down owing to sickness, and the total flu-related loss of production in the Crowsnest Pass alone by 15 November was 130,000 tons. The lowered production affected not only the mining companies but also businesses relying on that fuel. It was feared in Toronto that the coal shortage would soon be such that lay-offs would result.[44]

Services also suffered losses. Calgary's street railway estimated that its losses due to reduced passengers varied from $600 to $950 a day by the end of October and that its total deficit due to the flu would be close to $25,000. It was forced to shut down its remoter lines, thereby causing great inconvenience to the townspeople who remained healthy.[45] Other services which had difficult times meeting their obligations to the public included the telephones, so necessary to people in isolated areas but so reliant on a steady staff for regular service; the newspapers, which suffered not only reduced staffs, but shortages of newsprint when the epidemic closed some paper mills; the post office, which had even fewer people than usual to cope with the Christmas rush; and the federal government, which was finally compelled to grant paid sick leave even to temporary clerks.[46]

A significant amount of business losses was not due to the actual morbidity of the epidemic but to restrictions set up by health boards. In an attempt to limit the spread of contagion, to allow people time to volunteer for flu work and to remove any temptation that might lure the sick from their beds, Canadian health authorities, in general, restricted the hours of stores and businesses. Those considered unnecessary to human existence were closed outright: dance halls, pool rooms, dancing academies, cabarets, joy parlours, theatres, picture shows, roller skating rinks, secondhand clothing and furniture stores, auctions, rummage sales, and private furniture sales.[47] The most immediate victims of these restrictions were the owners of the places, such people as theatrical troupes and sports promoters who depended on such facilities being open, and the actual employees thrown out of work.[48] But the restrictions also added to the general economic malaise. On 8 November 1918, Dun's review of New York reported a general temporary slow-down in business in Canada due to the flu.[49]

As the epidemic began to wane, there were numerous complaints from those who felt they had been taken advantage of unfairly by the bans or other aspects of the fight against the flu. These included not only businessmen but city councils who felt their power had been undermined, people who felt they had been dealt with discourteously by those looking after them or had been overcharged by them, and even the churches, which had been closed in many centres and one of which intended to take up the case as a violation of freedom of religion as guaranteed by the Treaty of Paris.[50]

It is difficult to ascertain just how many problems the epidemic left in its wake. There are some obvious financial difficulties, the most important of which for most communities being who was to pay for the emergency facilities provided, for the extra staff, both professional and volunteer, and for the numerous little items needed to nurse the population through the flu.[51] Most industries had suffered during the epidemic but there was one which, like the municipalities, was left with a whopping bill after it was over—the insurance industry. Influenza accounted for 32.6 percent of all death claims against life insurance companies in Canada in 1918, compared with 20.95 percent for war claims. In 1919, the war claims had naturally dropped, to 4.64 percent, and so too had influenza claims, but only to 17.69 percent.[52] The Metropolitan Insurance Company alone paid over 83,000 death claims in Canada and the United States because of the influenza. In comparison, death claims against it stemming from World War I amounted to only 25,500. To add insult to injury, its overworked claims department was hit heavily by flu, forcing considerable overtime on the healthy. It is not surprising that one of the Metropolitan's first acts after it dug itself out was to organize the Influenza-Pneumonia Commission of specialists to study ways of combating these diseases.[53]

There was also severe loss on a personal level for some people. Arthur Lapointe, the Quebec soldier who survived two bouts of flu in Europe, returned home to find that he had lost three brothers and two sisters within nine days as a result of the epidemic.[54] Children's shelters offered record numbers of children for adoption and reported that, in addition, many orphans had already been taken over by relatives. Many families lost their chief wage-earner and charities reported that they had been called on as never before to provide necessities and little Christmas luxuries. A great number of the families added to the rolls had never asked for assistance before. People who had been laid off without pay during the epidemic also suffered financial loss, even though many of them, including theatrical troupers trapped in one centre or another, earned some small wage as flu volunteers.[55]

But in large part, though many people were sick, most recovered. They lost some time from work, felt very ill for from a week to a month, perhaps even went into hospital.

Those who were not sick helped out as best they could among their families and friends or volunteered their aid to total strangers. Those who had mild cases also were able to help out before and after their bouts. But the proof that life generally went on is that the health boards had to pass laws to limit the hours of or to close outright the concerns that they did. They were also forced to place bans on club meetings, labour rallies, wedding parties, and public funerals. The schools were closed, Hallowe'en calebrations cancelled, and official thanksgiving for the end of the war postponed.[56] But even these restrictions failed to keep people entirely at home. For example, the Dominion government may have decided to put off its victory celebrations until 1 December but the general populace went wild on 11 November, bringing a relapse of the epidemic in many centres. The majority of people simply did not hide in their houses peeping out at a hostile world. Some suffered tragedy, many underwent some financial loss, more suffered painful illness, and all encountered inconvenience. But the important point is that most survived and carried on their lives as normally as possible. There may have even been some advantages. For example, the effect of the epidemic on eastern grist mills meant that orders for the unpopular corn and rye substitutes for wheat flour could not be filled and government orders enforcing their consumption had to be lifted.[57]

Just how important was this pandemic that killed probably around twenty-two million people? That staggering figure of loss of life alone makes it an event on a par with any war. But there is a tendency to be carried away by it when discussing the social and economic effects of the flu. For one thing, the mortality was not evenly spread and the western industrial nations got off fantastically lightly when compared to India, which accounted for over twelve million of the deaths. Fatality inflicted by disease also has a basic difference from that inflicted by war. The latter is done with some political purpose in mind, the former is utterly random and its effects are not reached with any goal in mind. However, neither should the influenza epidemic be granted too little importance. It mattered.

Balfour and Scott, in their volume on health problems of the British Empire, coin the term "Imperial Diseases" and give the definition "any important communicable malady the presence of which exercises a markedly deleterious effect on the resources of the Empire," or more precisely:

> ... diseases transferable in a variety of ways from the sick person or from the so-called healthy carrier to the sound, existing as endemics, pandemics, or more especially as epidemics and possessed of such crippling or lethal powers that, taking the British Commonwealth as a whole, they interfere with progress and development, hinder trade and commerce, and occasion monetary loss.[58]

In their list of imperial diseases, flu shares the honours with ancylostomiasis, cholera, dysentery, enteric fever, malaria, plague, smallpox, tuberculosis, and venereal disease. But it is different from all the others in that it has attained this position solely through one disastrous epidemic, while the others have had years of endemic or regular epidemic existence. Balfour and Scott admit that flu would never have made the grade but for the 1918-19 pandemic:

> ... influenza cannot be said to be constantly sapping the health and vigour of the community, and it does not, as a rule, interfere with commerce. Neither is it much in evidence in tropical and subtropical lands under ordinary circumstances. And yet, as recent events have shown, and as a study of its history clearly indicates, there is no malady which better merits the title "imperial" than influenza in one of its great periodic outbreaks. It then sweeps like a pestilence from country to country, sparing no race, indifferent to climate, dislocating traffic, occasioning immense losses in lives and

money, and teaching anew the lesson that we are in large measure powerless against those communicable diseases whose true nature is still obscure, even if, as in the case of influenza, we have some idea as to the methods of spread and know in a general way how best to combat them.[59]

However, outside the general picture of misery and loss described above, it is a little difficult to attach any specific results to the epidemic. It might be thought that it would have had some effect on the outcome of the war. In some ways it did. Troops in large numbers on both sides became unable to fight. And the population at home was also affected in its ability to back them up. But no one gave up entirely. For example, although Victory Loan parades were cancelled, the loan campaigns themselves were not.[60] True, because of the terrible sickness and death in Canadian training camps and on troop ships, conscripts were no longer called up and volunteers were no longer taken after the epidemic became serious.[61] But the situation was just as bad in Germany, if not worse. That country suffered an estimated 2.75 million cases, with a death toll of 186,000 troops and 400,000 civilians.[62] By 28 October an estimated 45,000 railroad workers in Prussia and Hesse were off with flu.[63] By the same token, it cannot be assumed that sickness in Germany gave the allied powers any advantage. Not only were Canadian and United States troop supplies affected but Britain also suffered dreadfully, England and Wales recording 151,446 deaths from flu in the fifty-nine weeks starting 23 June 1918. Many of these were young and previously healthy adults.[64] And at the same time that German railroads were so debilitated, French rail companies reported 30 percent of their engineers and firemen were ill and daily express trains were to be suspended for ten days.[65]

It is likely that the epidemic shortened the war. The armies could fight no longer. During the allied march to the Rhine after armistice, evacuation of the sick was so huge a task that the added burden of battle casualties would have made matters impossible.[66] In addition, the military and its support organizations had to tend to large numbers of influenza-stricken civilians.[67] But the epidemic probably did not shorten the war by much. The victor had already been decided with United States entry into the war in 1917. That country still had more men to call up for soldiers, but the Germans had no reserves. They were exhausted and their troops demoralized. They could not fight much longer. In this matter, the epidemic inflicted more insult on them than injury. Had a ceasefire been called or forced until the flu had passed, the results would have been the same.

The positive achievements stemming from the flu come in other areas. It had been obvious to most people that the current organization of health services in Canada and other countries was, to say the least, faulty. No one wanted to be caught so short again. In fact, the International Red Cross gave the epidemic as one of three reasons for extending its activities into peacetime.[68] In Canada, communities voted funds for hospitals that had somehow never seemed that urgent before.[69] Calgary's civic elections at the beginning of December 1918 were dominated by health issues.[70] Nova Scotia established a public health nursing course at Dalhousie University.[71] And the United Farm Women's Association, meeting in Edmonton in January 1919, called for a system of medical and nursing aid to provide adequate health care, especially in rural areas, and a federal department of health.[72]

The UFWA was not the only organization to express this last wish. The Canadian Medical Association had been pushing for better federal health coordination since before the turn of the century. The federal government had always hung back, giving as excuse jurisdictional problems with the provinces. But with the epidemic, the popularity of the idea soared to politically expedient heights. The subject of favourable comments in both the Commons and the Senate,[73] the Department of Health Act received its first reading 26 March 1919. The department was staffed during the summer and was functioning by early autumn. There were many reasons for its inception: pressure from the medical profession, embarrassment over the poor degree of physical fitness among recruits, desire to increase the population through conquering communicable disease, worry over Canada's unusually high infant and maternal mortality rate, and, not least, the general euphoria of post-war reconstructionism.[74] But there can be no doubt that the flu was a major cause, and the most urgent one. The *Report to the Vice-Chairman of the War Committee of the Cabinet on the Establishment of a Federal Department of Public Health*, dated 25 October 1918, gives as a major reason for such a department the inadequacy and lack of coordination of current facilities:

> The recent epidemic of Spanish influenza points to the need of a Federal Health authority. Throughout this crisis there was no organization competent to handle the problem on a national scale. The control of the disease was necessarily left to local bodies, many of them ill-formed and all of them inevitably lacking in coordinated effort.[75]

Throughout the section of the *Report* devoted to the flu there is a portent of returning pestilence and in fact most authorities, and probably most of the population, expected the influenza to return. One of the most urgent matters taken up by the newly constituted Dominion Council of Health, the chief advisory organ of the new department, was preparations for a return of the epidemic. The measures it supported were a program of public education, a rapid expansion of hospital facilities up to 1 percent of the population, registration of all available nurses, emergency medical training of volunteers, and registration of any voluntary home helpers.[76] It was unable to propose anything more concrete until jurisdictional disputes could be ironed out with the provincial and local health authorities.

Other health organizations awaited the return of the flu. The Ontario Medical Association held a symposium on epidemic influenza at the end of May 1919, as did the Canadian Public Health Association and Ontario Health Officers' Association.[77] In fact, the Spanish flu did not leave until the mid-1920s and in April of that year, the *Canadian Medical Association Journal* still considered it widespread enough to refer to "the present epidemic."[78] But it never again flared up as it had in the fall and winter of 1918-19.

However, the precautions were not wasted. The flu had pointed out basic shortcomings in the facilities for the treatment of all diseases and related problems. The reforms it inspired gave not only Canada, but many countries, a firmer base from which to pursue better standards of health for the population.

Notes

1. It is also possible that the choice of name was further influenced by allied dislike of Spanish neutrality. Only slightly less repulsive than an outright enemy, Spain was seen as the sort of place likely to be diseased and to be indiscreet enough to pass it around. The same sort of psychology was involved centuries earlier in the French tagging syphilis "the English disease" and the English calling it "the French disease." In an interesting twist, *Maclean's Magazine* blamed the flu on the Germans who, it said, craftily named it Spanish flu before it could acquire its true name of German plague. *Maclean's Magazine* 32 (February 1919): 49.
2. Charles Graves, *Invasion by Virus: Can It Happen Again?* (London, 1969), pp. 17-22.
3. Arthur Lapointe, *Soldier of Quebec (1916-1919)*, trans. R. C. Fetherstonhaugh (Montreal, 1931), pp. 100-102.
4. Sir Andrew Macphail, *Official History of the Canadian Forces in the Great War, 1914-1919: The Medical Services* (Ottawa, 1925), p. 272; Public Archives of Canada (hereafter PAC), Records of the Department of Health and Welfare, RG 29, vol. 300.
5. Macphail, *Official History*, pp. 272-73.
6. PAC, RG 29, vol. 300.
7. Richard Collier, *The Plague of the Spanish Lady: The Influenza Pandemic of 1918-1919* (London, 1974), pp. 81-82; Calgary *Herald* (hereafter *Herald*), 2 October 1918.

8. J. P. Dickin McGinnis, "A City Faces an Epidemic," *Alberta History* 24 (Autumn 1976): 1-2.
9. *Herald*, 17 and 18 October 1918.
10. PAC, Records of the RCMP, RG 18, vol. 565.
11. PAC, RG 29, vol. 300.
12. PAC, RG 18, vol. 567, and Yukon Territorial Records, RG 91, vol. 67.
13. Adolph A. Hoehling, *The Great Epidemic* (Boston, 1961), p. 8.
14. Erwin H. Ackerknecht, *History and Geography of the Most Important Diseases* (New York, 1965), pp. 73-78.
15. Goldwin W. Howland, "The Nervous Conditions Associated with Influenza," *Canadian Medical Association Journal* (hereafter CMAJ) 9 (August 1919): 727-31.
16. John J. Heagerty, *Four Centuries of Medical History in Canada*, (Toronto, 1928): 213-14.
17. Ackerknecht, *History and Geography*, pp. 75-76.
18. T. H. Whitelaw, "The Practical Aspects of Quarantine for Influenza," CMAJ 9 (December 1919): 1071-72.
19. J. W. S. McCullough, "Influenza," *Public Health Journal* 10 (January 1919): 28-30.
20. Dickin McGinnis, "A City Faces an Epidemic," pp. 5-6.
21. Graves, *Invasion by Virus*, p. 201.
22. Collier, *The Plague*, p. 187; Dickin McGinnis, "A City Faces an Epidemic," p. 4; and PAC, RG 18, vol. 567.
23. Terry L. Chapman, "Drug Use in Western Canada," *Alberta History* 24 (Autumn 1976): 19-20.
24. E. A. Robertson, "Clinical Notes on the Influenza Epidemic Occurring in the Quebec Garrison," *CMAJ* 9 (February 1919): 159.
25. Andrew Balfour and Henry Harold Scott, *Health Problems of the Empire: Past, Present and Future*, vol. 5 of *The British Empire*, ed. Hugh Gunn (London, 1925), p. 219.
26. Major F. T. Cadham, "The Use of a Vaccine in the Recent Epidemic of Influenza," *CMAJ* 9 (June 1919): 519-27; John J. Heagerty, "Influenza and Vaccination," *CMAJ* 9 (March 1919): 226-28.
27. PAC, RG 29, vol. 300; and RG 18, vol. 567.
28. Heagerty, *Four Centuries* 1: 219-21; M. C. Urquhart and K. A. H. Buckley, eds., *Historical Statistics of Canada* (Toronto, 1965), p. 42; Alberta, *Annual Report of the Department of Public Health of the Province of Alberta, 1918* (Edmonton, 1919), p. 35; Alberta, *Annual Report of the Department of Public Health of the Province of Alberta, 1919* (Edmonton, 1920), pp. 8, 148.

29. See, for example, H. E. MacDermot, *History of the School for Nurses of the Montreal General Hospital* (Montreal, 1940), pp. 59-60.
30. For example, Montreal and Calgary. S. Boucher, "The Epidemic of Influenza," *CMAJ* 8 (December 1918): 1087-92; and Dickin McGinnis, "A City Faces an Epidemic," p. 6.
31. PAC, Records of RG 81, vol. 67.
32. For example, Montreal sent its leftovers to Alberta in recognition of the aid the city had received from an Alberta Red Cross official. *The McGill News*, 1 (December 1919): 55.
33. John Murray Gibbon, *The Victorian Order of Nurses for Canada* (Montreal, 1947), p. 73.
34. *Canadian Red Cross Bulletins*, no. 41 (December 1918-January 1919), pp. 38-40, 61.
35. G. W. L. Nicholson, *The White Cross in Canada* (Montreal, 1967), pp. 71-72.
36. Boucher, "The Epidemic," pp. 1090-91; Graves, *Invasion by Virus*, pp. 184-85; PAC, RG 29, vol. 300; RG 18, vols. 565, 567, and 568; Dickin McGinnis, "A City Faces an Epidemic," pp. 6-7.
37. PAC, RG 29, vol. 300.
38. PAC, RG 18, vol. 567.
39. PAC, RG 91, vol. 67; and RG 18, vol. 567.
40. PAC, RG 91, vol. 67; and RG 29, vol. 300. Wm. Perkins Bull, *From Medicine Man to Medical Man* (Toronto, 1934), p. 336; *Herald*, 12, 21, and 23 October, 28 November, 15 December 1918.
41. Arthur Bernier, "La Lutte contre la grippe," *Revue trimestrielle canadienne* 4 (février 1919): 356; Heagerty, *Four Centuries* 1: 218; "The Control of Influenza in Ontario," *Public Health Journal* 10 (January 1919): 47; *Herald*, 23 and 24 October 1918.
42. *Herald*, 24 October 1918.
43. *Herald*, 22 October to 3 December 1918.
44. *Herald*, 26 and 30 October, 15 November 1918.
45. *Herald*, 30 October, 6 November 1918, 9 January 1919.
46. *Herald*, 26 and 31 October, 6 November, 21 December 1918; PAC, RG 18, vol. 565.
47. *The Canada Year Book*, 1918 (Ottawa, 1919), p. 668; J. Castell Hopkins, *The Canadian Annual Review of Public Affairs*, 1918 (Toronto, 1919), p. 574; Dickin McGinnis, "A City Faces an Epidemic," p. 8; Antonio Drolet, "L'Epidémie de grippe espagnole à Québec en 1918," *Trois siècles de médecine québécoise* (Québec, 1970), p. 104.

48. *Herald*, 23 and 25 October, 15 November 1918; Collier, *The Plague*, p. 142.
49. *Herald*, 9 November 1918.
50. PAC, RG 18, vol. 567; *Herald*, 18 November, 4, 23, and 24 December 1918, 3 January 1919.
51. Calgary estimated its cost for flu care had reached $44,500 by the end of January. *Herald*, 31 January 1919. Minutes, 1914–19, of Finance, Special and Auditing Committees of Calgary Hospitals Board in Calgary Hospital Board Papers 1905-70, Glenbow-Alberta Institute, Archives.
52. *The Canadian Almanac, 1920* (Toronto, 1921), pp. 547, and ibid., p. 456.
53. Louis Dublin, *A Family of Thirty Million: The Story of the Metropolitan Insurance Company* (New York, 1943), pp. 74-75.
54. Lapointe, *Soldier of Quebec*, p. 114.
55. For example, Calgary. See *Herald*, 8 November 1918 to 8 January 1919. Capetown, S.A., estimated it had 2,000 new orphans as a result of the flu. *Herald*, 4 November 1918.
56. Ibid., 31 October, 15 November 1918.
57. Ibid., 4 November 1918.
58. Balfour and Scott, *Health Problems*, p. 188.
59. Ibid., pp. 214-15.
60. *Herald*, 29 October 1918.
61. Col. H. C. Parsons, "Official Report on Influenza Epidemic, 1918," *CMAJ* 9 (April 1919): 351; Drolet, "L'Epidémie," p. 104. Canada, however, certainly did not suffer as the United States in this regard. There, 17,000 flu deaths among troops who never left the United States compared with a total of 50,000 killed in action. See Graves, *Invasion by Virus*, p. 21. The young hero in Katherine Anne Porter's *Pale Horse, Pale Rider* (New York, 1939) is ordered not to return from leave because of the epidemic in the barracks. He is eventually called back for vaccination, contracts the disease, and dies.
62. Graves, *Invasion by Virus*, p. 61.
63. *Herald*, 29 October 1918.
64. Balfour and Scott, *Health Problems*, p. 218.
65. *Herald*, 25 October 1918.
66. Macphail, *Official History*, p. 395.
67. Mary MacLeod Moore, *The Maple Leaf's Red Cross: The War Story of the Canadian Red Cross Overseas* (London, 1919), p. 199.
68. Along with loss of human life through the war and the appalling degree of physical fitness revealed through medical examination of recruits. See John Murray Gibbon and Mary

S. Matthewson, *Three Centuries of Canadian Nursing* (Toronto, 1947), p. 342.

69. Bull, *From Medicine Man to Medical Man*, p. 336; and *Herald*, 21 December 1918, 15 and 18 January 1919.
70. *Herald*, 26 November, 3 December 1918.
71. PAC, RG 29, vol. 1192.
72. *Herald*, 21 January 1919.
73. Canada, House of Commons, *Debates*, 1919, 1: 94-95, 97, 301; and Canada, Senate, *Debates*, 1919, pp. 288-89.
74. These same causes, along with the flu, can also be applied to the inception of the Dominion Bureau of Statistics, the national laboratory, and much tighter narcotic and patent medicine laws which also came in during the immediate post-war period.
75. PAC, RG 29, vol. 19, page 14 of Report.
76. PAC, Records of the Dominion Council of Health, MG 28, Minutes of first meeting, 7-9 October 1919, pp. 3-4, microfilm reel C-9814.
77. A. H. W. Caulfeild and Capt. Donald T. Fraser, "Certain Bacteriological and Serological Aspects of Epidemic Influenza," *CMAJ* 10 (May 1920): 436; *Public Health Journal* 10 (May 1919): 236.
78. Editorial, *CMAJ* 10 (April 1920): 372.

Pragmatic Physicians: Canadian Medicine and Health Care Insurance, 1910-1945

ROBERT S. BOTHWELL
AND JOHN R. ENGLISH

It has become a ritual in Canada to view the medical profession as unalterably opposed to state-sponsored health insurance. It is usually assumed that this is so, was so, and has always been so. In fact, the history of the medical profession's attitude to health insurance belies this common stereotype.

The first mention of health insurance in the *Canadian Medical Association Journal* was in 1912. Lloyd George had just introduced his famous Insurance Act in Great Britain, and Canadian doctors took note of this new phenomenon. In the words of the editor of the *Journal*, the conservative Sir Andrew Macphail, "a spirit of charity will be replaced by a cold, official atmosphere. When physicians become civil servants, those who are peculiarly adapted for healing the sick will be automatically forced out of the service and into private practice." Prophetic words perhaps, and similar reservations were expressed in 1914 by Dr. A. R. Munroe of Edmonton, who claimed that Lloyd George was "exploiting the medical profession either in the name of charity or

Reprinted by permission from the *University of Western Ontario Medical Journal* 47, no. 3 (1976): 14-17.

religion." Nevertheless, Munroe believed that commercial methods of insurance should be studied and that the medical profession could agree on four points: universal access to medical care; no "charity" treatment; increases in doctors' incomes; the need to have insurance schemes calculated on the basis of "the medical schedule of fees." Munroe added that it was "worth every man's while studying."[1] Who could disagree?

Macphail and Munroe assumed that health insurance would be a long time coming to Canada. The First World War, however, created an atmosphere of mutual sacrifice and an acceptance of state involvement in a broader range of social services than hitherto contemplated. In 1917 the president of the CMA, Dr. A. D. Blackader, reflecting the anti-materialist sentiments so prevalent during the war, warned the CMA that it must avoid the imputation of "mercenary reasons" in its opposition to health insurance. Moreover, all doctors should now begin to prepare for the consideration of health insurance in Canada, and in this process the CMA should seize the initiative "to safeguard the true interests of our own profession."[2]

Still, by the war's end in 1918 no prominent Canadian doctor had explicitly stated a preference for state-directed medicine. But in 1919 Professor D. F. Harris told the Association of Medical Health Officers of Nova Scotia that since preventive medicine was already and properly the concern of the state, curative medicine should be a state concern as well. This was a fairly common attitude among public health doctors, who, being already civil servants, could see few terrors and no degradation in the prospect of universal state medicine. In the same year the first Royal Commission was appointed to study health insurance, in British Columbia, and its Report recommended a state-supported system of health insurance.[3]

The British Columbia government, however, took no action on the Royal Commission Report, because, as Premier Oliver informed the legislature, there was much doubt that health insurance was a provincial responsibility. The Royal Commission recommendation was therefore ignored, and medical insurance, like so many wartime social schemes, was all but forgotten during the 1920s. When the general secretary of the CMA, Dr. T. C. Routley, told Saskatchewan doctors in 1923 that health insurance was a serious proposition which deserved study, the secretary of the Saskatchewan Medical Society replied that he was "sure that this is just a flight of imagination in Dr. Routley's mind, and if he keeps quiet about it the country will never hear of it again."[4]

In fact, the country did begin to hear about health insurance again in 1928 and 1929 when a parliamentary committee held hearings in Ottawa to determine Canada's social security needs. Health insurance, the committee decided, was one of the needs, but the committee bowed to an advisory legal opinion which stated that social security was really the responsibility of the provinces. This did not prevent the House of Commons from debating health insurance, which it did annually, but it did insure that health insurance would be talked out every time.

The CMA itself discussed health insurance once again in 1929. In a debate at the annual meeting that year speakers indicated uncertainty, opposition and, in a few cases, support for health insurance. Dr. T. B. Green of British Columbia claimed that in his association meetings he had "never heard, with one exception, any voice favouring health insurance." On the other hand, Dr. George Wilson of Toronto stated his belief "that state medicine is coming and we need not fight against it. It behoves [*sic*] this Association to get behind it and direct it." Speakers from eastern Canada tended to be less specific than those from the West. One doctor from Saint John hoped that the idea of health insurance "will die before it reaches us," but was willing to support an investigation, providing that it was done "as quietly as possible, lest those [of us] in the East may hear of it."[5]

In the same year the British Columbia government abandoned its position that health insurance was a federal matter and appointed yet another Royal Commission to consider the possibilities of a provincial scheme. Before the commission submitted its report in 1932, a general economic depression had settled over the country, a depression which fundamentally altered both the state's and the medical profession's perspective on health insurance.

Quite suddenly the CMA began to perceive health insurance not as a threat but rather as an antidote for the economic ills of the profession. The CMA's Committee on Medical Economics pointed out how severely doctors were affected by the depression. In a survey of doctors in Hamilton, which the committee carried out in 1933, it was found that doctors' practices had declined in volume by 36.5 percent between 1929 and 1933. Even worse, in 1929 77.5 percent of doctors' work was remunerative; in 1932, the proportion had fallen to 50 percent. Almost half of the doctors surveyed claimed that their professional income was insufficient to pay their expenses and provide the necessities of life. The respondents estimated that only 30 percent of the population was willing to pay for medical care, and that many patients failed to secure medical attention early enough in cases of serious illness solely because they could not afford it.[6]

In rural areas the situation was reportedly even more desperate. Dr. Ward Woolner of Ayr, Ontario, described his own experience in an article in the *CMA Journal*:

> Since 1929, rural areas have many families who cannot pay anything to their doctor. Even farmers, who a few years ago were considered well to do—had electricity installed, had motor cars and telephones—cannot pay for medical care today. We are asked to accept all kinds of produce on our accounts. The writer received over twenty chickens, several ducks, geese, a turkey, potatoes and wood on account during last winter. Many country doctors have trouble collecting sufficient to purchase the bare necessities of life.[7]

Dr. Woolner concluded that only a province-wide scheme of medical care could alleviate the situation. Many others had come to the same conclusion.

In 1932 the Province of Quebec Medical Association recommended a system of compulsory health insurance to cover complete service, cash benefits, and the right to free choice of physician by the patient.[8] The B.C. Royal Commission set up before the depression reported in favour of a health insurance plan covering employed persons making less than $2,400 per annum. The unemployed, however, were still left to charity. This meant, inevitably, that indigents would continue to receive a considerable amount of free service from doctors, or continue to add to the municipal relief burden. Doctors generally found this to be intolerable, and, in response to the British Columbia proposals, the CMA instructed its economics committee to prepare its own health insurance plan.[9]

Medical care for the unemployed and payment for such care was the CMA's greatest concern. Accordingly in 1933, Dr. Routley, the CMA's general secretary, went to see Prime Minister Bennett about the problem. He pointed out to Bennett that the doctors were in effect providing their own subsidy to the unemployed by giving free service, but Bennett offered little hope of federal aid. With no solution in sight, the editor of the *Bulletin of the Vancouver Medical Association* called for the "socialization" of medicine. He urged doctors to accept a situation that was not only unavoidable, but actually desirable. A generous response from the medical profession would restore doctors' self-esteem and return "the medical profession to the pinnacle on which it once stood, and from which to a great extent . . . it has fallen."[10]

The CMA Committee on Economics finally presented its "Plan for Health Insurance in Canada" to the CMA's Council in 1934. The committee pointed out that provincial and municipal governments had shirked their responsibility for the provision of medical care for the indigent. The only solution to the problem was "State Health Insurance." State health insurance would be organized as a division of provincial departments of health and a central health insurance board, "representative of all interested parties," would furnish advice. The supervision of the plan would, of course, be handled by doctors, who would ensure that "the systematic practice of preventive medicine" would be properly carried out. The plan covered indigents, whose premiums would be paid for by the state, as well as single persons with incomes below $1,200 and families with incomes below $2,400. Above those income levels, participation in the plan would remain voluntary. The committee did not specify how doctors should be paid, although they noted that in sparsely populated rural areas doctors would have to rely on a contractual salary.[11]

In the same year, the president of the Toronto Academy of Medicine, Dr. E. A. McDonald, argued in his presidential address for state medicine. Doctors, he claimed, were "being driven into the indigent class" because they were forced to treat penniless patients free of charge. He advocated that Canada follow the British model for health insurance, but he recommended rather more generous salaries than the British paid. The general practitioner, McDonald suggested, "shall be paid a salary sufficient to enable him to live in comfort and continue his post-graduate studies to enable him to keep abreast of the progress of medicine, say, $6,000.00 per year." Specialists would be paid proportionately more, "say $8000 to $10,000 yearly." In 1930–31 the average male wage-earner in Canada was estimated to have earned only $927 per annum, and the salary of a member of Parliament was $4,000. It is therefore unlikely that McDonald's salary proposals met with much favour outside the medical profession.[12]

When British Columbia introduced a draft health insurance scheme in 1935, the medical profession began to realize that health insurance presented many difficulties which had not been anticipated. By the time the draft bill became law in 1936, the B.C. medical profession was thoroughly alarmed. The Health Insurance Act proposed a restricted coverage—

wage-earners making less than $150 a month, leaving out domestic servants, casual labourers, the indigent, part-time workers, and recipients of old age pensions and mothers' allowances. In short, those least likely to pay their accounts remained uninsured. The act was, the *Bulletin of the Vancouver Medical Association* declaimed, "a pale shadow of its former self, anaemic and paralyzed in its lower limbs, or its lower income levels, if you prefer." Equally disturbing was the act's failure to make specific provision for the rates and manner of payment and to give doctors a large role in the act's administration. Subsequent negotiations with the doctors failed to produce agreement, and the government postponed implementation of the scheme—indefinitely, as it turned out.[13]

The British Columbia experience, however, did not cause Canadian doctors to reject the concept of health insurance. Indeed, the problem was that governments were not prepared to go far enough. In some provinces, therefore, the medical associations took the lead in developing voluntary health care schemes. In 1937, Manitoba began the study of voluntary hospital insurance (Blue Cross) and by 1939 the plan was in operation. Other Canadian provinces soon followed. In Ontario, Associated Medical Services and the Windsor Medical Services were established in 1937; both were sponsored by the OMA. A similar scheme was put into operation in Regina in 1939.[14]

These plans were local in coverage and voluntary in nature, and it seems that the CMA regarded them as a stop-gap. In 1939, the CMA's Committee on Economics reported that it had completed a comprehensive study of the working of health insurance in other countries, but recommended that the task of completing a health insurance plan had to be left to the government: "the Government must be the lead horse and...the Canadian Medical Association should be an essential and recognized running mate."[15] The lead horse soon came round the corner, in the person of Dr. J.J. Heagerty, the director of public health for the federal Department of Pensions and National Health.

Before 1939, Pensions and National Health had failed to win, show, or place in the health insurance sweepstakes. It was regarded in Ottawa as a mediocre department filled with second-raters. Its functions were confined to house-keeping on the health side, and it had never developed a comprehensive approach to health insurance, which it believed was a provincial responsibility. But in September 1939, Pensions and National Health acquired a new minister, Ian Mackenzie, who had been hastily transferred from the sensitive Department of National Defence on the outbreak of war. Mackenzie was naturally anxious to re-establish his reputation, and within months he had adopted social welfare as his instrument.

In January 1941, the King government summoned a Dominion-Provincial Conference to discuss the recommendations of the Rowell-Sirois Royal Commission. One of the special studies prepared for the commissioners by A. E. Grauer dealt with public health, which Grauer reported was in dismal shape. As Ottawa prepared for the conference, Mackenzie approached the deputy minister of finance, Clifford Clark, to ask that "consideration [be] given to the possible inclusion of public health as one of the subjects for discussion." "Someone," Clark rudely noted, "has called his attention to Professor Grauer's report."[16] While Mackenzie did not succeed in having health insurance placed on the agenda, he did create the impetus within his own department for a re-examination of the possibilities of health insurance.

A small committee, chaired by Dr. Heagerty, reported in January 1941 that "The principle of health insurance is approved." Its recommendations were to form the nucleus of the future federal health insurance scheme. The committee urged that public health (Heagerty was a public health doctor) be "an integral part" of any health insurance plan, that coverage be universal below a certain income level, and that provincial departments of health administer the plan in consultation with medical practitioners.

In October 1941, the CMA's executive visited Ottawa, where they were informed by Mackenzie of the work in progress. Mackenzie emphasized that nothing had been decided as yet, and that he wished to keep in touch with the doctors. A subcommittee of seven, including Routley, was appointed for this purpose. More important, the CMA itself in the same year approved the principle of health insurance, expressing reservations mainly about direct employment of doctors by the state.

The stumbling block was not the medical profession but rather the federal Department of Finance. Pensions and National Health's early proposals envisaged a federal enabling act which would authorize federal contributions to provincially legislated plans. These plans would have to exclude indigents, but would allow fairly comprehensive medical treatment. In a letter to the minister of finance, Mackenzie estimated the cost of the program at $20 million, but alas, the Finance Department did not believe Mackenzie, and the minister's project was returned to him with a recommendation for more study.[17]

An exchange of letters in the *CMA Journal* of April 1942, between Heagerty and Routley, was intended to show that a health insurance bill was very near—something that was far from the truth. Dr. Routley sounded the alarm: the doctors must consider their position before it was too late. A great change was coming, and the CMA must be in the vanguard. Routley urged all doctors to join the CMA so that the CMA's answer to the anticipated question "Whom do you represent?" would not be too embarrassing. To the current wartime slogans of "Remember Hong Kong! Remember Pearl Harbor!" Routley suggested adding, "Remember Great Britain, and remember New Zealand when you think of Health Insurance!"[18]

At the annual meeting of the CMA in June 1942, the results of a questionnaire on health insurance were tabled. The 2,500 doctors who replied strongly supported the 1934 principles.

They wanted: "an independent Health Insurance Commission" in each province, "the majority of whom shall be representatives of organized medicine"; medical care for indigents paid for by the government; freedom of choice for physician and patient; remuneration "according to the method or methods of payment which [doctors] select." With this mandate the committee of seven could take the initiative in defining more precisely the association's attitude towards the prospective health bill.[19]

The next draft of Heagerty's bill reflected the CMA's concerns. There was to be both a dominion Council on Health Insurance and separate provincial councils, with a majority of the membership being practising doctors. There was to be fee for service payment, and all indigents were to be included. In effect, Heagerty's bill gave the doctors everything they wanted. As far as Pensions and National Health were concerned, the bill was complete by December 1942, "except as to matters relating to costs." But costs, as it turned out, were close to the heart of the matter.

On 18-19 January 1943, a special meeting of the CMA Council was convened in Ottawa. (Heagerty and his deputy minister, Dr. Wodehouse, were members of the council.) The meeting adopted two resolutions:

1. The Canadian Medical Association approves the adoption of the principle of health insurance.
2. The Canadian Medical Association favours a plan of health insurance which will secure the development and provision of the highest standard of health services, if such plan be fair both to the insured and to all those rendering the services.

The *CMA Journal* approvingly noted that Heagerty and Wodehouse's attitude throughout was one of satisfying frankness. While the council was pleased with the progress made to date, it nevertheless refrained from approving the specific plan put forward by Pensions and National Health.[20]

Heagerty and Wodehouse had achieved a qualified success on the medical front, but Mackenzie, their minister, had lost the political battle for immediate implementation of the plan. The day after the CMA Council approved the principle of health insurance, Mackenzie learned that the cabinet would not support the enactment of health insurance in 1943. Instead, Heagerty's draft bill would be sent to a House of Commons committee, the Committee on Social Security, for study.

The Special Committee on Social Security convened in March 1943. It held four months of frequently wild and woolly sessions as lawyer-MPs and medical MPs had at one another. Routley and Dr. A. E. Archer, the CMA president, appeared on behalf of the association. Routley repeated the conclusions of the special council meeting of the previous January: the doctors anticipated "great and in some respects unwelcome changes," but they had accepted the principle of health insurance. Reflecting a common fear among doctors that politicians would meddle in their daily work, Routley warned the committee that health insurance must be run by a "non-political independent commission."

Other medical opinions were given at the hearings. The Catholic Hospitals Council's representative told the committee that they feared a loss of autonomy and confessional identity in a national hospital scheme; the majority of Canadians, after all, were Protestants. The osteopaths, the chiropractors, the Christian Scientists, and even the "Anti-Vaccination and Medical Liberty League of Canada" came forward. The gist of their testimony was objection to the predominant role of doctors in the administration of health insurance, and the restriction of benefits to strictly medical forms of treatment. Heagerty firmly rejected their arguments, insisting on the control of all medical treatment by the medical profession.

Finally, in July, the committee reported to the House of Commons that it thought that the principle of health insurance was a good one, and that the government should scout

out the provinces' reactions. In the meantime the committee should be reconstituted next session. Heagerty's project had survived, chloroformed.[21]

The CMA, which may have been disturbed by the attitude of some who had appeared before the Social Security Committee, seemed to welcome this pause. An August 1943 editorial in the *CMA Journal* saw the delay in Ottawa as providing an opportunity to think things over. Archer echoed this sentiment in his presidential address, and while not repudiating the CMA's support for the principle of health insurance, he suggested that health insurance should be delayed until after the war.[22] The doctors' hesitations gained force in December 1943 when a financial committee on health insurance reported that health insurance would cost the federal government approximately $100,000,000, four times as much as Mackenzie's original estimate. This report undermined much of Heagerty's testimony to the Special Committee. This committee's conclusions did not become public for a few months and in the meantime, the *CMA Journal* described Heagerty's testimony on finance as "not always consistent." Heagerty, who must have known by this point that his financial estimates were unsound, tried to reply that the criticisms were "erroneous" and unjust. As the chairman of the B.C. Division of the CMA's Committee on Economics observed, "Dr. Heagerty's subsequent reaction has seemed to rather prove that we have hit a tender point."[23]

The tone of the discussion had changed, a fact noted by Dr. M. G. Burris in a letter to the *CMA Journal* in March 1944:

> The profession of Canada as a whole is only now realizing the true nature of the proposed Bill. In my opinion the section of the profession included within the Canadian Medical Association has been altogether too complacent and too compliant in the matter hitherto. We have proceeded apparently in the belief that State control was inevitable and as if the legislation had already been enacted. We have neglected to examine adequately

the theories underlying and the theorists responsible for the present situation. The philosophy of the proposal is as plain an example of National Socialism and State Control as one could imagine or desire.

The *Journal* also took note of the American Medical Association's hostile attitude on health insurance, an attitude quite unlike the CMA's "too complacent and too compliant" attitude. The *Journal* also began to publish unfavourable comments on the proposed measures for British health insurance, in one case repeating a warning issued to Canadian doctors by Lord Dawson of Penn, "Chief Physician to His Majesty the King."[24]

It was, however, the Health Insurance Act passed by the Saskatchewan legislature in the early spring of 1944 which crystallized doctors' fears about politicians and their use of health care schemes. The Saskatchewan medical profession strongly protested "the fact that no opportunity was given to make representations on this bill and the hasty manner in which it was rushed through in the last hours of the legislature." They were understandably alarmed that no provision had been made for the representation of doctors on the Health Insurance Commission. The responsible minister replied that the bill was merely an enabling act and that no health insurance could be set up immediately under its provisions. Nevertheless, the doctors treated this Saskatchewan experience as an evil omen. The profession, Saskatchewan doctors argued, had been subjected to slanders and abuse. Rather plaintively, they summed up their position: "We all know that individually, the doctor is everyone's friend but as a group we are regarded as anything but that."[25]

The fears of the Saskatchewan doctors were premature: there was no possibility that a poor province like Saskatchewan could finance a health insurance scheme without federal aid. Just as the Patterson government in Saskatchewan was passing its "innocuous enabling act," the federal scheme was collapsing in Ottawa, the victim of miscalculations and political exigencies. When the Mackenzie King government decided to proceed with family allowances, health insurance was abandoned and not revived as a separate measure. Far from being imminent and inevitable as CMA President Archer had claimed in 1943, a comprehensive health insurance scheme was a generation away. By the mid-1960s when the Pearson government introduced medicare, the Heagerty plan was all but forgotten; so too was the CMA's previous support for health insurance for Canadians.

The CMA's support for health insurance in the 1930s and early 1940s contrasted strongly with organized medicine's opposition to health insurance in the United States and Britain. Indeed, in the 1930s and even in the early 1940s, the most vocal supporters of health insurance were prominent members of the Canadian medical profession. It was always a qualified support and enthusiasm varied inversely with the economic condition of the profession. It also seems that the greater the degree of familiarity with the politician and his schemes, the greater were the doctors' doubts. Nevertheless, to the "indigent" medical profession of the 1930s, health insurance promised paid accounts and security. In the 1940s and 1950s there appeared to be better ways, and the medical profession then chose to confront the perils of prosperity alone, without the politician's help.

Notes

1. *Canadian Medical Association Journal* (hereafter *CMAJ*) 3 (1912): 228; ibid. 4 (1914): 1112.
2. Ibid. 7 (1917): 582.
3. H. E. MacDermot, *History of the Canadian Medical Association*, 2 (Toronto, 1958): 60–61.
4. Cited in ibid., p. 61.
5. A transcript of this discussion may be found in ibid., pp. 61–64.
6. *CMAJ* 31 (September 1934), Supplement: 51.
7. Ward Woolner, "Medical Economics in the Rural Districts of Ontario," *CMAJ* 30 (1934): 307.

8. *CMAJ* 31 (September 1934), Supplement: 51.
9. H. E. MacDermot, "A Short History of Health Insurance in Canada," *CMAJ* 50 (1944): 448–49.
10. Cited in ibid.
11. Report of the Committee on Economics, "A Plan for Health Insurance in Canada," *CMAJ* 31 (September 1934), Special Supplement: 25–62.
12. E. A. McDonald, "State Medicine," *CMAJ* 31 (1934): 666–67.
13. Reproduced in *CMAJ* 34 (1936): 685.
14. *Royal Commission on Health Services 1964* 1: 387–88.
15. Cited in MacDermot, *History of the CMA*, p. 73.
16. Clark to Alex Skelton, 23 December 1940, RG 19 E2C, v. 108, Public Archives of Canada. See, generally, R. S. Bothwell, "The Health of the People," Paper presented to Canadian Historical Association Annual Meeting, June 1975. Reprinted in John English and J. Stubbs, eds., *Mackenzie King: Widening the Debate* (Toronto: Macmillan, 1978), pp. 191–220.
17. See Bothwell, "Health of the People," pp. 11–13.
18. *CMAJ* 46 (1942): 390–91.
19. Ibid. 47 (1942), Special Supplement: 3–5.
20. Ibid. 48 (1943): 93.
21. Canada, House of Commons, Special Committee on Social Security, *Minutes*; *Journals of the House of Commons*, 23 July 1943.
22. *CMAJ* 49 (1943): 123–27.
23. Ibid. 50 (1944): 72, 174–75, 276.
24. Ibid., pp. 164–65, 276.
25. Ibid., pp. 273–74.

Suggestions for Further Reading

GENERAL AND REFERENCE WORKS

ABBOTT, MAUDE. *History of Medicine in the Province of Quebec.* Montreal: McGill University, 1931.

BIRKETT, HERBERT S. "A Short Account of the History of Medicine in Lower Canada." *Annals of Medical History,* 3rd series 1, no. 4, 1939.

BONENFANT, YOLANDE ET AUTRES. *Trois siècles de médecine québécoise.* Québec: Société historique de Québec, 1970.

BRAU, PAUL. *Trois siècles de médecine coloniale française.* Paris: Vigat, 1931.

CHARLTON, M. "History of Medicine in Lower Canada." *Annals of Medical History,* 1st series 5, nos. 2-3, 1923, and 6, nos. 2-3 1924.

DUBÉ, VIATEUR ET AL. *Bibliographie sur la prehistoire de la psychiatrie canadienne au dix-neuvième siècle.* Trois Rivières: University du Québec à Trois Rivières, 1976.

GODFREY, CHARLES M. *Medicine for Ontario: A History.* Belleville: Mika Publishing, 1979.

HEAGERTY, JOHN J. *Four Centuries of Medical History in Canada.* 2 vols. Toronto: Macmillan, 1928.

————. *The Romance of Medicine in Canada.* Toronto: Ryerson, 1940.

HOWELL, W. B. *Medicine in Canada.* New York: Paul Hoeber, 1933.

JAMIESON, H. C. *Early Medicine in Alberta: The First Seventy-Five Years.* Edmonton: Canadian Medical Association, Alberta, 1947.

KOUDELKA, J. B. "Bibliography of the History of Medicine of the United States and Canada." *Bulletin of the History of Medicine* 39, no. 6, 1965, and 40, no. 1, 1966.

LARGE, R. G. *Drums and Scalpel: From Native Healers to Physicians on the North Pacific Coast.* Vancouver: Mitchell Press, 1968.

LEA, R. GORDON. *History of the Practice of Medicine in Prince Edward Island.* Charlottetown: Prince Edward Island Medical Society, 1964.

MACDERMOT, H. E. *A Bibliography of Canadian Medical Publications.* Montreal: Renouf, 1934.

————. *One Hundred Years of Medicine in Canada, 1867-1967.* Toronto: McClelland and Stewart, 1967.

MCKECHNIE, ROBERT E. *Strong Medicine: A History of Healing on the Northwest Coast.* Vancouver: J.J. Douglas, 1972.

MILLER, GENEVIEVE. *Bibliography of the History of Medicine of the United States and Canada, 1939-1960.* Baltimore: Johns Hopkins Press, 1964.

————. "Bibliography of the History of Medicine of the United States and Canada." *Bulletin of the History of Medicine* 35, no. 6, 1961, and annually to 38, no. 6, 1964.

MITCHELL, ROSS. *Medicine in Manitoba: The Story of Its Beginnings.* Winnipeg: n.p. [1954].

ROLAND, CHARLES G. AND POTTER, PAUL. *An Annotated Bibliography of Canadian Medical Periodicals.* Toronto: Hannah Institute for the History of Medicine, 1979.

ROSE, T. F. *From Shaman to Modern Medicine: A Century of the Healing Arts in British Columbia.* Vancouver: Mitchell Press, 1972.

STEWART, W. B. *Medicine in New Brunswick.* St. John: New Brunswick Medical Society, 1974.

SWAN, ROBERT. "The History of Medicine in Canada." *Medical History* 12, no. 1, 1968.

EIGHTEENTH-CENTURY ORIGINS

CARON, WILFRID M. "The Early Surgeons of Quebec." *Canadian Journal of Surgery* 8, July 1965.

KELLY, A. D. "Health Insurance in New France." *Bulletin of the History of Medicine* 28, no. 6, 1954.

LEBLOND, SYLVIO. "La France et la médecine canadienne." *Revue de l'Université Laval* 4, no. 7, 1950.

MASSICOTTE, E.-Z. "Les Médecins, chirurgiens, et apothicaires de Montréal de 1701 à 1760." *Bulletin des recherches historiques* 27, nos. 3 and 11, 1921.

NICHOLLS, ALBERT G. "The Romance of Medicine in New France." *Dalhousie Review* 7, no. 2, 1927.

DEVELOPMENT IN THE NINETEENTH CENTURY

BUCKLEY, SUZANN. "Ladies or Midwives? Efforts to Reduce Infant and Maternal Mortality," in Linda Kealey, ed., *A Not Unreasonable Claim: Women and Reform in Canada, 1880-1920.* Toronto: Women's Press, 1979.

BULL, WILLIAM P. *From Medicine Man to Medical Man.* Toronto: Perkins Bull Foundation, 1934.

CANNIFF, WILLIAM. *The Medical Profession in Upper Canada, 1783-1850.* Toronto: Briggs, 1894.

CHAPMAN, TERRY L. "The Early Eugenics Movement in Western Canada." *Alberta History* 25, no. 4, 1977.

————. "Drug Use in Western Canada." *Alberta History* 24, Autumn 1976.

ELLIOT, J. H. "John Gilchrist, J.P., L.M.B.U.C., M.P.: A Pioneer New England Physician in Upper Canada." *Bulletin of the History of Medicine* 7, no. 7, 1939.

GODLER, ZLATA. "Doctors and the New Immigrants." *Canadian Ethnic Studies* 9, no. 1, 1977.

GROVES, ABRAHAM. *All in A Day's Work: Leaves from a Doctor's Casebook.* Toronto: Macmillan, 1934.

KELLEY, THOMAS P. *The Fabulous Kelley: He was King of the Medicine Men.* Toronto: Simon and Schuster, 1968.

MCFALL, W. A. "The Life and Times of Dr. Christopher Widman." *Annals of Medical History*, new series 4, no. 4, 1942.

PATTERSON, MARIAN A. "The Life and Times of the Hon. John Rolph, M.D. (1793-1870)." *Medical History* 5, no. 1, 1961.

RIDDELL, W. R. "Popular Medicine in Upper Canada a Century Ago." Ontario Historical Society, *Papers and Records* 25, 1929.

ROLAND, CHARLES G. "Diary of a Canadian Country Physician: Jonathon Woolverton (1811-1883)." *Medical History* 15, no. 2, 1971.

————. "Ontario Medical Periodicals as Mirrors of Change." *Ontario History* 72, no. 1, March 1980.

ROWLES, EDITH. "Bannock, Beans and Bacon: An Investigation of Pioneer Diet." *Saskatchewan History* 5, no. 1, 1952.

SEABORN, EDWIN. *The March of Medicine in Western Ontario.* Toronto: Ryerson Press, 1944.

SMITH, DOROTHY B., ed. *The Reminiscences of Doctor John Sebastien Helmcken.* Vancouver: University of British Columbia Press, 1976.

STANLEY, G. D. "Dr. John Rolph: Medicine and Rebellion in Upper Canada." Calgary Associate Clinic, *Historical Bulletin* 9, May 1944.

TOLMIE, WILLIAM F. *The Journals of William Fraser Tolmie, Physician and Fur Trader.* Vancouver: Mitchell Press, 1963.

TYRE, R. *Saddle-bag Surgeon: The Story of Murrough O'Brien, M.D.* Toronto: Dent, 1954.

THE TWENTIETH CENTURY

BARR, M. L. AND ROSSITER, R. J. "James Bertram Collip, 1892-1965." *Biographical Memoirs of Fellows of the Royal Society* 19, 1973.

BUCKLEY, SUZANN. "Efforts to Reduce Infant and Maternity Mortality in Canada Between the Two World Wars." *Atlantis* 2, Spring 1977.

CAMPBELL, MARJORIE FREEMAN. *Holbrook of the San.* Toronto: Ryerson Press, 1953.

CLUTE, KENNETH. *The General Practitioner: A Study of Medical Education and Practice in Ontario and Nova Scotia.* University of Toronto Press, 1963.

GIBSON, W. C. "Frank Fairchild Westbrook (1868-1918): A Pioneer Medical Educator in Minnesota and British Columbia."

Journal of the History of Medicine and Allied Sciences 22, no. 4, 1967.

HOWELL, W. B. *F. J. Shepherd—Surgeon: His Life and Times, 1851-1929*. Toronto: Dent, 1934.

JOHNSTON, WILLIAM VICTOR. *Before the Age of Miracles: Memoirs of a Country Doctor*. Toronto: Fitzhenry and Whiteside, 1972.

MACDERMOT, HUGH E. *Sir Thomas Roddick*. Toronto: Macmillan, 1938.

MACMILLAN, C. L. *Memoirs of a Cape Breton Doctor*. Toronto: McGraw-HIll Ryerson, 1975.

MURRAY, D. W. G. *Medicine in the Making*. Toronto: Ryerson Press, 1960.

PENFIELD, WILDER. "Edward Archibald, 1872-1945." *Canadian Journal of Surgery* 1, January 1958.

SHORTT, S. E. D. "Sir Andrew Macphail: Physician, Philosopher and Founding Editor of the *CMAJ*." *Canadian Medical Association Journal* 118, 4 February 1978.

WILLINSKY, A. I. *A Doctor's Memoirs*. Toronto: Macmillan, 1960.

THE WESTERN AND NORTHERN FRONTIER

COPLAND, DUDLEY. *Livingston of the Arctic*. Ottawa, 1967.

HARVEY, A. G. "Meredith Gairdner: Doctor of Medicine." *British Columbia Historical Quarterly* 9, no. 2, 1945.

KERR, JAMES LENNOX. *Wilfred Grenfell: His Life and Work*. New York: Dodd, Mead, 1959.

MCKERVILL, HUGH W. *Darby of Bella Bella*. Toronto: Ryerson Press, 1964.

MITCHELL, ROSS. "Doctor Cheadle in Western Canada." *Bulletin of the History of Medicine* 8, no. 1, 1940.

———. "Early Doctors of Red River and Manitoba." *Papers, Historical and Scientific Society of Manitoba*, series 3, no. 4, 1948.

MOODY, JOSEPH P. *Arctic Doctor*. New York: Dodd, Mead, 1955.

MOORE, PERCY, KRUSE, H. D. AND RISDALL, F. F. "Nutrition in the North." *The Beaver*, Outfit 273, March 1943.

PETERKIN, AUDREY AND SHAW, MARGARET, eds. *Mrs. Doctor: Reminiscences of Manitoba Doctors' Wives*. Winnipeg: Prairie Publishing, 1976.

RICH, E. E. "The Fur Traders: Their Drugs and Diet." *The Beaver*, Outfit 367, Summer 1976.

RICHARDS, R. L. "Rae of the Arctic." *Medical History* 19, no. 2, 1975.

STANLEY, GEORGE D. "Medical Pioneering in Alberta." *Alberta Historical Review* 1, Winter 1953.

THOMSON, COLIN. "Doc Shad." *Saskatchewan History* 30, no. 2, 1977.

THORINGTON, J. M. "Four Physician Explorers of the Fur Trade Days." *Annals of the History of Medicine*, new series 4, no. 4, 1942.

TOLMIE, S. F. "My Father: William Fraser Tolmie, 1812-1886." *B.C. Historical Quarterly* 1, no. 4, 1937.

MEDICINE AND THE NATIVE PEOPLES

BARBEAU, MARIUS. *Medicine-men on the North Pacific Coast.* National Museum of Canada, bulletin no. 152. Ottawa: 1958.

DAILEY, ROBERT C. "The Midewiwin, Ontario's First Medical Society." *Ontario History* 50, no. 3, Summer 1958.

DUFFY, J. "Smallpox and the Indians in the American Colonies." *Bulletin of the History of Medicine* 25, no. 4, 1951.

GRAHAM-CUMMINGS, GEORGE. "Health of the Original Canadians, 1867-1967." *Medical Services Journal, Canada* 23, February 1967.

HARRIS, WILLIAM R. *Practice of Medicine and Surgery by the Canadian Tribes in Champlain's Time.* Ottawa: King's Printer, 1915.

KEEHN, PAULINE. *The Effect of Epidemic Diseases on the Natives of North America: An Annotated Bibliography.* London: Survival International, 1978.

MACLEAN, JOHN. "Blackfoot Medical Priesthood." *Alberta Historical Review* 9, Spring 1961.

MAHR, AUGUST C. "Materia Medica and Therapy among the North American Forest Indians." *Ohio State Archaeological and Historical Quarterly* 60, no. 4, 1951.

MARGETTS, EDWARD. "Canada, Indian and Eskimo Medicine With Notes on the Early History of Psychiatry Among French and British Colonists." In John G. Howells, ed., *World History of Psychiatry.* New York: Brunner-Mazel, 1975.

PARKER, ARTHUR C. "Indian Medicine and Medicine Men." *Ontario, Report of the Minister of Education*, 1929. Appendix. Thirty-Sixth Annual Archaeological Report, 1928.

SMITH, HARLAN. *Materia Medica of the Bella Coola and Neighbouring Tribes of British Columbia*. National Museum of Canada, bulletin no. 56. Ottawa: 1929.

WALLACE, A. F. C. "Dreams and Wishes of the Soul: A Type of Psychoanalytic Theory among the Seventeenth-Century Iroquois." *American Anthropologist* 60, no. 2, 1958.

WALLIS, W. G. "Medicines Used by the Micmac Indians." *American Anthropologist* 24, no. 1, 1922.

WOMEN IN MEDICINE

ABBOTT, MAUDE. "Autobiographical Sketch (1928)." *McGill Medical Journal* 28, 1959.

BUCK, RUTH M. *The Doctor Rode Side-Saddle*. Toronto: McClelland and Stewart, 1974.

GODFREY, C. M. "The Origins of Medical Education of Women in Ontario." *Medical History* 17, no. 1, 1973.

HACKER, CARLOTTA. *The Indomitable Lady Doctors*. Toronto: Clarke, Irwin, 1974.

JACKSON, MARY PERCY. *On the Last Frontier*. London: Sheldon Press, 1933.

KEYWAN, ZONIA. "Mary Percy Jackson: Pioneer Doctor." *The Beaver*, Outfit 308, Winter 1977.

MACDERMOT, HUGH E. *Maude Abbott: A Memoir*. Toronto: Macmillan, 1941.

SCRIVER, JESSIE BOYD. "McGill's First Women Medical Students." *McGill Medical Journal* 16, no. 2, 1947.

SMITH SHORTT, ELIZABETH. "The Women's Medical College." *Queen's Review* 3, nos. 3, 4, and 5, 1929.

ALLIED HEALTH PROFESSIONS AND RESEARCH

Alberta Pharmaceutical Association, 1911-1961. Calgary: 1961.

EGGLESTON, WILFRID. *National Research in Canada: The N.R.C., 1916-1966*. Toronto: Clarke, Irwin, 1978.

GATTINGER, F. E. *A Century of Challenge: A History of the Ontario Veterinary College*. Toronto: Ontario Veterinary College, 1962.

GIBBON, J. M. AND MATHEWSON, M. S. *Three Centuries of Canadian Nursing*. Toronto: Macmillan, 1947.

GRIDGEMAN, N. T. *Biological Sciences at the National Research Council of Canada: The Early Years to 1952*. Waterloo: Wilfrid Laurier University Press, 1979.

GULLETT, D. W. *A History of Dentistry in Canada*. Toronto: University of Toronto Press, 1971.

MCDOUGALL, D. "The History of Pharmacy in Manitoba." *Papers, Historical and Scientific Society of Manitoba*, series 3, no. 11, 1956.

STREET, MARGARET M. *Watch-fires on the Mountains: The Life and Writings of Ethel Johns*. Toronto: University of Toronto Press, 1973.

YOUNG, E. GORDON. *The Development of Biochemistry in Canada*. Toronto: University of Toronto Press, 1976.

MENTAL HEALTH

GREENLAND, CYRIL. *Charles Kirk Clarke: A Pioneer of Canadian Psychiatry*. Toronto: Clarke Institute of Psychiatry, 1966.

————. "Ernest Jones in Toronto, 1908-13." *Canadian Psychiatric Association Journal* 6, no. 3, 1961.

————. "Richard Maurice Bucke, M.D., 1837-1902: A Pioneer of Scientific Psychiatry." *Canadian Medical Association Journal* 91, 22 August 1964.

————. "Services for the Mentally Retarded in Ontario 1870-1930." *Ontario History* 54, no. 4, 1962.

HORNE, JAMES. "R. M. Bucke: Pioneer Psychiatrist and Practical Mystic." *Ontario History* 59, no. 3, 1967.

LAVELL, A. E. "The Beginning of Ontario Mental Hospitals." *Queen's Quarterly* 49, Spring 1942.

STEVENSON, GEORGE H. "The Life and Work of Richard Maurice Bucke." *American Journal of Psychiatry* 18, no. 5, 1937.

DISEASES AND EPIDEMICS

ANDREWS, MARGARET W. "Epidemic and Public Health: Influenza in Vancouver, 1918-1919." *B.C. Studies*, no. 34, Summer 1977.

BILSON, GEOFFREY. "Cholera in Upper Canada, 1832." *Ontario History* 67, no. 1, 1975.

————. "The First Epidemic of Asiatic Cholera in Lower Canada, 1832." *Medical History* 21, no. 4, 1977.

DICKIN MCGINNIS, JANICE P. "A City Faces an Epidemic." *Alberta History* 24, Autumn 1976.

GODFREY, C. M. *The Cholera Epidemics in Upper Canada, 1832-1866.* Toronto: Seccombe House, 1968.

GREENWALD, ISIDOR. "The History of Goitre in Canada." *Canadian Medical Association Journal* 84, 18 February 1961.

KALISCH, PHILIP A. "Tracadie and Penikese Leprosuria: A Comparative Analysis of Societal Response to Leprosy in New Brunswick, 1844-1880, and Massachusetts, 1904-1921." *Bulletin of the History of Medicine* 47, no. 5, 1973.

PACK, MARY. *Never Surrender.* Vancouver: Mitchell Press, 1974.

RAY, ARTHUR. "Smallpox: The Epidemic of 1837-38." *The Beaver,* Outfit 306, Autumn 1975.

WHERRETT, GEORGE J. *The Miracle of the Empty Beds: A History of Tuberculosis in Canada.* Toronto: University of Toronto Press, 1977.

WRENSHALL, C. A., HETENYI, G. AND FEASBY, W. R. *The Story of Insulin: Forty Years of Success Against Diabetes.* London: Bodley Head, 1962.

MILITARY MEDICINE

CUMMINS, J. F. "The Organization of the Medical Services in The North-West Campaign of 1885." *Canadian Defence Quarterly* 2, January 1925.

DAVIS, DAVID B. "Medicine in the Canadian Campaign of the Revolutionary War: The Journal of Doctor Samuel Frisk Merrick." *Bulletin of the History of Medicine* 44, no. 5, 1970.

FEASBY, W. R. *Official History of the Canadian Medical Services, 1939-1945.* Ottawa: Queen's Printer, 1954.

MACPHAIL, SIR ANDREW. *Official History of the Canadian Forces in the Great War, 1914-1919: The Medical Services.* Ottawa: King's Printer, 1925.

NICHOLSON, G. W. L. *Seventy Years of Service: A History of the Royal Canadian Army Medical Corps.* Ottawa: Borealis Press, 1977.

POLITICS, HOSPITALS, AND PUBLIC HEALTH

AGNEW, G. HARVEY. *Canadian Hospitals, 1920 to 1970: A Dramatic Half Century*. Toronto: University of Toronto Press, 1974.

ANGUS, MARGARET. *Kingston General Hospital: A Social and Institutional History*. Montreal: Published for Kingston General Hospital by McGill-Queen's University Press, 1973.

BADGLEY, ROBIN F. AND WOLFE, SAMUEL. *Doctors' Strike: Medical Care and Conflict in Saskatchewan*. Toronto: Macmillan, 1967.

BLISHEN, BERNARD R. *Doctors and Doctrines: The Ideology of Medical Care in Canada*. Toronto: University of Toronto Press, 1969.

BOTHWELL, ROBERT S. "The Health of the People," in John English and John O. Stubbs, eds., *Mackenzie King: Widening the Debate*. Toronto: Macmillan, 1978.

COSBIE, W. G. *The Toronto General Hospital, 1819-1965: A Chronicle*. Toronto: Macmillan, 1975.

DEFRIES, R. D. *The Development of Public Health in Canada*. Toronto: Canadian Public Health Association, 1940.

————. *The Federal and Provincial Health Services in Canada*. 2nd ed. Toronto: Canadian Public Health Association, 1961.

GOFFMAN, IRVING J. "The Political History of National Health Insurance in Canada." *Journal of Commonwealth Political Studies* 3, July 1965.

LEWIS, D. SCLATER. *Royal Victoria Hospital, 1887-1947*. Montreal: McGill University Press, 1969.

MACTAGGART, K. *The First Decade: The Story of the Birth of Medicine in Saskatchewan*. Ottawa: Canadian Medical Association, 1973.

MATTERS, D. L. "A Report on Health Insurance: 1919." *B.C. Studies*, no. 21, Spring 1974.

MEDOVY, H. *A Vision Fulfilled, The Story of the Children's Hospital of Winnipeg, 1909-73*. Winnipeg: Peguis, 1979.

METCALFE, ALLAN. "The Evolution of Organized Physical Recreation in Montreal, 1840-1895." *Histoire Sociale/Social History* 11, no. 21, 1978.

PIVA, MICHAEL J. "The Workman's Compensation Board in Ontario." *Ontario History* 67, no. 1, 1975.

ROEMER, M. I. "Socialized Health Services in Saskatchewan." *Social Research* 25, no. 1, 1958.

SCRIVER, JESSIE BOYD. *The Montreal Children's Hospital: Years of Growth*. Montreal: McGill-Queen's University Press, 1979.

SHILLINGTON, C. HOWARD. *The Road to Medicare in Canada*. Toronto: Del Graphics, 1972.

TAYLOR, MALCOLM. *Health Insurance and Canadian Public Policy: The Seven Decisions that Created the Canadian Health Insurance System*. Montreal: McGill-Queen's University Press and the Institute of Public Administration of Canada, 1978.

PROFESSIONAL ORGANIZATION AND EDUCATION

ANDISON, A. W. AND ROBICHON, J. G. *The Royal College of Physicians and Surgeons of Canada*. Ste. Anne de Bellevue: Harpell's Co-operative Press, 1979.

BARR, MURRAY L. *A Century of Medicine at Western*. London: University of Western Ontario, 1977.

BOISSONNAULT, CHARLES-MARIE. *Histoire de la faculté de médecine de Laval*. Québec: Presses Universitaires Laval, 1953.

CLARKSON, F. A. "The Medical Faculty of the University of Toronto." Calgary Associate Clinic, *Historical Bulletin* 13, no. 2, 1948.

FERGUSON, JOHN. *History of the Ontario Medical Association, 1880–1930*. Toronto: Murray Printing, 1930.

GRAHAM, D. C. "The Canadian Medical Association: Its Genesis and Development." *Medical Journal of Australia* 49, 1962: 772–77.

JOHNSON, GEORGE R. "The History of Canadian Medical Schools. VIII. McGill University-Medical Faculty." Calgary Associate Clinic, *Historical Bulletin* 14, no. 3, 1949, and 15, no. 1, 1950.

KERR, ROBERT B. *History of the Medical Council of Canada*. Ottawa: Medical Council of Canada, 1979.

LAWRENCE, D. G. "'Resurrection' and Legislation, or Body-Snatching in Relation to the Anatomy Act in the Province of Quebec." *Bulletin of the History of Medicine* 32, no. 5, 1958.

LEWIS, D. SCLATER. *The Royal College of Physicians and Surgeons of Canada, 1920–1960*. Montreal: McGill University Press, 1962.

MACDERMOT, HUGH E. "Early Medical Journalism in Canada." *Canadian Medical Association Journal* 72, May 1955.
————. *History of the Canadian Medical Association 1867-1956*. 2 vols. Toronto: Murray Printing Co., 1935, 1958.
————. "The Fiftieth Anniversary of the Association Journal." *Canadian Medical Association Journal* 84, 7 January 1961.
MCNAB, ELIZABETH. *A Legal History of the Health Professions in Ontario: A Study for the Committee on the Healing Arts*. Toronto: Queen's Printer, 1970.
SPRAGGE, G. W. "The Trinity Medical School." *Ontario History* 58, no. 2, 1966.
STEWART, C. B. "One Hundred Years of Medical Education at Dalhousie." *Nova Scotia Medical Bulletin*, August 1968.
WOODS, DAVID. *Strength in Study: An Informal History of the College of Family Physicians of Canada*. Toronto: College of Family Physicians of Canada, 1979.

BIOGRAPHY

ALLAN, TED AND GORDON, SYDNEY. *The Scalpel, the Sword: The Story of Dr. Norman Bethune*. Toronto: McClelland and Stewart, 1952.
BETT, W. R. *Osler: The Man and the Legend*. London: Heinemann, 1951.
COMBER, W. M. *William Grenville, the Labrador Doctor*. London: Butterworth, 1950.
CUSHING, HARVEY. *The Life of Sir William Osler*. Oxford: Clarendon Press, 1925.
HARRIS, SEALE. *Banting's Miracle*. Philadelphia: Lippincott, 1946.
KERR, J. L. *Wilfred Grenville*. New York: Dodd Mead, 1959.
MACLEOD, WENDELL ET AL. *Bethune, the Montreal Years: An Informal Portrait*. Toronto: Lorimer, 1978.
REID, EDITH G. *The Great Physician: A Short Life of Sir William Osler*. London: Oxford University Press, 1931.
STEVENSON, LLOYD. *Sir Frederick Banting*. Toronto: Ryerson Press, 1946.
STEWART, RODERICK. *Bethune*. Toronto: New Press, 1973.
————. *The Mind of Norman Bethune*. Toronto: Fitzhenry and Whiteside, 1977.